Advancing Digital Humanities

# Advancing Digital Humanities

## Research, Methods, Theories

Edited by

Paul Longley Arthur
*University of Western Sydney, Australia*

Katherine Bode
*Australian National University, Australia*

palgrave
macmillan

First published 2014 by
PALGRAVE MACMILLAN

Palgrave Macmillan in the UK is an imprint of Macmillan Publishers Limited,
registered in England, company number 785998, of Houndmills, Basingstoke,
Hampshire RG21 6XS.

Palgrave Macmillan in the US is a division of St Martin's Press LLC,
175 Fifth Avenue, New York, NY 10010.

Palgrave Macmillan is the global academic imprint of the above companies
and has companies and representatives throughout the world.

Palgrave® and Macmillan® are registered trademarks in the United States,
the United Kingdom, Europe and other countries.

ISBN 978–1–137–33699–6 hardback
ISBN 978–1–137–33700–9 paperback

This book is printed on paper suitable for recycling and made from fully
managed and sustained forest sources. Logging, pulping and manufacturing
processes are expected to conform to the environmental regulations of the
country of origin.

A catalogue record for this book is available from the British Library.

Library of Congress Cataloging-in-Publication Data
Advancing digital humanities : research, methods, theories / edited by
    Katherine Bode (Australian National University, Australia), Paul Longley
    Arthur (University of Western Sydney, Australia).
        pages  cm
    Summary: "Advancing Digital Humanities moves beyond definition of
    this dynamic and fast growing field to show how its arguments, analyses,
    findings and theories are pioneering new directions in the humanities
    globally. Sections cover digital methods, critical curation and research
    futures, with theoretical and practical chapters framed around key areas
    of activity including modelling collections, data-driven analysis,
    and thinking through building. These are linked through the concept of
    'ambitious generosity,' a way of working to pursue large-scale research
    questions while supporting and enabling other research areas and
    approaches, both within and beyond the academy" — Provided
    by publisher.
    Includes bibliographical references.
    ISBN 978–1–137–33699–6 (hardback) —
    ISBN 978–1–137–33700–9 (paperback)
    1. Humanities—Data processing.   2. Humanities—Methodology.
    3. Humanities—Research.   4. Digital media.   5. Digital
    communications.   6. Information storage and retrieval systems—
    Humanities.   I. Bode, Katherine.   II. Arthur, Paul Longley.
    AZ105.A35 2014
    001.30285—dc23                                          2014024813

# Contents

## Part IV  Research Futures

# Figures and Tables

## Figures

## Tables

# Contributors

**Paul Longley Arthur** is Professor of Digital Humanities, University of Western Sydney. He was previously Deputy Director, Centre for European Studies, a joint initiative of the European Commission and Australian National University. From 2010–13 he was Deputy Director, National Centre of Biography, Australian National University, and Deputy General Editor, *Australian Dictionary of Biography*.

**Katherine Bode** is Senior Lecturer in Literary and Textual Studies at the Centre for Digital Humanities Research at the Australian National University. Her most recent monograph, *Reading by Numbers: Recalibrating the Literary Field* (2012), explores the critical potential of quantitative book historical and bibliographical methods for literary history.

**Axel Bruns** is an Australian Research Council Future Fellow and Professor at Queensland University of Technology. He is the author of *Blogs, Wikipedia, Second Life and Beyond: From Production to Produsage* (2008) and *Gatewatching: Collaborative Online News Production* (2005). His current work develops new methodologies for studying public communication in social media.

**Jean Burgess** is Associate Professor of Digital Media Studies, Director of Research Training for the Creative Industries Faculty, and Deputy Director of the Australian Research Council Centre of Excellence for Creative Industries & Innovation at Queensland University of Technology. Her research focuses on social and mobile media platforms.

**Mark Byron** teaches and publishes across the genres and practices of Modernism as well as textual and editorial theory. His current work developing digital scholarly editions of complex Modernist texts and their manuscripts includes the *Watt* module of the Samuel Beckett Digital Manuscript Project. He is the author of *Ezra Pound's Eriugena* (2014).

**Mark Coté** is Programme Director of the Masters in Digital Culture and Society at King's College London. Mark writes on social media, digital culture, and the relationship between the human and technology. He is currently examining 'big social data' through an Arts and Humanities Research Council-funded research project with Tobias Blanke.

**Øyvind Eide** is a lecturer and research associate at the Chair of Digital Humanities, University of Passau, Germany. His research interests focus on the modelling of cultural heritage information, especially as a tool for critical engagement with the relationships between texts and maps as media of communication.

**Jack Elliott** is a doctoral candidate at the University of Newcastle. His dissertation is on machine learning and romance novels.

**Julia Flanders** is Professor of Practice in English and Director of the Digital Scholarship Group at Northeastern University. She directs the Women Writers Project and serves as editor in chief of *Digital Humanities Quarterly*. Her research focuses on digital text representation and editing, and on theories of work in digital humanities.

**Tim Highfield** is a Research Fellow at Queensland University of Technology and Curtin University. His research examines political and cultural uses of social media, including information flows around breaking news and popular culture. His research website is located at http://timhighfield.net/.

**Alan Liu** is Professor of English at the University of California, Santa Barbara. His books include *The Laws of Cool: Knowledge Work and the Culture of Information* (2004) and *Local Transcendence: Essays on Postmodern Historicism and the Database* (2008). He is founder of the 4Humanities.org advocacy initiative.

**Willard McCarty** is Professor in the Department of Digital Humanities, King's College London, and in the Digital Humanities Research Group, University of Western Sydney; Editor of *Interdisciplinary Science Reviews* (2008–); founding Editor of *Humanist* (1987–); and recipient of the Roberto Busa Award (2013), Alliance of Digital Humanities Organizations. See www.mccarty.org.uk/.

**Richard Maltby** is Professor of Screen Studies and Executive Dean of the Faculty of Education, Humanities and Law at Flinders University, South Australia. His publications include *Hollywood Cinema* (2nd ed. 2003), *'Film Europe' and 'Film America': Cinema, Commerce and Cultural Exchange, 1925–1939* (1999), and *Explorations in New Cinema History: Approaches and Case Studies* (2011).

**Christopher Moore** is Lecturer in Digital Media and Communication in the School of Arts, English and Media at the University of Wollongong. He is a researcher in games studies and is currently investigating the role of online personae within indie and independent cultures of games production.

**Tara Murphy** is Senior Lecturer in the School of Physics at the University of Sydney. She is currently leading the VAST project to investigate astronomical objects that vary on rapid timescales. Tara is also interested in interdisciplinary applications of novel computer science techniques to data-intensive research in astronomy and beyond.

**Peter Robinson** is Bateman Professor of English at the University of Saskatchewan. He is developer of the texual editing program Collate, used by many textual editing projects worldwide, and of the Anastasia electronic publishing system.

He is active in the development of standards for digital resources and tools for collaborative editing.

**Ned Rossiter** is Professor of Communication at the Institute for Culture and Society at the University of Western Sydney and teaches in the School of Humanities and Communication Arts. He is currently working on a collective project entitled *Logistical Worlds: Infrastructure, Software, Labour* (logisticalworlds.org).

**Sydney J. Shep** is Reader in Book History at Victoria University of Wellington and The Printer at VUW's Wai–te–ata Press : : Te Whare Tā o Wai–te–ata. She directs the Print Culture eResearch Hub which hosts 'The Printers' Web', the New Zealand Reading Experience Database, and the Digital Colenso, a prosopographical collaboratorium.

**Tomoji Tabata** is Associate Professor of Language Informatics at the Graduate School of Language and Culture, University of Osaka. His primary research interests are in forensic stylometry and corpus–stylistic investigation of the language of eighteenth- and nineteenth-century British fiction with special reference to Charles Dickens.

**Paul Turnbull** is Professor of Digital Humanities at the University of Tasmania, and an Honorary Professor of eHistory at the University of Queensland. His digital research projects include 'South Seas', a major online resource focused on James Cook's Pacific voyaging; The Gugu Badhun Oral History; the Digital Guide to Sources in North Queensland History; and PaperMiner: Spatial Mapping of Australian Historical Newspapers.

**Deb Verhoeven** is Chair and Professor of Media and Communication at Deakin University. She is a founding member of the Australasian Association for the Digital Humanities (aaDH), Project Director of the Humanities Networked Infrastructure initiative (HuNI), and a member of the Tasmanian government's Digital Futures Advisory Committee.

**Dylan Walker** is a doctoral student in screen studies at Flinders University, South Australia, researching film distribution and exhibition in rural South Australia during the 1930s. He has published articles on rural cinema exhibition and his book, *Adelaide's Silent Nights* (1995), deals with the history of cinemas in Adelaide, South Australia, during the silent era.

**Mike Walsh** is Associate Professor in the Screen and Media Department of Flinders University in Adelaide, Australia. He has published regularly on Australian cinema and is currently completing a history of the South Australian Film Corporation. He is also a programmer and writer for the Adelaide Film Festival.

# 1

# Collecting Ourselves

*Katherine Bode and Paul Longley Arthur*

Digital humanities has become an influential and widely adopted term only in the past decade. Beyond the rapid multiplication of associations, centres, conferences, journals, projects, blogs, and tweets frequently used to signal this emergence, if anything characterizes the field during this time it is a concern with definition. This focus is acknowledged and reflected, for instance, in Matthew Gold's 2012 edited collection, *Debates in Digital Humanities*. The debates surveyed are overwhelmingly definitional: 'As digital humanities has received increasing attention and newfound cachet, its discourse has grown introspective and self-reflexive' (x). Questions that Gold identifies as central to and expressive of the emerging field include: Does one need to build or make things to be part of the digital humanities? 'Does DH need theory? Does it have a politics? Is it accessible to all members of the profession', or only those working at elite, well-funded institutions? 'Can it save the humanities? The university?' (xi).

The 2013 collection *Defining Digital Humanities: A Reader* (Terras et al. 2013) also reflects this focus, bringing together historical and contemporary readings on the act of defining digital humanities, many of which, not incidentally, are canonical in the field. Other areas of activity are equally self-reflexive, including the field's various manifestos[1] and the annual *Day of Digital Humanities*, where definitions are crowdsourced and participants are asked to document through text and image 'what digital humanists really do'. Despite this long-standing preoccupation, no clear agreement on a definition has emerged beyond broad references to research, teaching, and technical innovation at the intersection of humanities and computing. And within this broad description, commentators emphasize different aspects of the intersection—historical, institutional, political, economic, or social—as the aims and scope of digital humanities continue to be debated.

Why, then, is digital humanities so focused on defining itself, yet unable to arrive at an agreed-upon definition? Many have assessed this situation from a positive angle. Gold, for instance, suggests that such introspection simply marks 'a field in the midst of growing pains as its adherents expand from a small circle of like-minded scholars to a more heterogeneous set of practitioners who sometimes ask more disruptive questions' (Gold 2012, x–xi). Alan Liu (2013) identifies this focus as a characteristic that digital humanities shares with a number of past

1

fields, and thus, presumably, a relatively normal stage of development and matura-
tion. We could add that even the most mature disciplines have adapted and shifted
their boundaries in recent decades as the practices and rhetoric of interdisciplinary
research have extended the scope of traditional pursuits. The definitional debate
has also expressed many positive aims for digital humanities and the humanities
more broadly, including openness beyond the university; the importance of interdisciplinary and global connections, conversations, and collaborations; critiques
of established forms of hiring, peer review, and publication; and the importance
of valuing—and making a case for the value of—humanities scholarship.

Yet the coin has a negative side, too. The focus on definition has fed into
internecine and public battles about who is in and out of digital humanities—for
example, whether one needs to code, or just to 'build', or neither, to be considered a 'digital humanist' (Ramsay 2011). Such disputes make the field appear
cliquish and arguably occur at the expense of—or at the very least overshadow—
the actual work of doing digital humanities and advancing the field by showing,
rather than proposing or imagining, what can be achieved and discovered. This
criticism could be pushed further, as a number of commentators within and outside digital humanities have done, to describe the work in digital humanities thus
far as inadequate to constitute a field of humanities scholarship worth defining.

The most cogent and confronting expressions of this position come from
within digital humanities itself. For instance, Patrick Juola's 2008 analysis of article citations and author affiliations in the flagship journal *Computers and the
Humanities* (*CHum*) highlighted the 'minimal' impact of this research on mainstream humanities research. Building on this critique, in 2011 Andrew Prescott
described digital humanities as too focused on internal debates—definitional,
institutional, and technical—and displaying a lack of engagement with critical
theory that left the field 'perilously out of touch with the modern study of
the humanities' (69). The result, Prescott argues, is a 'collective failure to produce scholarship of outstanding importance and significance' (63). Liu's 2013
*PMLA* article encapsulated such criticisms as 'the meaning problem' in digital
humanities: the seeming inability for research in this area to move from data (or
textual models or visualizations) to arguments and interpretations that contribute
to knowledge and debates in the broader humanities.

The fact that major figures in digital humanities question whether the field has
made any real contribution is concerning enough; what makes these critiques even
more worrying is how closely they mirror earlier criticisms and supposed solutions.
Reflecting on the first 24 years of *CHum*, the same journal Juola analyses, in 1991
Rosanne Potter argued that most of its authors 'let the computer define what to
look for, and the statistician define what was significant' while 'neglect[ing] reading what others were doing and had done'; this 'toddler and teenager thinking'
produced a lot of counting, but not much in the way of insights relevant to mainstream humanities disciplines (427). A few years later, referring to this synopsis,
Mark Olsen—like Prescott—diagnosed the urgent need to 'address the issues surrounding the general failure of our discipline to have a significant impact on the
research community as a whole' (1993/1994, 309) by engaging with contemporary

theoretical insights and approaches.[2] The fact that the same problems—and purported solutions—remain despite more than two decades of work and a name change (from humanities computing) indicates the complexity of the 'meaning problem' for digital humanities.

A number of chapters in this collection continue and develop these and other critiques (see, for example, Bode and Murphy, Robinson, Rossiter, and Turnbull). But Willard McCarty's description of digital humanities' shortcomings is especially sobering, in part because his chapter was originally delivered as a lecture upon receiving the Busa Award, the most prestigious recognition of digital humanities scholarship offered by the Alliance of Digital Humanities Organizations:

> Make no mistake: we are *surrounded* by mature, subtle civilizations of enquiry, whose intellectual resources dwarf our own in volume, variety, and sophistication....We need far more than the luck of the moment, dozens of sessions at the MLA, THATCamps everywhere, millions of tweets, thousands of blogs, and so on and so forth. We need *resonance* with the intellectual cultures of the arts and humanities...and [of] the techno-sciences.

McCarty points to fear—of our confrontation with 'the uncanny *otherness* of computing' (this volume, 294) and of our being unable to emerge unscathed from this encounter—to explain why digital humanities (and humanities computing before it) has not achieved the stature of other areas of inquiry.

These criticisms of digital humanities provide a potential answer to the question of why the field has been so focused on definition, and why agreed-upon definitions, despite this effort, have not emerged. Instead of occurring at the expense of, or overwhelming, the work of doing digital humanities, it may well be that definition has been pursued as a stand-in for the insights and discoveries the field is not providing. Pursuing this line of reasoning, perhaps the unprecedented attention that digital humanities has received in recent years accounts for the current fever pitch of definitional debate. Heralded as the 'next big thing' (Pannapacker 2009)—or even just 'the thing' (Pannapacker 2011)—by many within and outside the academy, and even put in the position of saving the humanities from its own crisis of meaning (Liu 2013), the focus on definition may be an attempt to provide something—anything—for those who look to the field for salvation at a time of institutional and financial pressure, and even epistemological and ontological crisis.

This collection was conceived in the context of such criticisms of digital humanities—with the aim of advancing the field beyond definitional debates to show, rather than describe, what digital humanities is, what it can do, the contribution it makes to humanities research, and the role it can play in the future: its research, theories, and methods. To attempt this ambitious contribution, we embarked on the collection with two main ideas. First, rather than predetermine the areas we believed to be part of digital humanities, we sought contributions from a wide range of scholars who had self-identified with the field by attending the inaugural conference of the Australasian Association for Digital Humanities at the Australian National University in Canberra in 2012.

The result of this self-selecting approach is a collection that traverses some of the field's key fault lines. Indeed, quite unintentionally, the resulting collection demonstrates the broad version of digital humanities—its areas of need and promise—that Liu has been mapping out and advocating for a number of years (2011). Describing digital humanities from an ethnographic standpoint, Liu (2013) points to media studies—concerned with new media objects and networked, visual, and multimodal work—and traditional humanities computing—focused on technical questions and support—as neighbouring tribes to the core digital humanities, which arises mainly from traditional humanities disciplines and is predominantly concerned with textual materials as well as the examination and value of the old. This collection unites members of these 'neighbouring tribes' to demonstrate the importance of traditional and new scholarly objects and methods for digital humanities.

As is appropriate, given the emphasis internationally on literary studies in digital humanities research, that discipline provides one focus for this collection. However, such literary scholarship extends from established humanities computing areas of digital scholarly editing and stylistic analysis to book history and quantitative literary history. Moreover, these literary chapters sit alongside, and resonate productively with, a wide range of chapters relating to new media studies and theory, as well as contributions from researchers in film studies, history, cultural heritage, and even astrophysics. In addition, far from lacking the 'critical awareness of the larger social, economic, and cultural issues' at stake in humanities research (Liu 2011, 11)—a charge frequently levelled at digital humanities—this collection demonstrates a clear focus on relations of power and inequality, including their relation to gender, nationality, and global capital. Finally, while incorporating researchers from across the globe, the collection's origins give it an Australasian inflection, showcasing work from Australia, New Zealand, and Japan, and thus providing an important addition and corrective to the North American and European focus of many previous edited collections.

The second way we endeavoured to advance digital humanities beyond definition was to request contributions that did not merely describe digital humanities projects and methods but made an original contribution to research. The result is a collection of arguments, analyses, findings, and theories of relevance and value to multiple areas of the humanities. Such research has importance far beyond what it says about digital humanities, and we end this introduction by describing some of the specific ideas and arguments presented. Collected together, these chapters clearly demonstrate (rather than describe) the capacity of digital humanities to function as a site of rich conversations between and across disciplines.

What this collection also reveals, and what is particularly surprising given the diverse range of topics explored, is a set of significant commonalities in the approaches used and, more essentially, in the epistemological questions posed. Not all of these commonalities are new to our understanding of digital humanities, with themes such as the power of 'big data', the relationship of 'close' and 'distant' reading, and thinking through building all much discussed in recent years. Yet deployed in ways that advance our understanding of the world and our place in it, these common themes begin to indicate some of the intellectual possibilities of digital humanities: that is, not only how digital humanities can contribute to humanities disciplines, but what it does differently from these disciplines, and why and how this difference is important in understanding and analysing human culture and society now and in the future.

The core commonality that emerges is the *centrality of collections* as a product of, resource for, object of, and epistemological challenge in digital humanities research. While the meaning of collections has expanded in the digital age—here including digital archives and libraries as well as collections of images, documents, words, and metadata—its centrality to the humanities is long-standing. As the authors of *Digital_Humanities* write,

> Collection-building and curation have remained constants of humanistic knowledge production from remote antiquity through early modern courts to the academics of the Baroque era to late nineteenth century universities where chairs were typically associated with research collections. These domains became disjointed from the mainstream of scholarly practice only during the late print era, and are once again becoming integral to many forms of Digital Humanities practice.
>
> (Lunenfeld et al. 2012, 32)

Rather than simply continuing a tradition, the chapters in this book exemplify and interrogate how digital collections are motivating new ways of doing research—and indeed, of thinking—in the humanities.

The *critical potential of data-driven analysis* to enable new perspectives and insights provides another common thread. In a wide range of topics—including Harlequin Romance fiction (Elliott), the operations of Australian cinemas (Maltby et al.), and the 'digital human' created in assemblage with the smartphone (Coté)—these chapters demonstrate the capacity of data-driven analysis to indicate patterns and conjunctions that could not otherwise be perceived, and which enable us to understand cultural phenomena in revealing and challenging ways. As well as seeing culture from a 'distance', a number of contributors integrate data-rich analysis with exploration of particular instances: whether this means using data to highlight phenomena that are explored further by 'analogue' means (such as interviews, archival research, or textual analysis), or moving iteratively between these two levels of analysis. In combining what has been called 'close' and 'distant' reading, such research brings together modes of analysis that are in some quarters seen as paradigmatic of a supposed opposition of humanities and digital humanities, and takes a step that Liu (2013) identifies as vital for solving the 'meaning problem' in digital humanities.

Another commonality across the collection is a focus on *thinking through building*. While also an established theme in digital humanities—developed in discussions of the role of knowledge representation and modelling in the field—chapters in this collection realize the potential of this process by showcasing the intellectual, critical, and theoretical outcomes that thinking through building enables. The emphasis, in other words, is as much on thinking as on building, and these chapters highlight the iterative or dialogic movement between building and thinking, as models or prototypes prompt new questions and arguments that in turn motivate the creation of new models or prototypes, and so on. In his chapter in this collection, McCarty expresses ambivalence about the critical potential of modelling—a form of thinking through building that he himself did much to clarify—for digital humanities research, because it is 'unable to do more than work through consequences of interpretation that had already happened—elsewhere by other means' (this volume, 293). The work that follows shows the continuing importance and vitality of this approach, which in shifting our perceptions by degrees supports interpretations that would not be possible otherwise.

A key reason why the chapters in this collection succeed in using building to move beyond existing ways of thinking points to another commonality: *an explicitly self-conscious and critical approach to the nature and implications of collections*. As Julia Flanders explores in this volume, the current remediation of our cultural heritage into digital forms provides the opportunity to interrogate our assumptions about, and approaches to, collections before they become ingrained, normalized, and ultimately invisible. A number of chapters take up this challenge by highlighting the methodological and epistemological challenges and potential of analysing mediated objects, from mid-eighteenth-century documents used in the border negotiations between Denmark, Norway, Sweden and Finland (Eide), to the collective of Australian Twitter users (Bruns et al.) or national biographical datasets (Arthur). While Prescott criticizes digital humanities as atheoretical, even antitheory, if theory is 'a reasonably systematic reflection on our guiding assumptions' (Eagleton, cited in Prescott 2011, 68) then theorizing is precisely what the authors in this collection are doing. By interrogating how the organization of knowledge shapes what and how we can think—and using this awareness to imagine new modes of organization and, hence, new modes of thought—an explicitly self-conscious approach to collections manifests a dynamic mode of theoretical work.

A final commonality among chapters in this collection is a way of working that we term *ambitious generosity*. Ambition is clearly apparent in the scale and aims of these projects. Whether opening new areas for research or providing resources to reinvigorate and transform existing areas of scholarship, or the humanities as a whole, the authors in this book think big about the critical potential of digital techniques and technologies for humanities research. Much of this ambition relates to the focus on collections, which render these projects large in conception and membership, frequently involving not only a single researcher, or even a team of researchers, but multiple collaborators, many of whom will never meet or even know of each other, working on the same collection and thus contributing to the same broad agenda of expanding knowledge in a particular area or field.

What is remarkable about the ambition on display here is how closely and constitutively it is tied to generosity, a feature that is again intimately associated with the centrality of collections to such research. While the collections that underpin many of these projects were created to pursue particular questions or interests, they are also intended to support and enable a much wider range of research areas and approaches—and to be used by others, including academics as well as citizen scholars beyond the academy. Indeed, many of the chapters in this volume deliberately blur the distinction between these two groups, whether by creating resources that refuse to privilege traditional academic forms of knowledge or by proposing systems that make such knowledge practices accessible and employable by all. In their ambition and their generosity, and in the dynamically theoretical modes of scholarship the following chapters demonstrate, the authors involved in the research presented here collectively position digital humanities as moving beyond a concern with itself to making a productive—and potentially transformative—contribution to our knowledge of the world and our place in it.

*   *   *

While united by these common threads and a focus on research findings, the collection is divided into four sections representative of particular fields of investigation or topics of analysis. The first of these—'Transforming Disciplines'—features digital research from the traditional humanities disciplines of literature and history. In 'Exercises in Battology', Mark Byron demonstrates how a digital edition of Samuel Beckett's manuscript *Watt*—itself part of a large-scale collaborative project to digitize the complete manuscripts of Beckett's published literary oeuvre—both extends the complexity of, and clarifies, this important work. As well as being necessitated by the extensiveness of the manuscript, a digital edition has important benefits for hermeneutic and textual criticism: for instance, Byron shows how moving between 'textual features at different orders of magnitude and in various modes' can provide insights—for instance, into characterization—not previously possible (this volume, 16).

Tomoji Tabata's 'Stylometry of Dickens's Language' also analyses a canonical literary figure—in this case, Charles Dickens. Tabata uses mining techniques for stylometric differentiation and forensic analysis of text to provide a foundation for deeper understanding of Dickens's language. Dickensian keywords and markers are contrasted with those in the works of his contemporary Wilkie Collins, and Dickens's works are compared with a large reference set of eighteenth- and nineteenth-century texts. Arguing against the value of culling techniques such as clustering, Tabata applies a machine learning approach using the Random Forests classification algorithm to show how Dickens's language can be distinguished and to identify the elements that constitute Dickensian style. Jack Elliott's analysis, 'Patterns and Trends in Harlequin Category Romance', moves us to the realm of mass-market fiction, using bibliometric and stylometric methods to provide a number of important insights into this industry, including its authorship and production practices. In particular, Elliott's analysis of changes in the titles of these novels challenges the long-standing and prevailing view of the industry as static—offering a particular type of product and message to a specific type of reader—by identifying seismic shifts that significantly alter the narrative on offer.

In 'The Printers' Web', Sydney J. Shep describes the collaborative and interdisciplinary creation of a multidimensional digital biography of nineteenth-century printer Robert Coupland Harding, which is simultaneously an investigation into global print culture via the common practice of cut-and-paste journalism. Such journalism—presented as a predigital manifestation of open access as well as of viral texts and transnational readerships—is frequently described metaphorically as a network, web, or kaleidoscope. This project shows how digital methods and tools can be employed to investigate concrete manifestations of these hitherto metaphoric concepts by exploring the movement of texts through space and time, as well as the operations of a specifically printing-based culture and the life of an important historical figure. Paul Longley Arthur's chapter, 'Biographical Dictionaries in the Digital Era', approaches biography from a different perspective, reflecting on the complex transition from print to digital of a major national biographical dictionary and its reconceptualization as a virtual environment for social history and network analysis. This case study refers to historical, cultural, and technical factors to demonstrate how digital approaches have enabled a shift of emphasis away from the individual, focusing instead on tracing networks of associated lives—and in the process opening up new questions for biographical scholarship and extending the conventional role of biographical reference works in the digital environment.

The second section, 'Media Methods', presents digital humanities investigations into various forms and practices of media, both new and established. In 'Digital Methods in New Cinema History', Richard Maltby, Dylan Walker, and Mike Walsh describe and demonstrate a transition from film studies to new cinema history, where analysis of quantitative data shifts the focus from individual films, conceived as texts, to cinematic events and their circulation and consumption in local and global markets. Focusing on the AusCinemas database, the authors challenge prevailing assumptions about the history of cinema—for instance, the cause of cinema closure in Australia and that market's relationship with America—while also describing their experiments with crowdsourcing—their successes and failures—as a means of progressing such research and moving it beyond the academy.

The critical potential of data-rich analysis is also key to 'A "Big Data" Approach to Mapping the Australian Twittersphere' by Axel Bruns, Jean Burgess, and Tim Highfield, which takes a new approach to analysing Twitter, moving beyond discrete cases and investigation of particular topics and events via hashtag studies to explore the larger networked context in which this communication occurs. As the first attempt to identify, extract, analyse, and visualize the breadth and depth of a national portion of the Twittersphere, this study both explores key methodological challenges faced by large-scale analysis of proprietary systems and—in showing the distribution of particular topics across a wider network—analyses the operations of the Twittersphere and formation of social groups and identities online.

In 'iResearch', Mark Coté reports on an experiment that captures big social data (BSD) on mobile social media use in everyday interaction and communication. He argues that the data-constituted digital human—defined as 'a methodological covalence in the BSD database' and in terms of 'the human as always already in a constitutive relationship with technology' (this volume, 137)—should be a vital object of study in digital humanities. In particular, as we become 'native speakers' of technological syntax, BSD emerges as a cipher or a mediation of the digital human, thus providing a key area for understanding contemporary cultural heritage, society, and 'the structural complexity of the digital human and its cultural forms' (this volume, 132).

In 'Screenshots as Virtual Photography', Christopher Moore uses visualizations of the movement of video game screenshots—'a ubiquitous form of visual communication' (this publication, 141)—across social media platforms to investigate online identity formation and curation. The questions prompted by this process motivate new visualizations, investigations, and questions in a dialogic process that uses visual modelling as a basis for theorizing. Moore arrives at a conception of screenshots that challenges traditional hermeneutic and phenomenological interpretations derived from photography and instead highlights the performativity, materiality, affect, and motility of this form of online communication.

While apparent throughout the book, an explicitly self-conscious, critical approach to collections—whether of metadata, images, documents, or words—is foregrounded in the third section, 'Critical Curation'. In 'Rethinking Collections', Julia Flanders uses the language of modelling to situate the creation and coherence of collections not as neutral or standardized practices but as activities laden with specific intentions and driven by specific questions. Identifying the network and the patchwork as two dominant models for collections, Flanders considers the epistemological implications for the digital humanities of their different *modus operandi*: the former emphasizing connection, seamlessness, total commensurability, and increasing harmonization; the latter, assemblage, negotiation, and transaction.

This networked view of collections has the potential to support the positivist view of data—as truth or fact—that Katherine Bode and Tara Murphy critique in their chapter, 'Methods and Canons'. These authors analyse critical attention paid to Australian novelists and the issues of canon formation and cultural value relating to such judgements. However, to avoid the common association of data analysis with truth and comprehensiveness, Bode and Murphy publish their data along with a detailed account of the assumptions, arguments, and values that were involved in its creation. The approach they model emphasizes data's status as outcome, rather than unquestioned and unquestionable basis, of argument.

In 'Reading the Text, Walking the Terrain, Following the Map', Øyvind Eide likewise highlights the distance between, rather than equivalence of, data and the material world. Specifically, he employs computer modelling of maps and texts to identify and investigate the limitations of each as modes of representing the landscape. As Eide notes, all humanities scholars are aware that every medium has the capacity to represent only certain aspects of reality. However, modelling provides an enhanced understanding of both the nature of representation and mediation and how such systems play out at the micro level.

In 'Doing the Sheep Good', Deb Verhoeven investigates the role of databases in contemporary scholarly practices and knowledge formation. Far from being a neutral intervention, the 'production, organization, and communication of data' (this volume, 207) can encode its own implicit value system, fundamentally influencing how data is used and reused and the resultant conclusions that can be drawn. The author refers to case studies that link digital humanities with creative arts research, within and outside the academy, arguing for deeper and extended forms of engagement between modern academic work and wider publics.

In 'Materialities of Software', Ned Rossiter analyses the ways in which computational parameters increasingly mediate the production of knowledge, both in digital humanities itself and in the interests of global capital. According to Rossiter, existing computational methods—graphs, charts, digital maps, and so on—operate within and therefore have difficulty perceiving, let alone critiquing, the self-referentiality of data. In making a case for the need to invent new methods—relating to graphic design, game development, and digital visualization—Rossiter posits a mode of data analysis that resonates with Flanders's suggestion of a patchworked approach to collections: specifically, one that focuses not on equivalences or similarities—which 'integrate and make uniform data' in ways that erase geocultural differences—but on 'sites...where interoperability breaks down' as data rubs up against political, social, geographical, and material disruptions (this volume, 228).

In the book's final section, 'Research Futures', scholars who have for many years worked at the intersection of humanities and computing reflect on failings of the past to propose directions for the future. Peter Robinson's 'Digital Humanities' criticizes the dominant current model for digital humanities research—focused in centres and dependent on external funding—as unsustainable and argues instead for a future where an underlying infrastructure enables individual academics as well as scholar citizens to create and enrich materials over the Web. In 'Margins, Mainstreams and the Mission of Digital Humanities', Paul Turnbull asserts the need to challenge ingrained cultural mistrust of digital resources and technologies, while questioning the extent to which digitally based humanities research should be seen as distinct from the wider activities of humanities research that are increasingly informed by, and often integrally reliant on, the use of digital media and technology.

The major challenges and opportunities for digital humanities in the future are also the focus of the final two chapters, both of which have been published previously, Alan Liu's in French online journal *Ina*, and Willard McCarty's in *LLC: The Journal of Digital Scholarship in the Humanities*. In 'The Big Bang of Online Reading', Liu identifies online reading as equivalent for the digital humanities, and the humanities more broadly, to the 'big bang' in physics: an event unleashing 'a multiplicity of forces, materialities, forms, and dimensions' (this volume, 275). Liu argues that the resulting reconfigurations—of the media; of materiality; of literacy, in its sensory and social manifestations; and of cognition—together constitute a new research object in relation to which the digital humanities can offer important approaches and interventions.

In 'Getting There from Here', McCarty argues that the major challenge for digital humanities in the future is to realize we cannot avoid, and must instead embrace, being changed by the otherness of computing. Resting in—rather than retreating from—'the posthumanizing juncture where computing meets the humanities' will not divorce us from ourselves but help us to discover 'what it means to be human' (this volume, 306). By showcasing new approaches that harness not only the power of data but of our own humanity—in various forms of collectivity and ambitious generosity—this volume signals some of the ways in which digital humanities can work at this intersection, advancing discussion beyond a concern with definition to provide methodologically critical and dynamically theoretical modes of humanities research.

## Notes

1. See, for example, *A Digital Humanities Manifesto* (Manifesto) and its more recent manifestation, *A Digital Humanities Manifesto 2.0* (Manifesto 2.0), as well as *Digital_Humanities* (Lunenfeld et al.).
2. Similar arguments and observations had been outlined by Olsen (1991) and Kenny (1992).

## References

Gold, M. K. (2012). 'Introduction: The Digital Humanities Moment'. In *Debates in the Digital Humanities*, ed. M. K. Gold, ix–xvi. Minneapolis: University of Minnesota Press.

Juola, P. (2008). 'Killer Applications in Digital Humanities'. *Literary and Linguistic Computing* 23, no. 1: 73–83.

Kenny, Anthony. (1992). *Computers and the Humanities*. Ninth British Library Research Lecture. British Library, London.

Liu, A. (2011). 'The State of the Digital Humanities: A Report and a Critique'. *Arts and Humanities in Higher Education* 11, nos. 1–2: 8–41.

Liu, A. (2013). 'The Meaning of the Digital Humanities'. *PMLA* 128, no. 2: 409–23.

Lunenfeld, P., A. Burdick, J. Drucker, T. Presner, and J. Schnapp. (2012). *Digital_Humanities*. Cambridge, MA: MIT Press.

Manifesto. (2008). *A Digital Humanities Manifesto*. Available at: http://manifesto.humanities.ucla.edu.

Manifesto 2.0. (2009). *A Digital Humanities Manifesto 2.0*. Available at: http://manifesto.humanities.ucla.edu.

Olsen, Mark. (1991). 'What Can and Cannot Be Done With Electronic Text in Historical and Literary Research'. Paper for 'Modeling Literary Research Methods by Computer' session, Modern Language Association Annual Meeting, San Francisco, December.

Olsen, Mark. (1993/1994). 'Signs, Symbols and Discourses: A New Direction for Computer-Aided Literary Studies'. *Computers and the Humanities* 27, nos. 5–6: 309–14.

Pannapacker, W. (2009). 'The MLA and the Digital Humanities'. *Chronicle of Higher Education*, blog post, 28 December. Available at: http://chronicle.com/blogPost/The-MLAthe-Digital/19468/.

Pannapacker, W. (2011). 'Digital Humanities Triumphant'. *Chronicle of Higher Education*, blog post, 8 January. Available at: http://chronicle.com/blogs/brainstorm/pannapacker-at-mla-digital-humanities-triumphant/30915.

Potter, R. G. (1991). 'Statistical Analysis of Literature: A Retrospective on Computers and the Humanities, 1966–1990'. *Computers and the Humanities* 25, no. 6: 401–29.

Prescott, A. (2011). 'Consumers, Creators or Commentators? Problems of Audience and Mission in Digital Humanities'. *Arts and Humanities in Higher Education* 11, nos. 1–2: 61–75.

Ramsay, S. (2011). 'On Building'. Available at: http://lenz.unl.edu.

Terras, M., J. Nyhan, and E. Vanhoutte, eds. (2013). *Defining Digital Humanities: A Reader*. London: Ashgate.

# Part I
# Transforming Disciplines

# 2

# Exercises in Battology

## Digitizing Samuel Beckett's *Watt*

*Mark Byron*

Literary scholarship on the work of Samuel Beckett is cresting a wave brought about by the new availability of significant primary material—particularly the notebooks in which Beckett recorded his reading notes and early fragments of literary composition (Nixon and Van Hulle 2013; Nixon 2011; Feldman 2006b; Pilling 1992, 1999; Maxwell 2006; Bryden et al. 1998), as well as published volumes of letters (Beckett 2009, 2012). This heightened documentary awareness in Beckett studies has stimulated renewed attention to such hermeneutic matters as text structure, continuities of themes and tropes in Beckett's reading and note-taking, and the varieties of citation and allusion in his texts. Analogous forms of literary scholarship and critical interpretation also flourish, including a series of monumental annotative studies of specific Beckett texts (Pilling 2004; Ackerley 1998, 2005; Ackerley and Gontarski 2004). Consequently this activity has provoked new insights into aspects of Beckett's composition processes and the material state of his manuscripts and published works. Manuscript documents in particular provide a broader and richer framework within which to describe the Beckett 'text' as a literary event or process. Current efforts to digitize these documents and provide authoritative transcriptions of them compel acute reflections on the status of Beckett's texts and the editorial methods adequate to the task of establishing and representing them in scholarly editions. The narrator of Samuel Beckett's 1953 novel, *Watt*, neatly captures this tension between diachrony and formal repetition in narrative form and textual structure when he states: 'Watt's sense of chronology was strong, in a way, and his dislike for battology was very strong' (Beckett 1959, 165). Such an observation resonates alongside attempts to conceptualize and mark up complex narratives for digital presentation in scholarly editions. Textual criticism and hermeneutics have still to catch up with some of the formal and structural experiments of Beckett's texts.

Of the richly various experimental literary works of Modernism, *Watt* enjoys a singular reputation for its complex, fragmented narrative structure. Its emblematic status as an avant-garde challenge to literary convention is manifested in its many footnotes, musical scores, 'manuscript' perforations in the narrative, and extended prose sequences of 'battological' prose. This textual-material endowment is clarified further when the novel's very extensive manuscript archive is taken into account. This repository comprises nearly a thousand pages of drafts, revisions, and substantial narrative divergences from the published text. The manuscripts are famous in their own right as aesthetic objects—they are densely illustrated with Beckett's 'doodlings'—but very few scholars have read or studied them at any length, preliminary to any attempt to measure their evolution against published editions of the novel. The logic of a digital edition of this complex manuscript material is clear: to provide coherent ways of mapping the network of confluences and divergences between manuscript and published text, as a first, critical step towards exploring their semantic and hermeneutic implications. The sheer size of the manuscript record provides sufficient reason for digital representation, but a well-designed digital framework can go further: it can illuminate patterns and complexities in the material not otherwise readily evident in analogue form, presenting textual features at different orders of magnitude and in various modes (visual, statistical, diagrammatic, linguistic, and so on). This foundation opens up possibilities for further hermeneutic analysis and textual criticism, extending and challenging the ways in which this text and its manuscript have been understood both conceptually and as material objects.

The digital edition of the *Watt* manuscripts constitutes an early module in the Samuel Beckett Digital Manuscript Project (BDMP)—a large, international project that aims to digitize the complete manuscripts of Beckett's published literary works (Van Hulle 2011). Current work on the *Watt* module already suggests new modes of viewing and understanding the novel's narrative. The complex and often very subtle relationships between elements of the manuscript text—many of which do not appear in full or at all in the published text—are eminently conducive to digital display. The digital edition provides the careful reader with a more precisely calibrated appreciation for the reticulated networks of reference, association, and narrative lines in the manuscript material, and the implications of their recycled, revised, or omitted status in the published text. Such a digital remediation of archival documents provides benefits beyond the practical reach of print-based editions: the ability to visualize complex networks of citation and association across a large manuscript brings schematic focus to an otherwise bewildering document. Features such as multiple-page views aid in visualizing phases of composition, where doodles on verso pages, for example, often correlate to fluent, fractured, or otherwise distended prose on facing recto pages. XML-encoded information regarding patterns of emendation (the location of inserted material on the page, the nature of deletions, patterns of differently coloured inks, and so on) provides the tools by which to quantify, collate and interpret highly imbricated narrative material.

What kinds of benefits might accrue to the reader of such an edition? *Watt* is Beckett's most perplexing novel, presenting a turbulent text surface and a series of reticulated narrative digressions and redundancies. Consequently it has not received the same intensive critical attention as his other novels, despite its pivotal function as the transitional phase between the author's youthful, Joycean displays of learning (*More Pricks Than Kicks, Murphy*) and the mature investigations into subjectivity and identity (*Molloy, Malone Dies, The Unnamable*) for which he became famous. *Watt* also marks the shift in Beckett's language of composition, from English to French. Although written in English, the manuscript contains numerous Gallicisms and other grammatical and syntactic tendencies bearing a French linguistic imprimatur. The obvious merits of the *Watt* digital manuscript consist in providing mediated access to complex primary materials, opening up new zones of hermeneutic inquiry and textual scholarship in Beckett studies. But the potential benefits and consequences of the digital edition extend further: to the context of Modernist scholarship more generally (particularly the famous 'documentary turn' of recent years), to the theory and practice of textual scholarship, and to the ways in which these fields each negotiate the potential challenges and opportunities of the digital sphere.

By digitizing the eccentric manuscript of an elliptical, avant-garde text, the structure and content of its physical archive may be better understood, to a degree equalled only by a direct appraisal of the physical documents, offering a schematic account of their codicological and semantic features. A clearer understanding of the fractured and fragmented nature of the composition also situates *Watt* more precisely with regard to Modernist experimentalism and literary fragmentation. The literary fragment has, in a sense, always been a central fact of textual scholarship: from the preservation of ancient literary and biblical texts in papyrus fragments (such as the Nag Hammadi Library, or Oxford University's online Oxyrhynchus Papyrus project at http://www.papyrology.ox.ac.uk/POxy/), to the complementary discourses of fragment and ruin that shaped the contest between Classicism and Romanticism in the eighteenth century (McFarland 1981; Seyhan 1992; Harries 1994), to the disintegrations and dismantlings of literary forms and genres in the twentieth-century transatlantic avant-garde. The *Watt* digital edition provides a model for how these fragments, documents, and texts relate to one another, but also raises questions of how they calibrate with larger modes of experimentalism in Modernist aesthetics, and how textual scholarship might respond to these basic challenges to the literary artefact in adequate scholarly editions.

The BDMP is an important experiment in evaluating the relative value and costs of digital tools and methods in scholarly literary projects more generally. It is an evolving case study in how such digital innovations might function with traditional scholarly methods (such as stemmatics and philology), as well as ways in which newer methods are being developed (such as genetic editing techniques and corresponding Text Encoding Initiative [TEI] protocols). The enormous potential for digital literary scholarship dwells in large part in the scale-changing implications of large-batch processing of information—although this notion of rendering the literary artefact into raw data can catalyse scepticism towards large-scale (and costly) computer-aided humanities research. The present task is to strengthen a middle ground in scholarly practice and digital design, where digital humanities and traditional scholarly methods might interact productively and thus extend their respective zones of capability. In his review of *The Evolution of*

*Texts* (Macé et al. 2006), Tuomas Heikillä takes stock of the rapid advances in digital methods in textual scholarship:

> There has hardly ever been a period during which textual scholarship (or philology) has seen so many new challenges and opportunities as in the past few years. The computerization of the study of texts—be they ancient, medieval, or modern—the use of digital images, and the transformation of the concept of 'edition' have all played their part.
>
> (2007, 298)

Heikillä observes how computer-aided approaches to stemmatology reconfigure the theoretical and empirical landscape. He delineates the virtues of cross-disciplinary experimentation in developing new stemmatic and philological tools, such as phylogenetic methods adapted from biology and information theory. But these intersections work most effectively when digital methods are directed by critical insight: Heikillä notes that in one experiment described in *The Evolution of Texts*—in which a range of methodologies were deployed to attempt the generation of a stemmatic record of an artificial manuscript tradition—the obvious utility of digital tools when applied to very large datasets did not eclipse the accuracy and elegance of classical methods in stemmatology. A critically reflective digital (or analogue) edition is predicated on elegance of design, utility of function, and the explanatory power of its conceptual models, whether cutting-edge, classical, or hybrid.

## Reading with the *Watt* digital edition

The *Watt* digital manuscript edition aims to provide a mediated primary resource: the fullest representation of the *Watt* manuscript notebooks, housed at the Harry Ransom Center at the University of Texas at Austin, made accessible by way of an intuitive web interface (beckettarchive.org). The digital reproduction of the manuscript may be visualized in several ways—thumbnail images, parallel image-text functions, close-up images—and interacts with the XML-encoded transcription via a scrollover transcription function. The many doodles are presented schematically, recording their relationships with corresponding text material. These features allow for a more nuanced reading experience of the manuscript and illustrate how digital mediation can facilitate complex aspects of philology: stemmatic relationships between elements of a single document; the architecture of a literary object within a preliminary and evolving material form; and the complex interactions between word and image, often spatially disconnected or obliquely linked conceptually, otherwise invisible to all but the most assiduous codicologist. Examples of the word-image relation are abundant. Many of Beckett's doodles comprise humanoid figures, directly reflecting the evolution of the concept of character in the manuscript, and geometric figures visualize the permutative logic of several extended narrative phases.

The nearly 1,000 pages of Beckett's manuscript were composed from 1941 to 1945, mostly in the town of Roussillon in Vichy France following Beckett's abrupt departure from Paris upon its fall to the Wehrmacht. The notebooks vividly display the changing historical and aesthetic circumstances of their composition. They are famous among Modernist literary manuscripts for their floridly chaotic layout, mediated by the exacting, parodic logic and permutative strings of prose, a representative proportion of which survives in some form in the published text. The need for a coherent manuscript transcription becomes obvious, as a way of giving a context for—if not necessarily an answer to—the many riddles, non sequiturs, dangling references, and narrative digressions in the published text. The design and functionality of the *Watt* digital manuscript edition opens up newly available textual information and, consequently, new lines of research and hermeneutic inquiry. This level of access is of particular significance in the context of copyright issues surrounding Modernist texts, and, in the specific case of Beckett studies, indicates that both the Beckett estate and the Ransom Center (copyright holder of the material documents) are sensitive to the scholarly and pedagogical benefits of such access. The digital archive is proprietary in nature: it is available by subscription, which includes a monograph to accompany each module of the BDMP.

The *Watt* digital manuscript project prompts critical reflection on the nature and structure of primary materials in Modernist literature, their scholarly framework, and ways in which digital frameworks manifestly alter the landscape of literary studies. On the one hand, digital tools and techniques evolve rapidly, and on the other, the Anglophone editorial tradition has only begun to draw systematically from other theories and methods of editing, particularly the German philological tradition and French genetic criticism. As a way of framing the relation between the digital archive and text status in the case of *Watt*, two related questions might be posed. First, what scholarly need is being met by the production of a digital manuscript transcription? Second, what kinds of scholarly implications might there be by virtue of its digital delivery? Scholarly need might be justified by virtue of the famous inscrutability of this novel: the availability of primary materials establishes a wider critical context by which to understand the novel's (eccentric) composition process and its purported aesthetic aims. Its narrative is concerned with gnosis at various levels—not least with regard to the eponymous antihero in his quest for *any* meaning—but rather than dwelling in inscrutability, the reader is readily able to understand how such gnostic themes are developed in the published narrative, as well as in the framing textual apparatus that seems to thwart narrative integrity (the footnotes and Addenda, songs, and serial reference to a fragmented 'manuscript'). The reader may read beyond the surface of the published text with a deeper appreciation of how verbally artistic objects evolve, and how they codify aesthetic decisions in their creation. The second question concerning scholarly implications identifies specific and generalized potential gains for literary scholarship. The *Watt* digital manuscript (and literary projects with cognate aspirations) presents an opportunity to challenge the long-standing division between textual criticism and literary criticism in the Anglophone academy: any hermeneutic activity is fundamentally informed (overtly or otherwise) by the status of documents and texts and the methods of their representation. A coherent and comprehensive representation of manuscript documents aids specific interpretive work on *Watt* and also provides a focused opportunity to rethink the relationships between documents, texts, and works in literary scholarship more generally. The second half of this chapter illustrates both questions, but elsewhere I have given a more extensive account of the technical details of the project, albeit with reference to a previous interface now significantly updated (Byron 2010).

The *Watt* manuscript notebooks comprise a rich archive of primary documents for perhaps the most inscrutable of Beckett's works. Both the published text and its imbricated manuscripts display complex, uneven surface structures, which are replete with apparent non sequiturs, cryptic allusions, and references freighted with rhetorical significance, but seem to have lost their semantic anchors. The manuscript and the published text also share strong physical resemblances, most vividly in the disintegrating narrative surface and its documenting editorial voice: breaks towards the end of the narrative in the published text are punctuated by such comments as '(Hiatus in MS)' (Beckett 1959, 238), '(MS illegible)' (241), and extensive use of ellipses (239). A series of Addenda items follow the main narrative and compound this metafictional nod towards the presence of a manuscript within the narrative frame. Continuing this blurring of the real and fictive contingencies of the physical text (Beckett was in hiding from the Wehrmacht for several years), several of these Addenda items straddle a rhetorical divide between metafiction and authorial aides-mémoire: '*Watt learned to accept* etc. Use to explain poverty of Part III' (248), 'Note that Arsene's declarations gradually come back to Watt' (248), and the significant directive to 'change all the names' (253). Several of the Addenda items function as keys to sometimes much larger narrative episodes in the manuscript notebooks and typescript, and are not revisions or redactions in any conventional sense. They constitute a coded shorthand by which the author is able to register and preserve, at the level of concept or image, larger portions of his manuscript narrative, contained within physical documents that survived the war but, like their author, were by no means guaranteed to do so.

The nature of the documentary record makes the transcription of the manuscript notebooks an important scholarly exercise for a number of reasons. First, the material is valuable in its own right, comprising hundreds of pages of little-known compositional matter. The associations or, in some cases, direct correlation between manuscript and published text offer us a richly suggestive body of material by which to reconsider the published text of *Watt* and Beckett's compositional practices at this time. Second, the practical benefits of having a readable representation of this substantial material are significant when one considers the size of the archive and the difficulty of deciphering Beckett's orthography. The expense of producing a paper-based facsimile of the manuscript and its transcription, together with its size and complexity, present strong arguments for digital presentation. A Web-based transcription also offers scholars and students access to a representation of the manuscript material in the archives at the Harry Ransom Center at the University of Texas at Austin. Third, the relationship between archival material and published text is neither linear nor teleological. An adequate conceptual model for this complex literary manuscript is a necessary first step in a comprehensive model of the text, preliminary to any serious attempt at a scholarly edition. The singularities of the *Watt* archive present specific challenges to the current range of editorial practices. The blurred edges between archive and published text pose radical questions about the conceptual possibility of stable published texts. This profound reconfiguration of text status presents a basic challenge to editorial practice, even for the otherwise very conducive genetic text model, but it also provides a clear opportunity for digital tools and methods to represent the text in ways impractical or impossible in analogue forms.

This third point—the relation of archival material to published text—is best illustrated by means of an example taken from the transcribed notebooks. The *Watt* digital manuscript is encoded to display diplomatic and topographic transcription information (that is, a faithful representation of the manuscript page, including errors and the precise spatial distribution of linguistic material), as well as a full representation of additions, deletions, and *paralipomena* (manuscript material omitted in subsequent documents). Other potentially significant sources of information encoded in the XML markup include the kinds of writing tools used at specific points in the manuscript, such as the pink pencil Beckett used to change a string of names in Notebook 1. Such transcriptional trends bear potentially great hermeneutic significance, and a digitized manuscript is profoundly more easily searchable at this level of granularity. The very strong correlation between Notebook 6 and the published editions of *Watt* still contain clues to radical phases of emendation: the Juxta collation of pages 98–100 of Notebook 6 and the corresponding passages in the British and American editions of the text display the change of proper names in the episode, from Tully to Nolan and from Parnell to Gorman (Figure 2.1). The significance of these changes rests in what they tell us of Beckett's style of allusion. He decides to 'change all the names' in this episode (and we recall that this is alluded to in the novel's Addenda): from two historically significant figures (Tully being the Roman philosopher and orator Cicero, and Charles Stuart Parnell, the nineteenth-century Irish nationalist hero) to two generic Irish family names. This change diminishes or disguises the otherwise prominent intertextuality (the classical rhetorical tradition, and Irish nationalism in time of war), in a hallmark process of 'vaguening' for which Beckett's much later work is famous. These changes occur late in the final notebook, well after the Addenda directive to 'change all the names' appears in Notebook 3:62. This suggests that the Addenda item and the fact of Beckett's changing the names of his characters in the manuscripts are linked but are not one and the same: in other words, the 'archived' Addenda items encode specific events in the manuscripts, but also effect a metatextual commentary on them and give them a phantasmic textual afterlife.

The consequences of name changes in the manuscript record become more profound on closer consideration of dispersed documentary evidence across the archive and into the published text of *Watt*. Generating word clouds of the manuscript notebooks (deploying the resources available at wordle.net) provides a provocative visualization of the textual strategy of name changing. The word cloud of Notebook three, for example, is dominated by the word 'one', which is not surprising in a narrative so preoccupied with questions of identity. This word is

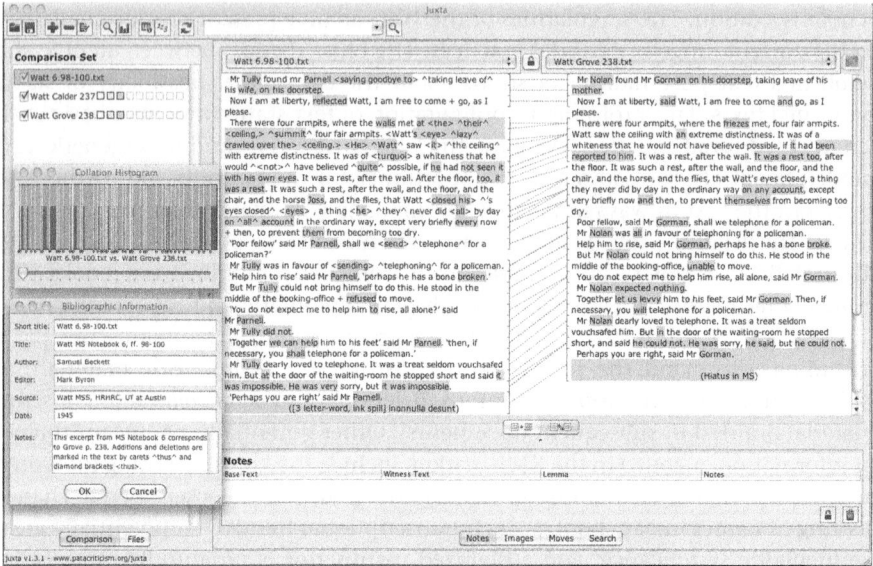

*Figure 2.1*  Juxta window of *Watt* MS 6:98–100 and *Watt* (1953/1959, 238), with collation histogram and comment apparatus

flanked by the names Watt, Lynch, Quin, Arsene, and Erskine, all of which appear in the published text with the exception of Quin (the character who is transformed into the more passive and enigmatic Knott in the published text). Names also dominate the word cloud of Notebook four—Watt, Hackett, and Nixon—reflecting the fact that this notebook contains the draft of what is to become Part I of the novel, where the decrepit character named Hackett first meets a couple, Goff and Tetty Nixon, at the park bench, before the novel's shambolic antihero makes his appearance nearby, disembarking from a tram. These two word clouds immediately recall the Addenda directive to 'change all the names'. One would expect the word cloud of a novel to be dominated by characters' names, but the changing emphasis on specific names in different notebooks may indicate that something else is afoot. The relationship between the two characters, Hackett and Watt, is a most lucid illustration of the complexities at work in the manuscript, an indication of its reticulated rather than teleological structure. The first-person narrator of the first three notebooks is transformed into the character Watt in the later notebooks and in the published text. But this earlier figure is not discarded altogether from the later evolution of the narrative. He becomes the elderly Hackett. This character appears only in the opening cameo scene of the published text but occupies a critically important place, allowing us to see exactly how the Addenda section functions in relation to manuscript change.

The opening scene of the novel has Mr Nixon unable to reconcile his uncanny associations of Hackett and Watt. When the latter appears at the tram stop, Nixon is at a loss to account for his familiarity. He first claims, 'I cannot say I really know him', and then 'I seem to have known him all my life, but there must have been a period when I did not' (18). The punch line comes with his confession to Hackett: 'The curious thing is, my dear fellow, I tell you quite frankly, that when I see him, or think of him, I think of you, and that when I see you, or think of you, I think of him. I have no idea why this is so' (19). With the aid of the digital manuscript transcription, and the visual clues offered by word clouds, the attentive reader knows precisely why Nixon finds himself in this uncanny predicament. It is because Hackett and Watt are different incarnations of the same fictional character, appearing together in the same place, contrary to all rules of naturalistic representation. Hackett is an archival revenant of the novel's antihero, visibly dessicating before Nixon, as physically fragile as the manuscript pages from which he emerges and to which his presence refers.

## Scholarly implications

The *Watt* digital manuscript provides a range of features to assist with traditional literary scholarship, opening new ways of thinking about Modernist literary texts in the contexts of book history, material culture, publishing, and new media of the early twentieth century. The module allows Beckett scholars to better understand the global and specific implications for text provenance in the documentary record of this text: the ways in which manuscript notes and episodes are transposed, sedimented, recycled, buried, and fragmented are various and by no means obvious, as the example above demonstrates. The digitized manuscript transcription allows for both global and granular searches: it is the means by which new thinking on text transformation and modes of allusion might inform an understanding of Beckett's published texts more generally. Additionally, by giving a schematic representation of the documentary record, specific aspects of Beckett's composition practices come into sharp focus: his processes of manuscript revision (distinct phases of which are indicated by different colours of ink), the relation between the extensive manuscript doodles and the processes of composition (where the kinds of doodles on verso pages can often be correlated to fluent, fractured, or otherwise distended prose composition on facing recto pages), and the submerged significance of Addenda entries in the published text can be threaded back to sometimes extensive networks of reference and composition at multiple points of the manuscript record.

The *Watt* digital manuscript also provides the first major step towards a scholarly edition of this crucial text within Beckett's oeuvre. The production of adequate critical editions of major Modernist texts is perhaps the most significant task yet to be properly engaged in Modernist studies, with a few notable exceptions (this situation is at least partly a consequence of copyright issues). That the texts of a figure of Beckett's stature remain available only in corrupt published editions is scandalous. In a close study of this problem, S. E. Gontarski quotes Beckett's lament to his biographer, James Knowlson, that 'my texts are in a terrible mess', and singles out *Watt* as 'perhaps the most egregious' example (Gontarski 1995, 190). The point could not be clearer: without adequately edited texts, even the most innovative work in Modernist studies will suffer deficiencies of empirical, formal, and conceptual varieties, many of which remain invisible until the rigorous work of textual scholarship has uncovered them. It is well known in the circles of textual studies and philology that a great variety of text models and techniques remain available but unused, largely stemming from the German philological tradition and its rich inheritance in the last century. Comprehensive digital representations of complex manuscripts seem perfectly suited to such textual models as the *Handschriftenedition*—the 'sui generis edition of working drafts and manuscripts' (Gabler 1995, 4) in which documents are represented as self-standing artefacts, rather than as clues to an ideal textual condition or a text 'intended' by its author to take forms other than those in material evidence. Recent work has sought to expand the Text Encoding Initiative's (TEI) editorial repertoire to include a tagging suite for genetic models of literary texts. This major step (Burnard et al. 2010) provides the means to expand the editorial repertoire whilst maintaining coherent standards of markup.

The Beckett Digital Manuscript Project thus aims to serve multiple utilities in literary studies. Its most immediate utility is to provide scholars with reliable transcriptions of Beckett's manuscripts, with searchable photographic reproductions and apparatus, in an intuitive digital environment. The consequence of success will be to provide scholars with access to (mediated) primary materials in such a way as to invoke new kinds of research questions, or else to provide the tools to considerably strengthen existing scholarship. A desirable consequence in the use of digital editions is to elucidate the kinds of decisions and methods employed by the transcriber-editor, and to make apparent the various freedoms and constraints of the digital platform, both at specific points and generally. By virtue of this project and others, Beckett studies is grappling with the old chestnut of the value of primary textual scholarship (or 'excavatory reason') when measured against, or in dialectic with, varieties of hermeneutic analysis. Recent debate over the roles of empirical research and theory-led research brings some of these methodological concerns at the very heart of literary scholarship to the surface (Feldman 2006a; Dowd 2008; Feldman 2008). Wide usage of digital tools in Beckett studies is already leading to a broader and theoretically nuanced understanding of the issues at stake in digital (and traditional) scholarly editorial work: since the launch of the BDMP at 'Beckett Out of the Archives', a conference at the University of York in 2011, the community has absorbed the initial allure of the 'shiny new toy' and is coming to grips with the functionalities and capabilities of a digitized manuscript. Even the most basic aspects of codicology—such as the relationship between the physical layout of a notebook or loose leaves and the distribution of written material, writing tools, patterns of handwriting and doodling, and modes of emendation—are coming into renewed focus by virtue of their digital dissemination. This powerful example shows how digital innovation and traditional textual studies mutually inform one another.

The present is an opportune moment for the re-evaluation of Anglophone scholarly editing techniques with regard to Modernism more generally, not least by drawing on the largely neglected German philological tradition. Modernist studies has undergone a revolution in the last two decades, adopting or inventing new theoretical paradigms and techniques of critical analysis—'bad' Modernisms (Mao and Walkowitz 2006), the event (Badiou 2005; Gibson 2007), the new materialism (Bornstein 2001)—and expanding into hitherto foreign territory—popular culture (Naremore and Brandlinger 1991), transnational literary and aesthetic culture (Gikandi 2006), mass media (Campbell 2006), advertising and celebrity (Jaffe 2005), and so on. This increased awareness of the variegations of the material objects, performances, and artworks at the centre of Modernist studies prompts reflection upon the tools and techniques that scholars use to represent and understand them. The hermeneutic task has been taken into hand in much of this new work, but the project of adequate curatorial and editorial methods is still in its adolescence. The Modernist text as a material process and object (whether dispersed, multiple, or unified) calls for just such methodological innovation, and recent work in digital stemmatics, large-batch collation, and digital editorial architectures indicates opportunity for significant advances in digital scholarly editing. The history of digital editorial projects—largely housed within university departments or centres—demands caution against overreaching ambition in design and overstatement in deliverable results, especially with regard to timing, resources, and cost. Yet it is equally clear that each side of the equation, as it were, is mandated to better understand and integrate what the other might offer: innovative digital tools and techniques, on the one hand, and an as-yet underexploited fund of textual theory and editorial methods on the other.

## Works cited

Ackerley, Chris. (1998). *Demented Particulars: The Annotated. Murphy*. Tallahassee, FL: Journal of Beckett Studies Books.

Ackerley, Chris. (2005). *Obscure Locks, Simple Keys: The Annotated. Watt*. Tallahassee, FL: Journal of Beckett Studies Books.

Ackerley, Chris, and S. E. Gontarski. (2004). *The Grove Companion to Samuel Beckett*. New York: Grove.

Badiou, Alain. (2005). *Being and Event*. Trans. Oliver Feltham. London: Continuum.

Beckett, Samuel. (1953/1959). *Watt*. New York: Grove.

Beckett, Samuel. (2009). *The Letters of Samuel Beckett*. Volume 1. *1929–1940*, ed. Martha Dow Fehsenfeld and Lois More Overbeck. Cambridge: Cambridge University Press.

Beckett, Samuel. (2012). *The Letters of Samuel Beckett*. Volume 2. *1941–1956*, ed. Martha Dow Fehsenfeld and Lois More Overbeck. Cambridge: Cambridge University Press.

Bornstein, George. (2001). *Material Modernism: The Politics of the Page*. Cambridge: Cambridge University Press.

Bryden, Mary, Julian Garforth and Peter Mills. (1998). *Beckett at Reading: Catalogue of the Samuel Beckett Manuscript Collection at the University of Reading*. Reading, UK: Beckett International Foundation.

Burnard, Lou, Fotis Jannidis, Elena Pierazzo, Malte Rehbein, Gregor Middell, and Moritz Wissenbach. (2010). 'An Encoding Model for Genetic Editions'. Available at: http://users.ox.ac.uk/~ lou/wip/geneticTEI.doc.html.

Byron, Mark. (2010). 'Digital Scholarly Editions of Modernist Texts: Navigating the Text in Samuel Beckett's *Watt* Manuscripts'. *Sydney Studies in English* 36: 150–69.

Campbell, Timothy. (2006). *Wireless Writing in the Age of Marconi*. Minneapolis: University of Minnesota Press.

Dowd, Garin. (2008). 'Prolegomena to a Critique of Excavatory Reason: Reply to Matthew Feldman'. In *Samuel Beckett Today/Aujourd'hui 20 'Des Eléments aux Traces/Elements and Traces'*, ed. Matthijs Engelberts, Danièle de Ruyter, Karine Germoni and Helen Penet-Astbury, 375–88. Amsterdam: Rodopi.

Feldman, Matthew. (2006a). 'Beckett and Popper, or, "what stink of artifice": Some Notes on Methodology, Falsifiability, and Criticism in Beckett Studies'. In *Samuel Beckett Today/Aujourd'hui 16, 'Notes Diverse Holo'*, ed. Matthijs Engelberts, Everett Frost, and Jane Maxwell, 373–91. Amsterdam: Rodopi.

Feldman, Matthew. (2006b). *Beckett's Books: A Cultural History of Samuel Beckett's 'Interwar Notes'*. London: Continuum.

Feldman, Matthew. (2008). 'In Defence of Empirical Knowledge: Rejoinder to "A Critique of Excavatory Reason"'.In *Samuel Beckett Today/Aujourd'hui 20 'Des Eléments aux Traces/Elements and Traces'*, ed. Matthijs Engelberts, Danièle de Ruyter, Karine Germoni and Helen Penet-Astbury, 389–99. Amsterdam: Rodopi.

Gabler, Hans Walter. (1995). 'Introduction'. In *Contemporary German Editorial Theory*, ed. Hans Walter Gabler, George Bornstein and Gillian Borland Pierce, 1–16. Ann Arbor: University of Michigan Press.

Gibson, Andrew. (2007). *Beckett and Badiou: The Pathos of Intermittency*. New York: Oxford University Press.

Gikandi, Simon. (2006). 'Modernism in the World'. Preface. *Modernism/Modernity* 13.3 (September): 419–24.

Gontarski, S. E. (1995). 'Editing Beckett'. *Twentieth Century Literature* 41.2 (Summer): 190–207.

Harries, Elizabeth Wanning. (1994). *The Unfinished Manner: Essays on the Fragment in the Later Eighteenth Century*. Charlottesville: University of Virginia Press.

Heikillä, Tuomas. (2007). 'Review of *The Evolution of Texts: Confronting Stemmatological and Genetic Methods. Proceedings of the International Workshop held in Louvain-la-Neuve on 1–2 September 2004*, ed. Caroline Macé, Philippe Baret, Andreas Bozzi, and Laura Cignoni'. *Variants* 6, 296–9.

Jaffe, Aaron. (2005). *Modernism and the Culture of Celebrity*. Cambridge: Cambridge University Press.

Macé, Caroline, Philippe Baret, Andreas Bozzi, and Laura Cignoni, eds. (2006). *The Evolution of Texts: Confronting Stemmatological and Genetic Methods*. Proceedings of the International Workshop Held in Louvain-la-Neuve on 1–2 September 2004. Pisa: Istituto editoriali e poligrafici internazionali.

Mao, Douglas, and Patricia E. Walkowitz, eds. (2006). *Bad Modernisms*. Durham, NC: Duke University Press.

Maxwell, Jane. (2006). 'Catalogue of the Samuel Beckett Manuscripts at Trinity College Library, Dublin'. In *Samuel Beckett Today/AujourdŠhui 16, 'Notes Diverse Holo'*, ed. Matthijs Engelberts, Everett Frost, and Jane Maxwell, 183–99. Amsterdam: Rodopi.

McFarland, Thomas. (1981). *Romanticism and the Forms of Ruin: Wordsworth, Coleridge, and Modalities of Fragmentation*. Princeton: Princeton University Press.

Naremore, James, and Patrick Brandlinger, eds. (1991). *Modernity and Mass Culture*. Bloomington: Indiana University Press.

Nixon, Mark. (2011). *Samuel Beckett's German Diaries, 1936–1937*. London: Continuum.

Nixon, Mark, and Dirk Van Hulle. (2013). *Samuel Beckett's Library*. Cambridge: Cambridge University Press.

Oxford Papyrology Online. Available at: http://www.papyrology.ox.ac.uk/POxy/.

Pilling, John. (1992). 'From a (W)horoscope to Murphy'. In *The Ideal Core of the Onion*, ed. John Pilling and Mary Bryden, 1–20. Reading, UK: Beckett International Foundation.

Pilling, John. (1999). *Beckett's Dream Notebook*. Reading, UK: Beckett International Foundation.

Pilling, John. (2004). *A Companion to Dream of Fair to Middling Women*. Tallahassee, FL: Journal of Beckett Studies Books.

Seyhan, Azade. (1992). *Representation and Its Discontents: The Critical Legacy of German Romanticism*. Berkeley: University of California Press.

Van Hulle, Dirk. (2011). *The Making of Samuel Beckett's Stirrings Still/Soubresauts and Comment dire/What Is the Word*. Beckett Digital Manuscript Project 1. Brussels: Academic and Scientific Publishers.

# 3

# Stylometry of Dickens's Language

## An Experiment with Random Forests

*Tomoji Tabata*

Textual analysis often begins with identifying 'key' words of a text, on the assumption that keywords reflect what the text is really about—and likely the stylistic features of the text as well. In corpus linguistics, 'key-words of a text, in the sense intended here, are words which can be shown to occur in the text with a frequency greater than the expected frequency (using some relevant measure), to an extent which is statistically significant' (Wynne 2007, 730). A popular method to measure 'keyness' is to calculate a log-likelihood ratio (LLR) score to assess the significance of difference between the expected and observed frequency of a word in a text (Dunning 1993; Rayson and Garside 2000).[1] However, one drawback of this approach emerges when we compare Dickens's texts with, for example, a set of texts by his contemporary, Wilkie Collins.[2] Table 3.1 lists 40 of the most significant keywords of Dickens as compared with Collins in descending order based on their LLR score. Words in boldface type appear only in one text, while words in italics are found in a very small number (two to four) of the texts in the corpus.

Although proper names such as *Dombey, Pecksniff,* and *Boffin* are ranked among the top 40 Dickensian 'key' words, none of these would normally be counted as important, at least from a stylistic perspective, apart from the fact that they represent a few peculiar Dickensian characters who appear only in a single text. Meanwhile, 19 of the top 100 entries on the list occur only in a single text. A close look at words listed as Collins's keywords reveals that 35 of the top 100 are from a single text. If words that occur only in a very small number of texts are included, the proportion becomes even greater. A less obvious drawback comes from the mathematical fact that LLR emphasizes high-frequency items: Indeed, high-frequency words predominate at the top of the list in Table 3.1, in comparison with words in lower-frequency strata.

Hoover (2003) suggests culling of variables to address the issue of peculiarly distributed words. In conducting a series of cluster analyses under a combination of different conditions, he found an improved accuracy in text clustering when culling at 80 per cent—that is, when removing from the analysis words for which a single text supplies more than 80 per cent of occurrences (Hoover 2003, 350–51). Hoover (2004) adopted a more stringent culling, at 70 per cent.

*Table 3.1* Forty most significant keywords of the Dickens corpus as compared with the Wilkie Collins corpus (sorted according to the log-likelihood ratios [LLR])

| Rank | Word | Frequency | In Files | Proportion % | LLR |
|---|---|---|---|---|---|
| 1 | upon | 12,990 | 24 | 0.27 | 8871.058 |
| 2 | and | 176,688 | 24 | 3.65 | 8215.058 |
| 3 | Mr | 31,312 | 24 | 0.65 | 5151.845 |
| 4 | very | 14,312 | 24 | 0.30 | 3639.361 |
| 5 | so | 20,986 | 24 | 0.43 | 3479.701 |
| 6 | a | 109,288 | 24 | 2.26 | 2666.071 |
| 7 | but | 26,202 | 24 | 0.54 | 2580.812 |
| 8 | said | 30,698 | 24 | 0.63 | 2457.399 |
| 9 | *Pickwick* | 2,198 | 2 | 0.05 | 2373.409 |
| 10 | great | 6,975 | 24 | 0.14 | 2015.407 |
| 11 | much | 7,268 | 24 | 0.15 | 1912.053 |
| 12 | *Nicholas* | 1,740 | 4 | 0.04 | 1878.858 |
| 13 | they | 17,630 | 24 | 0.36 | 1863.395 |
| 14 | Tom | 1,846 | 21 | 0.04 | 1712.521 |
| 15 | **Dombey** | 1,420 | 1 | 0.03 | 1533.321 |
| 16 | replied | 3,875 | 24 | 0.08 | 1447.446 |
| 17 | John | 2,113 | 24 | 0.04 | 1432.579 |
| 18 | **Pecksniff** | 1,250 | 1 | 0.03 | 1349.755 |
| 19 | gentleman | 4,601 | 24 | 0.10 | 1344.429 |
| 20 | or | 16,102 | 24 | 0.33 | 1278.461 |
| 21 | king | 1,687 | 21 | 0.03 | 1275.183 |
| 22 | Joe | 1,172 | 17 | 0.02 | 1251.145 |
| 23 | Martin | 1,121 | 7 | 0.02 | 1210.460 |
| 24 | **Boffin** | 1,105 | 1 | 0.02 | 1193.183 |
| 25 | being | 6,904 | 24 | 0.14 | 1181.222 |
| 26 | though | 3,841 | 24 | 0.08 | 1180.777 |
| 27 | *Sam* | 1,210 | 4 | 0.02 | 1143.636 |
| 28 | many | 4,225 | 24 | 0.09 | 1141.551 |
| 29 | down | 8,408 | 24 | 0.17 | 1088.151 |
| 30 | *Weller* | 992 | 2 | 0.02 | 1071.165 |
| 31 | *Dorrit* | 971 | 2 | 0.02 | 1048.489 |
| 32 | 'em | 1,331 | 21 | 0.03 | 1047.537 |
| 33 | old | 9,624 | 24 | 0.20 | 1041.342 |
| 34 | **Nickleby** | 939 | 1 | 0.02 | 1013.936 |
| 35 | **Clennam** | 938 | 1 | 0.02 | 1012.856 |
| 36 | were | 17,745 | 24 | 0.37 | 989.771 |
| 37 | indeed | 2,503 | 24 | 0.05 | 966.672 |
| 38 | such | 7,351 | 24 | 0.15 | 961.150 |
| 39 | *Florence* | 1,083 | 4 | 0.02 | 940.432 |
| 40 | **Squeers** | 861 | 1 | 0.02 | 929.711 |

*Note*: Words in **boldface** appear only in a single text, while words in *italics* are found in a very small number (2–4) of the texts in the corpus.

Another form of culling is seen in Ishikawa (2008), where words that occur with less than 50 per cent relative document frequency, or those found in fewer than 50 per cent of the total number of samples, were culled from the word-frequency list.

While culling techniques were used also in Eder and Rybicki (2009), Rybicki (2009), Eder (2010), and Rybicki and Eder (2011), among others, to improve accuracy in authorship attribution testing, Burrows (2005, 2007) is cautious in interfering with evidence, noting that 'the compelling objection to ad hoc forms of culling is that they make it too easy to tip the balance in one direction or another' (Burrows 2007, 28). I concur with Burrows in opting out of culling on the ground that setting a threshold for culling at a particular level is a highly arbitrary decision. This study, therefore, does not use ad hoc forms of culling, but instead adopts a machine-learning approach as a better and more intellectually robust approach to identifying keywords of Dickens.

## Random Forests as a stylometric tool

Random Forests (RF; Breiman 2001) is a very efficient classification algorithm based on ensemble learning from a large number of classification trees (thus 'forests') randomly generated from the dataset. As RF builds a classification tree from a set of bootstrap samples, about one-third of the cases are excluded each time to function as an internal unbiased estimate of the classification error. The process is iterated until the $n$th (500th by default) tree is added to the forests, there being no need for cross-validation or a separate test (Breiman and Cutler n.d.). One of the most prominent features of RF is its high accuracy in respect to classification of datasets. In the experiments reported by Jin and Murakami (2007), RF was unexcelled in accuracy among other high-performance classifiers—such as $k$ Nearest Neighbor, Support Vector Machine, Learning Vector Quantification, Bagging, and AdaBoosting—in distinguishing between 200 pieces of texts written by ten modern Japanese novelists. In my own experiments, RF consistently achieved accuracy rates as high as 96–100 per cent in distinguishing Dickens's texts from the control set of texts.[3]

RF is capable of handling thousands of input variables and running efficiently on a large database (Brieman and Cutler n.d.). The first series of experiments with RF in this study were on a set of 24 Dickens texts versus a comparable set of 24 Wilkie Collins texts, with variables ranging from more than 5,000 words to as few as 50. The results were fairly consistent, with over 96 per cent accuracy. The best results emerged when 300 input variables were used (see Table 3.2). The out-of-bag (OOB) estimate of error rate was 0 per cent, or 100 per cent accuracy, in distinguishing between Dickens's and Collins's texts.

RF computes proximities between pairs of cases that can be visualized in a multidimensional scaling diagram, as in Figure 3.1. Dickens's texts and Collins's texts, respectively, form distinct clusters, with two unusual pieces by Collins shown as outliers: *Antonina* (1850), which is set in ancient Rome, and the travel book *Rambles beyond Railways* (1851).

*Table 3.2* A result of running Random Forests

Call:
randomForest(formula = dat$AuthGroup ~., data = dat[,2:301],
proximity = T, importance = T, mtry = 20)

| Type of random forest | Classification |
|---|---|
| Number of trees | 500 |
| Number of variables tried at each split | 20 |
| OOB estimate of error rate | 0% |
| Confusion matrix | |

| | Collins | Dickens | Classification error |
|---|---|---|---|
| Collins | 24 | 0 | 0 |
| Dickens | 0 | 24 | 0 |

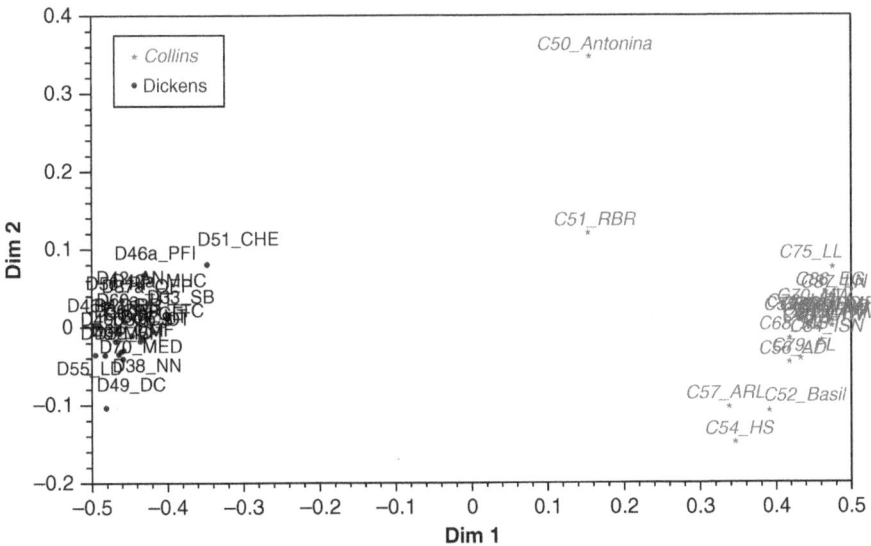

*Figure 3.1* A multidimensional scaling plot based on the proximity matrix generated by RF:
Dickens versus Collins

Note: Figures following either C_ (for Collins) or D_ (for Dickens) indicate the last two digits of the year
of publication: i.e., 18xx).

A further advantage of RF is the ability to highlight the lexical items that contribute most strongly to authorial classifications. RF shows the importance of
variables in two measures: mean decrease in accuracy (MeanDecreaseAccuracy)
and mean decrease in the Gini index when a particular variable is left out
of the analysis (MeanDecreaseGini). The former indicates the mean decrease
in the accuracy of classification when a particular variable is excluded from
analysis. The latter shows the mean decrease in the Gini index, an index of
uneven distribution of a particular variable between the groups, when the variable in question is left out of the analysis. The two indices are comparable to

*Table 3.3*   Important variables: Dickens markers and Collins markers
(in order of importance)

---

**Dickens markers**
very, many, upon, being, much, and, so, with, a, such, indeed, air, off,
but, would, down, great, there, up, or, were, head, they, into, better,
quite, brought, said, returned, rather, good, who, came, having, never,
always, ever, replied, boy, where, this, sir, well, gone, looking, dear,
himself, through, should, too, together, these, like, an, how, though,
then, long, going, its

**Collins markers**
first, words, only, end, left, moment, room, last, letter, to, enough,
back, answer, leave, still, place, since, heard, answered, time, looked,
person, mind, on, woman, at, told, she, own, under, just, ask, once,
speak, found, passed, her, which, had, me, felt, from, asked, after, can,
side, present, turned, life, next, word, new, went, say, over, while, far,
London, don't, your, tell, now, before

---

each other. Table 3.3 lists marker words of Dickens and Collins, respectively, in the order of importance (sorted according to the mean decrease in the Gini index).

A close comparison of Table 3.3 with Table 3.1 shows how RF helps identify words with high discriminatory power. Proper nouns and words distributed unevenly in each set now have effectively made way for words that are consistently more frequent in one author than the other. While the results outlined in Table 3.3 invite further scrutiny of how Dickens markers are contrasted with Collins markers, this study will seek to compare Dickens's texts with a larger and more representative corpus of writings in order to highlight Dickens's stylistic features in a wider perspective.

## Comparing and contrasting Dickens with a reference corpus of eighteenth- and nineteenth-century authors

In the following analysis, the set of 24 Dickens texts was compared with a reference corpus consisting of 24 eighteenth-century texts and 31 nineteenth-century texts. With 300 input variables being used, the OOB estimate of error rate fell to 1.28 per cent—that is, with 98.72 per cent of runs correctly distinguishing Dickens from the reference set of texts. Figure 3.2 distinguishes between the Dickens cluster and the control cluster. One seeming anomaly is the position of *A Child's History of England* (1851) as an outlier. This history book for children is considerably different in style from other works by Dickens. Therefore, this outcome is not unexpected, and is consistent with previous multivariate studies based on other linguistic variables, such as collocates of *gentleman* (Tabata 2009),—*ly* adverbs (Tabata 2005), and part-of-speech distribution (Tabata 2002).

Table 3.4 arrays major Dickens markers in descending order of importance (sorted according to the mean decrease in the Gini index). The most important

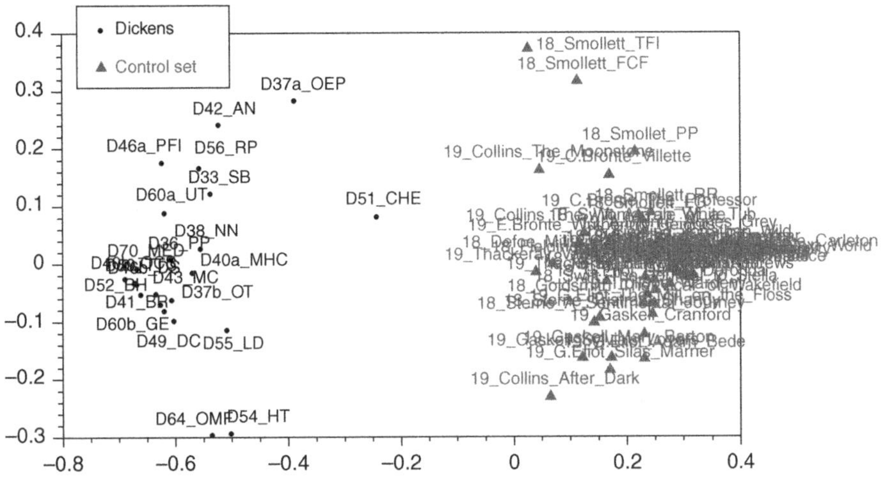

*Figure 3.2* A multidimensional scaling plot based on the proximity matrix generated by RF: Dickens versus reference corpus

*Table 3.4* Important V: Dickens versus the reference corpus (in order of importance)

---

**Positive Dickens markers** (words significantly *overused* by Dickens)
*eyes, hands, again, are, these, under, right, yes, up, sir, child, looked, together, here, back, it, at, am, long, quite, day, better, mean, why, turned, where, do, face, new, there, dear, people, they, door, cried, in, you, mrs, very, way, man*

**Negative Dickens markers** (words significantly *underused* by Dickens)
*lady, poor, less, of, things, leave, love, not, from, should, can, last, saw, now, next, my, having, began, our, letter, had, I, money, tell, such, to, nothing, person, be, would, those, far, miss, life, called, found, wish, how, must, more, herself, well, did, but, much, make, other, whose, as, own, take, go, no, gave, shall, some, against, wife, since, first, them, word*

---

positive markers for Dickens—'eyes' and 'hands', for example—were considerably 'underevaluated' in the traditional 'key' words analysis (based on log-likelihood ratio) carried out on the Dickens set versus the control set, being ranked 129th and 216th, respectively. On the other hand, a word like 'gentleman', seemingly a Dickensian word with the 38th highest LLR (or the eighth in the content word category), does not make it into the list of important variables highlighted by the RF run. This result indicates that *gentleman* does not contribute in a consistent way to the differentiation between the Dickens set and the control sets.

Although relationships among these words are complex enough to defy simple generalization, the predominance of words related to description of actions—typically bodily actions—or postures of characters rather than words denoting abstract ideas is clear. Words such as 'eyes', 'hands', 'saw', 'looked', and 'back' in particular have caught the eyes of critics such as Hori (2004) and

Mahlberg (2007a, 2007b), which suggests that the present methodology is well grounded. Stubbs states,

> Even if quantification only confirms what we have already known, this is not a bad thing. Indeed, in developing a new method, it is perhaps better not to find anything too new, but to confirm findings from many years of traditional study, since this gives confidence that the method can be relied on.
>
> (2005, 6)

In order to determine the local textual functions (Mahlberg 2007a, 2007b) performed by each of these words, researchers must return to the texts and examine the words in local contexts with the help of other tools such as concordance, collocation, and *n*-grams.

## Keywords in frequent *n*-grams

Mining techniques can open up a pathway to deeper textual analysis. As an example, this section will attempt to examine the local textual functions of two keywords identified by RF, 'eyes' and 'hands'.

Table 3.5 shows frequent 5-grams in Dickens's corpus incorporating 'eyes', one of the most important variables identified as a result of RF (Table 3.4). If we compare Table 3.5 with Tables 3.6 and 3.7, lists of frequent 5-grams with 'eyes' in each of the eighteenth- and nineteenth-century corpora respectively, we see the abundance as well as the greater variety of five-word sequences involving 'eyes' in Dickens.

A closer look at Table 3.5 reveals some overlaps of word sequences in the frequent 5-grams in Dickens; frequent *n*-grams tend to be either part of, or variations of, a larger phrasal unit. Major patterns include the following:

(1) (*with*) GENITIVE *eyes fixed on/upon* ... (65 instances found in 16 texts)
    Five instances were recorded in the eighteenth-century corpus, and 58 in the nineteenth-century corpus.
(2) *with* GENITIVE *eyes on/upon* ... (54 instances found in 12 texts)
    No instance was found in the eighteenth-century corpus; four were in the nineteenth-century corpus.
(3) EVALUATION *in the eyes of* EVALUATOR (42 instances found in 20 texts)
    Twenty-three instances (in 11 texts) were found in the eighteenth-century corpus, and 64 in the nineteenth-century corpus.
(4) (with) (the) *tears in* [ONE's]/*the eyes* (*of*) (46 instances found in 18 texts)
    Thirty-nine instances were found in the eighteenth-century corpus, and 33 (in 17 texts) in the nineteenth-century corpus.
(5) VERB *his/her eyes to* OBJECT (92 instances found in 20 texts)
    The constructions, VERB his/her eyes to ACTION-VERB (for example, Tom sat up in bed, and *rubbed his eyes to dispel* the illusion [*Pickwick Papers*]) are not counted in this category. Fourteen instances appeared in the eighteenth-century corpus, and 29 (in 18 texts) in the nineteenth-century corpus.

*Table 3.5*   Frequent 5-grams including 'eyes' in the Dickens corpus

| Rank | 5-grams | Frequency |
|------|---------|-----------|
| 1 | his *eyes* fixed on the | 22 |
| 2 | with his *eyes* fixed on | 20 |
| 3 | with his *eyes* on the | 16 |
| 4 | in the *eyes* of the | 15 |
| 4 | with tears in his *eyes* | 15 |
| 6 | her handkerchief to her *eyes* | 13 |
| 6 | his *eyes* with his hand | 13 |
| 8 | raising his *eyes* to the | 12 |
| 9 | his *eyes* fixed upon the | 10 |
| 9 | the corners of his *eyes* | 10 |
| 9 | with his *eyes* wide open | 10 |
| 12 | he raised his *eyes* to | 9 |
| 12 | his *eyes* to the ceiling | 9 |
| 12 | with his *eyes* fixed upon | 9 |
| 15 | his *eyes* on the fire | 8 |
| 15 | with tears in her *eyes* | 8 |
| 17 | cast down her *eyes* and | 7 |
| 17 | *eyes* fixed on the ground | 7 |
| 17 | he fixed his *eyes* on | 7 |
| 17 | his *eyes* from the ground | 7 |
| 17 | his *eyes* on the ground | 7 |
| 17 | his *eyes* upon the ground | 7 |
| 17 | raised his *eyes* to the | 7 |
| 17 | raising his *eyes* from the | 7 |
| 17 | she raised her *eyes* to | 7 |
| 17 | with her *eyes* upon the | 7 |

*Table 3.6*   Frequent 5-grams including 'eyes' in the eighteenth-century corpus

| Rank | 5-grams | Frequency |
|------|---------|-----------|
| 1 | with tears in his *eyes* | 19 |
| 2 | tears gushed from his *eyes* | 8 |
| 3 | up his hands and *eyes* | 8 |
| 4 | he lifted up his *eyes* | 7 |
| 4 | her handkerchief at her *eyes* | 7 |
| 4 | up his *eyes* to heaven | 7 |

*Table 3.7*   Frequent 5-grams including 'eyes' in the nineteenth-century corpus

| Rank | 5-grams | Frequency |
|------|---------|-----------|
| 1 | in the *eyes* of the | 19 |
| 2 | her handkerchief to her *eyes* | 14 |
| 3 | her *eyes* fixed on the | 12 |
| 4 | the *eyes* of the world | 10 |
| 5 | with her *eyes* fixed on | 10 |
| 6 | with tears in her *eyes* | 9 |
| 7 | her *eyes* were fixed on | 8 |
| 7 | the tears in her *eyes* | 8 |
| 9 | handkerchief to her *eyes* and | 7 |
| 9 | her *eyes* filled with tears | 7 |
| 9 | her *eyes* on him with | 7 |
| 9 | his *eyes* fixed on the | 7 |
| 9 | with her *eyes* fixed upon | 7 |

(6) *her (pocket-)handkerchief to her eyes* (14 instances found in eight texts)

All seven cases in the eighteenth century are from Richardson, while 19 instances are identified with this pattern in the nineteenth-century corpus.

When the eighteenth- and nineteenth-century corpora are searched for the five frequent patterns, the major Dickens phraseologies are either absent or account for very few hits in the eighteenth-century corpus, while some of the frequent patterns in Dickens's work—Types (1), (3), and (4)—are found fairly commonly in the nineteenth-century corpus.

Within phrases used by Dickens, some variations can be found in a particular time period in his career as a novelist: Type (1) phrases, for example, predominantly occur in the early half of Dickens's career. Fifty-seven out of 65 instances of *GENITIVE eyes fixed on/upon*... are found in texts published in the 1830s and 1840s (see Appendix 3.5). Of further interest, from a stylistic viewpoint, is that the phrase 'eyes fixed on/upon...' is imbued with typical semantic prosodies: the phraseology is used predominantly to describe a character brooding over something *with his/her eyes (up)on* an object, a character with suppressed emotions, or one with a calm determination. A similar use is associated with the Type (2) phrases. A marked contrast, however, emerges when we compare Dickens's use of Type (2) (see Appendix 3.6 for the concordance lines) with Type (1). While Type (1) predominantly occurs in his early works, Type (2) is typically used in his later works—*Our Mutual Friend*, in particular.

Unfortunately, at the time of writing, no diachronic corpus of British English comprising a large enough collection of fiction texts of the age in question is available in the public domain. The present study therefore employed the *Corpus of Historical American English* as a reference for comparison. Taking differences between British and American English into careful account, the following section examines Dickens phraseologies in a diachronic light.

| SECTION | 1810 | 1820 | 1830 | 1840 | 1850 | 1860 | 1870 | 1880 | 1890 | 1900 | 1910 | 1920 | 1930 | 1940 | 1950 | 1960 | 1970 | 1980 | 1990 | 2000 |
|---|---|---|---|---|---|---|---|---|---|---|---|---|---|---|---|---|---|---|---|---|
| FREQ | 0 | 7 | 21 | 17 | 32 | 28 | 33 | 27 | 34 | 24 | 13 | 13 | 11 | 6 | 5 | 3 | 0 | 0 | 1 | 1 |
| PER MIL | 0.00 | 1.01 | 1.52 | 1.06 | 1.94 | 1.64 | 1.78 | 1.33 | 1.65 | 1.09 | 0.57 | 0.51 | 0.45 | 0.25 | 0.20 | 0.13 | 0.00 | 0.00 | 0.04 | 0.03 |

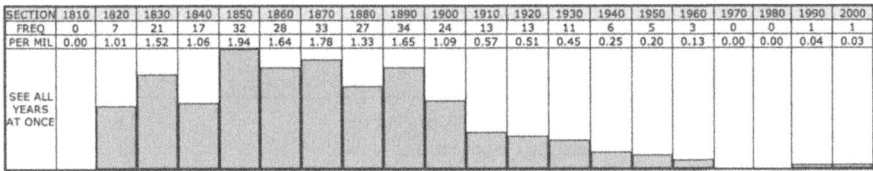

*Figure 3.3*    Result of a COHA search: *with his/her eyes fixed on/upon*

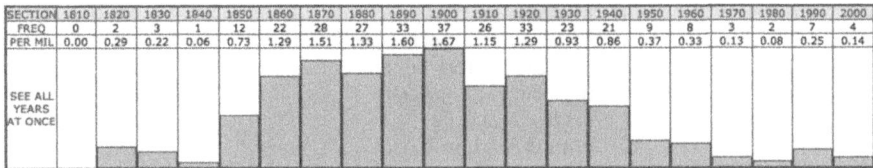

| SECTION | 1810 | 1820 | 1830 | 1840 | 1850 | 1860 | 1870 | 1880 | 1890 | 1900 | 1910 | 1920 | 1930 | 1940 | 1950 | 1960 | 1970 | 1980 | 1990 | 2000 |
|---|---|---|---|---|---|---|---|---|---|---|---|---|---|---|---|---|---|---|---|---|
| FREQ | 0 | 2 | 3 | 1 | 12 | 22 | 28 | 27 | 33 | 37 | 26 | 33 | 23 | 21 | 9 | 8 | 3 | 2 | 7 | 4 |
| PER MIL | 0.00 | 0.29 | 0.22 | 0.06 | 0.73 | 1.29 | 1.51 | 1.33 | 1.60 | 1.67 | 1.15 | 1.29 | 0.93 | 0.86 | 0.37 | 0.33 | 0.13 | 0.08 | 0.25 | 0.14 |

*Figure 3.4*    Result of a COHA search: *with his/her eyes on/upon*

Figures 3.3 and 3.4, retrieved from the 400-million-word *Corpus of Historical American English*, are consonant with the diachronic pattern just described, indicating Dickens was among the early adopters of *with * eyes (fixed) on* . . . phrases as rhetorical devices for fiction. Another word that discriminates strongly in favour of Dickens is 'hands', which is also used consistently in a few frequent phrasal units. Tables 3.8, 3.9, and 3.10 list frequent 5-grams including 'hands' in the Dickens corpus, eighteenth-century and nineteenth-century sets, respectively ($n \geq 7$). Quite obviously, 'hands' 5-grams are much more common and varied in Dickens than in the control sets. The top three 5-grams have considerable overlaps between them, with *his hands in his (pockets)* as a common core.

Among the Dickens 5-grams listed, the phrasal pattern *(with) his hands in his (pockets/etc.)* attracts special attention. As the concordance lines in Appendix 3.7 illustrate, the phrase is fairly evenly distributed throughout Dickens's career, unlike the phrases involving 'eyes'. A close inspection of the concordance lines shows that the phrase is not simply used as a description of a character's posture/action, but rather employed with a specific local textual function (i.e., used as a rhetorical device for characterization in most cases). The following quotations are typical instances of a character described as being *with his hands in his (pockets)*: someone who is, for example, idle, audacious, indifferent, insensitive, arrogant, impolite, or slouchy:

Joe Gargery kept a journeyman whose name was Orlick. He was a broad-shouldered, looselimbed, swarthy fellow of great strength. On working-days he would come slouching, *with his hands in his pockets* and his dinner loosely tied in a bundle round his neck, and dangling on his back.

—*Great Expectations* (emphasis added)

'Coachman, are you going or not?' bawled Mr Minns, with his head and half his body out of the coach window.

*Table 3.8*　Frequent 5-grams including 'hands' in the Dickens corpus

| Rank | 5-grams | Frequency |
| --- | --- | --- |
| 1 | his *hands* in his pockets | 92 |
| 2 | with his *hands* in his | 62 |
| 3 | *hands* in his pockets and | 41 |
| 4 | with his *hands* behind him | 20 |
| 5 | the palms of his *hands* | 18 |
| 6 | his *hands* into his pockets | 17 |
| 7 | his *hands* on his knees | 14 |
| 8 | *hands* into his pockets and | 13 |
| 9 | her *hands* before her face | 12 |
| 9 | his face with his *hands* | 12 |
| 9 | his *hands* as if he | 12 |
| 9 | put his *hands* in his | 12 |
| 13 | putting his *hands* in his | 10 |
| 13 | thrust his *hands* into his | 10 |
| 15 | her face with her *hands* | 9 |
| 15 | his head upon his *hands* | 9 |
| 15 | their *hands* in their pockets | 9 |
| 18 | his *hands* behind him and | 8 |
| 18 | his *hands* upon his knees | 8 |
| 18 | with his *hands* on his | 8 |
| 18 | with their *hands* in their | 8 |
| 22 | and his *hands* in his | 7 |
| 22 | her face in her *hands* | 7 |
| 22 | his face in his *hands* | 7 |
| 22 | in the *hands* of the | 7 |
| 22 | shook *hands* with him and | 7 |

*Table 3.9*　Frequent 5-grams including 'hands' in the eighteenth-century corpus

| Rank | 5-grams | Frequency |
| --- | --- | --- |
| 1 | into the *hands* of the | 33 |
| 2 | fall into the *hands* of | 13 |
| 3 | in the *hands* of the | 13 |
| 4 | fallen into the *hands* of | 12 |
| 5 | into the *hands* of a | 11 |
| 6 | falling into the *hands* of | 9 |
| 7 | fell into the *hands* of | 8 |
| 7 | from the *hands* of the | 8 |
| 7 | in the *hands* of a | 8 |
| 7 | out of the *hands* of | 8 |
| 7 | the *hands* of the enemy | 8 |
| 7 | up his *hands* and eyes | 8 |

*Table 3.10* Frequent 5-grams including 'hands' in the nineteenth-century corpus

| Rank | 5-grams | Frequency |
| --- | --- | --- |
| 1 | his *hands* in his pockets | 25 |
| 2 | with his *hands* in his | 20 |
| 3 | in the *hands* of the | 14 |
| 4 | *hands* in his pockets and | 10 |
| 5 | was in the *hands* of | 8 |
| 6 | her face with her *hands* | 7 |
| 6 | out of the *hands* of | 7 |
| 6 | with his *hands* behind him | 7 |

'Di-rectly, sir,' said the coachman, *with his hands in his pockets*, looking as much unlike a man in a hurry as possible.

—*Sketches by Boz* (emphasis added)

'When you think every one has retired to rest to-night', said Evenson very pompously, 'if you'll meet me without a light, just outside my bedroom door, by the staircase window, I think we can ascertain who the parties really are, and you will afterwards be enabled to proceed as you think proper.'

Mrs Tibbs was easily persuaded; her curiosity was excited, her jealousy was roused, and the arrangement was forthwith made. She resumed her work, and John Evenson walked up and down the room *with his hands in his pockets*, looking as if nothing had happened. The game of cribbage was over, and conversation began again.

—*Sketches by Boz* (emphasis added)

Since Figures 3.5 and 3.6 were derived from the *Corpus of Historical American English*, we must be careful in applying any findings in a study of British English. The two diagrams, nevertheless, demonstrate diachronic movements of the two 5-grams well. Again, these pieces of quantitative information, taken together with Tables 3.8, 3.9, and 3.10, can be interpreted as evidence of Dickens as a very early adopter of the phrase *with his hands in his pockets* for use as a rhetorical device in his novels.

The phrases including 'eyes' and 'hands' were hardly new in Dickens's day—they were certainly already in the inventory of the English language. However, Dickens

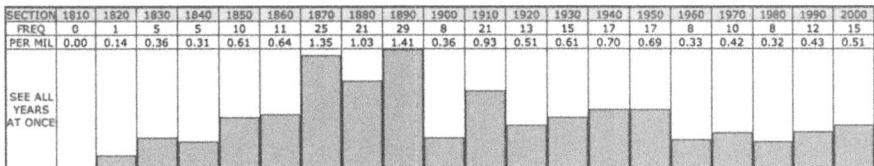

| SECTION | 1810 | 1820 | 1830 | 1840 | 1850 | 1860 | 1870 | 1880 | 1890 | 1900 | 1910 | 1920 | 1930 | 1940 | 1950 | 1960 | 1970 | 1980 | 1990 | 2000 |
| --- | --- | --- | --- | --- | --- | --- | --- | --- | --- | --- | --- | --- | --- | --- | --- | --- | --- | --- | --- | --- |
| FREQ | 0 | 1 | 5 | 5 | 10 | 11 | 25 | 21 | 29 | 8 | 21 | 13 | 15 | 17 | 17 | 8 | 10 | 8 | 12 | 15 |
| PER MIL | 0.00 | 0.14 | 0.36 | 0.31 | 0.61 | 0.64 | 1.35 | 1.03 | 1.41 | 0.36 | 0.93 | 0.51 | 0.61 | 0.70 | 0.69 | 0.33 | 0.42 | 0.32 | 0.43 | 0.51 |

*Figure 3.5* Result of a COHA search: *with his hands in his*

| SECTION | 1810 | 1820 | 1830 | 1840 | 1850 | 1860 | 1870 | 1880 | 1890 | 1900 | 1910 | 1920 | 1930 | 1940 | 1950 | 1960 | 1970 | 1980 | 1990 | 2000 |
|---|---|---|---|---|---|---|---|---|---|---|---|---|---|---|---|---|---|---|---|---|
| FREQ | 0 | 0 | 5 | 6 | 13 | 17 | 34 | 38 | 51 | 26 | 62 | 42 | 27 | 50 | 45 | 22 | 26 | 25 | 35 | 32 |
| PER MIL | 0.00 | 0.00 | 0.36 | 0.37 | 0.79 | 1.00 | 1.83 | 1.87 | 2.48 | 1.18 | 2.73 | 1.64 | 1.10 | 2.05 | 1.83 | 0.92 | 1.09 | 0.99 | 1.25 | 1.08 |

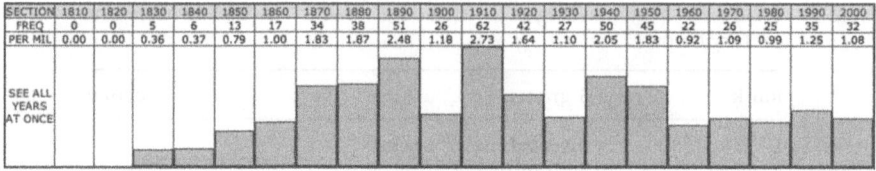

*Figure 3.6*   Result of a COHA search: *his hands in his pockets*

was among the earliest adopters of such phraseology in fiction, and he seems to have used the expression fully so as to perform specific local texual functions (characterization, cues for readers to expect a particular type of character, etc.).

## Conclusion

This application of RF in stylometric differentiation of texts to highlight important keywords of a text, set of texts, author, and so on, demonstrates that with RF, words with a peculiarly skewed distribution have a significantly lower chance of being included as important variables than is the case with traditional keyword detection techniques such as LLR. The words identified as important variables in this study can in turn lend themselves to further analysis of stylistic function: frequent *n*-grams in which the keywords appear illustrate typical phraseologies of the target texts. More importantly, given RF's high accuracy in attributing texts to authors, the technique could arguably be usefully applied to cases of disputed authorship or forensic identification of a text, although few studies have used the technique for such purposes. This pathway from text mining to textual analysis shows how the machine-learning approach can provide humanists with revealing insights into stylistic properties of text.

## Appendix 3.1 Dickens corpus (Dickens component of ORCHIDS)

| No. | Author | Texts | Abbr. | Category | Date | Word-Tokens |
|---|---|---|---|---|---|---|
| 1 | Dickens | *Sketches by Boz* | (D33_SB) | Sketches | 1833–36 | 187,474 |
| 2 | Dickens | *The Pickwick Papers* | (D36_PP) | Serial fiction | 1836–37 | 298,887 |
| 3 | Dickens | Other Early Papers | (D37a_OEP) | Sketches | 1837–40 | 66,939 |
| 4 | Dickens | *Oliver Twist* | (D37b_OT) | Serial fiction | 1837–39 | 156,869 |
| 5 | Dickens | *Nicholas Nickleby* | (D38_NN) | Serial fiction | 1838–39 | 321,094 |
| 6 | Dickens | *Master Humphrey's Clock* | (D40a_MHC) | Miscellany | 1840–41 | 45,831 |
| 7 | Dickens | *The Old Curiosity Shop* | (D40b_OCS) | Serial fiction | 1840–41 | 217,375 |
| 8 | Dickens | *Barnaby Rudge* | (D41_BR) | Serial fiction | 1841 | 253,979 |

| 9 | Dickens | *American Notes* | (D42_AN) | Sketches | 1842 | 101,623 |
|----|---------|------------------|----------|----------|------|---------|
| 10 | Dickens | *Martin Chuzzlewit* | (D43_MC) | Serial fiction | 1843–44 | 335,462 |
| 11 | Dickens | *Christmas Books* | (D43_CB) | Fiction | 1843–48 | 154,410 |
| 12 | Dickens | *Pictures from Italy* | (D46a_PFI) | Sketches | 1846 | 72,497 |
| 13 | Dickens | *Dombey and Son* | (D46b_DS) | Serial fiction | 1846–48 | 341,947 |
| 14 | Dickens | *David Copperfield* | (D49_DC) | Serial fiction | 1849–50 | 355,714 |
| 15 | Dickens | *A Child's History of England* | (D51_CHE) | History | 1851–53 | 162,883 |
| 16 | Dickens | *Bleak House* | (D52_BH) | Serial fiction | 1852–53 | 354,061 |
| 17 | Dickens | *Hard Times* | (D54_HT) | Serial fiction | 1854 | 103,263 |
| 18 | Dickens | *Little Dorrit* | (D55_LD) | Serial fiction | 1855–57 | 338,076 |
| 19 | Dickens | *Reprinted Pieces* | (D50_RPR) | Sketches | 1850–56 | 91,468 |
| 20 | Dickens | *A Tale of Two Cities* | (D59_TTC) | Serial fiction | 1859 | 136,031 |
| 21 | Dickens | *The Uncommercial Traveller* | (D60_UT) | Sketches | 1860–69 | 142,773 |
| 22 | Dickens | *Great Expectations* | (D60_GE) | Serial fiction | 1860–61 | 184,776 |
| 23 | Dickens | *Our Mutual Friend* | (D64_OMF) | Serial fiction | 1864–65 | 324,891 |
| 24 | Dickens | *The Mystery of Edwin Drood* | (D70_ED) | Serial fiction | 1870 | 94,014 |

Sum of word-tokens in the set of Dickens texts: 4,842,337

## Appendix 3.2 Collins corpus

| No. | Texts | Abbr. | Category | Date | Word-Tokens |
|-----|-------|-------|----------|------|-------------|
| 1 | *Antonina, or the Fall of Rome* | (C50_Ant(onina)) | Historical | 1850 | 166,627 |
| 2 | *Rambles Beyond Railways* | (C51_RBR) | Sketches | 1851 | 61,290 |
| 3 | *Basil* | (C_52_Basil) | Fiction | 1852 | 115,235 |
| 4 | *Hide and Seek* | (C_54_HS) | Fiction | 1854 | 159,048 |
| 5 | *After the Dark* | (C_56_AD) | Short stories | 1856 | 136,356 |
| 6 | *A Rogue's Life* | (C_57_ARL) | Serial fiction | 1856–57 | 47,639 |
| 7 | *The Queen of Hearts* | (C_59_QOH) | Fiction | 1869 | 145,350 |
| 8 | *The Woman in White* | (C_60_WIW) | Serial fiction | 1860 | 246,916 |
| 9 | *No Name* | (C_62_NN) | Serial fiction | 1862 | 264,858 |

(Continued)

| No. | Texts | Abbr. | Category | Date | Word-Tokens |
|-----|-------|-------|----------|------|-------------|
| 10 | *Armadale* | (C_66_Armadale) | Serial fiction | 1866 | 298,135 |
| 11 | *The Moonstone* | (C_68_MS) | Serial fiction | 1868 | 196,493 |
| 12 | *Man and Wife* | (C_70_MW) | Fiction | 1870 | 229,376 |
| 13 | *Poor Miss Finch* | (C_72_PMF) | Serial fiction | 1872 | 162,989 |
| 14 | *The New Magdalen* | (C_73_TNM) | Serial fiction | 1873 | 101,967 |
| 15 | *The Law and the Lady* | (C_75_LL) | Serial fiction | 1875 | 140,788 |
| 16 | *The Two Destinies* | (C_76_TD) | Serial fiction | 1876 | 89,420 |
| 17 | *The Haunted Hotel* | (C_78_HH) | Serial fiction | 1878 | 62,662 |
| 18 | *The Fallen Leaves* | (C_79_FL) | Serial fiction | 1879 | 133,047 |
| 19 | *Jezebel's Daughter* | (C_80_JD) | Fiction | 1880 | 101,815 |
| 20 | *The Black Robe* | (C_81_BR) | Fiction | 1881 | 107,748 |
| 21 | *I Say No* | (C_84_ISN) | Fiction | 1884 | 119,626 |
| 22 | *The Evil Genius* | (C_86_EG) | Fiction | 1886 | 110,618 |
| 23 | *Little Novels* | (C_87_LN) | Fiction | 1887 | 148,585 |
| 24 | *The Legacy of Cain* | (C_89_LOC) | Fiction | 1888 | 119,568 |

Sum of word-tokens in the set of Collins texts: 3,233,926

## Appendix 3.3 Eighteenth-century component of ORCHIDS

| No. | Author | Texts | Date | Word-Tokens |
|-----|--------|-------|------|-------------|
| 1 | Defoe | *Captain Singleton* | 1720 | 110,916 |
| 2 | Defoe | *Journal of Prague Year* | 1722 | 83,494 |
| 3 | Defoe | *The Military Memoirs of Captain George Carleton* | 1728 | 80,617 |
| 4 | Defoe | *Moll Flanders* | 1724 | 138,094 |
| 5 | Defoe | *Robinson Crusoe* | 1719 | 232,453 |
| 6 | Fielding | *A Journey from this World to the Next* | 1749 | 45,024 |
| 7 | Fielding | *Amelia* | 1751 | 212,339 |
| 8 | Fielding | *Jonathan Wild* | 1743 | 70,086 |
| 9 | Fielding | *Joseph Andrews* | 1742 | 126,342 |
| 10 | Fielding | *Tom Jones* | 1749 | 347,219 |
| 11 | Goldsmith | *The Vicar of Wakefield* | 1766 | 63,076 |
| 12 | Richardson | *Clarissa* | 1748 | 939,448 |
| 13 | Richardson | *Pamela* | 1740 | 439,562 |

| | | | | |
|---|---|---|---|---|
| 14 | Smollett | *Peregrine Pickle* | 1751 | 330,557 |
| 15 | Smollett | *Ferdinand Count Fathom* | 1753 | 157,032 |
| 16 | Smollett | *Humphrey Clinker* | 1771 | 150,281 |
| 17 | Smollett | *Sir Launcelot Greaves* | 1760 | 89,010 |
| 18 | Smollett | *Roderick Random* | 1748 | 191,539 |
| 19 | Smollett | *Travels through France and Italy* | 1766 | 121,032 |
| 20 | Sterne | *A Sentimental Journey* | 1768 | 41,028 |
| 21 | Sterne | *Tristram Shandy* | 1759–67 | 184,428 |
| 22 | Swift | *A Tale of a Tub* | 1704 | 44,225 |
| 23 | Swift | *Gulliver's Travels* | 1726 | 103,806 |
| 24 | Swift | *A Journal to Stella* | 1710–13 | 191,740 |

Sum of word-tokens in the set of 18th-century texts: 4,493,348

## Appendix 3.4 Nineteenth-century component of ORCHIDS

| No. | Author | Texts | Date | Word-Tokens |
|---|---|---|---|---|
| 1 | A. Brontë | *Agnes Grey* | 1847 | 68,352 |
| 2 | Austen | *Emma* | 1815 | 160,899 |
| 3 | Austen | *Mansfield Park* | 1814 | 159,921 |
| 4 | Austen | *Northanger Abbey* | 1803 | 77,810 |
| 5 | Austen | *Persuasion* | 1816 (1818) | 83,380 |
| 6 | Austen | *Pride and Prejudice* | 1813 | 121,874 |
| 7 | Austen | *Sense and Sensibility* | 1811 | 119,793 |
| 8 | C. Brontë | *Jane Eyre* | 1847 | 188,092 |
| 9 | C. Brontë | *The Professor* | 1857 | 88,281 |
| 10 | C. Brontë | *Villette* | 1853 | 193,819 |
| 11 | Collins | *After Dark* | 1882 | 136,356 |
| 12 | Collins | *The Moonstone* | 1868 | 196,506 |
| 13 | Collins | *The Woman in White* | 1859 | 246,917 |
| 14 | E. Brontë | *Wuthering Heights* | 1847 | 117,344 |
| 15 | G. Eliot | *Adam Bede* | 1859 | 215,253 |
| 16 | G. Eliot | *Brother Jacob* | 1864 | 16,693 |
| 17 | G. Eliot | *Daniel Deronda* | 1876 | 311,400 |
| 18 | G. Eliot | *Middlemarch* | 1871–72 | 317,975 |
| 19 | G. Eliot | *Silas Marner* | 1861 | 71,449 |

(Continued)

| No. | Author | Texts | Date | Word-Tokens |
|-----|--------|-------|------|-------------|
| 20 | G. Eliot | *The Mill on the Floss* | 1860 | 207,505 |
| 21 | Gaskell | *Cranford* | 1851–53 | 71,037 |
| 22 | Gaskell | *Mary Barton* | 1848 | 161,098 |
| 23 | Gaskell | *Sylvia's Lovers* | 1863 | 191,176 |
| 24 | Thackeray | *Barry Lyndon* | 1844 | 125,986 |
| 25 | Thackeray | *Vanity Fair* | 1848 | 303,530 |
| 26 | Trollope | *Bachester Towers* | 1857 | 197,691 |
| 27 | Trollope | *Can You Forgive Her* | 1865 | 316,349 |
| 28 | Trollope | *Doctor Thorne* | 1857 | 220,867 |
| 29 | Trollope | *The Eustace Diamonds* | 1873 | 269,981 |
| 30 | Trollope | *Phineas Finn* | 1869 | 263,393 |
| 31 | Trollope | *The Warden* | 1855 | 72,068 |
| | | Sum of word-tokens in the set of 19th-century texts: 5,292,795 | | |

## Appendix 3.5 Concordance Lines: (with/etc.) GENITIVE eyes fixed on/upon

| No. | Concordance Lines | Text |
|-----|-------------------|------|
| 1 | hrown off the bonnet and veil, and now stood with *her eyes fixed upon* him. Her features were those of a woman about fi | D33_SB |
| 2 | n old box, with his head resting on his hand, and *his eyes fixed on* a wretched cinder fire that was smouldering on th | D33_SB |
| 3 | nflamed appearance. He was smoking a cigar, with *his eyes fixed on* the ceiling, and had that confident oracular air | D33_SB |
| 4 | atio, with his hair brushed off his forehead, and *his eyes fixed on* the ceiling, reclining in a contemplative attitud | D33_SB |
| 5 | lying on his back in the middle of the road, with *his eyes fixed on* the sky. I thought he was dead; but no, he was a | D33_SB |
| 6 | lying on his back in the middle of the road, with *his eyes fixed on* the sky. I thought he was dead; but no, he was a | D33_SB |
| 7 | a stout broker in a large waistcoat, who had kept *his eyes fixed on* this luminary all the time he was speaking. "Ah | D33_SB |
| 8 | case, and the little man, with his mouth open and *his eyes fixed upon* his face, looked on with an expression of bewilde | D33_SB |
| 9 | dark hair trailed over his arm, and *her beautiful dark eyes fixed themselves upon* his face when she recovered, he felt so strange | D36_PP |

| | | |
|---|---|---|
| 10 | reet." At this point, Sam Weller, who had had *his eyes fixed hitherto on* Mr Namby's shining beaver, interfered. "Are | D36_PP |
| 11 | ng the "TIZER, vill you:" and then he'd set vith *his eyes fixed on* the clock, and rush out, just a quarter of a mini | D36_PP |
| 12 | tter, who walked at his side in silence. Job kept *his eyes fixed on* the ground for some time. Sam, with his glued to | D36_PP |
| 13 | y on his errand, with his hands in his pocket and *his eyes fixed on* the ground. "Rum feller, the hemperor," said | D36_PP |
| 14 | onds. Dumkins confidently awaited its coming with *his eyes fixed on* the motions of Luffey. "Play!" suddenly crie | D36_PP |
| 15 | nearly concealed from view. Sam was sitting with *his eyes fixed upon* the dust-heap outside the next gate to that by wh | D36_PP |
| 16 | Mr Alfred Jingle; his head resting on his hands, *his eyes fixed upon* the fire, and his whole appearance denoting miser | D36_PP |
| 17 | etical young gentleman is lounging on a sofa with *his eyes fixed upon* the ceiling, or sitting bolt upright in a high-ba | D37a_OEP |
| 18 | fearful of irritating the housebreaker, sat with *her eyes fixed upon* the fire, as if she had been deaf to all that pas | D37b_OT |
| 19 | his best obeisance. He had been wondering, with *his eyes fixed on* the magistrates' powder, whether all boards were | D37b_OT |
| 20 | gentleman paused; Monks was biting his lips, with *his eyes fixed upon* the floor; seeing this, he immediately resumed: | D37b_OT |
| 21 | denly upon me at the inn," said Oliver. "We had *our eyes fixed full upon* each other; and I could swear to him." "They | D37b_OT |
| 22 | s engaged, and the two men sat by in silence with *their eyes fixed upon* the floor, a pattering noise was heard upon the s | D37b_OT |
| 23 | ed. And there was one looker-on, who remained *with eyes fixed upon* the spot where the carriage had disappeared, long | D37b_OT |
| 24 | d remained with his head resting on one hand, and *his eyes fixed moodily on* the ground. This departure from his regular a | D38_NN |
| 25 | f his right hand inserted between the leaves, and *his eyes fixed on* a very fat old lady in a mob-cap evidently the | D38_NN |
| 26 | that one with the thick trunk and there, with *his eyes fixed on* me, he stood!" "Only reflect for one moment, | D38_NN |
| 27 | hind him. The man remained on the same spot with *his eyes fixed upon* his retreating figure until it was lost to view, | D38_NN |
| 28 | s gloves with great precision and nicety, keeping *his eyes fixed upon* Mr Ralph Nickleby all the time, he adjusted his h | D38_NN |
| 29 | , honest-looking countryman on the box, who, with *his eyes fixed upon* the dome of St Paul's Cathedral, appeared so wrap | D38_NN |
| 30 | body bent forward as if in profound respect, and *his eyes fixed upon* the face of his worthy client. "Well, Nickle | D38_NN |
| 31 | with his wife, who sat trembling in a corner with *her eyes fixed upon* the ground, the little man planted himself before | D40b_OCS |
| 32 | ny deviation or omission. Richard Swiveller kept *his eyes fixed on* his visitor during its narration, and directly it | D40b_OCS |
| 33 | arance) Mr Swiveller leant back in his chair with *his eyes fixed on* the ceiling, and occasionally pitching his voice | D40b_OCS |
| 34 | , with the accustomed grin on his dirty face, and *his eyes fixed upon* the ceiling. He certainly did not glance at Kit | D40b_OCS |
| 35 | with little understanding for the words, but with *his eyes fixed upon* the child and if she smiled or brightened with | D40b_OCS |
| 36 | ey both looked narrowly at the old man, who, with *his eyes fixed upon* the fire, sat brooding over it, yet listening eag | D40b_OCS |

(Continued)

| No. | Concordance Lines | Text |
|-----|-------------------|------|
| 37 | found gravity, and in a deep silence, each having *his eyes fixed on* a huge copper boiler that was suspended over the | D41_BR |
| 38 | urely in his seat, but he kept his head erect and *his eyes fixed on* the fire, then, and always. The road was dang | D41_BR |
| 39 | speaking by fits and starts, often stopping with *his eyes fixed on* the ground, moving hurriedly on again, like one d | D41_BR |
| 40 | dumb; but kept riding on quite comfortably, with *his eyes fixed on* the horizon. "Did you ever try a fall with a | D41_BR |
| 41 | e suddenly dropped into a whisper as he repeated, *with eyes fixed upon* the locksmith, "he has been at neither." "I | D41_BR |
| 42 | hest upon the shore, without anybody heeding them *all eyes fixed upon* the boat. It comes alongside, is made fast, the | D42_AN |
| 43 | a creature of ill omen, sat the aged clerk, with *his eyes fixed on* some withered branches in the stove. He rose and | D43_MC |
| 44 | e so agreeable to Mr Pecksniff that he stood with *his eyes fixed upon* the floor and his hands clasping one another alte | D43_MC |
| 45 | " said the Doctor. Marion had stood apart, with *her eyes fixed upon* the ground; but, this warning being given, her yo | D43b_CB |
| 46 | sitting in his chair in the chimney-corner, with *his eyes fixed on* the ground, and his son was leaning against the o | D43b_CB |
| 47 | ad been harshly agitated, quieted down; while her dark eyes, fixed upon the fire, exchanged the reckless light that had a | D46b_DS |
| 48 | g round. "Shall I tell you," she continued, with *her eyes fixed on* her mother, "who already knows us thoroughly, an | D46b_DS |
| 49 | te of repose becoming a good smoker; but sat with *his eyes fixed on* Florence, and, with a beaming placidity not to be | D46b_DS |
| 50 | se mild tones Robin started and disappeared, with *his eyes fixed on* his patron to the last. "You don't remember that | D46b_DS |
| 51 | ade to him; and having swallowed his liquor, with *his eyes fixed on* the messenger, and his face as pale as his face c | D46b_DS |
| 52 | ere heard without. But not by him. He sat with *his eyes fixed on* the table, so immersed in thought, that a far hea | D46b_DS |
| 53 | ing for some time silently rubbing his chin, with *his eyes fixed upon* her, "and a brave lad, and a good lad?" Flore | D46b_DS |
| 54 | handed him out of the room; and Rob, keeping *his round eyes fixed upon* his patron to the last, vanished for the time bei | D46b_DS |
| 55 | t quite silent and still during this speech, with *her eyes fixed on* the ground; her cousin standing near her, and loo | D49_DC |
| 56 | this intelligence; but sat severely silent, with *his eyes fixed on* the ground. Long after the subject was dismissed | D49_DC |

| | | |
|---|---|---|
| 57 | ceived it." He remained calm and silent, with *his eyes fixed on* the ground, and the tip of every finger of his ri | D49_DC |
| 58 | d with which she has caught it, and standing with *her eyes fixed on* the fire, puts it about and about between her own | D52_BH |
| 59 | he morning and stand before the beer-engine, with *her eyes fixed upon* him like an accusing spirit, strikes him dumb. | D52_BH |
| 60 | d a dread of me when I came up, standing with *his lustrous eyes fixed upon* me, and even arrested in his shivering fit. I | D52_BH |
| 61 | avour to follow, and to comprehend?" She kept *her eyes fixed upon* him with a frown. "Yes." "Further, I am a | D55_LD |
| 62 | y to him as he could. Arthur was sitting with *his eyes fixed on* the floor, recalling the past, brooding over the | D55_LD |
| 63 | solicitude at her father, Doctor Manette keeping *his eyes fixed on* the reader, Madame Defarge never taking hers from | D59_TTC |
| 64 | or regret or grief.'" As he said these words with *his eyes fixed on* the writer, his hand slowly and softly moved down | D59_TTC |
| 65 | after he was gone, Herbert said of himself, with *his eyes fixed on* the fire, that he thought he must have committed | D60b_GE |

## Appendix 3.6 Concordance Lines: with GENITIVE eyes on/upon

| | | |
|---|---|---|
| 1 | r more, Mr Swiveller, lying sometimes on his back *with his eyes upon* the ceiling, and sometimes half out of bed to cor | D40b_OCS |
| 2 | anxious to know, an't you?" returned Mrs Varden, *with her eyes upon* the print. "You, that have not been near me all | D41_BR |
| 3 | had been his accustomed place five years before, *with his eyes on* the eternal boiler; and had sat there since the c | D41_BR |
| 4 | that." "It was took off," muttered Mr Willet,*with his eyes upon* the fire, "at the defence of the Salwanners, in | D41_BR |
| 5 | ts feet, the Phantom stood, immovable and silent, *with its eyes upon* him. Ghastly it was, as it had ever been, but n | D43b_CB |
| 6 | k her in his madness and keeping close to him, *with her eyes upon* his face, and his arm about her, led him out to a | D46b_DS |
| 7 | I was, and as I am." Still upon her knees, and *with her eyes upon* the fire, and the fire shining on her ruined beau | D46b_DS |
| 8 | there again. While he thus walked up and down *with his eyes on* the ground, Mrs Brown, in the chair from which sh | D46b_DS |
| 9 | eet, or even out into the street. It sat down, *with its eyes upon* the empty fireplace, and as it lost itself in tho | D46b_DS |
| 10 | ietly on the ground, *with my touch upon your arm, with my eyes upon* your face, you may believe that there is no commo | D46b_DS |
| 11 | of doing good; and if I could spare my brother," *with her eyes upon* me, "perhaps the time could not." "What I a | D49_DC |

48

(Continued)

| 12 | les sat upon the sofa affecting to read the paper *with his eyes on* the ceiling; and I looked out of the window to gi | D49_DC |
| 13 | nod, paused when I had done, and sat considering, *with his eyes upon* my face, and his hand upon my knee. "Doctor | D49_DC |
| 14 | s, I sat revolving it still, at past one o'clock, *with my eyes on* the coffee-room fire. I was so filled with th | D49_DC |
| 15 | narrow, that but two men could cross it abreast. *With his eyes upon* this bridge, Wallace posted the greater part of h | D51_CHE |
| 16 | e it was quite said and whispered. His lordship, *with his eyes upon* his papers, listened, nodded twice or thrice, tur | D52_BH |
| 17 | king intently at him, and Louisa stood coldly by, *with her eyes upon* the ground, while he proceeded thus: "Jupe, | D54_HT |
| 18 | he question; said the eminently practical father, *with his eyes on* the fire, "in what has this vulgar curiosity its | D54_HT |
| 19 | y Flintwinch. Hey, old intriguer?" Jeremiah, *with his eyes upon* his mistress, made no reply. Rigaud looked from | D55_LD |
| 20 | "Why should I look at him?" returned Estella, *with her eyes on* me instead. "What is there in that fellow in the | D60b_GE |
| 21 | nfused. Estella, pausing a moment in her knitting *with her eyes upon* me, and then going on, I fancied that I read in t | D60b_GE |
| 22 | have drawn his salary when that came round and *with his eyes on* his chief, sat in a state of perpetual readiness | D60b_GE |
| 23 | shed the book over to me, as Provis stood smoking *with his eyes on* the fire, and I read in it: "Young Havisham' | D60b_GE |
| 24 | 'And when don't you, you know?" Herbert threw in, *with his eyes on* the fire; which I thought kind and sympathetic of | D60b_GE |
| 25 | icks and barns. He always slouched, locomotively, *with his eyes on* the ground; and, when accosted or otherwise requi | D60b_GE |
| 26 | rence to the venerable figure standing before him with eyes upon the ground: "What a Monster of an Israelite this | D64_OMF |
| 27 | ntion in Mrs Lammle's face as she said some words *with her eyes on* Mr Lammle's waistcoat, and seemed in return to re | D64_OMF |
| 28 | ls' dressmaker sat in her corner behind the door, *with her eyes on* the ground and her hands folded on her basket, ho | D64_OMF |
| 29 | giana?" inquired Mrs Lammle, still smiling coolly *with her eyes upon* her lunch, and her eyebrows raised. "YOU kno | D64_OMF |
| 30 | er. It shaded off into a cool smile, as she said, *with her eyes upon* her lunch, and her eyebrows raised: "You are | D64_OMF |
| 31 | wink. "I must own," returned the dressmaker, *with her eyes upon* her work, "that we are not good friends at prese | D64_OMF |
| 32 | und, as she meditated more and more thoughtfully, *with her eyes upon* his beaming face. "Still," said Bella, after | D64_OMF |
| 33 | ) "I a lady!" Lizzie went on in a low voice, *with her eyes upon* the fire. "I, with poor father's grave not even | D64_OMF |
| 34 | y. I don't complain of him." As she said it, *with her eyes upon* the fire-glow, there was an instantaneous escape | D64_OMF |
| 35 | accepted." "I do not doubt it," said Lizzie, *with her eyes upon* the ground. "I have sometimes had it in my t | D64_OMF |
| 36 | suspicions are, Miss," she asked after a silence, *with her eyes upon* the ground. "It's not an easy thing to tell | D64_OMF |
| 37 | l, neither Mr and Mrs Boffin said a word. He sat *with his eyes on* his plate, eating his muffins and ham, and she sa | D64_OMF |

| 38 | our family friends." ("Oh!" thinks Twemlow, *with his eyes on* Podsnap, "then there are only two of us, and he' | D64_OMF |
|---|---|---|
| 39 | u might have overlooked that," retorted Fledgeby, *with his eyes on* Riah's beard as he felt for his own; "having com | D64_OMF |
| 40 | ng grey hair as he stood on the verge of the rug, *with his eyes on* the acceptable fire. With a plunge of enjoyme | D64_OMF |
| 41 | lated rock in a stormy sea," said Eugene, smoking *with his eyes on* the fire, "Lady Tippins couldn't put off to visi | D64_OMF |
| 42 | ressed in the strange man's manner, and he walked *with his eyes on* the ground though conscious, for all that, of | D64_OMF |
| 43 | d, but, aware of his employer's suspicions, stood *with his eyes on* the ground. Mr Fledgeby was thus amiably enga | D64_OMF |
| 44 | s visitor sat down, resting his chin on his hand, *with his eyes on* the ground. And very remarkably again: Riderhood | D64_OMF |
| 45 | " "Are they, by George!" muttered Riderhood, *with his eyes on* the passion-wasted face. "Your working days mus | D64_OMF |
| 46 | fectly quiet, though his jaw was heavily squared; *with his eyes upon* Riderhood; and with traces of quickened breathing | D64_OMF |
| 47 | Boffin sitting in the arm-chair hugging himself, *with his eyes upon* the fire, acted as a restorative. Counterfeiting | D64_OMF |
| 48 | e suspicion crossed him as he rested in a doorway *with his eyes upon* the Temple gate, that perhaps she was even concea | D64_OMF |
| 49 | reign between his fingers. Slouching at his side *with his eyes upon* the towing-path, Riderhood held his left hand ope | D64_OMF |
| 50 | le. "No." They both lapsed into silence, *with their eyes upon* the fire. "You don't need to be told I am he | D64_OMF |
| 51 | should take it very kindly." Rosa intimated, *with her eyes on* the ground, that she thought a substitute might b | D70_MED |
| 52 | very great, though," said Mr Grewgious at length, *with his eyes on* the fire. Edwin nodded assent, with HIS eyes | D70_MED |
| 53 | th his eyes on the fire. Edwin nodded assent, *with HIS eyes on* the fire. "And let him be sure that he trifl | D70_MED |
| 54 | fter a little. His memory grew DAZED." Mr Tope, *with his eyes on* the Reverend Mr Crisparkle, shoots this word out, | D70_MED |

## Appendix 3.7 Concordance Lines: with his hands in his...

| 1 | ow. "Di-rectly, sir," said the coachman, *with his hands in his pockets*, looking as much unlike a man in a hurry | D33_SB |
|---|---|---|
| 2 | ork, and John Evenson walked up and down the room *with his hands in his pockets*, looking as if nothing had happened. The | D33_SB |
| 3 | left the room, and departed slowly on his errand, *with his hands in his pocket* and his eyes fixed on the ground. "Ru | D36_PP |
| 4 | g of the real state of the case. Mr Pickwick, *with his hands in his pockets* and his hat cocked completely over his le | D36_PP |
| 5 | logue was cut short by the entry of Master Bates, *with his hands in his breeches-pockets*, and his face twisted into a loo | D37b_OT |
| 6 | t cocked, as usual; Master Bates sauntering along *with his hands in his pockets*; and Oliver between them, wondering where | D37b_OT |

(Continued)

| 7 | ally substantial breakfasts. Mr John Browdie, *with his hands in his pockets*, hovered restlessly about these delicacie | D38_NN |
|---|---|---|
| 8 | this kind that Mr Ralph Nickleby gazed, as he sat *with his hands in his pockets* looking out of the window. He had fixed | D38_NN |
| 9 | u had gone at the right time, Mr Wackford Squeers *with his hands in his pockets*. Mr Squeers's appearance was not prep | D38_NN |
| 10 | nd wrapped up from his boots to his chin; and Sam *with his hands in his pockets* and his hat half off his head, remonstrat | D40a_MHC |
| 11 | s into the mud when the tide was out, to standing *with his hands in his pockets* gazing listlessly on the motion and on th | D40b_OCS |
| 12 | and looking at the roofs of the opposite houses, *with his hands in his pockets*; "he has an extraordinary flow of langua | D40b_OCS |
| 13 | meals. "Now," said Dick, walking up and down *with his hands in his pockets*, "I'd give something if I had it t | D40b_OCS |
| 14 | It seemed that Mr Chuckster had been standing *with his hands in his pockets* looking carelessly at the pony, and occas | D40b_OCS |
| 15 | e family over Mr Quilp's head, and Quilp himself, *with his hands in his pockets*, smiled in an exquisite enjoyment of the | D40b_OCS |
| 16 | l, who had attended Edward to the door, came back *with his hands in his pockets*; and, after fidgeting about the room in a | D41_BR |
| 17 | Mrs Varden complied. The locksmith followed *with his hands in his pockets*, and Mr Tappertit trundled off with the c | D41_BR |
| 18 | aid the officer, who had been lounging in and out *with his hands in his pockets*, and yawning as if he were in the last ex | D41_BR |
| 19 | iples of Christianity! Meanwhile the Lord Mayor, *with his hands in his pockets*, looked on as an idle man might look at a | D41_BR |
| 20 | fast asleep; and so sat leaning back in his chair *with his hands in his pockets* until his son's return caused him to wake | D41_BR |
| 21 | it, as his fancy dictates; leans against the door *with his hands in his pockets* and stares at you, if you chance to be a | D42_AN |
| 22 | om stirred from behind Mr Jinkins's chair, where, *with his hands in his pockets*, and his legs planted pretty wide apart, | D43_MC |
| 23 | le dialogue, Jonas had been rocking on his chair, *with his hands in his pockets* and his head thrown cunningly on one side | D43_MC |
| 24 | as a short man, he was round and broad, and stood *with his hands in his pockets*, and his legs just wide enough apart to e | D43b_CB |
| 25 | falling back in his chair, and surveying the Firm *with his hands in his pockets*. "Deep in love." "And not with an he | D43b_CB |
| 26 | er," muttered William, looking at him grudgingly, *with his hands in his pockets*. "I don't know what good you are, mysel | D43b_CB |
| 27 | "Ha ha ha! laughed the Doctor thoughtfully, *with his hands in his pockets*. "The great farce in a hundred acts!" | D43b_CB |
| 28 | Tugby tried philosophy. "Come, come!" he said, *with his hands in his pockets*, "you mustn't give way, you know. That | D43b_CB |
| 29 | say so: and he beamed on his audience afterwards, *with his hands in his pockets*, and excessive satisfaction twinkling in | D46b_DS |
| 30 | e, to find Mr Brogley sitting in the back parlour *with his hands in his pockets*, and his hat hanging up behind the door. | D46b_DS |
| 31 | . The Captain in his own apartment was sitting *with his hands in his pockets* and his legs drawn up under his chair, on | D46b_DS |
| 32 | t his feelings best by withdrawing: when he said, *with his hands in his coat pockets*, into which it was as much as he cou | D49_DC |

| 33 | me or any of us, he sat on the edge of his table *with his hands in his pockets*, and one of his splay feet twisted round | D49_DC |
| 34 | ious." Mr Micawber, leaning back in his chair *with his hands in his pockets*, eyed us aside, and nodded his head, as m | D49_DC |
| 35 | his sister sat herself at her desk. Mr Quinion, *with his hands in his pockets*, stood looking out of window; and I stood | D49_DC |
| 36 | a private word to you?" Mr Tulkinghorn rises *with his hands in his pockets* and walks into one of the window recesses | D52_BH |
| 37 | t me, and brightened, and came and sat down again *with his hands in his pockets*. "I told you this was the growlery, | D52_BH |
| 38 | d." "Ah!" He began to walk about the room *with his hands in his pockets*, showing that he had been thinking as muc | D52_BH |
| 39 | ng up." "Whether," said Gradgrind, pondering *with his hands in his pockets*, and his cavernous eyes on the fire, "wh | D54_HT |
| 40 | far, that's true enough," assented Mr Bounderby, *with his hands in his pockets* and his hat on. "But I have known you p | D54_HT |
| 41 | he words, "By your leaves, gentlemen!" walked in *with his hands in his pockets*. His face, close-shaven, thin, and sallo | D54_HT |
| 42 | to acquire any fashion of wearing his hat and *with his hands in his pockets*, sauntered out into the hall. "I never | D54_HT |
| 43 | this, Tom Gradgrind," said Bounderby, standing up *with his hands in his pockets*, "that you are of opinion that there's w | D54_HT |
| 44 | my love, and gone away again." Mr Bounderby, *with his hands in his pockets*, walked in impatient mortification up and | D54_HT |
| 45 | xpiration of that term sauntered back one evening *with his hands in his pockets*, and incidentally observed to his sister | D55_LD |
| 46 | id as he was ordered. The man remained standing, *with his hands in his pockets*, and towered between Clennam and the pros | D55_LD |
| 47 | e best account." "Just so," said Mr Meagles, *with his hands in his pockets*, and with the old business expression of | D55_LD |
| 48 | had got back into his corner, where he now stood *with his hands in his pockets*, taking breath, and returning Mrs Clennam | D55_LD |
| 49 | s hat from his head, and stood defiantly lounging *with his hands in his pockets*. "You villain of ill-omen!" said Art | D55_LD |
| 50 | ot wet, was a shabby man in threadbare black, and *with his hands in his pockets*, who fascinated me from the memorable ins | D56_RP |
| 51 | od knows. It was my way, I suppose." He sat, *with his hands in his pockets* and his legs stretched out before him, lo | D59_TTC |
| 52 | d a case in hand, anywhere, but Carton was there, *with his hands in his pockets*, staring at the ceiling of the court; the | D59_TTC |
| 53 | im: and nearly opposite another wigged gentleman *with his hands in his pockets*, whose whole attention, when Mr Cruncher | D59_TTC |
| 54 | at other bowl of punch?" said Stryver the portly, *with his hands in his waistband*, glancing round from the sofa where he | D59_TTC |
| 55 | fferent way; the lion for the most part reclining *with his hands in his waistband*, looking at the fire, or occasionally f | D59_TTC |
| 56 | the identical greengrocer appeared on the steps, *with his hands in his pockets*, and leaning his shoulder against the doo | D60a_UT |
| 57 | ing days would come slouching from his hermitage, *with his hands in his pockets* and his dinner loosely tied in a bundle r | D60b_GE |
| 58 | laughed outright, and sat laughing in our faces, *with his hands in his pockets* and his round shoulders raised: plainly s | D60b_GE |

(Continued)

| | | |
|---|---|---|
| 59 | , eh!" retorted Mr Jaggers, lying in wait for me, *with his hands in his pockets*, his head on one side, and his eyes on th | D60b_GE |
| 60 | tating aloud in his garden at Camberwell. Orlick, *with his hands in his pockets*, slouched heavily at my side. It was very | D60b_GE |
| 61 | w," said the Deputy Lock, shrugging his shoulders *with his hands in his pockets*, and shaking his head in a sulkily ominou | D64_OMF |
| 62 | and them I learned her." The gloomy Eugene, *with his hands in his pockets*, had strolled in and assisted at the latt | D64_OMF |

## Notes

1. The equation to calculate log-likelihood ratio (LLR or *G2*) is as follows:

   $$-2\log\lambda = 2\left\{\sum_i O_i * \log\left(\frac{O_i}{E_i}\right)\right\}$$ where $E_i$ is the expected frequency of the word $i$ and $O_i$ the

   observed frequency of the word $i$. It is also possible to calculate *G2* in the following way:

   1) Calculate for each word in the corpus $X$ how many times that word occurs in the corpus ... (*a*)
   2) Calculate the total number of the words in the corpus $X$ ... (*c*)
   3) Calculate for each word in the corpus $Y$ how many times that word occurs in the corpus ... (*b*)
   4) Calculate the total number of words in the corpus $Y$ ... (*d*)

   $$G^2 = 2\left(a\log\left(\frac{a}{\left(\frac{c(a+b)}{(c+d)}\right)}\right) + b\log\left(\frac{b}{\left(\frac{d(a+b)}{c+d}\right)}\right)\right)$$

2. The list of texts incorporated in the Dickens and Collins corpora are given in Appendices 3.1 and 3.2, respectively.
3. RF analyses in this study were carried out under R, a language and environment for statistical computing and graphics (the R Foundation for Statistical Computing; http://www.r-project.org/index.html).

## Works cited

Breiman, L. (2001). 'Random Forests'. *Machine Learning* 45: 5–32.

Breiman, L., and A. Cutler. (n.d.). 'Random Forests'. Available at: http://stat-www.berkeley.edu/users/breiman/RandomForests/cc_home.htm.

Burrows, J. (2005). 'Who Wrote *Shamela*? Verifying the Authorship of a Parodic Text'. *Literary and Linguistic Computing* 19, no. 4: 453–75.

Burrows, J. (2007). 'All the Way Through: Testing for Authorship in Different Frequency Strata'. *Literary and Linguistic Computing* 22, no. 1: 27–47.

Dunning, T. (1993). 'Accurate Methods for the Statistics of Surprise and Coincidence'. *Computational Linguistics* 19, no. 1: 61–74.

Eder, M. (2010). 'Does Size Matter? Authorship Attribution, Small Samples, Big Problem'. *Digital Humanities 2010 Conference Abstracts*, King's College London, 132–5.

Eder, M., and J. Rybicki. (2009). 'PCA, Delta, JGAAP, and Polish Poetry of the 16th and the 17th Centuries: Who Wrote the Dirty Stuff?' *Digital Humanities 2009 Conference Abstracts*, University of Maryland, College Park, 242–4.

Henry, A., and R. L. Rooseberry. (2001). 'Using a Small Corpus to Obtain Data for Teaching Genre'. In *Small Corpus and ELT*, ed. M. Ghadessy, A. Henry, and R. L. Roseberry, 93–133. Amsterdam: John Benjamins.

Hoover, D. L. (2003). 'Correspondence: Multivariate Analysis and the Study of Style Variation'. *Literary and Linguistic Computing* 18, no. 4: 341–60.

Hoover, D. L. (2004). 'Testing Burrows's Delta'. *Literary and Linguistic Computing* 19, no. 4: 453–75.

Hori, M. (2004). *Investigating Dickens' Style: A Collocational Analysis*. New York: Palgrave Macmillan.

Ishikawa, S. (2008). *Eigo Corpus to Gengo Kyouiku—Data toshite no text* [English corpora and language pedagogy: Texts as data]. Tokyo: Taishukan.

Jin, M., and M. Murakami. (2007). 'Random Forest hou ni yoru bunshou no kakite no doutei [Authorship identification using Random Forests]'. *Toukei Suuri* (*Proceedings of the Institute of Statistical Mathematics*) 55, no. 2: 255–68.

Mahlberg, M. (2007a). 'Corpus Stylistics: Bridging the Gap Between Linguistic and Literary Studies'. In *Text, Discourse and Corpora: Theory and Analysis*, ed. M. Hoey, M. Mahlberg, M. Stubbs, and W. Teubert, 217–46. London: Continuum.

Mahlberg, M. (2007b). 'Clusters, Key Clusters, and Local Textual Functions in Dickens'. *Corpora* 2, no. 1: 1–31.

Rayson, P., and R. Garside. (2000). 'Comparing Corpora Using Frequency Profiling'. *Proceedings of the Workshop on Comparing Corpora, Held in Conjunction with the 38th Annual Meeting of the Association for Computational Linguistics* (*ACL 2000*), 1–8 October, Hong Kong, 1–6. Available at: http://www.comp.lancs.ac.uk.

Rybicki, J. (2009). 'Translation and Delta Revisited: When We Read Translations, Is it the Author or the Translator that We Really Read?' *Digital Humanities 2009 Conference Abstracts*, University of Maryland, College Park: 245–7.

Rybicki, J., and M. Eder. (2011). 'Deeper Delta Across Genres and Languages: Do We Really Need the Most Frequent Words?' *Literary and Linguistic Computing* 26, no. 3: 315–21.

Stubbs, M. (2005). 'Conrad in the Computer: Examples of Quantitative Stylistic Methods'. *Language and Literature* 14, no. 1: 5–24.

Tabata, T. (2002). 'Investigating Stylistic Variation in Dickens Through Correspondence Analysis of Word-Class Distribution'. In *English Corpus Linguistics in Japan*, ed. T. Saito, J. Nakamura, and S. Yamasaki, 165–82. Amsterdam: Rodopi.

Tabata, T. (2005). 'Profiling Stylistic Variations in Dickens and Smollett Through Correspondence Analysis of Low-Frequency Words'. *ACH/ALLC 2005 Conference Abstracts*, Humanities Computing and Media Centre, University of Victoria, Canada: 229–32.

Tabata, T. (2009). 'More about Gentleman in Dickens'. *Digital Humanities 2009 Conference Abstracts*, University of Maryland, College Park: 270–5.

Wynne, M. (2008). 'Searching and Concordancing'. In *Corpus Linguistics: An International Handbook*, ed. A. Lüdeling and M. Kytö, 706–37. Berlin: Mouton de Gruyter.

# 4
# Patterns and Trends in Harlequin Category Romances

*Jack Elliott*

## Introduction

Romance fiction is dominated by a single publisher, Harlequin Mills and Boon, which publishes roughly half of all romantic fiction worldwide, selling over four books a second (Harlequin Public Relations Office 2012). The line-up is divided into different categories, sequentially numbered imprints that empha-size a different aspect or brand of romance, such as 'Medical' for romance in the health industry, 'Intrigue' for romance with an element of suspense, and 'Nocturne' for romance with a supernatural twist. Each category publishes any-where from two to eight titles a month—thousands of novels a year in total (Harlequin Public Relations Office 2011). Harlequin has been in business for over 60 years, producing a monumental back-catalogue that cannot easily be char-acterized, so critical opinion has diverged, describing the company variously as a savvy mercantile player (Grescoe 1997), regressive manipulator of socio-sexual norms (Modleski 1982), or faithful reproducer of women's desires (Krentz 1992). However, the size of its publication list—with over 110 titles every month worldwide—renders this body of work impervious to more traditional forms of literary analysis.

Bibliographic analysis of title and authorship data turns this overabundance of publication on its head, allowing researchers to make sense of a great number of novels (Moretti 2005). Authorship, national origin and changes throughout time can all be explored using bibliographic analysis. Studying changes over time using bibliographic information is not novel. It has been shown that, in response to mar-ket pressures, the length of titles of British novels contracts over the course of the eighteenth century (Moretti 2009). It has also been demonstrated that, contrary to prevailing academic wisdom, Irish-American literature did not contract during the 1920s (Jockers 2013, 35–47). These other studies have looked at the evolution of titles over time by analysing the rise and fall of keywords by publication date. This study refines the methodology slightly by automatically discovering the keywords to analyse and the periods in which they are popular.

Bibliographic analysis shows that the majority of category romance is written by a minority of authors. These authors tend to live in countries such as Australia and the United Kingdom, not in the United States or India where the works are sold. The titles of the novels can be used to divide categories into distinct periods. These transitions in the titles can be directly tied to financial shocks as Harlequin reacts to changing market conditions. Overall, study of the bibliographic data shows a company driven by crisis, reacting to changes in romance purchasing habits by radically manipulating its titles to better deliver what its customers want.

Harlequin distributes its novels in over 127 markets worldwide, and translates its titles into 27 different languages, so one book can have many different titles. Even the publisher and its imprints are known under different names in different markets. In the interests of simplicity, this study uses the titles and imprint names of Harlequin's largest market—the United States (Harlequin Public Relations Office 2011). Bibliographic information was taken from Fiction DB (Fiction DB 2012), which provides the ability to search by category, and reconciled against the information on the Romance Wiki (Romance Wiki Editorial Team 2011). Publishing eight novels every month, the most prolific of all the categories, and the focus of this study, is Harlequin Presents, which has been continuously published since 1973. Harlequin Presents is the most glamorous of the Harlequin imprints, promising to snatch the reader 'away to exclusive jet-set locations to experience smouldering intensity and red-hot desire' (Harlequin Corporation 2012a).

## Authorship of Harlequin Presents novels

Authorship of Harlequin Presents is dominated by a few 'super-authors'. Figure 4.1 matches the author's rank (that is, the most prolific author appears on the far left, followed by the next-most prolific author), with their output (the number of Harlequin Presents novels they have published).

The top 20 authors, out of 190, are responsible for roughly half the novels. Almost all the names in the sample are pseudonyms, although often widely known ones. Women write almost all these novels; men are a rounding error. In fact, only two authors are known to be men: Madelyne Ker, who has written 20 novels, and Victoria Gordon, who has written one. Far from being a mundane activity dominated by housewives, Figure 4.1 shows Harlequin Presents authorship is primarily undertaken by 'super-authors', capable of rolling out multiple novels every year.

## Country of origin of Harlequin presents

To study any national trends in authorship, nationality was assigned by googling each author in turn, and choosing the nation where they spent the most time. Figure 4.2 shows the relative contribution of each country to Harlequin Presents. While Harlequin has sourced roughly equivalent amounts of fiction from the United States, United Kingdom, Australia and New Zealand, Harlequin's third-largest market, India (Flesch 2004, 48), is not represented at all. New Zealand is extremely over-represented, as authors from this nation of four-and-a-half million people have written almost as many novels as Australia, with roughly five times the population.

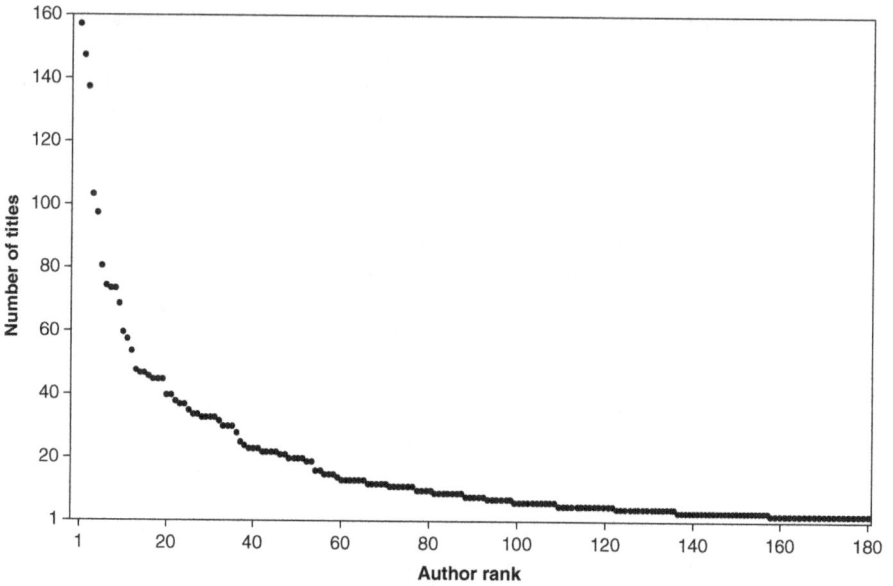

*Figure 4.1*   Author rank plotted against the number of novels by that author
Note: The most prolific author here, to the far left, is Penny Jordan.

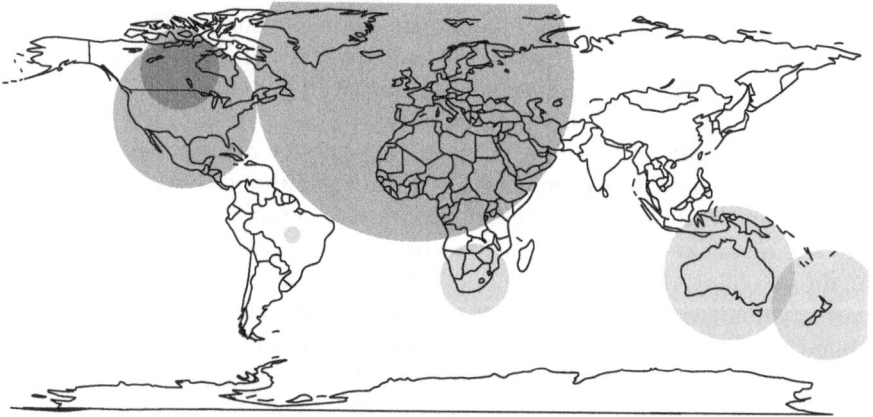

*Figure 4.2*   Bubble plot of writers by country, matching nationality to output
Note: The larger the circle around each country, the greater the output of that country. Here the United Kingdom has been treated as a single country, as contributions from Scotland, Wales and Northern Ireland get overwhelmed by the output from England.

Figure 4.3 plots the origin of the novels published in the United States since Harlequin Presents was founded in 1973. Some former Commonwealth countries, notably South Africa and Canada, were more important in the past than now. Conversely, Australia and New Zealand have gone through periods where they

**Harlequin presents by country 1973–2012**

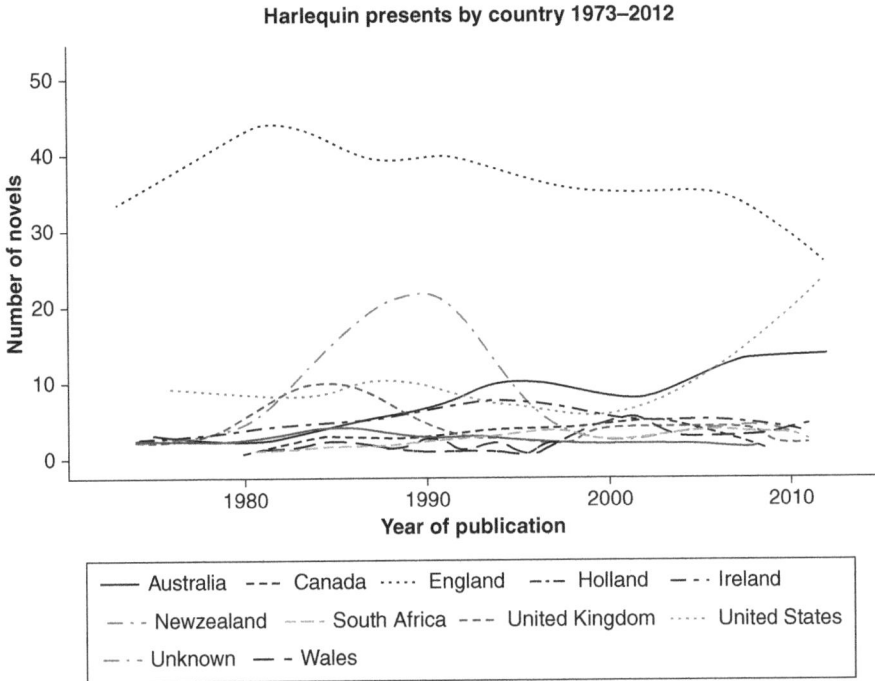

*Figure 4.3* Publications per country by year

*Note*: Countries with a total contribution of fewer than ten novels (Brazil and Scotland) have been elimi-nated. Lines are drawn with Friedman's Super Smoother (Friedman 1984), using a span of 0.3. The United Kingdom is the contribution of all United Kingdom authors who could not be located in one of the con-stituent kingdoms or principalities of the United Kingdom. Breaking out the United Kingdom shows the surprising lack of contribution from Scotland, while highlighting the surprising output of Wales.

were not represented at all. Strikingly, the amount of Harlequin Presents written worldwide is currently evenly divided between England, Australia and the United States, although the United States is by far Harlequin's largest and most lucrative market.

Harlequin acts, in effect, as a cultural importer, taking stories from countries where profits are thin, and publishing them in larger markets. This has impor-tant implications for researchers of national bibliographies; the greatest impact of some genres may be foreign rather than domestic. The trends in Figure 4.3 suggest that the introduction of a commissioning editor in the Australian office in 2006 (McWilliam 2009) was driven by a desire to better manage an important source of raw material.

Bibliographic studies of national printed data sometimes understate the contribution of romance authors and Harlequin to their country's cultural output. The AustLit Database of Australian bibliographic data (AustLit 2012), for exam-ple, currently understates the contribution of Melanie Milburne, an Australian author, omitting 24 Milburne titles to date.[1] Studies based on the AustLit informa-tion, such as Bode's 'From British Domination to Multinational Conglomeration', argue that Harlequin fell from publishing the most Australian fiction of any pub-lisher during the 1980s and 1990s to the fifth most important by volume after the year 2000 (Bode 2009). The increasing importance of Australian authors to Harlequin Presents after 2000 suggests that any perceived decline is probably due to incomplete information in the AustLit database. Other national databases of bibliographic information that rely on self-reporting should be approached with similar caution.

For countries such as the United Kingdom, Australia and New Zealand, Harlequin provides a valuable export opportunity. Works are bought in these countries and redistributed in the United States and India. Historical analysis shows that this is not something to be treated with complacency; Harlequin is a self-interested player, and can always treat these producing countries as they did South Africa, abandoning them when they no longer produce the product Harlequin needs.

## Trends in title data

The most important source of information in bibliographic data is the titles them-selves (Moretti 2009, 134). Aggregating the titles published each year into a single body of text allows the titles to be analysed year by year. A tree diagram, also called a cluster dendrogram, allows a computer to group these years together into clumps. The cluster dendrogram works by measuring the distance between each year (the more words they have in common, the 'closer' the years) and then applies a clustering algorithm to lump these years into groups. The clustering method used here, Ward's Distance Measure, can be thought of as growing a bub-ble around each point. As the bubble around any year touches any other bubble, the two years are linked together. These years now share a 'super-bubble' represent-ing them as a group. If two super-bubbles touch, the two groups are also linked. Bubbles are grown until all the data is inside the one bubble, linking all the years together. Two years with a great similarity to one another will be joined by lines close to the bottom of the diagram. A year with nothing in common with any other year would be joined to all other years by a single line near the top of the diagram (Everitt, Landau, and Leese 2009). This is a so-called 'unsupervised' learn-ing procedure, as the algorithm is not conscious of anything beyond the content of the years; it is not aware that the years are sequential, and it draws inferences without any input from the user.

Figure 4.4 groups the years into early, middle and late periods. The early period (on the right-hand side of the plot) runs from the founding of the imprint in 1973 until 1994; the middle period, from 1995 until 2003; and the late period, from 2004 on. Note the anomalous allocation of 2011 into the wrong group—trends in the titles were changing in this year.

It is possible to inspect the changes in time more closely using a technique called Principal Components Analysis (PCA), commonly applied in computational

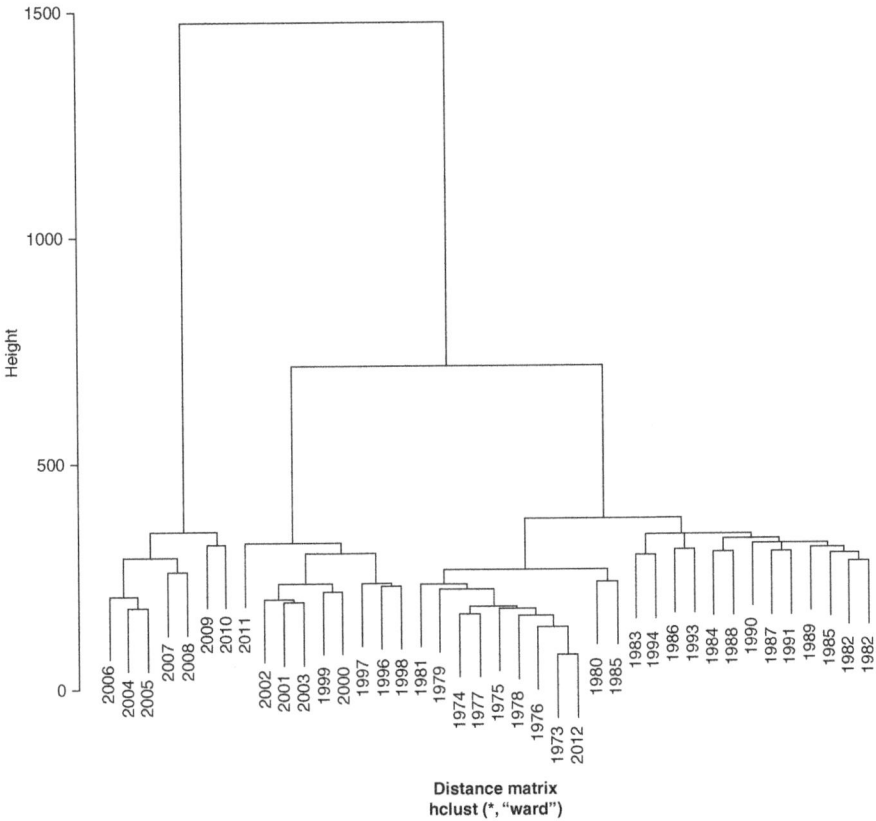

*Figure 4.4* Cluster dendrogram of Harlequin Presents novels by year

stylistics (Craig 2004), which constructs synthetic 'dimensions' to try to account for most of the variance in the data. Each of these dimensions gives every word a weight, accounting for the variation across time for that word. Words that account for most of the variation will tend to be heavily weighted. Words that vary at the same rate as a headline word, but with a lower amplitude, will be assigned a much lower weight. The arrows in Figure 4.5 show the direction each year will move when plotted: more titles with the word 'marriage' in them drive a year to the top right of the plot; years with more titles containing the word 'love' will move to the top left of the panel; and years with the word 'bride' will be placed to the right (Smith 2002).

Years from 2006 onward are very strongly clustered to the top right of the plot. 1996–2005 are at the bottom of the plot. Years before the mid-1990s are to the left. We can see that 'marriage' is a middle period word, 'bride' is a late period word, and 'love' is the quintessential early period word. There is a little bleeding between the groups found by cluster analysis and those found by PCA: 1996, for example, seems to want to break away from the middle period and join the early

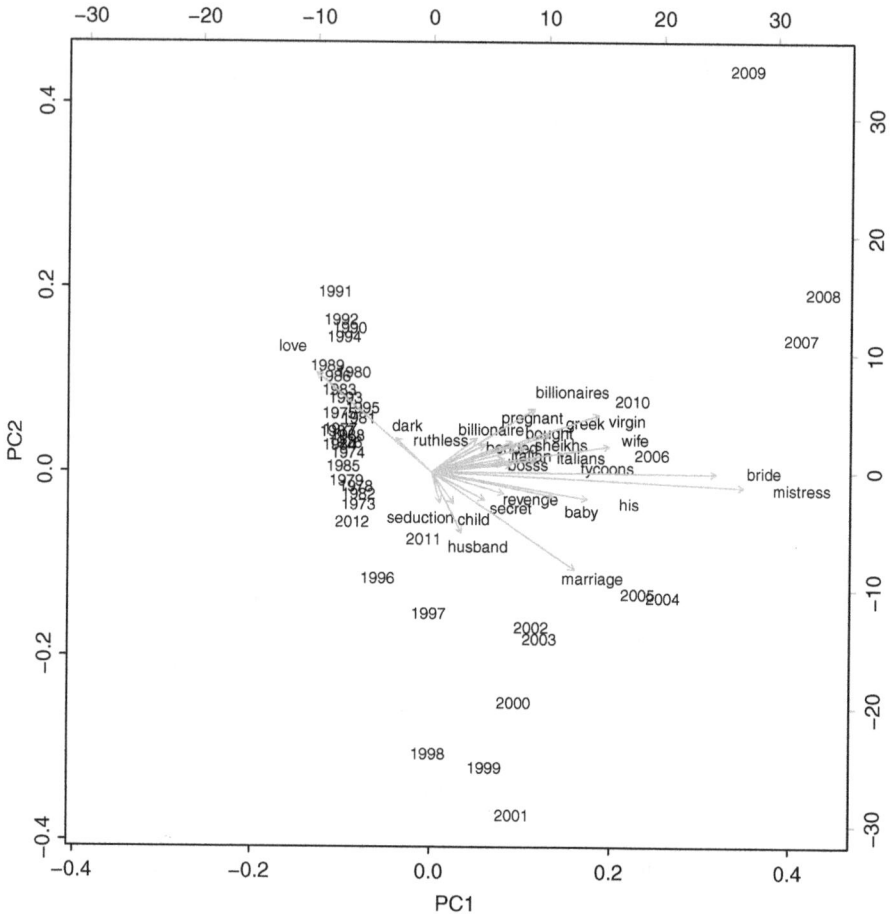

*Figure 4.5*   Principal Components Analysis of Harlequin Presents, with years overlaid. Words with an absolute weight less than 0.1 in either components 1 or 2 have been removed from the plot

*Note*: The early period found by cluster analysis is to the top left of the plot; the middle period is towards the bottom; late period years are in the top right.

period (cluster analysis classifies 1996 as a middle period year). What is striking is the way that PCA has found our distinct periods, and assigned a word to each period.

PCA does not simply give us the archetypal word for each period; it also reduces the contribution of words that covary at the same rate as the headline word. We can tease out other words that belong to the same period by selecting all words that vary at something like the same rate as the headline word. In a technical sense, we are taking the words with a correlation greater than 0.5 with our archetypal word. Heuser and Le-Khac studied the variation of words using correlations (Heuser and Le-Khac 2012, 56), but took their keywords from an OED thesaurus; these keywords are extracted directly from the plot in Figure 4.5. Only words that appeared in more than one year were analysed. Plotting the incidence of these words over time sheds light on the period the archetypal word represents.

Plotting all these words together on a timeline gives us a sense of the words rising and falling together. For these plots, I have used Friedman's Super Smoother, which must be approached with caution for tasks such as predicting the next in a series or reconstructing missing data (Friedman 1984). For the purposes of divining patterns and trends from complete information, however, it is easily one of the better tools available[2].

Figure 4.6 shows words correlated with 'love' for Harlequin Presents. These words are 'touch', 'heart' and 'dark'. 'Touch' has a dash of sensuality, 'heart' is a tip to the emotions and the potpourri is spiced by the addition of 'dark'. The hero is not yet the selling point he will become in later periods. The only anomaly is 'dark', with its hint of danger. Behind all these words stands the rock of 'love', casting a long shadow over the period and clearly invoked to sell more books than the others combined (Figure 4.7).

Figure 4.7 has 'bride' as its archetypal word. The words correlated here are more exciting in flavour, as 'revenge', 'contract' and 'blackmail' join the mix. This combination of words lends the imprint a more escapist, fantastical feel and also

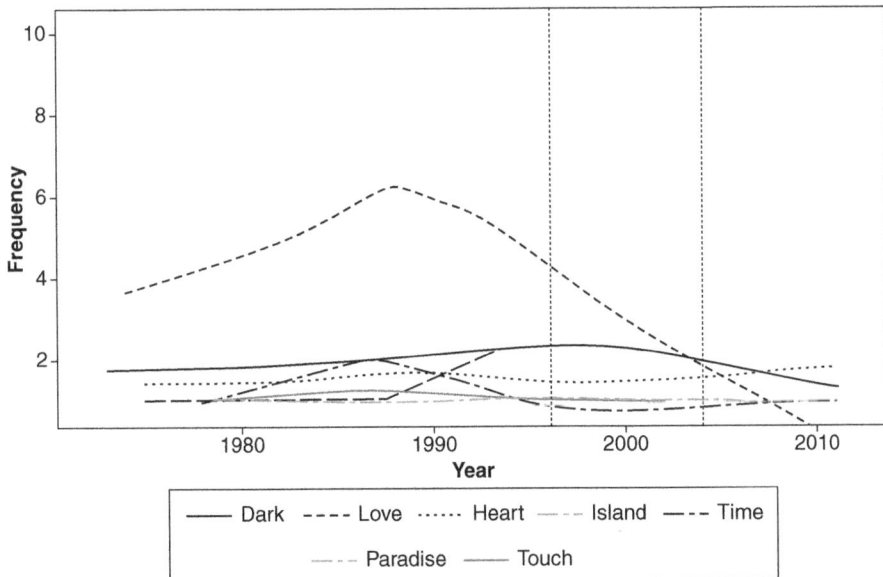

*Figure 4.6* Early period words in Harlequin Presents

*Note*: Vertical lines demark the periods (1996 onwards and 2004 onwards) predicted by cluster analysis and confirmed by PCA.

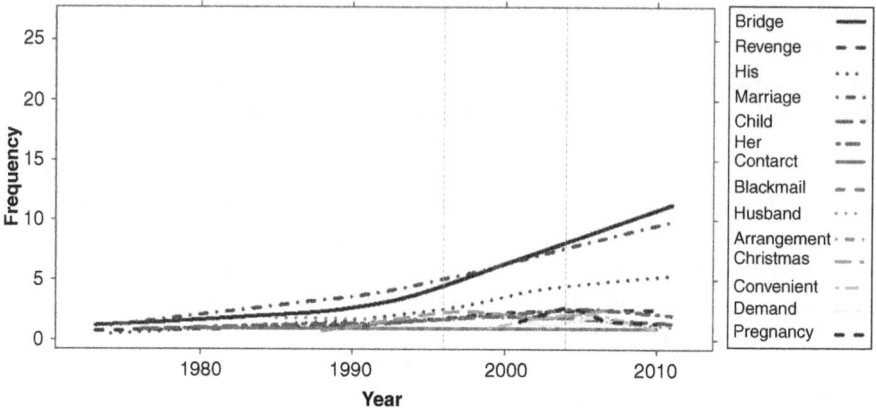

*Figure 4.7*  Middle period words in Harlequin Presents

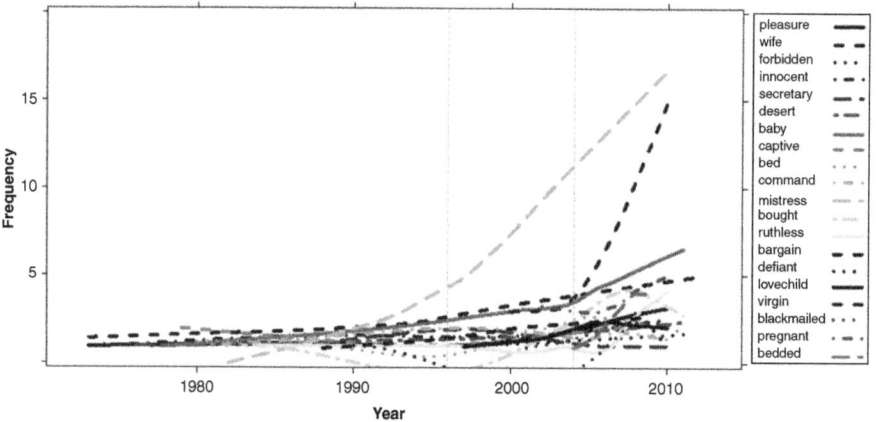

*Figure 4.8*  Late period 'non-status' words in Harlequin Presents

serves to more clearly delineate Harlequin Presents from other imprints. The trend for these words is to increase in usage throughout our middle and late period—they tend not to drop off in popularity like the early period words (Figures 4.8. and 4.9).

The final period is busier than the earlier periods, but the words can be divided into two types—'status' words such as 'billionaire', 'sheikh' and 'tycoon' in Figure 4.9, and the non-status words in Figure 4.8. The profile of the non-status words is markedly different; words like 'love-child', 'bargain' and 'defiant' all increase markedly throughout the period, but do so without trending downward. The status words such as 'billionaire', 'Greek' and 'boss's' all move upwards before sharply collapsing. This trend is not universal ('millionaire' and 'millionaire's' are still popular words at the end of the late period), but is shared by the overwhelming majority of status words.

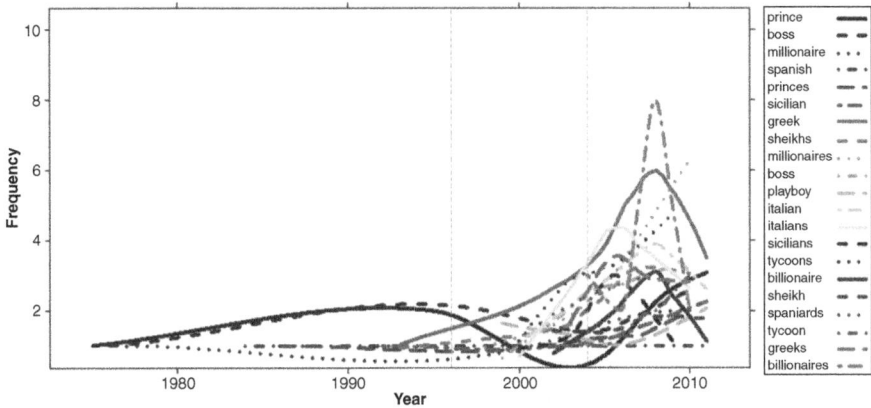

*Figure 4.9* Late period 'status' words in Harlequin Presents

Figure 4.9 also highlights the use of the possessive. 'Boss's', 'prince's' and other possessives all belong to the same period as their non-possessive counterparts. With the exception of 'sheikh's', these possessive forms are never as popular as the non-possessive form, but they share the same profile.

Though these title words are unique to Harlequin Presents, two other imprints, Harlequin Romance and Harlequin Superromance, display almost precisely the same periods when subjected to cluster analysis. The title words for these other imprints are, of course, different. Superromance, an imprint with a more 'realistic' flavour, differentiates itself by focusing on families in the middle period, then introduces cowboys in the late period. This imprint also shifts from a feminine focus ('daughter', 'mom' and 'wife') in the middle period to a more masculine one ('father', 'son' and 'cowboy') in the late period. Harlequin Romance, with stories that, according to the submissions guidelines, 'could really happen to you' (Harlequin Corporation 2012b), concentrates on weddings and marriage in the middle period and has its share of sheikhs and tycoons in the late period, but also adds more family words just at the time Superromance de-emphasizes the family. In all cases the imprints move from generic titles in the early period, to imprint-specific titles in the middle period, to emphasizing the hero in the late period.[3]

## Analysis

Analysis of the title data supports the theory that category romance can be divided into distinct periods. These shifts can be tied to financial crises at the publisher Harlequin, and suggest that changes in the genre are dominated by financial concerns of the publisher rather than some mysterious cultural force. Changes in romance generally have had a profound effect on the academic criticism, at once informing and frustrating it as critics have grappled with a hugely prolific genre only to have it shift from under their grasp. Consensus within the academic community is often driven by periods of stability in the genre, allowing ideas to be fully developed on a stable genre. Periodization is so strong that it can be discovered by cluster analysis and then unpicked using PCA—it is the dominant force in title generation.

The first major change in Harlequin Presents titles occurred during the mid-1990s, when Harlequin lost more and more of its authors to publishers of so-called 'single title', as opposed to category, romance. Because a minority of writers are responsible for a majority of the output in Harlequin Presents, the loss of even a few key writers can jeopardize an imprint. Figure 4.10 shows each year together with the number of authors that published for the first time and the last time for the Harlequin Presents line. In 1989, Harlequin Presents added a record number of new authors to their line-up, with very little in the way of loss. The period 1991–3 was a different story, as more writers left than were added. Clearly 1994, when a huge number of writers left but no new ones came on board, was a disaster. Harlequin's response was to create, in 1994, the Mira imprint focusing on single-title romance. Authors wishing for a canvas broader than 50,000 words, or a setting less constricting than the traditional imprints, were encouraged to move to Mira.

Mira drained off authors from the other Harlequin imprints and allowed the editorial team to sharpen the focus of each imprint. They began to give the readers more revenge, blackmail, demands and marriage. More, in short, of what the readers wanted from the imprint. Draining off writers from the top of the pool may also have left the imprints with more junior writers who were happy to relinquish control over the names of their novels.

The second shift in the titles comes in the mid-2000s, a particularly challenging time for Harlequin, as readers moved away from category romance. 'Our principal challenge in 2004 was Harlequin which had a difficult year' admitted the CEO, but 'Harlequin's management team, led by Donna Hayes, has a strategy for stabilising and then growing the business again' (Prichard 2004, 4). The solution to the crisis was, in part, to change up the title mix. More emphasis was placed on the hero, and the titles were made more masculine.

Although these title changes were probably undertaken with other marketing and publication initiatives, by 2005 Harlequin's profits had largely recovered (Prichard 2005, 4). One thing Harlequin did not do as part of its revamp was alter its line-up of authors—Figure 4.10 shows the number of authors publishing for the last time to be stable over the years 2004–05.

The collapse in so many of the title words, particularly status words associated with heroes, towards the end of our late period can also be explained by a recent shock at Harlequin. In particular, Harlequin is being forced to adapt to the new world of digital publishing. According to the most recent Chairman's Letter: 'Excluding the impact of foreign exchange and acquisitions, the revenue was down slightly from 2010 with digital revenue growth not offsetting declines in print revenue in the overseas markets that were in part affected by fragile economic conditions' (Prichard 2011, 4). In particular, the latest Management Report notes

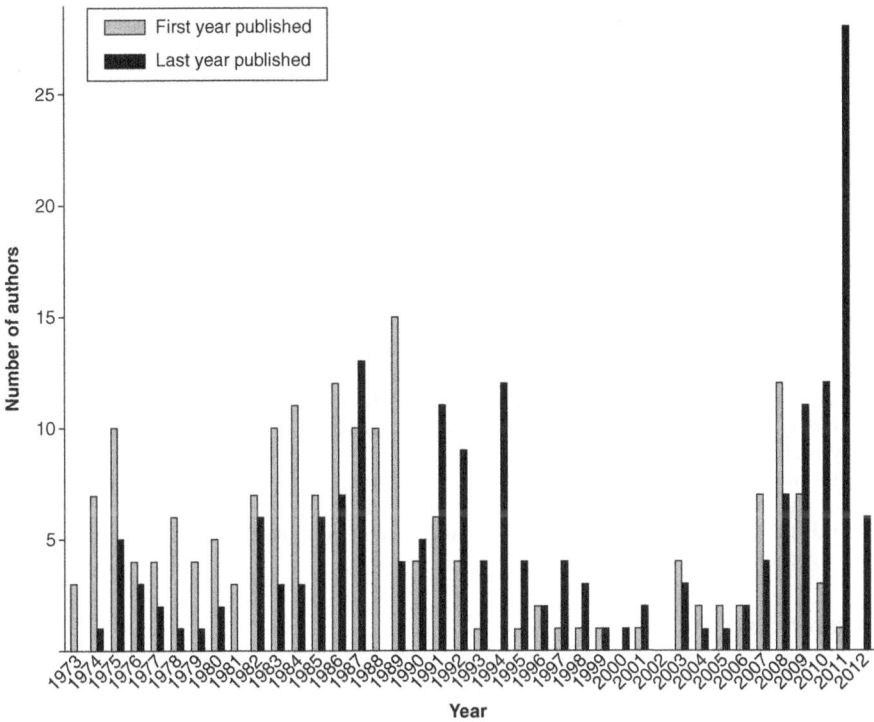

*Figure 4.10* Number of authors publishing their first title and last title in the Harlequin Presents line

*Note*: The plot towards the end of the timeline gets a little chaotic: it is not unusual for a writer to go a year or so without publishing, so the far right-hand side may be overestimating the loss of authors to Harlequin Presents.

that foreign exchange losses, particularly a large fourth-quarter loss in 2011, are placing strain on the business (Torstar Management 2011).

Academic criticism often seeks to place shifts in category romance in the context of wider social changes (Dixon 1980, 6–8). Title data analysis adds a further nuance to this picture—changes are swing-shifts that pivot on certain years and sweep through the genre. The changes are primarily driven by crisis at Harlequin, not by artistic innovation or authorial direction. Harlequin titles only indirectly reflect the fears and desires of everyday readers, refracted through the market calculations of Harlequin.

Distant reading of category romance imprints shows a creative industry in action and demonstrates that the dynamics are driven by short-term shocks rather than long-term trends. The international nature of this industry is key, as Harlequin sources novels from peripheral markets such as Australia and New Zealand and sells them into core markets such as India and the United States. Of particular importance is the nature of authorship—the catalogue is dominated by a few super-authors, capable of publishing many novels a year, sometimes for decades at a stretch. While this mode of authorship is essential in delivering the quantity of material the industry needs, it can lead to instability if enough of these super-authors alter their publication schedules or leave category romance altogether. Furthermore, the industry is currently undergoing a crisis as it tries to adapt to a changing economic and technological climate.

## Notes

1. Even allowing AustLit to be complete only up to the year 2007, the database is missing *Back In Her Husband's Bed* (2006), *The Greek's Bridal Bargain* (2006) and *The Virgin's Price* (2006). All were published in Australia.
2. The Super Smoother was used with a span of 0.8, to correct for the relative scarcity of the data. This was the smallest span that would still allow the lines on all plots to be drawn. Uncorrected smoothing is best done on series with datapoints greater than 40. Although Harlequin Presents has been published for longer than 40 years, individual title words typically do not span the period.
3. For more detail on the Harlequin Superromance and Harlequin Romance imprints, see the supplementary materials (Elliott 2012). The Superromance imprint has 'Texas' and 'babies' in the middle period, whereas Harlequin Romance has 'weddings' and 'engagements'.

## References

AustLit 'AustLit Database'. (2012). Available at: http://www.austlit.edu.au (visited on 21 January 2012).

Bode, Katherine. (2009). 'From British Domination to Multinational Conglomeration? A Revised History of Australian Novel Publishing 1950–2007'. In *Resourceful Reading: The New Empiricism, eResearch, and Australian Literary Criticism*. Ed. Katherine Bode and Robert Dixon. Sydney: Sydney University Press.

Bode, Katherine. (2010). 'Publishing and Australian Literature: Crisis, Decline or Transformation?' In *Cultural Studies Review* 16, no. 2: 24–48.

Craig, Hugh. (2004). 'Stylistic Analysis and Authorship Studies'. In *A Companion to Digital Humanities*. Oxford: Blackwell: 243–88.

Dixon, Jay. (1980). *The Romance Fiction of Mills & Boon 1909–1990s*. London: Routledge.

Elliott, Jack. (2012). 'Love Falls Out of Style: Supplementary Materials'. Available at: http://jackelliott.net/papers/CategoryRomanceSupplementaryMaterials.pdf (visited on 1 May 2012).

Everitt, Brian, Sabine Landau, and Morgan Leese. (2009). *Cluster Analysis*. Chichester:Wiley.

Fiction DB. (2012). 'Fiction DB'. Available at: http://www.fictiondb.com (visited on 3 October 2011).

Flesch, Juliet. (2004). *From Australia With Love: A History of Modern Australian Popular Romance Novels*. Fremantle, WA: Fremantle Arts Center Press.

Friedman, Jerome. H. (1984). 'A Variable Span Smoother'. In *Technical Report LCS5*. Palo Alto: Stanford University.

Grescoe, Paul. (1997). *The Merchants of Venus: Inside Harlequin and the Empire of Romance*. Vancouver: Raincoast Books.

Harlequin Corporation. (2012a). 'Harlequin Presents Submissions Guidelines'. Available at: http://www.harlequin.com/articlepage.html?articleId=547&chapter=0 (visited on 20 April 2012).

Harlequin Corporation. (2012b).'Harlequin Romance Submissions Guidelines'. Available at: http://www. harlequin.com/articlepage.html?articleId=1573&chapter= (visited on 20 April 2012).

Harlequin Public Relations Office. (2012). 'Harlequin Enterprises Limited: A Global Success Story'. Available at: http://www.eharlequin.com/store.html? cid=2659 (visited on 20 April 2012).

Heuser, Ryan and Long Le-Khac. (2012). 'A Quantitative Literary History of 2,958 Nineteenth-Century British Novels: The Semantic Cohort Method'. Available at: http://litlab.stanford.edu/LiteraryLabPamphlet4.pdf (visited on 8 June 2013).

Jockers, Matthew. (2013). *Macroanalysis*. Chicago: University of Illinois Press.

Krentz, Jayne Ann. (1992). 'Introduction'. In *Dangerous Men and Adventurous Women*. Philadelphia: University of Pennsylvania Press.

McWilliam, Kelley. (2009). 'Romance in Foreign Accents: Harlequin-Mills & Boon in Australia'. In *Continuum* 23, no. 2: 137–45.

Modleski, Tania. (1982). *Loving With a Vengeance: Mass-produced Fantasies for Women*. Oxford: Clarendon Press.

Moretti, Franco. (2005). *Graphs, Maps, Trees*. New York: Verso.

Moretti, Franco. (2009). 'Style, Inc. Reflections on Seven Thousand Titles (British Novels, 1740–1850)'. In *Critical Inquiry* 36, no. 1: 134–58.

Prichard, J. Robert. S. (2004). 'Letter to Shareholders'. In *Torstar 2004 Annual Report*.

Prichard, J. Robert. S. (2005). 'Letter to Shareholders'. In *Torstar 2005 Annual Report*.

Prichard, J. Robert. S. (2011). 'Letter to Shareholders'. In *Torstar 2011 Annual Report*.

Romance Wiki Editorial Team. (2011) 'Romance Wiki'. Available at: http://www.romancewiki.com (visited on 3 October 2011).

Smith, Lindsay. (2002). 'A Tutorial on Principal Components Analysis'. Available at: http://www.cs.otago.ac.nz/cosc453/student_tutorials/principal_components.pdf (visited on 28 April 2012).

Torstar Management. (2011). 'Managements Discussion and Analysis'. In *Torstar 2011 Annual Report*.

# 5

# The Printers' Web

## New Tools to Crack Old Chestnuts

*Sydney J. Shep*

On Tuesday, 17 March 1868, the youthful Robert Coupland Harding set out from his father's printing establishment on Hastings Street, Napier, to walk overland to his uncle John's farm in Waipukurau, some 80 miles away. Apart from visiting relatives, the primary reason was to hand-deliver the weekly country edition of the daily newspaper, the *Hawkes Bay Times*, which had been overlooked in the scramble to bundle up the papers for the Cobb and Co. coach earlier that morning. As Harding's diary records, the rhythms of walking provide a singular opportunity for observing in vivid and minute detail the world around him: from various signposts in the landscape, both familiar and foreign, to chance meetings with acquaintances; from getting lost and fording streams in the Big Bush to meeting a Maori woman who gives him a watermelon; from encountering three tramps sleeping rough who share a cup of strong coffee to bushwhacking through Scotch thistles. His jottings also include this wonderfully evocative description:

> I left at 12:52, and the first thing I noticed on the road were the telegraphic wires,—the first time I had seen them. I soon became conscious of a most extraordinary humming which I heard at intervals, gradually rising, and then gradually dying away. It could not be the sea, and I was puzzled. Before I passed the houses, however, I found that it proceeded from the vibrations of the telegraphic wires, causing the posts to give forth a musical sound, and the ground to quake around them,—quite in the style of the Aeolian harp. Where the wires were at all loose there was an awful rattle. It struck me as being astonishing how tight the wires were drawn between the posts, being almost horizontal. I took notes of the milestones, and the time I reached them, as follows:—1. 1.3; 2, 1.18; 3, 1.32; 4, 1.50; 5, 2.6; 6, 2.21; 7, 2.37; 8, 2.55; 9, 3.12; 10, 3.30; 11, 3.47; 12, 4.5; 13, 4.20; 14, 4.40; 15; 4.59; 16, 5.15; 17, 5.34; 18, 5.53.

Harding's encounter with the telegraph immediately results in a desire to mimic the stenography of sound, suspending the narrative by a marking of time and place that overwrites and encodes the landscape in numerical sequences. Later that evening when he tosses and turns in bed at the halfway house of his friends, the Fosters, he writes, 'I still seemed to be taking quick and regular strides, and the music of the telegraph wires rose and fell on my ears just as it had done for the first fourteen miles of my journey' (Harding 1867–68).

The conjunctions and disjunctions of this moment are several: walking to hand-deliver a hand-typeset, hand-printed newspaper in a landscape already infiltrated by that exemplar of progress and speed, the telegraph; listening to the hum of the wires that deliver, in the end, not sound, but writing; and writing that, in turn through the print medium, recrosses delivery lines that depend, variously, on coach roads, railways, steamships, electrical impulses, and the rhythms of walking. This technological moment also exemplifies how the newspaper and periodical press in the long nineteenth century functioned as part of a global communication network. Molded by the interrelationships of hand and machine, walking and telegraphic transmission, slow reading and the illusion of instantaneity (Hofmeyr 2013), this flexible and fluid web of empire (Ballantyne 2012) was reliant upon the cut-and-paste economy of trade exchanges, repurposing snippets of information for domestic consumption, and sending the results out once more into the great sea of textual circulation.

The Printers' Web, a Royal Society of New Zealand Marsden-funded project, uses twenty-first-century tools to unpick the thread and glue binding nineteenth-century typographical journals in order to understand the structures and rhythms of global communication networks in the printological world, and how they contributed to social and cultural cohesion amongst a highly mobile workforce in an era of mass industrialization. New imperial historians use metaphors such as webs and kaleidoscopes to describe this interconnected world of global interchange and globalizing sensibilities; they talk about migration and circulation as key elements. However, they rarely acknowledge the potential of a linked open data model or deploy methods from digital history or humanities computing that provide a perfect fit for the topic under consideration. The Printers' Web is a test bed for exploring alternative, digitally mediated modes of data collection, analysis, and visualization that turn metaphor into practice.

Digital history is an internationally recognized approach to historical studies that is defined as the application of digital technologies to investigating and representing the past. As both a field and a method (Sword in Cohen et al. 2008), it relies on an increasing breadth of Web-delivered digitized resources that enable scholars and students 'to make, define, query, and annotate associations in the human record of the past' (Seefeldt and Thomas 2009), often in the context of Web 2.0 social media and gaming interfaces. A focus on tool building for resource discovery, analysis, and visualization is at the heart of this enterprise. Stephen Ramsay has coined the phrase 'algorithmic criticism' to describe this shift in humanities research from 'criticism to creation, from writing to coding, from book to tool' (Ramsay 2011). In his 2011 monograph, *Reading Machines*, Ramsay notes,

'Algorithmic criticism' sounds for all the world like a set of methods for exploiting the sudden abundance of digital material related to the humanities. If not a method, then perhaps a *methodology* for coping with it, handling it, comprehending it. But in the end, it is simply an attitude toward the relationship between mechanism and meaning that is expansive enough to imagine building as a form of thinking.

(Ramsay 2011)

Sitting at the centre of the Printers' Web is Robert Coupland Harding. Born in Wellington, New Zealand, in 1849, burnt out of house and home in Wanganui in 1858, he arrived in Ahuriri, Napier, with his parents and siblings in 1859, where he survived extreme poverty and the spectre of scurvy. At age 11, he met a curious gentleman at an auction who gave him a book, remarking,

'I have seen enough to know that you are fond of books.... You were disappointed, I know. I hope this will please you.' It was a classic in its way— St. Pierre's 'Paul and Virginia' and 'Indian Cottage', with over a hundred wood-cuts by French artists. It has long since gone the way of all picture books in a large family.

(Harding 1899)

Some months later, when Harding began an apprenticeship at the local print shop, he discovered that the man was William Colenso, a remarkable Victorian polymath who became both a close friend and mentor, and who considered the young lad to be his intellectual heir. In 1864 Harding's father, Thomas Bennick Harding, a London-trained bookbinder and printer, bought out the *Hawkes Bay Times* and turned it into the first daily on the East Coast. Coupland—or 'Coup', as he was called—signed up with the Napier Rifle Volunteers and served as one of New Zealand's first war correspondents; later he spent time as a court recorder for the Hawkes Bay Native Lands Alienation Commission hearings in Napier. Evidenced by the extant manuscript volumes of his notes, he doodled profusely, building up a visual lexicon that informed his practice and exemplified a passion for type and fine printing. From an early age he also read voraciously, collecting typographical journals and type specimens, and corresponding with the leading type founders and printers around the globe.

And yet, in contrast to many migrant printers of his age, Harding was not an imperial careerist, colony-hopping through the white settler dominions as warranted by economic circumstances or encouraged by an adventuresome spirit. He was not like Jack Farrell, otherwise known as 'Australian Jack' or 'Transvaal Jack', who was born in Ireland, immigrated to Australia, worked in New Zealand and America, and finally fetched up in South Africa, where he became the inaugural President of the South African Typographical Union, launched the *South African Typographical Journal*, and was one of the Twelve Apostles sent to establish the Government Printing Office after the fall of Pretoria in 1901. Nor was he like Hugh Finlay, who was born in New Brunswick, Canada; fought for the Confederates during the American Civil War; was captured at the Battle of Vicksburg and paroled to New Orleans; returned to Saint John to set up a printing house, establish the local International Typographical Union no. 85, and produce *The Printers' Miscellany*;

and who, later in life, worked in Boston, then Vancouver, and finally returned once again to Saint John.

Instead, Harding travelled the world solely through the empire of print. After taking over and then selling his father's newspaper, he cut his display teeth on jobbing printing, and in 1887 he produced the first issue of the internationally acclaimed *Typo: A Monthly Newspaper and Literary Review*. *Typo* joined a legion of journals dedicated to the black arts that thrived on the Victorian journalistic penchant for cut-and-paste—scissoring and scrapbooking. Predating news syndication and affordable cable feeds, 'infectious texts' could go 'viral' (Cordell 2013) through the simple expedient of 'writing with scissors' (Garvey 2013). As an early mix-'n'-mash artist, Harding participated fully in this world of 'open access' text: open to whomever had the skills and capital to reset, print, and circulate the text anew; open insofar as the idea of copyright for these journalistic snippets was internally policed by a gentlemanly code of attribution, even as the original moved further and further away from its source and opportunities for plagiarism and misattribution increased exponentially. In many respects, too, *Typo* is the primary archive of Harding's personal and professional career. Until the discovery of an unknown, but still patchy, archive in 2011–12, his life was glimpsed through fragments of print, a few letters, and some memorial reconstructions. His business archives followed the way of most records: tossed out, pulped, destroyed. But this is no different from the bulk of historical evidence of the nineteenth-century printing and allied book trades—hence the importance of their journals.

The typographical press played a critical role in manufacturing, disseminating, and sustaining the trade identity and sociocultural memory practices of printers. Unlike printers' manuals that revealed the arcana of the trade, or printing house magazines that were advertising fora for products and services, the typographical journal was a rich miscellany of domestic and international printological news from the sublime to the eccentric. It included trade union and technical information, pension and benefit schemes, book reviews and notices of printers' library acquisitions, trade advertisements, reports of social activities, the results of sporting events, literary works and quotations, lists of typos and howlers, and memorials of one sort or another to the human fragment: obituaries, biographies of prominent trade personalities, lists of union members in arrears, and information purveyed or solicited about mobile members and friends. Farrell and Finlay, like countless other journeymen printers, physically travelled the world but left their traces for all to view in the pages of this typographical press. The journals built up a picture of a profession comfortable in the skin of writing and reading, and conscious of its aristocratic heritage amongst skilled artisans.

New Zealand printers and their trade journals contributed to the reciprocating translocal textual cultures of colonialism, imperialism, and globalization in multiple and complex ways. As local producers of information that circulated throughout the Anglo world and beyond through ever-increasing and far-reaching tentacles of transport, communication, and migrant networks, printers and members of the allied book trades fashioned a global economy of print. At any one time, for example, Harding subscribed to, exchanged, and scissored from over

80 journals, including the usual Anglo, French, and German suspects, but more intriguingly, also from far-flung places like Romania and Argentina. By selecting the choicest morsels for his audience, typesetting them anew, reprinting them in the pages of *Typo*, and sending that journal back into the world, Harding helped to create and sustain a community of practice that consolidated its identity through shared information networks. Such documentary activities of decontextualizing and recontextualizing information through cut-and-paste worked in tandem with the communal activities that knitted the printing trades together across space and through time. The detailed reportage of the trade's rituals—the archaic chapel system that organized each printing house's workforce and workflows, wayzgoose festivals that provided occasions to socialize beyond the workplace, and trade union parades that put books, literacy, and the civilizing power of print on the public stage—connected printers with their peers as well as their past, evoking history while manufacturing memory.

As a site of memory, a *lieu de mémoire* (Nora 1989), the typographical journal and the typographical press system functioned as 'a vehicle for collective memory, forging a community's self-definition in relation to its past' (Gaunt 2009, 80). The practice of scissoring and scrapbooking was intimately related to the archival project of recovering context by marking the sites of informational exchange and transmission, and the creation of a global communication network was firmly rooted in the local particularities of people, places, and textual objects. Preliminary archival research identified several questions about the cut-and-paste economy of the typographical press. What kinds of information were being circulated through the typographical press? What topics, speed and rhythms of exchange, or journals acted as primary nodes or secondary conduits? What forms did this information exchange take: was the citation in full text or snippet view, framed and reframed by an editor who naturalized it for a local audience? What were the authority structures embedded in or divorced from this scissors-and-paste, mix-'n'-mash culture, a research practice that has not changed appreciably for centuries? How did attribution work, and what happened when data was severed from metadata in what Tim Hitchcock has termed 'the deracination of knowledge' (Hitchcock 2007)?

To answer these research questions, the Printers' Web took a hybrid, collaborative, and linked open-data approach. Could the process of identifying and analysing more examples of the mix-'n'-mash journalistic practice across a wider range of publications be sped up or gathered differently using digital tools? Could tentative conclusions derived from traditional archival research be generalizable with a greater quantity and breadth of data? Would digitally mediated modes of analysis enable the evidence to speak in similar or different ways? As the project developed, juggling these two modalities of research practice became an important exercise in understanding how they could intersect, complement, or supplant each other. Increasingly, we foregrounded prototype research (Siemens 2010) as a generative and creative scholarly activity and to emphasize building as a way of knowing; like Harding's rhythmic milestones, we could document work in progress, but also pause to reflect on the way forward, the paths not taken, and new ways of approaching the project and its archive, in much the same manner as grounded theory and its recursive methodologies (Glaser and Strauss 1967; Strauss and Corbin 1998).

Consequently, in addition to traditional desk-based archival research and printed scholarly outputs, the research team built a digital collection of nineteenth-century typographical journals, created or reconfigured digital tools to engage with that corpus, and developed prototype Web-based, interactive publications to tell digitally the many stories of our project. Research assistants Max Sullivan, Sara Bryan, and Sam Callaghan used the Text Encoding Initiative (TEI) markup to enhance our corpus of digitized and OCR-scanned typographical journals, and populated EATS, an Entity Authority Tool Set, built by our developer, Jamie Norrish (Norrish 2013). Tim Sherratt designed several prototype tools and interfaces to realize some of the more experimental possibilities of the project. Throughout the life of the project, we examined Harding's personal and professional worlds through the lens of social network analysis; traced the impact of his thinking through text, mining the typographical press as well as historical newspapers; and mapped his career in Napier and Wellington using geospatial tools. One research project, led by Meghan Hughes, reconstructed Harding's library through *Library Thing* in order to understand book-collecting practices in late-nineteenth- and early-twentieth-century New Zealand. Another, undertaken by Polly Cantlon, delved into typographical nationalism and the emergence of a New Zealand graphic design aesthetic shaped, in part, by Harding's visual practice and pedagogy. A third, conducted by Flora Feltham, used mapping tools and Omeka-Neatline to tell geotemporal stories about Harding's career and analyse his business decline and failure in relation to the book trade terrain of Wellington in the 1890s. Finally, Sara Bryan combined Harding's *Press Notices* clipping book with BatchGeo to map the contemporary New Zealand reception of his journal, *Typo*.

Like all projects aspiring to algorithmic criticism, data preparation is everything, but the key to a project of this scale and scope was developing a technical infrastructure based on a robust ontology to support the project's linked open-data approach. Having been involved with the New Zealand Electronic Text Centre (NZETC) from its inception, we adopted their technical infrastructure, metadata standards, and workflows. Foundational work was undertaken in 2000–01 with *The Print History Project: Wellington's Book Trades, 1840–2000*. This electronic monograph was an early digital collection that surveyed the local printological terrain through a suite of temporal snapshots opening into selected digital objects that formed the basis of an interpretive narrative achieved through contextual captioning. However, certain items on our wish list were not achieved: linking objects spatially to georeferenced historical maps of Wellington, for example, and digitizing Robert Coupland Harding's *Typo*, or at the very least, creating a digital edition of his landmark series of essays, 'Design in Typography'. Almost ten years later, the NZETC initiated the Digital Typo project. The pages of *Typo* from Victoria University of Wellington's bound edition were captured in high-resolution TIFFs, then OCR scanned with basic TEI encoding. Edmund King experimented with volume one, enhancing the TEI markup, dealing with challenges such as image-rich pages (before genetic or facsimile TEI really came along), devising snippet views with transcribed text for advertisements, and creating logical descriptive categories of the multiple genres of textual and visual matter populating the informationally dense pages of this monthly newspaper and literary review. At its simplest, the TEI encoding enabled us to machine-read the text and extract patterns such as the proportion of advertisements to original features to scissored text across the whole journal, in any one year, or in any one issue. The balance between these divisions then became a reflection of the time and copy demands in the printshop as well as an indication of the financial health of the periodical, reliant as it was upon subscriptions and advertising revenue. By marking up names, we could also identify at a glance which journals formed the bulk of the clipping enterprise and their country of origin, and whether there were reciprocal links. King's prototyping work provided the intellectual and technical foundation for the Marsden project's digital corpora, bolstered by Callaghan's entity type relationship model and Norrish's Web-based authority access and control application designed to provide persistent, unique, and resolvable identifiers for entities in the form of universal resource identifiers (URIs). By supporting multiple identifiers for the same entity, EATS was useful for linking together resources (or sets of resources) that referred to common entities but used different identifiers, thus enabling the project to link its own digital objects to relevant Web-based resources external to the project.

The Printers' Web digital repository of typographical journals currently consists of a complete TEI-encoded edition of *Typo*; the same 1887–97 time slice extracted from digital files of the *Australasian Typographical Journal*; the earlier New Zealand journal *Griffin's Colonial Printers' Register and New Zealand Press News* (1876–79; 1879–80); test samples from the *Canadian Printer & Publisher* (est. 1892); and the 1887–97 decade of an American journal, the *Inland Printer*. We experimented training up the open-source and natural-language processing software GATE (General Architecture for Text Engineering) to map entities already identified in *Typo* onto the other journals in the corpora, but the success rate was unpredictable. Ideally, we should have added the *Scottish Typographical Circular* in the first tranche since it was frequently mentioned in all the press organs and was one of the earliest and longest-running journals. However, no complete set exists, or in a single repository; furthermore, the logistics of remotely coordinating and centralizing the digitization activity were massive, even with funding in hand. Another key journal, the *Printers' Miscellany* (1864–72), has been digitized by canadiana.org, but the full-access portal is currently only open to those at participating Canadian cultural heritage and tertiary education institutions. Given that Harding's personal and professional network can be documented in over 80 journals, our project cannot, given the original time frame and funding allocation, reconstruct this complete intertextual landscape. Were any of these already digitized, our task would simply involve dealing with multiple formats and disparate metadata. But such is the nature of the periodical press: under the radar of the Internet Archive, Google Books, and the Hathi Trust or, if digitized, not fully available outside the Anglo-American bloc. Public funding bodies increasingly refuse to fund digitization, assuming that the data already exists in the digital form(s) required; they want research outputs, and quickly. So, despite some lobbying, this genre of trade publication is not yet on the wish lists of ProQuest or Gale Cengage, which have done so much to raise the profile of nineteenth-century British periodicals and newspapers. And if it were, as subscription-based commercial collections, we would remain embedded in the digital divide, where access is less a product of technological infrastructure and more the power of big corporations to act as the gatekeepers of knowledge. Such large collections wittingly or otherwise reinscribe the canon, recolonizing rather than decolonizing cyberspace; impede research capability; and inhibit knowledge transfer. Understandably crowdsourcing has become the mantra of the decade, and this approach may be a way to expand our corpora in the project's afterlife. Certainly, we envisage that our project webspace, data standards, and prototyping approach will be a magnet for such future collaborative endeavours.

These challenges notwithstanding, if research follows record, what can we do with what we have? Although much of the project time was spent on building the digital corpora, prototype research provided a way of interacting with the data at formative stages. We contextualized and extended the interpretative possibilities of the typographical journals by identifying and linking resources external to our digital corpora: Australian and New Zealand historical newspapers such as those found in *Trove* and *Papers Past*, already digitized and prime candidates for cultural hacking; all the provincial volumes of *The Cyclopedia of New Zealand* available now through the NZETC; the metadata from about 130 cultural heritage institutions delivered through *Digital NZ*; the *Dictionary of New Zealand Biography* available through the *Te Ara* portal; a database of printers' registrations compiled by Ian Morrison; and local street directory information for the 1880–1920 period compiled by Flora Feltham. In a linked open-data world, however, will this be 'big data' enough? Do we even have the 'infinite archive' Bill Turkel describes as requiring a new methodology (Turkel 2008)? It is no coincidence that many of the conceptual and technical breakthroughs in digital humanities have occurred in the context of classical and mediaeval literature, where extant texts are relatively few and their genetics almost completely mapped; or in eighteenth-century studies, where the majority of English-language texts have already been digitized, whether through EEBO, EECO, the Old Bailey Online, or the Oxford Enlightenment Project, to name but a few. If one of Marsden's five overarching research objectives was to identify the dominant nodes and links constituting the printers' web, mapping the relationships between people (personal, professional), textual objects (letters, journals, books), and practices (rituals, commemorations, social activities), how could we handle the scraps, pars, clippings, and odd sorts of our data—'the world of the infinitely little' (Ramsay 2011)? At what point can a linked open-data model function effectively given all the fragmentation, messiness, and fuzziness of historical data?

With its fate pending as an archive relegated to inaccessible deep preservation, Flora Feltham repurposed the digital assets from the *Print History Project*, combined them with the Printers' Web corpus, and created a suite of visualizations using a combination of out-of-the-box tools such as xCharts, MapBox, TileMill, Timeliner, and Leaflet to talk about people, places, and things. By mapping the locations of printers and members of the allied book trades in Wellington in the 1890s, for example, she identified an important ecosystem. Printing jobs, by necessity, had to move around the terrain to capitalize on technological capabilities, timing of work, and availability of trained staff. When Robert Coupland Harding moved to the big smoke in 1891 his office was located on the corner of Ballance and McGinnity streets. Not only was he in full view of the bustling docks, the epicentre of trade and information exchange, but the Government Printing Office was a mere stone's throw away. Lyon & Blair's steam press and lithographic printery was just down the road on Lambton Quay; booksellers, stationers, and the General Post Office were a short walk away. As Harding hustled for jobs, he used his social networks to leverage work, transferring his membership in the Hawkes Bay Philanthropic Society to Wellington, corresponding voluminously with William Colenso (a correspondence for which we have only the Colenso half), and maintaining contact with Edward Tregear and his parliamentary and Theosophical circles. Life also revolved around the Presbyterian Church, where Harding was a respected elder, and the Wellington Athenaeum and Mechanics' Institute, that hub of workingmen's book learning and intellectual debate. Once Harding moved his business to Farish Street, at the edge of the porous membrane of this complex space of 'printerdom', his capacity for survival was compromised. He uncharacteristically embarked on a disastrous electioneering rag titled *X-Rays*, alienated powerful political allies, bullheadedly continued to produce *Typo* at a loss, and eventually sold up in 1897. After a short spell as a time-work compositor for the Government Printing Office, he moved his family to the suburbs and retired gracefully into the position of literary editor for the *Evening Post* and became an avid book collector.

Feltham's visualizations exemplify what the project terms 'tools for thinking'— that is, early interventions with digital tools to provide a quick, synoptic, or bird's-eye view of the evidence as a strategy to refine research questions or follow leads that would not necessarily have been recognized so soon in the analytical process. Like a sketch on a restaurant dinner napkin, they can reinforce what the researcher already knows or capture a breakthrough moment. These moments of insight are also part and parcel of traditional research activity, but the shift from data collection, content analysis, and prose narrative to geotemporal visualizations using structured digital resources constitutes a different kind of research activity. As a result, we now want to gather and map more contextual data, view the material through the lens of economic history, and generate a more nuanced interpretation of Harding's decline and fall from business grace. That being said, the power of spatial tools to represent place is contested in contemporary literature, so as Feltham moves her story into the world of Omeka-Neatline, she remains attuned to the narrative possibilities as well as challenges of digital storytelling.

Meghan Hughes's project titled 'Books as Social Currency: The Library of Robert Coupland Harding' had three main components: writing a history of book collecting in New Zealand during the turn of the twentieth century; investigating Harding's private library and situating him in a circle of fellow collectors; and analysing a small sample of individual books in his collection in order to illustrate his unique book-collecting identity. In the process she demonstrated how his collection and collecting habits impacted, or were impacted by, his professional life as a significant figure in printing and typography in New Zealand and internationally. Rather than being relegated to the position of a 'minor' collector or branded either a 'connoisseur' or 'colonial' collector, Harding's social networks enabled him to move seamlessly through the book-collecting world, acquiring works opportunistically and providing a conduit by which other collectors could satisfy their needs. By grounding her study in Bourdieu's theory of capital and cultural production, Hughes examined the premise that books played a significant role as social currency as well as symbolic capital in the field of book collecting. Although Harding's financial circumstances did not enable him to compete in the high-stakes marketplace, he was an astute purchaser of key titles and used his later career as literary editor and book reviewer to acquire New Zealand works that would have otherwise been beyond his means. Finally, she developed a model of book-collecting practices that combined the collecting trajectory of acquisition-preservation-dispersal with a rhizomatic network of collector types and transactions.

Central to this line of research was the auction catalogue of Harding's library, comprising over 5,000 works. While it was common that large and prestigious book collections were auctioned off in their entirety, many serious collectors selfconsciously crafted collections that were bequeathed to an institution, whether a university, a civic space, or a national repository. Since Harding's library did not end up as a named collection in a public institution, Hughes's investigation started at its posthumous dispersal in 1920. Some of Harding's personal copies with signature, stamp, or bookplate were discovered in local repositories—notably in the Horace Fildes collection at Victoria University of Wellington Library's JC Beaglehole Room—obtained through local booksellers' networks, and viewed in private collections around New Zealand. With world enough, money, and time, Harding's library could be brought together again physically, but as both a research instrument and research output for the twenty-first century, Hughes reconstructed the dispersed library in the virtual environment, using the legacy library function of *Library Thing*. This online social network site enables the creation and sharing of personal libraries as well as the capture and enhancement of historic libraries by uploading digitized collection catalogues. Given that only two antipodean legacy libraries with substantial New Zealand imprints have been built to date, connections between collectors and collections were less apparent than with, for example, the large sample of American legacy libraries where researchers could assess the popularity of specific titles in libraries over time, collection formation by socioeconomic imperatives, and the conjunction of various print genres. Nevertheless, Hughes's database enabled easy correlation and display of publication dates with collecting chronologies, and the metadata field structure was expansive enough to support bibliographic annotations of copy-specific features.

One book was used as a testing ground for Hughes's model building in order to illustrate the benefits of a linked open-data approach overlaid on the traditional book history life cycle of production, distribution, and reception—and, in turn, the relationship between digital interventions and traditional archival research. William Miles Maskell was a globally recognized authority on the subject of noxious insects, and his chief publication is still in print: *An Account of the Insects Noxious to Agriculture and Plants in New Zealand: Scale Insects* (1887). Using FRBR's (Functional Requirements for Bibliographic Records) differentiation between work, expression, manifestation, and item, the intellectual content of the work was rendered conceptually separate from the specific artefact or individual item, tracked through online library catalogues, and entered in Hughes's legacy library. The author was linked to his biography in the online *Dictionary of New Zealand Biography* version in *Te Ara* rather than Wikipedia (drawn down from metadata in DigitalNZ, but not complete), his obituary in *Papers Past*, and his bibliography in the National Library of New Zealand catalogue. Harding obtained a copy of *Scale Insects* because it was given to him to be reviewed in *Typo*. The original review appears online in the digitized *Typo*; additional newspaper reviews are found in *Papers Past*. Because the physical copy we bought for the VUW library contains Harding's signature as well as his stamp, we added these material traces to other recorded marks of provenance, including his distinctive bookplate. Additional links are found in Harding's probate, which cites individual book titles, and in family-owned copies that belonged to Harding or were bought by Harding on their behalf. Each of these resources is digitized, marked up, and given a URI. Linking all this evidence drives refinements to a model that not only helps to illuminate the history of the work and the biography of the artefact but adds value by charting connections between this artefact and others in Harding's library, as well as providing insights into his book-collecting habits and collecting identity. When all her case studies are mapped in this way, Hughes anticipates being able to identify clusters and patterns that would not have been apparent, or perhaps detected at all, without using a model of linking digital data.

Digital media provide powerful tools to extend and enhance research on a previously unimagined scale, generating new research questions as much as new findings. The serendipity of traditional research methods can be enlivened by using 'tools for thinking', including QueryPic, devised by Tim Sherratt originally to mine Australian historical newspaper collections (Sherratt 2011–12). QueryPic is a word or phrase harvester that uses an API to search digital corpora and presents data in frequency graphs using JavaScript Highcharts, which display actual numbers of hits or ratios over time. Each graph point is hyperlinked to the actual text, enabling the user to drill down into content and context; multiple terms can be graphed in an additive exercise to facilitate first-order comparisons and contrasts. QueryPicNZ was launched at a Marsden-sponsored Digital History Workshop in March 2012. Since then, Norrish, who has experimented with n-grams to track the scissors-and-paste movement of text between periodicals, extended the visualization possibilities of QueryPic by ingesting our typographical journals collection. Such a tool is useful for distant reading—that is, identifying and observing trends or patterns in large corpora—and for providing an alternative search and retrieval strategy, often resulting in the discovery of hitherto undocumented resources or networks. When searching on the terms 'Napier' and 'Wellington', for example, we can see how through the pages of *Typo* Harding dramatically shifted focus from the parochial to the urban, from the regional to the global once he physically moved to Wellington and retailored his international magazine to embrace a different local readership. Similarly, a change in the spelling of 'fount' to 'font' in 1891 registers a shift in Harding's attention from talking about English-made types to those manufactured in America, the home of the artistic printing movement Harding wished to emulate and promote. This evidence can be triangulated with the TEI name-entity markup for fonts to examine how and when Harding introduced these American types to his international audience in *Typo* and how he discussed them in hard-hitting yet astute critiques in the *Inland Printer*—critiques that were so effective that American type foundries lobbied successfully to have his 'Recent Type Specimens' column discontinued, claiming loss of business.

The suite of Voyant tools devised by Stéfan Sinclair and Geoffrey Rockwell has also been useful to gain high-level insights into change over time, with snapshots of thematic foci visualized by the word cloud builder Voyant Cirrus and the collocation tool Voyant Links demonstrating some of the relational networks occurring in specific texts. Providing a word-in-context approach, Voyant Cirrus identifies the frequency of individual words linked to full text. As Harding refashioned *Typo* for the Wellington market, different subjects emerged in comparison with the same time slice of the *Australasian Typographical Journal*; whereas Wellington was all about news and the London papers, Melbourne in 1893 focused on the local typographical society and trade unionism. Another 'tool for thinking' is the timeline visualization function in Zotero, a Web-based and stand-alone tool for harvesting, enhancing, and exporting bibliographic resources. Using the metadata in our Zotero bibliography, a time slice of William Colenso's personal correspondence with Robert Coupland Harding isolated a node of interest to feed into advanced social network analysis tools. At first glance, Harding is part of a coherent, multidimensional network that included important and influential people like James Hector and Joseph Dalton Hooker but not Edward Tregear. Therefore, asking Tregear for a letter of reference for the post of Superintendent of the Government Printing Office was not the way to get ahead; when Harding finally did get part-time employment at the GPO, it was as a lowly compositor.

In its foregrounding of prototype research, the Printers' Web project has also prioritized building as a way of knowing. The Digital NZ Magic Squares tool conceptualized by Shep, built by Sherratt, and launched at the National Digital Forum in Wellington in 2012 combines the possibilities of serendipity with a playful, interactive interface in order to explore the richness of digitized collections (Sherratt 2012). It addresses two research needs—one methodological, the other conceptual: how to deal with search and discovery in big data sources that often deliver masses of unfiltered hits and whose subsequent systematic reorganization mirrors existing knowledge structures or assumptions; and how to conceptualize digital biography using a tool that, rather than scripting the narrative, furnishes 'an experience for users—a process, an active, spatial, virtual reality encounter with the past' (Murray 1997). As Elizabeth Podnieks has remarked, today 'the two greatest changes notable in biography arise both from technologies that allow for radical new ways of producing, disseminating, and theorizing the genre and from an expansion of the definition of what constitutes biographical expression' (Podnieks 2009, 2). Magic Squares was developed from research undertaken on the algorithms underpinning historic magic squares, particularly those devised by the eighteenth-century polymathic printer Benjamin Franklin. In this Enlightenment version of Sudoku, each row and column of Franklin's eight-by-eight square had the magic constant of 260. Each half column or row added up to 130, that is, half of 260: the four corners plus the middle totalled 260. Moreover, each half diagonal, or bent row, repeated the magic constant of 260. At the time, it was called a panmagic or diabolic square. But Franklin did not stop there; in a stunning tour de force he also created a 16-by-16 grid: 'the most magically magical of any square ever made by any magician' (Franklin 1771/1856). Translated into the world of contemporary humanities computing, the Digital NZ Magic Squares has brought previously unrelated digitized items together, breaking down the predetermined structure of the archive and its metadata, as well as the defaults of standard search engines and search strategies. The result has been sometimes surprising associations that compel us to ask new questions of our data or reframe our assumptions. Currently designed to work over Digital NZ metadata, it will be reconfigured for the Printers' Web resources. The attraction of such an approach is evidenced by Serendip-o-matic, a project of the 2013 One Week/One Tool hackfest at the Roy Rosenzweig Center for History and New Media at George Mason University. Like Magic Squares, 'the tool is designed mostly for inspiration, search results aren't meant to be exhaustive, but rather suggestive, pointing you to materials you might not have discovered. At the very least, the magical input-output process helps you step back and look at your work from a new perspective' (Serendip-o-matic 2013).

Alan Liu recently advocated for the rapprochement of close and distant reading practices, and Julia Flanders has proposed that we rethink collections in the world of the infinitely little as the crafted assemblage of a patchwork quilt rather than a systems-based network. Our Marsden project reveals that we can do research under the sign of both, using a contemporary e-research workflow and technological interface to investigate a corresponding historical practice, and undertaking traditional archival research at the same time as harnessing the potential of digital research modes. As a result, the Printers' Web is turning as much into a project about the 'informal, open, multiple, competing, and dynamic' (Potter 2007, 622) nature of global communication networks in the long nineteenth century as a multidimensional digital biography of the man who helped fashion them—a man who left a prosperous Napier business to try his luck in the big city; a man who, once bankrupt, returned to his original trade as a compositor; a man whose passion for collecting books meant often only an apple on the family table for dinner; a man's whose enormous typographic legacy is at odds with the paucity of extant historical sources; a man who, incidentally, like Benjamin Franklin, devised and printed magic squares. By using digital tools to think through the square and beyond the square, many of the questions our team is exploring are also meta-questions about the nature of linked open-data projects, the role of prototyping in digital research, and digital humanities if not digital culture in general. As such, the Printers' Web joins Luke Tredinnick in posing the ultimate question: 'What does the past look like through the lens of digital culture?' (Tredinnick 2013, 39).

## Works cited

Ballantyne, Tony. (2012). *Webs of Empire. Locating New Zealand's Colonial Past*. Wellington: Bridget Williams Books.

Cohen, D. J., M. Frisch, P. Gallagher, S. Mintz, K. Sword, A. M. Taylor, W. G. Thomas III, and W. Turkel. (2008). 'Interchange: The Promise of Digital History'. *Journal of American History* 95, 2 (September): 452–91.

Cordell, Ryan. (2013). *Infectious Texts: Viral Networks in 19th-Century Newspapers*. Available at: http://www.viraltexts.org/.

Franklin, Benjamin. (1771/1856). *The Works of Benjamin Franklin*, vol. 6, ed. Jared Sparks. Boston: Whittmore, Niles and Hall.

Garvey, Ellen Gruber. (2013). *Writing With Scissors: American Scrapbooks From the Civil War to the Harlem Renaissance*. New York: Oxford University Press.

Gaunt, Heather. (2009). 'Social Memory in the Public Historical Sphere: Henry Savery's "The Hermit in Van Diemen's Land" and the Tasmanian Public Library'. *Library and Information History* 25, no. 2: 79–96.

Glaser, B. G., and A. L. Strauss. (1967). *The Discovery of Grounded Theory: Strategies for Qualitative Research*. Mill Valley, CA: Sociology Press.

Harding, Robert Coupland. (1867–68). Unpublished Diary. Private Collection.

Harding, Robert Coupland. (1899). 'William Colenso: Some Personal Reminiscences'. *The Press* (Christchurch, NZ), 27 February: 5.

Hitchcock, Tim. (2007). 'Digital Searching and the Re-Formulation of Historical Knowledge'. In *The Virtual Representation of the Past*, ed. Mark Greengrass and Lorna Hughes. Farnham: Ashgate.

Hofmeyr, Isabel. (2013). *Gandhi's Printing Press: Experiments in Slow Reading*. Cambridge, MA: Harvard University Press.

Hughes, Meghan. (2013). 'Books as Social Currency: The Library of Robert Coupland Harding'. Digital Humanities Australasia conference presentation, March 2012; MA thesis, Victoria University of Wellington.

*Legacy Libraries*. Available at: http://www.librarything.com/legacylibraries.

Murray, J. H. (1997). *Hamlet on the Holodeck: The Future of Narrative in Cyberspace*. Cambridge, MA: MIT Press.

Nora, Pierre. (1989). 'Between Memory and History: *Les Lieux de Mémoire*'. *Representations* 26 (Spring): 7–25.

Norrish, Jamie. (2013). Entity Authority Tool Set. Available at: http://eats.readthedocs.org/en/latest/.

Podnieks, Elizabeth. (2009). 'Introduction: "New Biography" for a New Millennium'. *a/b: Auto/Biography Studies* 24, no. 1 (Summer): 1–14.

Potter, Simon. (2007). 'Webs, Networks, and Systems: Globalization and the Mass Media in the Nineteenth- and Twentieth-Century British Empire'. *Journal of British Studies* 46 (July): 621–46.

The Printers' Web. Available at: http://www.victoria.ac.nz/wtapress/research/printers-web.

*The Print History Project: Wellington's Book Trades 1840–2000*. Available at: http://www.victoria.ac.nz/wtapress/research/print-history.

Ramsay, Stephen. (2011). *Reading Machines: Toward an Algorithmic Criticism*. Urbana: University of Illinois Press.

Seefeldt, D., and W. G. Thomas III. (2009). 'What Is Digital History? A Look at Some Exemplar Projects'. University of Nebraska-Lincoln, *Faculty Publications, Department of History*. Paper 98. Available at: http://digitalcommons.unl.edu.

Serendip-o-matic. 2013. Available at: http://serendipomatic.org/.

Sherratt, Tim. (2011–12). 'Mining the Treasures of Trove'. Available at: http://discontents.com.au/mining-the-treasures-of-trove-part-1/; http://discontents.com.au/mining-the-treasures-of-trove-part-2/.

Sherratt, Tim. (2012). *DigitalNZ Magic Squares*. Available at: http://wraggelabs.com.

Siemens, Ray, et al. (2010). 'Underpinnings of the Social Edition'. In *Online Humanities Scholarship: The Shape of Things to Come*, ed. Jerome McGann, 8 May. Available at: http://cnx.org.

Strauss, A. L., and J. Corbin. (1998). *Basics of Qualitative Research: Techniques and Procedures for Developing Grounded Theory*. London: Sage.

Tredinnick, Luke. (2013). 'The Making of History: Remediating Historicized Experience'. In *History in the Digital Age*, ed. Toni Weller: 39–60. London: Routledge.

Turkel, William. (2006). 'Methodology for the Infinite Archive'. Available at: http://digitalhistoryhacks.blogspot.co.nz/.

*Typo: A Monthly Newspaper and Literary Review*. (1887–97). Napier: Harding. Available at: http://nzetc.victoria.ac.nz.

# 6
# Biographical Dictionaries in the Digital Era

*Paul Longley Arthur*

By any measure biography is popular today. With films, dedicated television channels, books, magazines, and multiple forms of social media disseminating biographical information online at an unprecedented rate and feeding an ever-escalating interest in the lives of real people, intense public engagement with biography may be considered a defining feature of the early-twenty-first-century cultural landscape. Not coincidentally, interest in biography has soared from the mid-1990s alongside the phenomenon of mass public access to the World Wide Web, and especially since the emergence of Web 2.0 and social media in the past decade.[1]

National dictionaries of biography provide a compelling demonstration of the benefits of computer-assisted research methods. These online biographical dictionaries and reference resources are increasingly allowing quick access to information while providing enhanced data-rich environments for sophisticated analysis and visualization, enabling new research findings in fields of biography, prosopography, genealogy, family history, and social history more broadly. Major national dictionaries of biography have been migrated online in the last decade and a half. The *American National Biography* (1999), *Dictionary of New Zealand Biography* (2001), *Dictionary of Canadian Biography* (2003), and the *Oxford Dictionary of National Biography* (2004) were first to move online, then the *Australian Dictionary of Biography* (2006), followed by the Swedish, Welsh, Ulster, and Irish national biographies (a notable exception is the *Diccionario Biográfico Español*, 25 vols, 2011, which remains in print only [Carter 2013]). In their digital forms these dictionaries have taken different approaches (chronological and sequential volumes, as in the case of Australia and Canada, or complete series as for the American and UK examples). Their interfaces and priorities have also varied, driven by different histories, epistemologies or technical considerations (Carter 2013).

In this chapter I focus on the transition from print to digital of the *Australian Dictionary of Biography* (ADB), a 50-year print publishing project that was first launched online in 2006 and substantially redeveloped in 2010–13. Now conceived of as a virtual research environment in its own right, ADB online allows for user analysis of complex biographical and historical datasets, including faceted searching, relationship mapping, and visualization of search results.[2] The ADB is a working example of key issues that need to be considered in migrating any major project from print to digital form.

I begin this chapter by outlining the ADB's history in order to establish the context for its publication online and subsequent redevelopment. Although the online product was designed for speed and ease of use, the process has been time-demanding and involves an ongoing program of manual indexing that is providing a solid foundation for future applications, including social network analysis, data mining, and dataset interoperability.

## Background

Established as a national project in 1959 (Griffiths 2013), the first volume of the ADB was published in 1966; however, the concept of the dictionary has its roots in the 1950s and was discussed as early as 1947 (Nolan 2013b; Moyal 2013). The ADB followed the lead of the *Oxford Dictionary of National Biography* and had similarities with the *Dictionary of Canadian Biography*, which was established in the same year as the ADB, also at a university (Nolan 2013b).[3] From the outset, the ADB's innovation was not specifically in its format but rather in the model for national collaboration via a distributed expert network that it set in place, which remains unique among national biographical projects worldwide. This model lends itself particularly well to the connectivity that digital tools for collaboration now offer. To date there have been over 4,000 authors, and at any time more than 100 people serve on working parties in Australian states and territories and the national editorial board (Roe 2013). The ADB has recently been recognized as 'the largest and most successful cooperative research enterprise in the humanities and social sciences in Australia' (Griffiths 2013).[4] The text of the ADB currently consists of more than 12,500 concise, scholarly biographies. Eighteen volumes and one supplementary volume, plus an index (1991), have been published under the Melbourne University Press (MUP) imprint. Volume 18 (covering subjects who died between 1981 and 1990, surnames beginning L to Z) was published at the end of 2012. ADB articles range from a minimum of approximately 500 words to a maximum upwards of 6,000 words, with the longest word-length allocations usually reserved for those judged to be particularly significant in Australian history and who have made a major and usually very visible social contribution, such as prime ministers or other notable public figures.

By 1999 it was clear that the CD-ROM version of the ADB, which had been published by Melbourne University Press in 1996, should be superseded by an online edition.[5] 'Progressive and provisional publication' had been mentioned as early as 1986 (Nolan 2013a), but planning for an online version did not begin until 2000. This step was prompted in part by the example and experience of the *American National Biography* (ANB) online (1999) and the *Oxford Dictionary of National Biography* (ODNB)—a soon-to-be-released, fully rewritten and expanded online edition of the definitive British biographical dictionary (initially including 55,113 entries, with a series of annual updates planned). ODNB had taken 12 years to complete and was ultimately launched in 2004 (Carter 2013); both ODNB and

ANB are Oxford University Press publications. The 2001 launch of the *Dictionary of New Zealand Biography* online added further impetus.

## ADB online

Digitization of the print volumes of the ADB for the CD-ROM edition provided a basis for the online publication, and yet the digitized version was found to contain a great many errors that first needed correcting, which proved to be a laborious process (Bennet 2013). Nevertheless, the ADB online (http://adb.anu.edu.au/) was completed on schedule and was launched in 2006 by governor-general of Australia Michael Jeffery. The first iteration of the ADB online was built on the Online Heritage Resource Manager (OHRM) software developed by Gavan McCarthy at the University of Melbourne's Australian Science and Technology Heritage Centre (later, eScholarship centre).[6] It was funded through successive Australian Research Council Linkage Infrastructure and Equipment Fund (LIEF) project grants involving, initially, six university partners, which then-deputy general editor Darryl Bennet managed.

The print and digital versions of national biographical dictionaries have sometimes appeared simultaneously, as was the case for the ADB and the ODNB (Carter 2013). ADB online replicated all the material from the print volumes, although for a time it excluded, for contractual reasons with the print publisher, content from the very latest volume. The online ADB also added digital images. The intent was to feature a portrait for each subject, something that had not been feasible in print. In some cases images were not available, but for those that were, a link was provided to the digitized file in the National Library of Australia's Picture Australia online collection,[7] with a persistent identifier and stable URL provided by the library. The ADB was the first to use this new service, which was intended to provide a framework for collaboration between national institutions and datasets.[8] This single enhancement of the text through the addition of a visual dimension provided instant evidence of the capacity of online formats to deliver new benefits. In some cases links were also made to the digital records of the National Archives of Australia.

ADB online quickly became one of the most widely consulted resources for the study of Australian history and society, with 70 million hits annually reported by 2009 (Chubb 2009). Key ADB users include school children, family historians and specialist researchers across the full range of academic disciplines. Because it is freely available in online form, ADB is routinely consulted by the general public in Australia and internationally. Yet the situation could have been different. In 1992, during contractual negotiations, then-general editor John Ritchie ceded all publishing rights to Melbourne University Press, including those relating to the new World Wide Web (Bolton 2013). Only later would the terms of the contract be renegotiated to give the Australian National University (ANU) digital publication rights (with MUP retaining the right to publish new print works that may be produced from the online dictionary) (Nolan 2013b). As in the case of the ADB's Canadian and New Zealand counterparts, the digital version was always intended to be accessible freely rather than via paid subscription, which has clearly encouraged its use and expanded its reader base (Bennet 2013).[9]

Although there were no immediate plans to abandon the print work, a basic motivation for moving from print to digital was to enable greater user access and increased public and academic engagement. This has particular resonance in Australia, where those in remote or sparsely populated regions do not necessarily live in close reach of public libraries. While open access, in digital form, has been recently mandated in some countries or jurisdictions, a decade or more ago, when the ADB online was in planning, this was a choice rather than a requirement, and a revenue-based model was considered (Bennet 2013). Online publication also allowed more flexibility in the way information could be presented, the capability to correct and update efficiently, and the means for users to locate information quickly and accurately.

I was employed in 2010–13 to oversee the completion of Volume 18 of the *Australian Dictionary of Biography*, in print and online, as the dictionary's managing editor (deputy general editor), and to contribute to the ADB's development at a time of change and expansion as it transitioned from a print publication to a fully online and enhanced digital research resource.[10] All staff at the ADB during that period contributed in different ways to the rethinking and redeveloping of the editorial systems and processes as the group reviewed the very role of a biographical dictionary in the digital era. My responsibilities included aspects of planning and production, from research editing and monitoring of workflow through to the point of print and online publication, as well as addressing strategic issues relating to matters such as negotiating intellectual property rights, archiving policies, public engagement, and developing relationships with other national digital projects, including planning for dataset interoperability.[11] At critical points the tension between old and new ways generated its own challenges. In many cases it was difficult to let go of tried-and-true procedures, but the shift to digital methods required some of these to be abandoned rather than modified. As in most large projects, the whole ADB team undertook all this work collaboratively.[12]

## Creating a virtual research environment

In 2010 the ADB also employed a full-time computer programmer, Scott Yeadon, effectively in place of a senior research editor, signalling a major shift towards emphasizing the digital dimensions of the project and creating the opportunity to rethink the underlying database structure and redevelop it to meet current and future needs. The vision of general editor Melanie Nolan was that

> Future users of the *ADB* online would be able to search the database using each of the fielded categories or a combination of them to identify the biographical subjects relevant to a research project. Moreover, it would be possible to explore the interactions and relationships between factors such as class, ethnicity, religion, region, and period in Australian history.
>
> (Nolan and Fernon 2013, 198)

ADB bibliographer Christine Fernon had already taken on new responsibilities in the role of online manager and has been closely involved with the digital evolution of the dictionary at each stage (Bennet 2013).[13] For most of the production of Volume 18 the group experimented with a freely available cloud-based document management system, Windows Live, renamed Skydrive and now Onedrive, a Microsoft online service. We needed an effective system and simple interface to collaborate and share documents. First launched in Australia in mid-2010, the ADB used this service to track editorial workflow and as a content management system until 2012, when it was replaced with the custom-developed Biographical Information Management System (BIMS). Designed to fully integrate with the online publication workflow, including supporting metadata fielding and other indexing, BIMS superseded the Online Heritage Resource Manager that had been used in the first iteration of the ADB online. It built in much of the collaboration functionality of the Windows Live system and also had the advantage of allowing ADB data to be stored locally on university servers, which became a policy requirement. An equally significant factor was the move from proprietary to open source platforms, and the flexibility this opened up.

A key feature of the current BIMS system is that it has provided the ability to more fully describe and hence also visualize the relationships between individuals and with related entities such as places, properties, awards, or military service—or a wide range of other categories. The metadata recorded in the first iteration of the ADB online included name, gender, life span, date and place of birth and death, occupation, religious and cultural affiliation, workplace, and year or range of years of occupation. In the second iteration, using BIMS, far greater detail is being recorded for newly edited entries. Articles are now systematically indexed to also include cause of death, education, military service, awards, association with organizations, major events, rural properties and homes, and where relevant, legacies created in a person's name, as well as other information (a metadata schema that is being constantly expanded). Obituaries Australia (http://oa.anu.edu.au/), a companion website to the ADB launched in 2011, which shares its newly reconfigured database, has used the BIMS system from the outset, and all new ADB articles now use BIMS indexing guidelines. Obituaries Australia and the Women Australia and Labour Australia websites were created to complement and enhance the ADB as a research resource (for example, multiple obituaries are now being linked with the relevant ADB entries). A full view of the shared database is provided through the overarching People Australia website, launched in 2012 (http://peopleaustralia.anu.edu.au/).

The process of meticulously gathering rich metadata and indexing has allowed for experiments in visualizing relationships through family trees as well as, more recently, social network graphs showing spousal relations. As the ADB general editor has explained, 'The NCB/*ADB* is amassing a large body of comprehensively indexed biographical records of Australian families for our community....There is also research potential in the new online capacity to study the associational patterns of Australians and their place in biographical history' (Nolan 2013a, 392). In terms of user interface, perhaps the most visible change between the first and second iteration of the ADB online is that relationships between biographical subjects are now being described discretely. The in-text hyperlinks between entries for related biographical subjects in the first iteration of the ADB online have been replaced with a panel of links separate from the main text that specifically name the relationships (mother, father, sister-in-law, business associate, friend, gang member, to mention only a few of the many relationship descriptors in use). The current research and editorial process gathers not only metadata about individual relationships but also this information about links with other people, places, institutions, and events. The very latest fields to be included in the metadata schema are marital status, year of marriage and place of residence.[14] The approach taken to indexing has been to describe subjects comprehensively, consistently, and as accurately as possible. This work is manually focused, requiring the location, interpretation, and recording of information from multiple text-based sources. Substantial benefits, however, can be gained from such an investment of time and labour. The entry for chief justice and legislator Sir Alfred Stephen (1802–94) in People Australia is an example the ADB has often used to illustrate the value of the chosen approach. In addition to the ADB article (http://adb.anu .edu.au/biography/stephen-sir-alfred-1291), data has been obtained from a set of obituaries relating to Sir Alfred and his relatives, drawn from documents in Obituaries Australia. The family tree (http://peopleaustralia.anu.edu.au/treeview/1291) and spousal relations network graph (http://peopleaustralia.anu.edu.au/families/ 1291/0) generated based on this data are highly detailed, due partly to the indexing regime but also because the subject had two wives and ultimately 18 children, all of whom are recorded in the BIMS system as individual, linked entities. The ADB online manager reported that she had been able to find obituaries for 12 of Sir Alfred's children and for five generations of Stephens. While this is not a typical case in that it is a particularly large family, the example shows the value of visualizing such complex interconnections. This research work and resultant indexing is enriching the people and relationship data in the ADB, Obituaries Australia and related websites and hence allowing for relationship mapping and research into the degrees of connection or separation of families that would have previously been impossible.

The manual indexing and classification approach avoids much of the ambiguity in presenting data that can result from techniques such as automated text mining of sources where, because the context is not accessible to automated processes, important information may be missed, misrepresented, or recorded incorrectly. The naming of people and places, for example, may be unclear, and relationships may be difficult to ascertain out of context. Using the manual approach allows even entries with only basic information to be included and indexed as thoroughly as possible. The indexing guidelines include established authority lists and controlled vocabularies. While the goal is to create a high-quality dataset for researchers, supporting the ADB's commitment to and reputation for historical accuracy, the approach does not preclude alternative future strategies for enriching the data, for example through crowdsourcing or social linking.[15]

Access to detailed metadata allows a researcher to potentially pose and answer questions such as those involving the degrees of separation between network members and how densely or loosely networks are connected. These may be family groups, clubs, or various kinds of communities. Identifying cliques and clusters within social networks also becomes possible. In developing the companion website Obituaries Australia and linking this with the ADB, it already has been possible to trace a number of families, including those who came to Australia as convicts or assisted immigrants, through multiple generations.

## Conclusion

The ADB remains 'at a watershed as it moves from a book to a digital culture. Its future promises the possibilities of advanced indexing, network analysis, visualisations, inclusion of supporting resources and e-research' (Nolan 2013b, 32). The print version of the ADB may eventually be abandoned; yet, as in the case of newspapers transitioning online, there continues to be a demand for both in order to serve particular segments of the community and for contractual reasons. In this the ADB represents a very clear and self-contained example of the sorts of issues that confront every kind of print-based activity as it moves into the digital realm. Despite its versatility, there are arguably drawbacks to the approach taken to date, precisely because the metadata schema is tailored specifically for the ADB. The capacity to interlink with other projects or datasets, for example, may be limited. However, the recent integration of ADB data into the Humanities Networked Infrastructure (HuNI) Virtual Laboratory project (along with 28 other nationally significant Australian cultural datasets, many of them using entirely different systems and metadata schemas), supports the argument for maintaining the unique identity and bespoke functionality of major digital resources even as they aim for closer alignment to create collaborative platforms for interdisciplinary research.[16]

In the arena of national biography, the print-to-digital transition certainly represents much more than a change of medium. In fact, the digital environment can be seen to have had an impact on the ADB's core role. Whereas the ADB had aimed to remedy the paucity of knowledge of Australians in history, the ADB's ability to counteract the overabundance of information is now proving most valuable for many.[17] The ADB performs a curatorial role, typical of well-developed large digital projects, of sifting, presenting, framing, and containing biographical information as a collection that is growing and changing. It has become much more than a dictionary; it is a powerful research tool. As Philip Carter, a lead editor at the ODNB, asks,

> To what extent are researchers willing to treat online dictionaries not just as 'super-accessible print' but as new resources in which the ability to make connections between people shifts perspectives from biography to history; from, in effect, discrete biographies of those who shaped a nation to a nation's history told through the lives of its people?
>
> (Carter 2013, 346)

This arguably represents the most empowering change that the highly complex migration from a print to an online environment has brought to the ADB and also arguably the point at which it became a digital humanities project. The capacity to trace and map connections between individual lives and their wider historical contexts, and with other lives—to an extent that was unimaginable in the past—and the way that this in turn is changing users' approach to ADB information, indicates that this is now much more than a dictionary.[18]

The story of the ADB's move online is one of many; others' stories may be very different. No formula exists for successful transition. It is an iterative process—not a 'step' but rather an ongoing series of cultural as well as technical shifts. They impact not only the product but also patterns of work, professional identity, and organizational priorities and dynamics. For example, the ADB replacing a research editor with a computer programmer was a sign of the reality of the resourcing required to support digital research ventures, but there was a substantial resultant loss in senior editing capacity within the group. Timing is an issue, too. As the current general editor envisaged it, the dictionary was ripe for the collective approaches that digital environments facilitate. An awarded collective biographer, Nolan provided the impetus for this change, one that would have been unattainable without the culture of computer-aided research that was being established (Nolan 2013a).

New research capabilities and methods being developed in online national biographies such as the ADB are productively contributing to an accelerating change that is profoundly transforming every branch of the humanities in these first two decades of the twenty-first century. Overall, however, the main message that emerges from the ADB experience is that moving into digital ways of producing work in the humanities involves much more than adopting new technical tools. Each place and project requires its own tailor-made steps and strategies for the shift to digital methods. They also require a cultural change in the way work is done at the initiating level—new rhythms, workflows, and priorities, and letting go of traditional trusted and familiar patterns of daily work—an aspect that is critically important during times of major transition in an organization.

## Notes

1. See Arthur 2010.
2. The editorial and research unit that produces the *Australian Dictionary of Biography* (ADB) has been led by general editor Professor Melanie Nolan since 2008. In that year, the National Centre of Biography (NCB) was established at the Australian National University (ANU) to extend the work of the ADB and to serve as a focus for the study of life writing in Australia, supporting the highest standards in the field, nationally and internationally. The NCB is a growing community made up of research editors, PhD students, postdoctoral and research fellows, senior academics and adjunct appointments, together with administrative support staff, a website developer, and an online manager.
3. The ADB is distinctive for being housed at a national university with recurrent university funding, and for its national cooperative structure. The *Dictionary of Canadian Biography* had been established with substantial private funds.

4. The ADB first established its reputation as the largest project in the social sciences in Australia in 1966. See Walsh 2001.

5. Interestingly, when the online version of the ADB was first proposed, there was not a sense that ADB online would be a national resource of value to the ANU and its mission (Roe 2013).

6. http://www.esrc.unimelb.edu.au/about-us/informatics-lab/ohrm/.

7. Picture Australia is now incorporated within the library's Trove service (http://trove.nla .gov.au/general/australian-pictures-in-trove).

8. Copyright holders were consulted and agreed to waive copyright fees on the condition that the ADB online would be freely available (Bennet 2013).

9. While all the content is effectively available for public access, republication of articles and data reuse for research purposes require permission.

10. In the College of Arts and Sciences at ANU at the time, the terms 'e-research' and 'e-scholarship' were being used in policy rather than 'digital humanities', although a Digital Humanities Hub had recently been established.

11. This planning led to the ADB's participation in the Humanities Networked Infrastructure (HuNI) virtual laboratory and tools project, funded by the NeCTAR Super Science programme of the Australian government in 2012–14 and involving collaboration between 28 nationally significant cultural datasets—the largest interdisciplinary project of its kind attempted worldwide—for which I was the Australian National University project lead.

12. At the time there were approximately 15 research and professional staff members who formed the ADB unit and worked within the larger framework of the National Centre of Biography.

13. Fernon was assistant project manager to the initial ADB online project and had been working with the ADB first as research editor (1999) and then bibliographer (2000–) before becoming online manager in 2009 (see Nolan and Fernon 2013). As is often the case with long-running projects, the energy and long-term dedication of individuals is equally as important as larger collaborative frameworks.

14. 'Enhancements to NCB Websites' (2013).

15. During my employment at the ADB, crowdsourcing was discussed but was not considered a priority given the existing opportunities for public input and the extent of correspondence received; part of my job was to respond to such correspondence daily.

16. For case study discussion of HuNI, see p. 211 in this volume.

17. 'The *ADB* served a particularly important role when there was little in the way of authoritative published Australian history in the 1950s and 1960s. It is important again, in the twenty-first century, when there is so much information on the Internet' (Nolan 2013b, 32).

18. One example of a change in user behaviour is that most readers of the ADB now find entries directly through a web search, rather than by navigating through the ADB home page. This change has implications for usability and interface design (providing options for onward navigation to related pages, for example, is essential) and also poses gatekeeping problems (such as users not routinely seeing the standard 'front page' warning about culturally sensitive information in the dictionary relating to images of deceased Aboriginal subjects).

## Works cited

Arthur, Paul Longley. (2010). 'Digital Biography: Capturing Lives Online'. *Auto/Biography Studies* 24, no. 1: 74–92.

Bennet, Darryl. (2013). 'The Di Langmore Era, and Going Online, 2002–2008'. In *The ADB's Story*, ed. Melanie Nolan and Christine Fernon, 181–212. Canberra: ANU E Press.

Bolton, Geoffrey. (2013). 'John Ritchie: Consolidating a Tradition, 1987–2002'. In *The ADB's Story*, ed. Melanie Nolan and Christine Fernon, 153–80. Canberra: ANU E Press.

Carter, Philip. (2013). 'Opportunities for National Biography Online: The Oxford Dictionary of National Biography, 2005–2012'. In *The ADB's Story*, ed. Melanie Nolan and Christine Fernon, 345–72. Canberra: ANU E Press.

Chubb, Ian. (2009). 'The ADB: Honouring Its Foundational Culture'. *Biography Footnotes*, December.

Enhancements to NCB Websites. (2013). *Biography Footnotes*. 12 December: 3.

Griffiths, Tom. (2013). 'Foreword'. In *The ADB's Story*, ed. Melanie Nolan and Christine Fernon, xi–xii. Canberra: ANU E Press.

Moyal, Ann. (2013). 'Sir Keith Hancock: Laying the Foundations, 1959–1962'. In *The ADB's Story*, ed. Melanie Nolan and Christine Fernon, 49–100. Canberra: ANU E Press.

Nolan, Melanie. (2013a). 'From Book to Digital Culture: Redesigning the ADB'. In *The ADB's Story*, ed. Melanie Nolan and Christine Fernon, 373–96. Canberra: ANU E Press.

Nolan, Melanie. (2013b). ' "Insufficiently Engineered": A Dictionary Designed to Stand the Test of Time?' In *The ADB's Story*, ed. Melanie Nolan and Christine Fernon, 5–48. Canberra: ANU E Press.

Nolan, Melanie, and Christine Fernon, eds. (2013). *The ADB's Story*. Canberra: ANU E Press.

Roe, Jill. (2013). 'National Collaboration: The ADB Editorial Board and the Working Parties'. In *The ADB's Story*, ed. Melanie Nolan and Christine Fernon, 277–98. Canberra: ANU E Press.

Walsh, Gerald. (2001). ' "Recording the Australian Experience": Hancock and the Australian Dictionary of Biography'. In *Keith Hancock: The Legacies of an Historian*, ed. D. A. Low. Carlton, Victoria: Melbourne University Press.

# Part II
# Media Methods

# 7
# Digital Methods in New Cinema History

*Richard Maltby, Dylan Walker, and Mike Walsh*

During the last decade a new direction has emerged in international research into cinema history, shifting focus away from analysing the content of films to considering their circulation and consumption, and examining the cinema as a site of social and cultural exchange. This body of work distinguishes itself from previous models of film history that have been predominantly constructed as histories of production, producers, authorship, and individual films most commonly understood as texts. This approach has now achieved critical mass and methodological maturity, and has developed a distinct identity as the 'New Cinema History'.[1] In this chapter we describe the emergence and concerns of New Cinema History and its relationship with digital methods and technologies through a discussion of several case studies and projects, focusing particularly on the 'Mapping the Movies' project, which has developed a geodatabase of Australian cinemas, covering the period from 1948 to 1971. The project's data is used to examine the effects of the introduction of television on the Australian cinema industry, while its structure raises questions about the relationship between the microhistories of particular venues and the individuals attached to them, and larger-scale social or cultural history represented by the cinema industry's globally organized supply chain.

New Cinema History focuses on the questions that surround the social history of the experience of cinema rather than on the histories of individual films.[2] Its underlying premise is that cinema cannot adequately be studied in isolation from its social, cultural, and economic context. Its research practice seeks to engage contributors from different points on the disciplinary compass. Projects have examined the commercial activities of film distribution and exhibition, the legal and political discourses that craft cinema's profile in public life, and the social and cultural histories of specific cinema audiences. In doing so, they have deployed a range of information—from insurance maps and building ordinances, transport timetables and screening schedules drawn from newspaper advertisements to oral histories—that extend the object and scope of cinema research. As the sources of information expand and diversify, the need increases for more complex and powerful tools with which to accumulate and analyse data. Although the concern to write what Jeffrey Klenotic has evocatively called 'a people's history of cinema' long pre-existed the 'computational turn', the practice of New Cinema History and its capacity to take cinema research in new directions and ask new questions depends on techniques of digital curation and research.[3]

Projects such as Klenotic's study of Springfield, Massachusetts or Robert Allen's investigation of silent cinema in North Carolina employ databases, spatial analysis, and geovisualization to compile and analyse information previously too time- and labour-intensive to acquire.[4] Some New Cinema History projects provide opportunities for crowdsourcing; almost all are collaborative, presenting opportunities for film studies to escape the confines of textual analysis, to overcome the self-perpetuating insularity of 'middle-level' accounts of film's medium specificity, and to begin to speak with other disciplines in the humanities and social sciences.[5]

Focused as it has been on the individual text, film history has predominantly served an evaluative, classificatory, or curatorial purpose. As such, it has had to ignore or deny the transitory nature of any individual film's commercial existence. Indeed, its remit has to a great extent been to disavow the ephemerality of cinema. When seeking to place films into a wider historical context, its most common approach has been to treat films as involuntary testimony, bearing unconscious material witness to the *mentalité* or zeitgeist of the period of their production.[6] This mode of analysis turns the movies themselves into proxies for the missing historical audience, in the expectation that an interpretation of film content will reveal something about the cultural conditions that produced it and attracted audiences to it.

This symptomatic film history pays little attention to the actual mode of cinema's circulation at any time and is largely written without acknowledging the material circumstances of that circulation or the transitory nature of any individual film's exhibition history. Motion picture industries require audiences to cultivate the habit of cinemagoing as a regular and frequent social activity. From very early in their industrial history, motion pictures were understood to be consumables, viewed once, disposed of and replaced by a substitute providing a comparable experience. The routine change of programme was a critical element in the construction of the social habit of attendance, ensuring that any individual movie was likely to be part of a movie theatre audience's experience of cinema for three days or less, with little opportunity to leave a lasting impression before it disappeared indefinitely. Sustaining the habit of viewing required a constant traffic in film prints, ensuring that the evanescent images on the screen formed the most transient and expendable element of the experience of cinema.

Every screening was the successful outcome of negotiations exchanged by mail, telegraph, or telephone, and a sequence of physical journeys by air, sea, road, and rail, in order to enable the audience's cultural encounter with a film's content through the delivery of a film print. This logistical history of product flow—the contractual history of cinema—is expressed archivally in multiple discursive forms of involuntary testimony: theatre records, business correspondence, newspaper reviews, the trade press, legislation, and government policy.

Oral histories with cinema audience members consistently tell us that the local rhythms of motion picture circulation and the qualities of the experience of cinema attendance were place-specific and shaped by the continuities of life in the family, the workplace, the neighbourhood, and the community. These accounts confirm Robert Allen's proposition that for most of cinema's history, the experience of cinema has been 'social, eventful and heterogeneous', and that the history of the experience of cinema is consequently a social history.[7] Stories that cinemagoers recall return repeatedly to the patterns and highlights of everyday life, its relationships, pressures, and resolutions. Only the occasional motion picture proves to be as memorable, and it is as likely to be memorable in its fragments as in its totality.

Focusing on the social and commercial history of cinema, New Cinema History seeks to engage scholars from more diverse disciplinary backgrounds, who have not been schooled in the professional orthodoxy that the proper business of film studies is the study of films. From the perspective of historical geography, social history, economics, anthropology, or population studies, the observation that cinemas are sites of social and cultural significance has as much to do with the patterns of employment, urban development, transport systems, and leisure practices that shape cinema's global diffusion, as it does with what happens in the transient encounter between an individual audience member and a film print. New Cinema History uses quantitative information to advance a range of hypotheses about the relationship of cinemas to social groupings in the expectation that these hypotheses must be tested by other, qualitative means.

Arguing for a 'triangulation of data, theory and method', Daniel Biltereyst, Philippe Meers and Lies Van de Vijver have explored ways in which longitudinal databases that track programming and exhibition patterns, ethnographic and oral history research into audience behaviour and memory, and archival research in corporate records and the local and trade press can be integrated in order to produce a social geography of cinema.[8] The oral histories add a subjective layer to their map of cinema in Flanders from 1985 to 2004, illuminating the ways in which people's choice of venue reflected their attachment to community, their sense of social and cultural distinction, and their awareness of geographical stratification.[9]

Jeffrey Klenotic, who has pioneered the use of a geospatial component in the compilation of exhibition databases, argues that the social history of cinema is also a spatial history.[10] In such an account, cinema is an event: each occasion of cinema a unique convergence of multiple individual trajectories upon a particular social site, each event an unpredictable and irreproducible conjunction of undocumented purposes and meanings. Historical engagements with the circumstances of individual cinemas suggest the rich possibilities that a spatial history of cinema can provide in aiding our understanding of the shifting forms of exhibition and moviegoing. A spatial history of cinema must aim to map the routes by which films circulated as commodities and the geographic constraints and influences on the diverse set of social experiences and cultural practices constituted by going to the movies. In such a map, movie theatres are the nodal points at which cinema takes on material form.

At one level, New Cinema History describes a highly localized activity, involving particular sites and the individuals attached to them. But these individuals were also part of a globally organized supply chain, the profitability of which was dependent on the predictability of their behaviour. The particularity of these individual accounts confronts the New Cinema historian with the question of whether and how microhistorical research from one location can generate findings that are usable elsewhere and by others. In this respect, New Cinema History provides an example of the more general historical project in an ecology of information abundance, enlarging the scope of what has previously been dismissed as merely local or community history into new, quantitatively engaged forms of history from below.

The fact that the larger comparative analysis that New Cinema History can provide will rest on a foundation of microhistorical inquiry requires its practitioners to work out how to undertake small-scale, practicable projects that, whatever their local explanatory aims, also have the capacity for comparison, aggregation, and scaling. With common data standards and protocols to ensure interoperability, comparative analysis across regional, national, and continental boundaries will become possible as each 'local history' contributes to a larger picture and a more complex understanding of what Karel Dibbets, in his Dutch 'Culture in Context' project, has called 'the infrastructure of cultural life'.[11]

## Auscinemas: The Australian cinemas map

In parallel with the European and American projects we have described, the Australian Cinemas Map (AusCinemas) database has been developed as a part of the Mapping the Movies research project, which explores the significance of Australian cinemas as sites of social and economic activity.[12] Its immediate purpose is to provide tools for investigating Australian cinemas in the period from 1950 to 1970. This period witnessed considerable changes in the number, nature, and geographic distribution of cinemas in Australia, and our research has focused on interrogating the conventional explanation for those changes—the appearance of television as a functional alternative to cinema—and on examining a range of other factors that might have contributed to the relative decline in cinema attendance over the period. The longer-term aim of the project is to combine archival, social, and spatial data with oral histories to construct a geodatabase of cinema venues and their neighbourhoods, creating maps of distribution practices and audience movements in order to analyse the responsiveness of cinemas and their audiences to social and cultural change. Mapping locations is, however, only a starting point for the spatial analysis of cinema. Klenotic argues that, as a research tool, GIS operates best as a form of bricolage, in which knowledge is constructed through a trial-and-error research process of rearranging layers of spatial and temporal information.[13] These visualizations enable us to discern patterns in the location of cinemas and in their relation to other features, such as public transport routes or population groups. Conceived of in this way, the geodatabase can allow for the interaction of quantitative and qualitative methods. It also provides a platform on which marginalized voices and competing historical perspectives can be presented, compared, and tested. Our aim is to create an open access resource that enables researchers, students, and the public to explore the relationships that surround the occasion of cinema, whether they conceive of their practice as 'research' or not.

Of course, this is a far more ambitious agenda than one grant-funded project can achieve, and our work to date might best be viewed as an initial enabling device for our larger and longer-term goals. Our initial data has been taken from the yearly listings of cinema venues published in *Film Weekly's Motion Picture Directory*, from 1948 until the demise of the trade paper in 1971. These listings provide basic information on the ownership, location, and capacity of approximately 4,000 screening venues.[14] In using this dataset, we have prioritized consistency over accuracy. The *Film Weekly* information is industry-sourced data, collected and published for industry use. Its virtues are its volume, national coverage, and uniformity. We also know, however, from the other research in our project, that its data is not always accurate. It does not, for example, capture the opening or closing dates of cinemas with any degree of accuracy: closure is simply recorded by a cinema's absence from the list in a given year (Figure 7.1).

The question of data accuracy has preoccupied the project's internal debates. The Mapping the Movies project's original database, the Cinema Audiences in Australia Research Project (CAARP), has retained a high level of exactitude and a much greater level of detail in the data that we have stored in it, with data entry only provided by the project researchers.[15] One consequence has been that CAARP has covered smaller areas and narrower periods of time than the intended national reach of AusCinemas. Our pragmatic solution to the dual requirements of gathering data in quantity and retaining precision has been to keep the two datasets separate, but also to allow the AusCinemas site to access CAARP data, and for CAARP to have the capacity to ingest AusCinemas data when we are sufficiently confident about its reliability.

Creating a map from the *Film Weekly* listings involved scanning the original pages for the first year's data, performing optical character recognition (OCR) on the scanned pages, transferring the OCR data to a spreadsheet, and checking it for accuracy against the original. Our data included *Film Weekly's* classification of each cinema by its physical type (for example, conventional indoor or 'hardtop', drive-in, open-air cinema, or travelling show venue) and by a locational schema (central business district, suburban, rural). Street addresses for each cinema were then entered manually so that each location could be geocoded. Where street addresses were not available—mainly for rural venues—we used the central point of the postcode area as the location. Each year of data provided a template for the next year, with any alterations in venue, name, seating capacity, or management being entered manually. The data was then exported into a purpose-built geodatabase for display via Google Maps (Figure 7.2).[16]

The second aim of AusCinemas has been to visualize the changes in cinema locations over time. As the initial scope of the project was to create a tool for researching the post-war changes in Australian film exhibition, we commenced our data visualization with the 1947–48 listings and entered every available year thereafter. The time-based slider that we built for our implementation in Google Maps can be employed to animate the data, providing a visualization of the

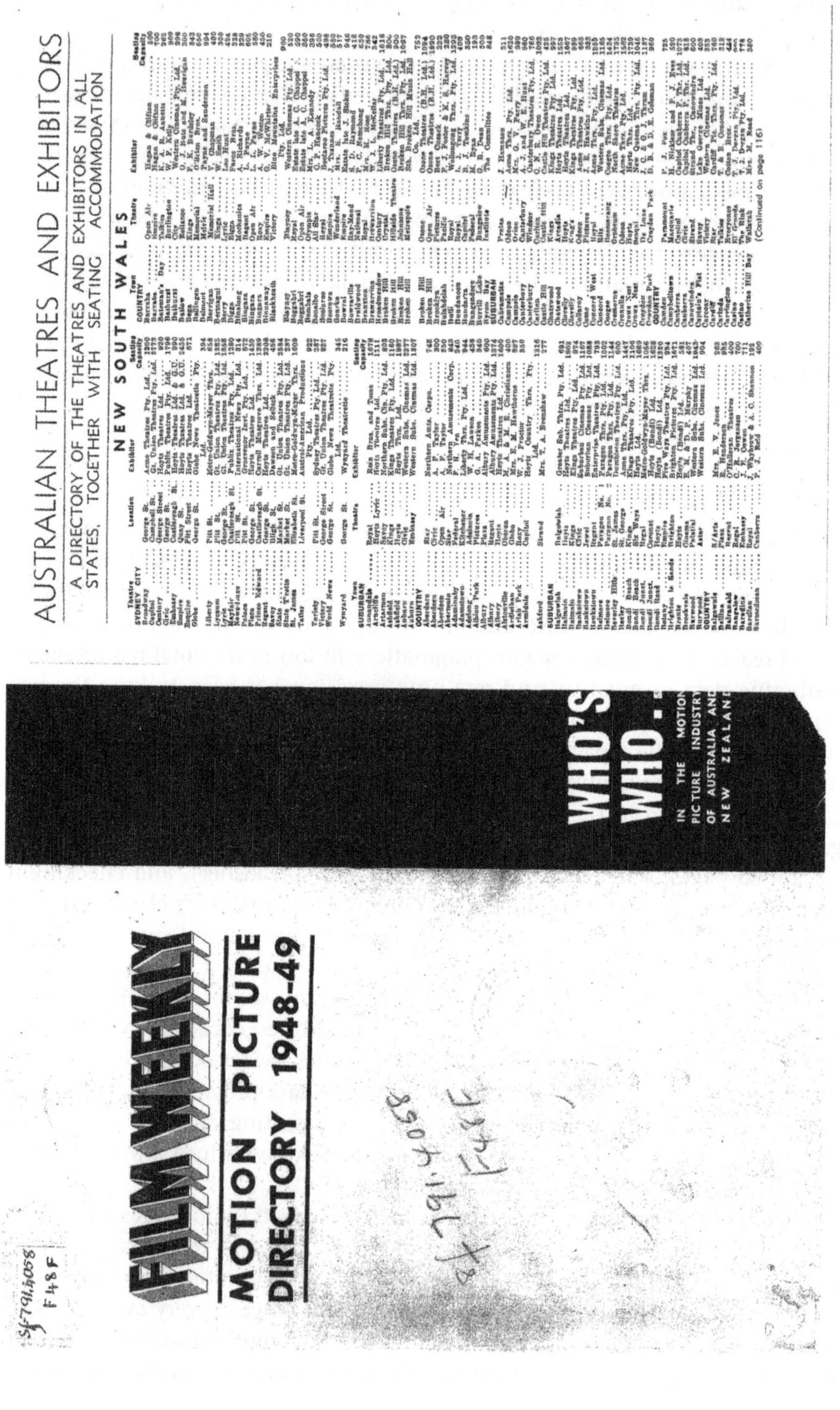

*Figure 7.1*  *Film Weekly* 1948–49 cover and page 1

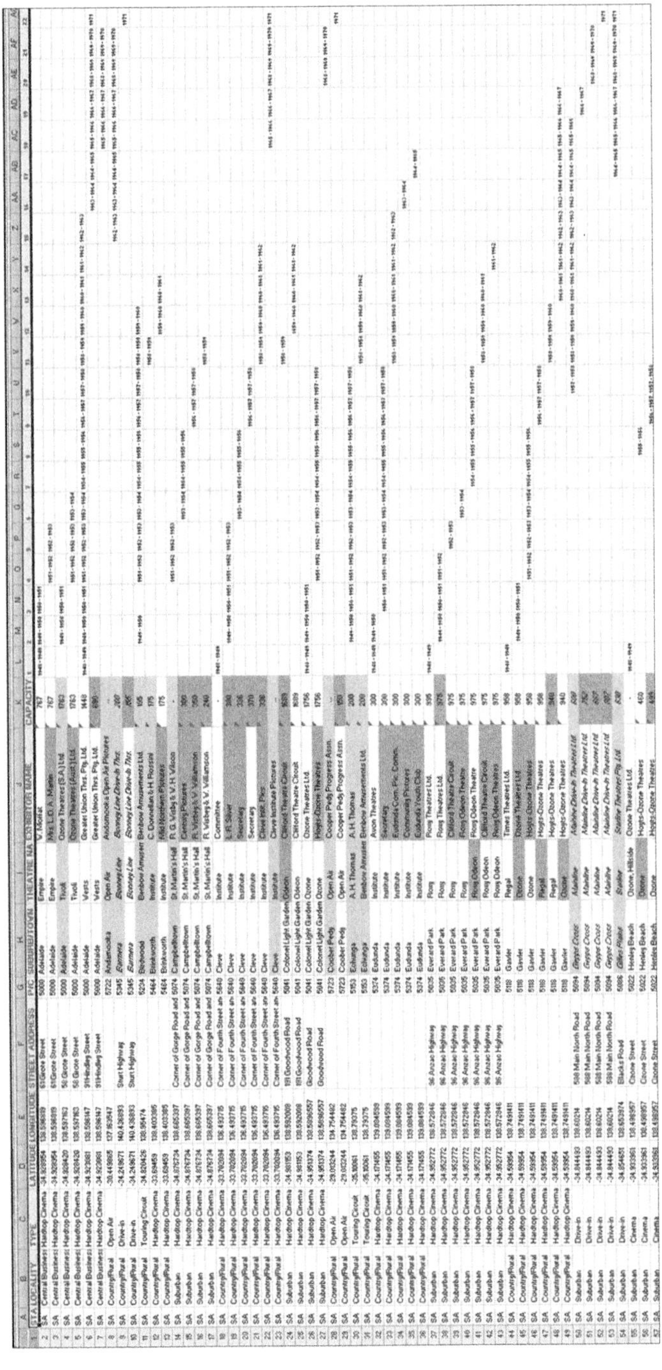

*Figure 7.2* *Film Weekly* data extracted to spreadsheet

appearance and disappearance of venues. This visualization makes clear that the closure of cinema venues in the decade between 1955 and 1965 was far from indiscriminate: while the introduction of television was a major factor in the overall decline in attendance, it cannot adequately explain the closure of any individual venue or the pattern of closure in any city. Closure rates were highest in cities' inner suburbs, reflecting both population movements and the growth of car ownership, as well as the theatre chains' decision to preserve their city-centre venues at the expense of their smaller suburban operations. In her detailed analysis of patterns of closure in Melbourne, Alwyn Davidson has demonstrated that cinemas that did not change capacity—usually to incorporate widescreen projection—had much higher rates of closure, while almost all the venues that survived experienced some change.[17] Although television came later to Queensland and South Australia than to Victoria and New South Wales, the cumulative effect of cinema closures from state to state reduced the size of the national market and with it the viability of marginal operations, including touring circuits that might have served locations well beyond the reach of television transmission. The growth of outer suburban drive-in cinemas in this period indicates that within the overall contraction of the audience, demographic shifts prompted a relocation and partial renewal of cinema venues (Figure 7.3).

Our third aim has been to provide a resource in which other information pertinent to the venue can be collected and accessed. To this end, each venue is linked to a pop-up information window that collects and displays a list of information about the venue's history and the range of other relevant resources. The *Film Weekly* listings provide annual information on the management of the cinema and its seating capacity. Changes in either of these are registered within the pop-up window as part of the venue archaeology. The window also incorporates links to any other information that can be gathered through crowdsourcing. Photographs, document collections held in archives, websites, essays contributed by students or other historians, or reminiscences gleaned through oral histories can be shown here through hyperlinks to materials held either internally within a wiki hosted on the AusCinemas server or externally at other websites. Each cinema window also contains a link to the CAARP database, which holds screening data for some of the venues.

An example of the information that a researcher can find on a particular cinema through AusCinemas comes from the record for the Capri, a suburban Adelaide cinema. Opened as a purpose-built cinema, the New Goodwood Star, in 1941, it is still in use as a single-screen cinema. The AusCinemas' links provide photographs ranging from 1941 to 2012, newspaper articles, digital images of financial records (including admission prices) held at the National Archives of Australia, information on the official records held at the State Records of South Australia, directions to where the original architectural plans can be viewed, information on the building and architect's history, screening data (stored in CAARP), and ephemera such as the opening night's programme. An example of a rural cinema is the Ozone in Victor Harbor, a seaside resort township one hour from Adelaide. Opened as the Victa Theatre in 1923, like the Capri it is still in operation as a

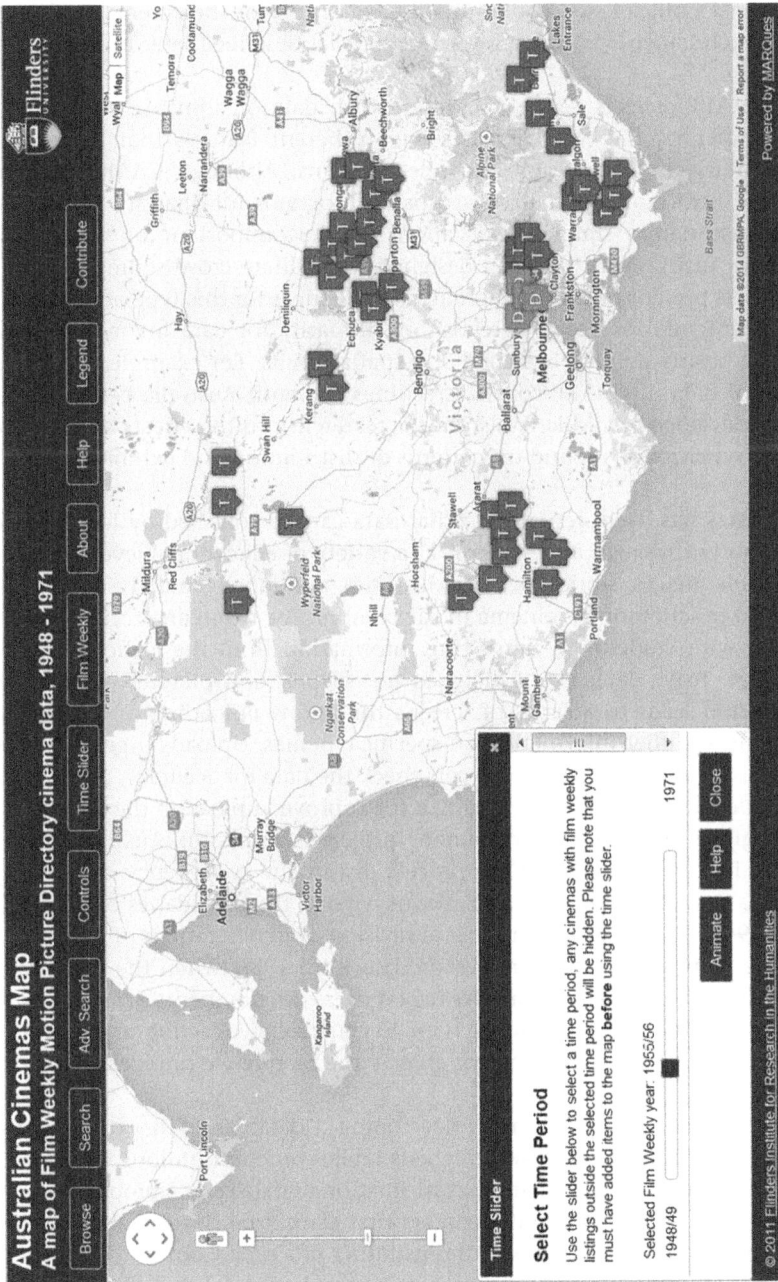

*Figure 7.3* Drive-ins and touring circuits in Victoria, 1955–56

cinema today. Anyone researching the cinema's history through AusCinemas is linked to similar resources to those for the Capri, with additional material such as the cinema's official site, containing a brief history of the cinema, and a student's research paper from the crowdsourcing trial described later in the chapter (Figure 7.4).

While CAARP collects venue data along with data on films, screenings, and related companies, the two databases have different features that make them complementary in their design and research aims. Although CAARP data can be exported into more specialized geospatial programs for analysis, it does not allow for AusCinemas' simple visualization. The most important difference, however, is that AusCinemas has been designed to facilitate crowdsourcing of data. Large datasets present one of the significant challenges for this type of endeavour. CAARP is designed for use as a repository primarily for data involving screenings during clearly defined temporal and spatial limits. For example, the largest collection of data in CAARP covers screenings in South Australia between 1928 and 1931, developed by Mike Walsh in his research into the effects of the introduction of synchronous sound on patterns of distribution and exhibition in that state.[18]

AusCinemas has been designed so that data can be collected by local historians, amateur enthusiasts, and students at a variety of educational levels. The aim is to assemble images, stories, personal histories, and more generally, accounts of the role and function of the cinema in the community, to augment the work that we will do with students in harvesting information from the National Library of Australia's Trove database of digitized newspapers and pictures.[19] The 'Contribute' button leads to a series of screens that allow uploading of documents, photographs, or other information on specific cinemas. Uploads trigger an email to the database administrators, who can check the data for accuracy, duplication, and format consistency before releasing it for approved upload to the site.

We recognize that if our crowdsourcing project is successful, AusCinemas will grow from its base data and in the process distort the consistency of the original dataset. Crowdsourcing will also take us beyond the boundaries of our initial period of 1948–71, requiring a number of revisions and reiterations of the original site; we are planning to add *Film Weekly* data from 1936, when the trade paper published its first annual directory. We regard these developments as an inevitable consequence of the research, and we hope to generate a collection of microhistories that will correct, amplify, and complicate the picture we can create from the existing data.

One of the problems inherent in developing a database with extensive geographical and historical coverage, which also relies on contributions from a wide range of potential sources, is that the confirmation of data can be problematic. If a contributor makes a claim about a cinema that cannot be confirmed from other sources, how should the database administrators proceed? Contributions by cinema enthusiasts often cannibalize existing sources, leading to the perpetuation of inaccuracies, while students are prone to errors such as the confusion of one venue with another. These issues were identified in the crowdsourcing trial.

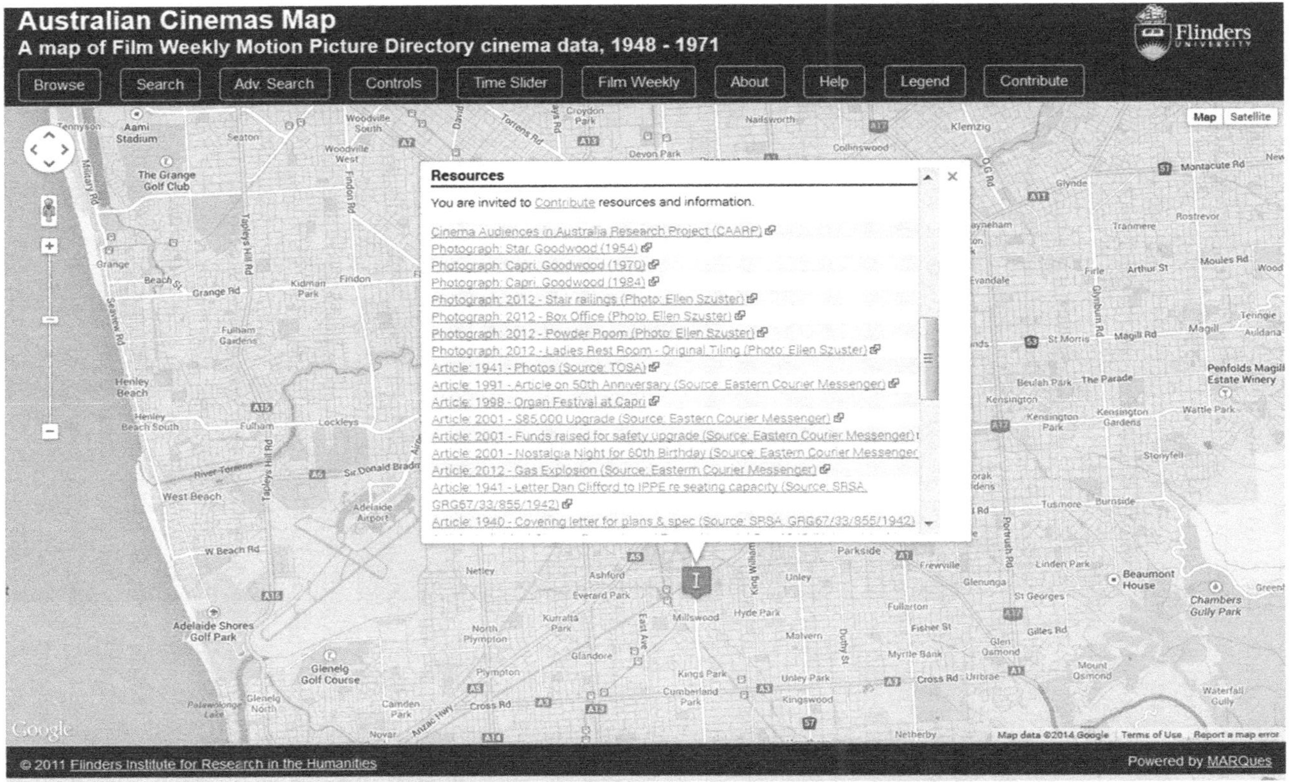


*Figure 7.4* Capri cinema, Goodwood

## A crowdsourcing trial

In order to trial the use of these functions, we used the database in a Flinders University undergraduate class in which each student was assigned a South Australian cinema and required to write a report on the cinema's history and contribute their research materials to AusCinemas. Students were given training in the use of Trove and were introduced to archival record collections held at the State Records of South Australia, the State Library, and the Architecture Museum of the University of South Australia.[20] This exercise also engaged with the need to devise curriculum strategies and models that enable our students to develop the practical skills involved in using archival data, integrating quantitative information within qualitative analysis and representing their research in terms of spatial databases and maps as well as conventional historical narratives.

The student exercise produced 140 contributions from 20 students, with 44 contributions from one particularly enthusiastic student. Items inputted included photographs (either found on the Web or taken by the students), copies of official documents found in the State Records, newspaper clippings from Trove and from other libraries and private collections, architectural plans, opening-night programmes, and information on cinema staff.[21] While the majority of students drew from sources we had already identified at the beginning of the course, some explored further afield and were able to unearth material not found in institutional archives.

Unsurprisingly, the quality and relevance of the contributions varied considerably, necessitating our use of a quality assurance process before uploading the information. Our students' experience demonstrates that online search engines require their users to have skills comparable to those needed in 'analogue' archival research: a broad historical knowledge of their subject and a familiarity with specific vocabularies relevant to their enquiries. In a few instances, students posted newspaper articles or photographs that did not specifically relate to the cinema in question, or provided poor quality pictures taken with little regard for framing and focusing. More commonly, we had to address issues concerning the provenance of the material provided. Some students lacked a sufficient understanding of copyright issues, particularly when they used photographs sourced from the Web. Others cut and pasted material they found on websites into an attachment, and correcting these practices sometimes required the database administrator to duplicate the search in order to identify the link for posting. Our solution to these issues has been to provide external links to such materials rather than include them within the AusCinemas database itself. This approach has the additional practical advantage of reducing the size of the database, and is sufficiently robust when the linked information is held on a secure site, but it does raise issues about the longevity of links to websites maintained by enthusiasts or organizations relying on volunteer support.

We envisage that embedded links can take a researcher directly to primary sources held in archives and museums. A recent test involved ordering online digital images of select cinema-related financial records from the late 1940s held by the National Archives of Australia (NAA). For example, a researcher interested in the trading results of the South Australian Clifford suburban cinema circuit in the 1940s could look up any of the circuit's cinemas on AusCinemas and click on the link displayed in the pop-up window. This screen will then display a digital copy of the file containing the trading results from 1939 up until the circuit was taken over by Greater Union Theatres in early 1947. The potential also exists to provide direct links to digital images of architectural plans and photographs of cinemas held in architecture museums throughout Australia.[22]

As well as clarifying a number of issues in managing crowdsourced information, the student exercise produced much valuable material. The more enthusiastic students visited their assigned cinema, taking interior and exterior photographs. They tracked down newspaper clippings covering major events in the life of the cinema and found relevant materials in archives, museums, and private collections. Several students developed a sense of ownership over the history of a building of which they were previously unaware. This sense of historical attachment is clearly a significant feature of cinema preservation and restoration projects and might be cultivated in gaining broader public input into the project, particularly through encouraging the project's take-up by local historical societies and schools.

We conducted a further trial of crowdsourcing by asking the same students to gather data on all the screenings for their cinema for the year 1954, for inputting into the CAARP database. To maintain the integrity of CAARP, we again employed a quality assurance process before uploading data. Students entered the screening data they had found in local newspapers into a spreadsheet, using a template we devised. A random sample of these entries was checked on each submission, with further checking if any errors or omissions were found. The size of each spreadsheet would depend on the business operations of the particular cinema. Where a cinema screened two features six days each week, the spreadsheet could contain 624 lines of data, or more if the matinee programme differed from the evening sessions. In the case of a rural venue that might only screen on a Saturday and the occasional public holiday, the spreadsheet would be more likely to contain about 120 lines. Once all spreadsheets had been verified for quality, they would be consolidated for a single data export to CAARP.

Random checks revealed that all the sheets submitted required detailed checking and correction, sometimes to a significant degree. The exercise highlighted a number of issues that need to be addressed before students again take a large-scale collection of screening data. Searching Trove through its advanced search facility encounters the limitations of OCR failing to recognize the name of a cinema either because of the poor quality of the newspaper copy or because the advertisement featured the cinema's logo rather than its name in block print. Some spreadsheets fell short of the number of data lines expected, with one listing only 19 days of screenings when that particular cinema advertised on 312 days. Other issues arose as a result of students' lack of knowledge of exhibition advertising style and terminology, which might result in a newsreel or promotional line being entered as a feature film, or a reference to 'three serials' being interpreted as describing the number of screening sessions.

The exercise netted screening data for 36 venues (approximately 15,500 data lines). It has provided us with a much clearer understanding of the challenges involved in crowdsourcing reliable screening data when it is presented in such variable formats, as well as reminding us of the scale of the enterprise we are studying.

## Results

The exercise with our students proved extremely valuable, as much for what it told us about the process of data collection as for what it showed about the microhistory of exhibition and distribution in South Australia. The mass of students were able to unearth a wider spread of information than a small number of trained academics, even if the information needed to be evaluated by the supervising academics.

The screening data entered into CAARP provides a valuable commentary on exhibitors' sense of the popularity of specific films among their audiences, and also on the shifting sets of relations between distributors and exhibitors. CAARP shows at a glance which cinemas were the first to show films during their suburban release, and hence it allows us to reconstruct the detail of exhibition contracts at this time. This provides a much more nuanced understanding of the way that exhibitors juggled contracts with specific distributors and helps dispel prevailing accounts of distributor-exhibitor relations in Australia as an American hegemony.[23]

Mapping the location of central business district and suburban cinemas immediately reveals the extent to which venues clustered together. Almost all of Adelaide's first-run cinemas were located on a single street (albeit one that, confusingly, has two separate names). The AusCinemas map also allowed us to isolate cinemas from the two suburban circuits, known as the Ozone and the Star. In several instances, the map provided clear evidence of the extent to which these circuits shadowed each other by locating rival cinemas within a short distance of competitors in order to constitute a cinemagoing 'district' in which cinemas could take advantage of spillover business. In Adelaide, as in Melbourne, the closure of cinemas in the 1960s was not a simple process, with many venues closing temporarily and reopening in new configurations and under different management, often with new names and screening policies.

The close empirical detail derived from the study also provided a sense of the complexity of pricing structures. We have accessed pricing information for individual cinemas from Trove and from government documents and linked these to the cinema record. Both sources indicate how finely differentiated were the pricing policies of many of the first-run cinemas, which adjusted prices for different sections of their auditoria on a session-by-session basis during the week. Documents from the National Archive detailing South Australian cinema admission charges for 1942 and 1943 provide us with the most comprehensive compilation of admission charges for a particular period unearthed to date. They indicate that the complexity of a cinema's pricing system was based on the time and seating location of each individual audience member's viewing, rather than on the content or quality of the film being viewed. In 1943 the Metro, MGM's first release house in the Adelaide CBD, had seven admission rates (excluding the concessional rates for children), ranging from one shilling and threepence to five shillings and threepence—a variation of over 400 per cent. Prices were determined by a combination of three variables: session (four per day), seating location (five areas for three sessions and seven for the evening session), and day of the week (weekday, weekend, and public holiday). In total, there were 70 different possible pricing permutations. Examining the economic rationale for operating such a complex pricing system leads us to suggest that in first-run city-centre venues, at least, the cinema audience was highly differentiated, while the products that they viewed were regarded as interchangeable.[24]

As this chapter has indicated, New Cinema History is a quilt of many methods and many localities. As a practice of historical enquiry it is decentred, exploratory, and open, requiring that the subjectivities of oral history converse with the quantitative data of economic history and the resources of the archive to answer the apparently simple question, 'What was cinema?' In refocusing that question on the circulation and consumption of cinema rather than on its production or aesthetics, New Cinema History situates itself within the trajectory by which historians have, in Krzysztof Pomian's phrase, 'shifted their gaze from the extraordinary to the everyday', from history's exceptional events to the large mass of its commonplaces.[25] It seeks to make use of quantitative information without rendering the audiences it studies as merely data for a statistical series. With E. P. Thompson, we view our task as historians as being to understand 'how past generations experienced their own existence'.[26] In examining the social experience of cinema, our practice has affinities with the new histories described by Peter Burke as studying topics not previously thought to possess a history: childhood, death, madness, climate, cleanliness, reading.[27] Like many of these other versions of the sociocultural history of experience, New Cinema History raises issues of definition, evidence, method, and explanation, as well as the challenge of relating everyday life to larger events or long-term trends. Methodologically, histories of the everyday present the issue that they must literally be interested in every day, and that as a result they generate datasets that grow exponentially, presenting researchers with fresh sets of problems concerning the organization, standardization, and verification of data. We view the AusCinemas project as an early, tentative address to these issues.

## Notes

1. See Maltby 2011; Maltby and Bowles 2009.
2. See Allen 2006.
3. See Klenotic 2007.

4. See http://www.mappingmovies.com/; http://docsouth.unc.edu/gtts/.
5. See Bordwell 1996.
6. See Kracauer 1947, 6, 8; Ferro 1988, 30–31.
7. See Allen 2011, 51.
8. See Biltereyst et al. 2011.
9. For further information on The Enlightened City Project, see http://www.cims.ugent.be/research/past-research-projects/-enlightened-city. For other examples of related research conducted by the History of Moviegoing, Exhibition, and Reception (HOMER) project, see http://homerproject.blogs.wm.edu/projects/.
10. See Klenotic 2011.
11. See Dibbets 2007; 2010.
12. This project forms part of the output for an ARC Discovery project involving Deb Verhoeven, Mike Walsh, Kate Bowles, Colin Arrowsmith, and Jill Matthews called Mapping the Movies: The Changing Nature of Australia's Cinema Circuits and Their Audiences. The project was, in turn, a continuation of a previous Discovery project, Regional Markets and Local Audiences: Case Studies in Australian Cinema Consumption, 1928–80. The Australian Cinemas Map project is at http://auscinemas.flinders.edu.au/.
13. Klenotic 2011, 60.
14. The *Film Weekly* Directory began publication in 1936. The AusCinemas dataset currently includes data from this source from 1948 onwards; as noted below we intend to include earlier data in a subsequent development of the dataset.
15. The CAARP database is at http://caarp.flinders.edu.au/.
16. One of our original intentions was to develop the geodatabase as a lightweight and reusable piece of software for digital humanities researchers wanting to map relatively small-scale datasets in order to answer research questions. The aim was to develop an open source system that supports many of the standard activities that a mapping system must provide, including search and browse interfaces and the capacity to view and manage map markers. The MARQues (Maps Answering Research Questions) system supports the definition of objects with metadata, allowing additional objects to be added to the system without the need to make significant changes to the underlying database structure. The system is focused on easy implementation and management, needing high-level IT skills for only brief periods in the establishment of a project, to define objects in the database and in the programming code, and to customize the user interface to meet researchers' specific needs. The core of the system is built around the Lithium framework using the PHP scripting language. For more information, see the MARQues project wiki at http://code.google.com/p/marques-project/.
17. See Davidson 2011.
18. See Walsh 2077.
19. http://trove.nla.gov.au/.
20. http://www.archives.sa.gov.au/; http://www.slsa.sa.gov.au; http://www.unisa.edu.au/Business-community/Arts-and-culture/Architecture-Museum/.
21. For examples of the types of information contributed by the students, see entries on the Star Adelaide, the Star Unley, Wests Adelaide, and the Strand Glenelg at http://auscinemas.flinders.edu.au/.
22. For example, the Architecture Museum of the University of South Australia has in its collection donated architectural plans of a number of CBD, suburban, and rural cinemas; see http://www.architectsdatabase.unisa.edu.au.
23. See Walsh 2011.
24. See Maltby 1999.
25. See Pomain 1978.
26. See Thompson 1963, 12; 1972.
27. See Burke 2001, 3.

# Works cited

Allen, Robert C. (2006). 'Relocating American Film History'. *Cultural Studies* 20, no. 1: 48–88.

Allen, Robert C. (2011). 'Reimagining the History of the Experience of Cinema in a Post-Moviegoing Age'. In *Explorations in New Cinema History: Approaches and Case Studies*, ed. Richard Maltby, Daniel Biltereyst, and Philippe Meers, 41–57. Malden, MA: Wiley-Blackwell.

Biltereyst, Daniel, Philippe Meers, and Lies Van de Vijver. (2011). 'Social Class, Experiences of Distinction and Cinema in Postwar Ghent'. In *Explorations in New Cinema History: Approaches and Case Studies*, ed. Richard Maltby, Daniel Biltereyst, and Philippe Meers, 101–24. Malden, MA: Wiley-Blackwell.

Bordwell, David. (1996). 'Contemporary Film Studies and the Vicissitudes of Grand Theory'. In *Post-Theory: Reconstructing Film Studies*, ed. David Bordwell and Noël Carroll, 26–30. Madison: University of Wisconsin Press.

Burke, Peter. (2001). *New Perspectives on Historical Writing*. 2nd ed. University Park: Pennsylvania State University Press.

Davidson, Alwyn. (2011). *A Method for the Visualisation of Historical Multivariate Spatial Data*. PhD thesis, RMIT University, Melbourne.

Dibbets, Karel. (2007). 'Culture in Context: Databases and the Contextualization of Cultural Events'. Paper presented at 'The Glow in Their Eyes': Global Perspective on Film Cultures, Film Exhibition, and Cinemagoing conference, Ghent University, December 2007.

Dibbets, Karel. (2010). 'Cinema Context and the Genes of Film History'. *New Review of Film and Television Studies* 8, no. 3: 331–42. Available at: http://dx.doi.org/10.1080/17400309 .2010.499784.

Ferro, Marc. (1988). *Cinema and History*. Trans. Naomi Greene. Detroit: Wayne State University Press.

Klenotic, Jeffrey. (2007). ' "Four Hours of Hootin' and Hollerin": Moviegoing and Everyday Life Outside the Movie Palace'. In *Going to the Movies: Hollywood and the Social Experience of Cinema*, ed. Richard Maltby, Robert Allen, and Melvyn Stokes, 130–54. Exeter: University of Exeter Press.

Klenotic, Jeffrey. (2011). 'Putting Cinema History on the Map: Using GIS to Explore the Spatiality of Cinema'. In *Explorations in New Cinema History: Approaches and Case Studies*, ed. Richard Maltby, Daniel Biltereyst, and Philippe Meers, 58–84. Malden, MA: Wiley-Blackwell.

Kracauer, Siegfried. (1947). *From Caligari to Hitler: A Psychological History of the German Film*. Princeton: Princeton University Press.

Maltby, Richard. (1999). 'Sticks, Hicks, and Flaps: Classical Hollywood's Generic Conception of Its Audience'. In *Identifying Hollywood's Audiences: Cultural Identity and the Movies*, 23–41. London: British Film Institute.

Maltby, Richard. (2011). 'New Cinema Histories'. In *Explorations in New Cinema History: Approaches and Case Studies*, ed. Richard Maltby, Daniel Biltereyst, and Philippe Meers, 3–40. Malden, MA: Wiley-Blackwell.

Maltby, Richard, and Kate Bowles. (2009). 'What's New in the New Cinema History?' In *Remapping Cinema, Remaking History*, ed. Hilary Radner and Pam Fossen, 7–21, 14th Biennial Conference of the Film and History Association of Australia and New Zealand. Otago: University of Otago.

Pomian, Krzysztof. (1978). 'L'histoire des structures'. In *La Nouvelle Histoire*, ed. Jacques Le Goff, Roger Chartier, and Jacques Revel, 115–16. Paris: CEPL.

Thompson, E. P. (1963). *The Making of the English Working Class*. London: Gollanz.

Thompson, E. P. (1972). 'Anthropology and the Discipline of Historical Context'. *Midland History* 1, no. 3 (Spring): 48–49.

Walsh, Mike. (2007). 'Cinema in a Small State: Distribution and Exhibition in Adelaide at the Coming of Sound'. *Studies in Australasian Cinema* 1, no. 3: 299–313.

Walsh, Mike. (2011). 'From Hollywood to the Garden Suburb (and Back to Hollywood): Exhibition and Distribution in Australia'. In *Explorations in New Cinema History: Approaches and Case Studies*, ed. Richard Maltby, Daniel Biltereyst, and Philippe Meers, 159–70. Malden, MA: Wiley-Blackwell.

# 8

# A 'Big Data' Approach to Mapping the Australian Twittersphere

*Axel Bruns, Jean Burgess, and Tim Highfield*

The widespread adoption of leading social media platforms such as Facebook and Twitter in much of the developed world has also led to a rise in research projects across the humanities and social sciences that seek to investigate and analyse the emerging uses of these platforms. A substantial number of such research projects have applied existing communication and cultural research methodologies to this task, including qualitative approaches (for example, the close reading of textual and communicative artefacts sourced from these platforms, or the ethnographic study of specific users and user communities) and quantitative methods (such as surveys of users to examine their attitudes and activities, in order to explore larger behavioural patterns).

However, the increasing—if not always comprehensive—availability of structured data on user activities through the Application Programming Interfaces (APIs) of such social media platforms has also enabled the development of a range of new research methods that see the intersection between humanities-oriented Internet studies and the 'big data' paradigm and accompanying debates (Burgess and Bruns 2012). Research that builds on such API data is potentially able to access much larger datasets on user activities and to develop more systemic perspectives on the uses of social media than previous approaches have been able to do; along with other developments in the 'new' digital humanities, this is seen by some scholars as representing a 'computational turn' (Berry 2011, 2012), while others portend the development of more scientistic models in media, cultural, and communication studies (for example, Manovich 2012; Hartley 2009).

Social media platforms provide API access to user activity data in the first place to enable the development and use of third-party tools and applications that are able to enhance the user experience and provide additional functionality (for example, to high-end and professional as opposed to casual users). However, the availability of such data has also supported the development of social media analytics as a field of industry as well as scholarly research. Such research has been able, inter alia, to examine the uses of social media for everyday communication (for example, boyd et al. 2010; Papacharissi 2011; Marwick and boyd 2011), as a back channel to live and televised events (Deller 2011; Dröge et al. 2011; Weller et al. 2011; Harrington et al. 2012; Highfield et al. 2013), in crisis communication

(Lotan et al. 2011; Bruns et al. 2012; Mendoza et al. 2010; Palen et al. 2010), and for political campaigning (Bruns and Burgess 2011; Burgess and Bruns 2012a; Christensen 2011; Larsson and Moe 2011; Stieglitz and Dang-Xuan 2013).

In the case of Twitter, a substantial amount of existing research that draws on the Twitter API deals with relatively discrete case studies. Such case studies typically capture tweets relating to specific Twitter hashtags (keywords prefixed with the hash symbol '#', which enable users to search for and track topical conversations more easily), and usually draw upon datasets that range from several hundred to a few million tweets. The 'hashtag studies' approach is especially useful for the analysis of key communicative activities in the context of identified events or topics: to include a hashtag in one's tweet constitutes a process of self-selection on behalf of the user, so hashtag datasets contain only those tweets that their authors felt were relevant to a specific topic, from users who were familiar with the hashtag concept overall and knew the appropriate hashtag to use for their specific topic. For tweeting about one-off events, especially televised content, and subjects that strongly promote their related hashtags (such as the Occupy activist movement or crisis relief efforts), focusing on hashtags is an appropriate methodological choice, since communication is directed towards these markers.

While these hashtag-based datasets can be very large (far too large for a single researcher or even a small team to deal with using manual content analysis, for example), and a proper treatment of the sociocultural phenomena to which they relate can be very 'thick' indeed, the need to delimit the corpus in advance (through the selection of the hashtag) means that such studies rarely provoke the same epistemological and methodological shifts as more radically data-driven 'big data' studies do. Further, hashtag datasets are unable to capture the wider communicative activities around the topic or event described by the hashtag (for example, posts between individual users who refer to the topic, but choose not to make their tweets visible more widely by hashtagging them); while little comparative research into such matters has been conducted so far, our own explorations show that four times more tweets contained the keyword 'tsunami' than the hashtag '#tsunami' in the immediate aftermath of the major earthquake in northeastern Japan in 2011, for example (an unknown and unknowable, but still larger, number of tweets would have referred to the event in yet other ways, without using 'tsunami' or '#tsunami' at all). Even where hashtag datasets like #tsunami or #occupy grow very large in their own right, they continue to represent only a self-selecting subset of all tweets that are related to their areas of interest.

Further, even when a prominent hashtag has developed for recurring topics of interest on Twitter, the longevity of these hashtags means that patterns of use have changed in ways that do not necessarily affect the briefer, more focused discussions in response to televised events, for instance. The #auspol hashtag, denoting tweets about Australian politics, offers a prime example; while the hashtag remains widely used, its notoriety for inflammatory comments and replies, for trolling, and for the dominance of a small number of overwhelmingly active users, has led other Twitter users with an interest in politics to not include it in their own tweets.

A hashtag-based research approach also depends crucially on the existence of a common and widely adopted hashtag in the first place, of course. Hashtag research is especially valuable, therefore, in the context of foreseeable events (with foreseeable hashtags), such as elections, sports, conferences, or media programming, or for unforeseen events for which a dominant hashtag quickly emerges (such as some political crises and natural disasters). It is far less able to address more general themes of discussion (music fandom, the state of the economy, the progress of scholarly research) unless a group of lead users in any such area promotes a preferred hashtag for the discussion of their interests—and in doing so, erects a new barrier between committed and more casual users, similar to the #auspol example above. Hashtag datasets are therefore especially unable to shed light on everyday communicative activities that are linked only loosely to any one specific topic—yet such everyday activities constitute a substantial part of Twitter activity and (if researched) may offer valuable new insight into fundamental communication patterns on Twitter.

Thus, perhaps the most significant limitation of hashtag datasets for the study of Twitter and its uses is the fact that these datasets necessarily contain all relevant tweets matching the hashtag or hashtags chosen for analysis (subject only to server failures or API rate-limiting, they are comprehensive) but provide no information whatsoever on the broader communicative context surrounding these hashtags on Twitter. A hashtag dataset on a major event may contain several hundred thousand tweets, but it is impossible to determine from the dataset itself whether at the height of its activity the hashtag was widely visible across the entire Twitter network (for example, as a 'Trending Topic'—a hashtag or theme identified by Twitter itself to have experienced a rapid growth in volume), or whether it represented one of several other major themes being discussed on Twitter concurrently. Indeed, beyond the limited and somewhat vague information occasionally released by Twitter itself—for example, Usain Bolt's 100m final at the 2012 Olympics generated over 80,000 tweets per minute (Twitter 2012a)—it remains very difficult for researchers to place their observations about individual hashtag datasets in a wider context. If the 2010 Australian federal election on 21 August 2010 generated 94,000 tweets on election day alone, for example, does this represent activity by a considerable percentage of all Australian Twitter users? How does election day tweeting compare with tweeting during the final episode, say, of popular reality TV cooking show *Masterchef*, or the Rugby League or Australian Football League (AFL) grand finals?

One approach to addressing such questions is to pursue a greater number of comparative studies across hashtag datasets, which also requires developing a range of standardized metrics for the quantitative description of Twitter user activities, to provide a reliable basis for such cross-comparisons. Such metrics (Bruns and Stieglitz 2012, 2013) enable the identification of stable patterns of user activity across comparable events, indicating, for example, that communicative patterns are different when Twitter is used as a back channel for televised events, compared to its use in crisis communication. But even this does not address the more fundamental problem of comparing hashtag activities against the full range of public communication that takes place on Twitter at any one moment.

Most fundamentally, hashtags are unable to shed much light on how every-day users may encounter information on Twitter. While it is possible for users to deliberately track the content of hashtags themselves, of course, and thereby to encounter tweets even from other users of whom they had not previously been aware, this serves as only one possible layer of communicative exchanges on Twitter (Bruns and Moe 2014). By contrast, the most common and most central path of message transmission on Twitter is through the networks of interconnection between individual Twitter users (as followers and followees of one another, and not necessarily in a reciprocal connection). Hashtag datasets provide information on what tweets were marked with a hashtag, but their packaging as a unified dataset is a convenient fiction for the researcher rather than representing the lived experience of most Twitter users, for whom hashtagged and nonhashtagged tweets appear alongside each other in their Twitter feeds. Such datasets cannot tell us how many users such tweets may have reached; information on the shape of follower/followee networks on Twitter provides a more direct understanding of how far individual messages would have been visible throughout the platform.

Additionally, in many cases it will also be desirable to understand user activity across hashtags not against the backdrop of all other Twitter communication but rather in more local (for example, national) contexts. Australian uses of Twitter, for instance, are likely to be dwarfed by the total volume of tweets being posted at any one point in time, and such comparisons are therefore less than useful. It would be more appropriate to establish a baseline of everyday Australian user activity, filtered from the total 'firehose' of global Twitter communication, in order to situate individual hashtags within this national context. Possible in principle, if difficult in practice due to the increasingly commercialized nature of large-scale Twitter data (an issue to which we return in the final section of this chapter), such a comprehensive identification and analysis of the public communication activities of Australian Twitter users would constitute a 'big data' initiative in its scale, and a more 'data-driven' one in its approach.

Such an approach, in turn, crucially relies on identifying at least the majority of Australian Twitter users, so that their tweets can be extracted from the global firehose of tweets. This constitutes a substantial methodological challenge in its own right: while profile information about individual users is readily available from the Twitter API, alongside their tweets, there is no direct way of retrieving a list of all Australian users from the API, nor is there even reliable data about the full extent of the Australian Twittersphere. Available industry estimates (which rarely identify the rationale for their figures) range between 1.8 and 2.2 million Australian accounts (for example, Bull 2010).

In response to these challenges, in this chapter we outline our approach to developing a reliable picture of the Australian Twittersphere, demonstrate the utility of these baseline data in shedding new light on existing hashtag datasets, and map further steps towards a more comprehensive analysis of Twitter use in Australia. Finally, we position this work as an example of the computational turn in the digital humanities and discuss the practical and conceptual challenges that lie ahead.

## Mapping the Australian Twittersphere

Studying the wider Australian Twittersphere provides the opportunity to look beyond isolated topical and event-based communication on Twitter, by instead examining how these discussions overlap across a national population of Twitter users. Do users who tweet about politics, parenting, or sport primarily follow users with these same topics of interest? Are a user's home town and state, for example, also factors that may be reflected in who they follow on Twitter? A wealth of new information comes out of such research; as the first detailed study of the Australian Twittersphere, the identification of the size of the Australian Twitter user base and its topics of interest invites further exploratory and comparative work around other national Twitterspheres—and their interlinkages. To date, while research into communication on Twitter has covered a variety of contexts, as noted above, attempts at mapping the structural follower/followee relationships between a national Twitter population—in particular, identifying communities of interest and comparing these implicit topical clusters with the ad hoc publics arising from tweeted discussions—are more limited. Our research into the Australian Twittersphere, then, also establishes a framework that future studies may adopt for analysing national as well as international Twitter activity.

The first step in developing a more comprehensive picture of the Australian Twittersphere is to identify individual users as Australian, within acceptable margins of certainty. Twitter provides users with a number of means to identify their location or nationality: they may do so in the free text description attached to their profile, state the town or city where they are located, or provide geolocation coordinates attached to their Twitter profile. These datapoints are of limited use for our purposes, however, given their inconsistent use: descriptions provided by the users themselves may be vague or ambiguous. Users may say they are in 'Australia', 'Victoria', 'Perth', or 'Paddington', but several such names could also point to locations outside of Australia; or they state their location as 'Oz', 'Out West', or 'BrisVegas', or a wide range of other alternatives that could not always be reliably identified. Indeed, during the protests against manipulations of the 2009 Iranian election, many Twitter users worldwide set their location to Tehran or other Iranian cities (Burns and Eltham 2009), in order to make it more difficult for Iranian authorities to identify domestic users; free text location information may be gamed, therefore. Geolocation, on the other hand, is not widely used on Twitter (Wilken 2013) and would identify only a small percentage of the total Australian user base.

A further datapoint available through the Twitter API provides a more useful alternative: in setting up their profiles, users are also able to set their home time zone; due to the diversity in Australian time zones and daylight savings regimes, Twitter provides specific time zone options for Perth, Adelaide, Darwin, Brisbane, Canberra, Hobart, Melbourne, and Sydney. Perhaps not least also because this setting appears in fourth place in the Twitter website's 'Basic Account Settings' page (after the username, email address, and language settings), ahead of many more minor settings options, a substantial number of Twitter users do appear to make use of this customization option, as we will see; in turn, this provides a means not only to identify users as Australians (or at least as based in Australia) but even to pinpoint their likely home state.

Our approach to identifying Australian Twitter accounts is premised on the use of the time zone information in each user profile, therefore; this clear and unambiguous datapoint can be captured and evaluated by automated means. Using this datapoint, we could—in theory—request information about each and every Twitter user from the Twitter API, and divide Australian from non-Australian accounts. However, this brute-force approach would be highly wasteful, as it would require us to test several hundred million Twitter accounts in order to find an estimated two million Australian accounts. Instead, based on the assumption that most Australian Twitter users are more likely on average to connect with other Australians than with international accounts, we proceed by performing a snowball crawl of the Australian Twitter network; this approach also has the advantage of generating additional information about the shape of that network, which will be valuable in its own right.

Over the course of 2011 and 2012, we engaged in such a snowball crawl of the network. We began with a seed list of Twitter accounts that participated in hashtag conversations on particularly Australian topics, including #ausvotes (for the 2010 Australian election), #auspol (a continuing discussion of Australian politics), #qldfloods (for the 2011 south-east Queensland floods), and #masterchef (for the popular television cooking program). Accounts appearing in these hashtag datasets were first tested to examine whether they had set an Australian time zone in their profiles; for those accounts accepted as 'Australian' by that criterion, we then retrieved their follower and followee lists. (Any 'private' accounts, whose tweets and network connections are not publicly available, were ignored in this process.) We then tested the time zone settings of each of these followers and followees in turn, and repeated the process with each newly identified account that had set an Australian time zone.

Due to significant access restrictions that Twitter places on its API, this is a slow process: at present, only 15 follower or followee lists may be retrieved from the API during any one 15-minute window (Twitter 2012b), and for users with more than 5,000 connections, the API counts such retrieval procedures as multiple requests. (These rate limits have changed several times over the course of our research project.) To date, we have tested more than four million Twitter accounts for our time zone criterion, identified more than one million of these accounts as Australian, and retrieved their follower/followee connections. The network crawl continues at the time of writing, and the decelerating rate at which we are identifying additional Australian accounts is consistent with a total population of some two million Australian Twitter accounts. However, on the basis of the data retrieved so far, identifying the accounts themselves and their network connections, it is already possible to sketch the overall shape of the Australian

Twittersphere as we have constructed it here—with the rather large caveat that there is no necessary correspondence between the topography of this network and any user's lived experience of a Twittersphere, or 'networked public', from a (literally, not pejoratively) egocentric point of view (boyd 2010).

In the first place, based on the network information that we have retrieved, it is possible to visualize the total network of interlinkages between accounts. To simplify the discussion and visualization of results for the purposes of this chapter, we concentrate here on those accounts that have at least 20 incoming or outgoing connections to the rest of the network (i.e., degree = 20 or above). This (necessarily arbitrary) cut-off removes users from the network who have yet to follow or be followed by more than a handful of others, including especially very recently created Twitter accounts whose connections are still forming; the removal of such recent users, in particular, also removes any distortions of the overall network structure that the inclusion of such still-nascent follower relationships would introduce. What remains, instead, are the most connected 120,000 of all identified Australian accounts.

Using the Force Atlas 2 algorithm provided by the network visualization software *Gephi* (Gephi.org 2012), which simulates gravitational attraction between connected nodes in a network, we arrange these accounts in line with their strength of interconnection with other accounts: accounts that belong to a cluster of highly interconnected accounts will be placed close to those clusters, while accounts and clusters that share few common connections will repel one another. Force Atlas 2 is especially useful for our purposes because it is able to visualize large and complex networks and is optimized to highlight densely interconnected clusters in the networks it visualizes; this is important for the visualization of the large dataset of Australian Twitter users' connections we are addressing. It should be noted in this context, however, that a large number of other network visualization approaches are available both within *Gephi* and in other network visualization tools, and that there is no one 'true' representation of any network dataset; our results using Force Atlas 2 provide one approach to viewing the network, but other visualizations are also possible. In Jacomy et al. (2011), the authors of the Force Atlas 2 algorithm discuss the respective advantages and drawbacks of their approach in comparison to other popular algorithms. We refer here also to critical work on the performativity of algorithms that construct and represent networks such as that of Tarleton Gillespie (2014); while Gillespie is writing of algorithms such as that used by Klout to calculate popularity, in relation to network visualization, too, we must note 'the friction between the "networked publics" forged by users and the "calculated publics" offered by algorithms' (Gillespie 2014). In what follows, then, we attempt to represent our network visualizations as tools for exploration, not as literal or total representations of social realities.

Several network clusters and multicluster structures emerge through this network analysis process. Further qualitative exploration of these clusters, which examines the accounts that are central to each cluster, is able to provide a rationale for each of these clusters; for example, one densely interlinked section of the network contains the leading Australian news organizations, political

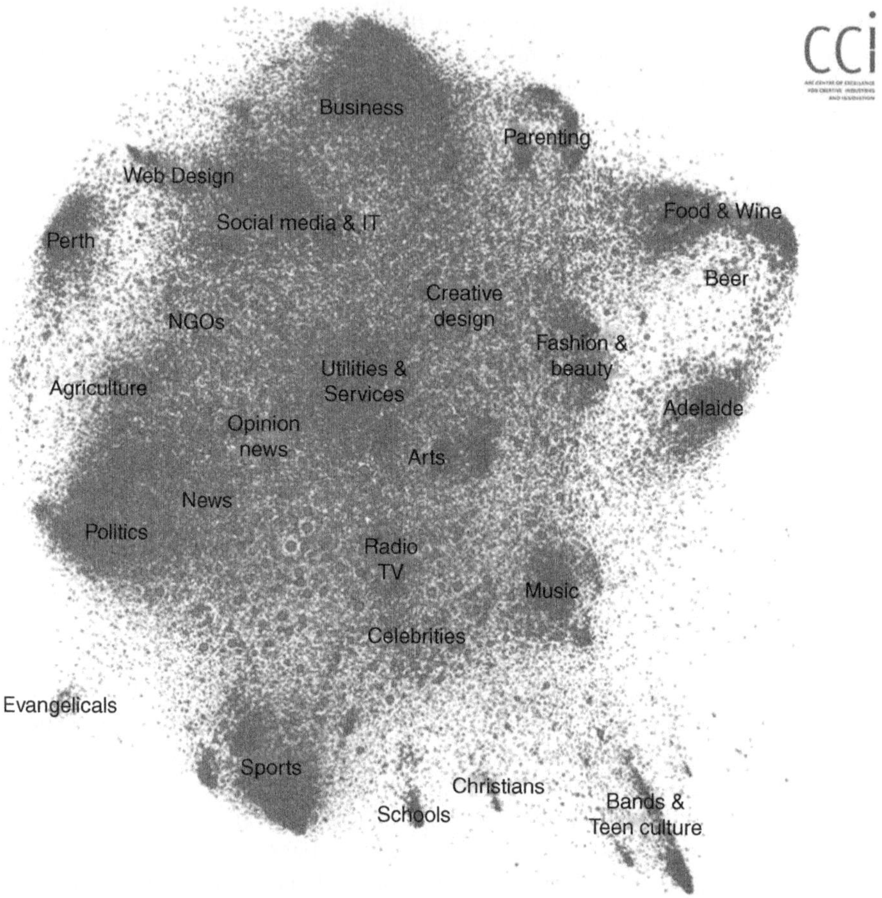

*Figure 8.1* Thematic clusters in the Australian Twittersphere
*Note*: Based on network information for the 120,000 most connected users in the overall network.

journalists, politicians, and political activists, and further subdivides into areas dominated by various conservative and progressive party interests, or feature accounts related variously to social policy, environmental concerns, or agricultural interests. Another is dominated by sports-related accounts, and subdivides into a range of different sports and sporting codes. Figure 8.1 presents this preliminary map of the Australian Twittersphere and labels the different clusters, while Figure 8.2 provides additional detail by indicating the subdivisions in the large politics cluster.[1]

For Figure 8.1, note that it is based on follower/followee network information, not on data about these accounts' tweeting activities. It indicates that clustering in follower relationships in the Twitter network is based largely on thematic affinity, rather than on family relationships or personal friendships (as may be the case for a network such as Facebook), and provides a reasonable approximation of the

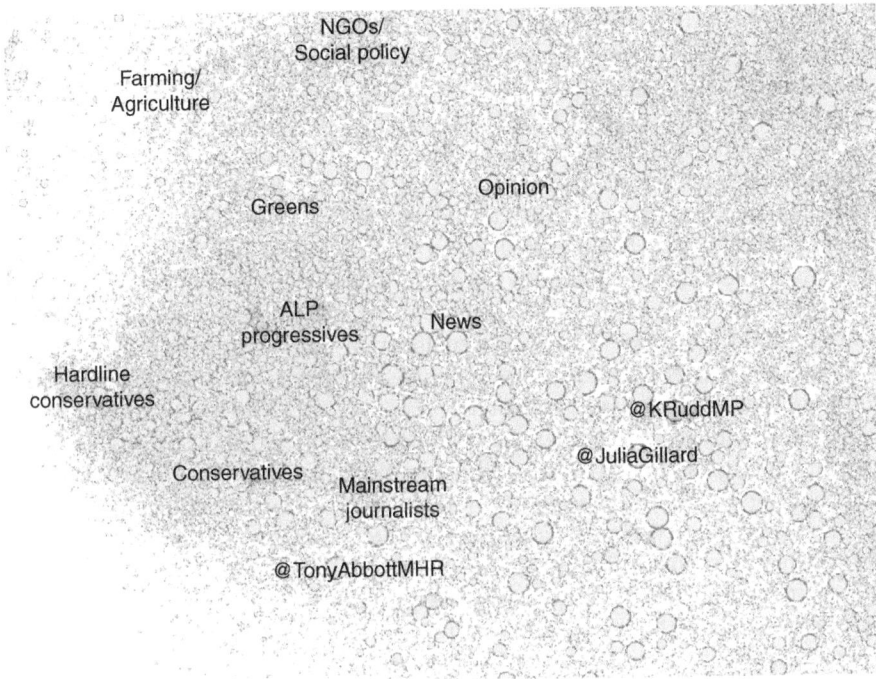

NGOs/
Social policy

Farming/
Agriculture

Opinion

Greens

ALP
progressives          News

Hardline
conservatives

@KRuddMP

@JuliaGillard

Conservatives     Mainstream
journalists

@TonyAbbottMHR

*Figure 8.2*   Subdivisions within the politics cluster of the overall network map

major themes of everyday Australian Twitter discussions and their relative centrality to the network: politics, business, lifestyle, the arts, and sports, subdivided into
a range of smaller and more specific themes. This does not mean that the accounts
placed in each cluster *exclusively* discuss such themes in their day-to-day activities,
nor that they *only* link to other members of the same cluster; nor is there any
reason that users who do not belong to a specific cluster would not occasionally
touch on themes that the cluster would cover more frequently. The small 'beer'
cluster in the top right of the map, for example, represents a tightly interlinked
network of craft breweries, specialist retailers, and related accounts whose primary
raison d'être for networking is beer culture; other accounts in the network may
also refer to beer on occasion, but this is not the core purpose of their Twitter
presence. Indeed, while the network clusters themselves are clearly evident, most
are also far from distinctly separated from one another, suggesting a considerable
overlap in membership. Notably, a range of accounts representing key utilities
and services organizations (from @abcnews to @Telstra to @Qantas) are found at
the very centre of the graph, indicating that accounts from across the map are
equally likely to connect with them.

In itself, the map provides an argument against suggestions that online communication as such and social media in particular must necessarily lead to a
fragmentation of the public sphere into separate interest groups that act as sealed

echo chambers; the considerable interconnection between virtually all major clusters shows that there are substantial overlaps between almost all groups represented here but also indicates that certain combinations are more likely than others: politics and business, for example, go together more readily than religion and lifestyle pursuits. Notably, only two geographically based clusters can be readily identified, pointing to an overall lack of regional divisions in the Australian Twittersphere; the two regional clusters (centred around Perth and Adelaide) appear at least in part to be related to a strong uptake of Twitter by specific local business interests (public relations for Perth, tourism and wine for Adelaide), and may point to deliberate strategies in these industries to use Twitter to strengthen informal local networks. For the vast majority of users who appear on the map, and for the clusters they form around shared interests, the interlinkages across communities are strong and widespread.

Several notable minor clusters can be identified at a distance from the main map, including various flavours of Christianity, teen culture, and education. The fact that these clusters are separate from the mainstream Australian Twitter network is likely due to their stronger orientation towards international interests that are not represented on this Australian map: Australian fans of teen stars Justin Bieber or the Jonas Brothers are more likely to use Twitter to connect with their peers elsewhere in the world than with other Australian users; Australian evangelical Christians network with fellow believers in the United States and Europe. Although they may appear isolated on the map in Figure 8.1, they may nonetheless be part of rich Twitter networks that exist beyond this specific geographical space.

## Networks in action

These new data on the shape and extent of the overall Australian Twitter user base, which Figure 8.1 represents, may now be used to shed new light on the Twitter user activities that hashtag datasets describe. Where previously it was possible to determine the total volume of activity within a hashtag, or to count the total number of unique users participating in the dataset, we are now able to develop a considerably more detailed picture of the spread of a hashtag, both in total and over time. Figure 8.3 illustrates these opportunities by comparing participation patterns in the #auspol and #ausvotes hashtags (in darker colours) against the backdrop of the overall map (in light grey): participants in #auspol are recruited largely from that part of the overall network that we have previously identified as being centred around politics, news, and journalism, and the level of participation in the hashtag is strongest in a small cluster to the left of the network that closer qualitative analysis of key accounts and their tweets reveals to be dominated by particularly hard-line conservative views (one such user threatens in his profile description that he will block any left-winger who tries to follow his tweets, for example). Participation in #ausvotes during the 2010 election campaign, on the other hand, while still especially strong in the news and politics area of the overall map, is distributed considerably more evenly across all areas of the network; this

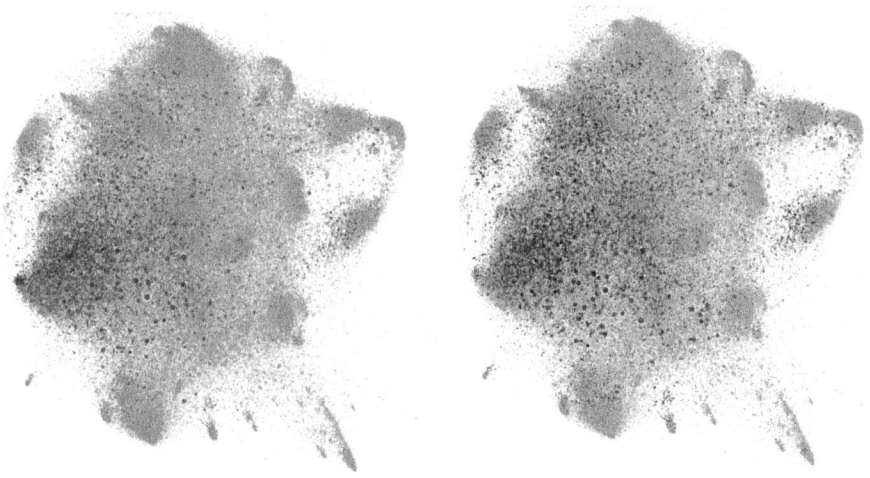

*Figure 8.3* Participation by Australian users in the hashtags #auspol (left) and #ausvotes (2010, right)

is due perhaps to the fact that compulsory voting requires all eligible Australians to participate in the election at least to a minimal extent, as well as to the fact that Twitter was also used as an important back channel to election-night television coverage (Burgess and Bruns 2012a); both these factors appear likely to engender a more widespread use of the #ausvotes hashtag beyond established 'political junkies' (Coleman 2006). Notably, activity by users in the hard-line conservative cluster is substantially quieter in #ausvotes than it is in #auspol.

Further analysis, which is beyond the scope of this chapter, can further break down these overall patterns—for example, by distinguishing the various phases of the election. It is able to document the differences in widespread popular engagement in the #ausvotes hashtag, between the early days of the election campaign and the final event of election night itself, or to show how actively different participants in #auspol react to the events of the day. Similarly, by using hashtag data to show which users tweet it at what point, it is possible to trace how specific information (for example, links to new articles about political matters, retweets, or other viral memes) is disseminated across the network over time. A useful metaphor to explore the potential of such approaches is the brain scan: it can be used to show how specific electrical impulses (tweets) traverse the synaptic structures of the brain (the Australian Twitter network) in response to various external stimuli.

While hashtags such as #auspol and #ausvotes are necessarily centred mainly around already identified thematic clusters in the overall network, other hashtags behave considerably differently; this is true, for example, for major televised events that draw participation from a wide range of the Twitter audience (and increasingly incorporate such back channel activities deliberately; see Harrington et al. 2012). Figure 8.4 shows the user activity patterns in the hashtags for popular

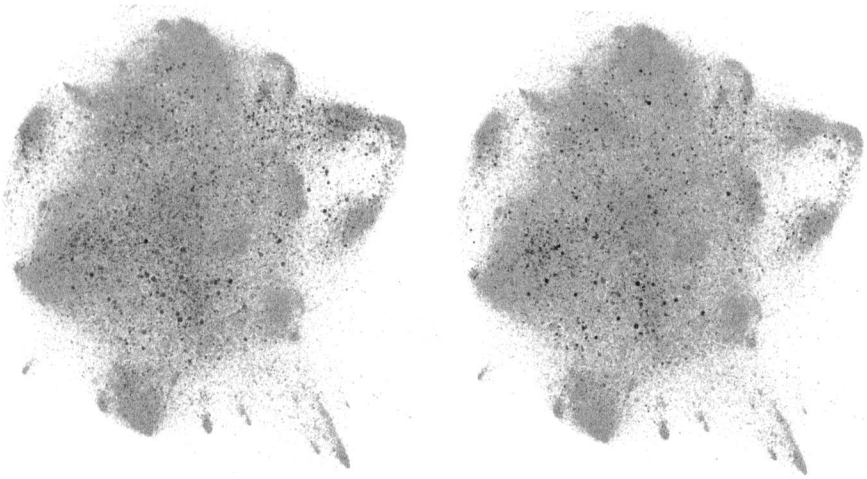

*Figure 8.4*  Participation by Australian users in the hashtags #masterchef (left) and #royal-wedding (right)

Australian cooking show *Masterchef* (#masterchef) and for the 2011 wedding of Prince William and Catherine Middleton (#royalwedding). These examples indicate substantial levels of activity across the overall map, pointing to the fact that these events and their coverage reach mass audiences rather than specific interest groups.

This investigation of both the depth (volume) and breadth (network spread) of Twitter participation also has immediate practical value for media researchers and media organizations: it provides a useful indication of the specific target audiences for diverse media events, and of the broadcasts' ability to engage with and enlist such audiences in active participation. Such research extends well beyond the hashtag datasets that we have explored so far; instead, it also becomes possible to examine the spread of key terms, of references to specific organizations or individuals, and of links to particular websites (at the domain or URL level). This style of analysis therefore also has substantial applications in marketing and brand communication.

To illustrate this potential, Figure 8.5 compares the sharing of links to the websites of the Australian Broadcasting Corporation (abc.net.au; ABC News sections only) and middle-of-the-road news site news.com.au, including in tweets where such URLs were shortened using t.co, bit.ly, or other URL shorteners, during February 2013. This figure shows the relative distribution of audiences for both sites across the overall network and its interest-based clusters: as one of the leading providers of news on state and federal politics in Australia, ABC News has a significant footprint especially amongst the politics-related clusters in the network; news.com.au, by contrast, has a less central role in such discussions and instead provides a greater range of general, entertainment, and sports news, resulting in a more scattered presence throughout the map. This indicates the relative strengths

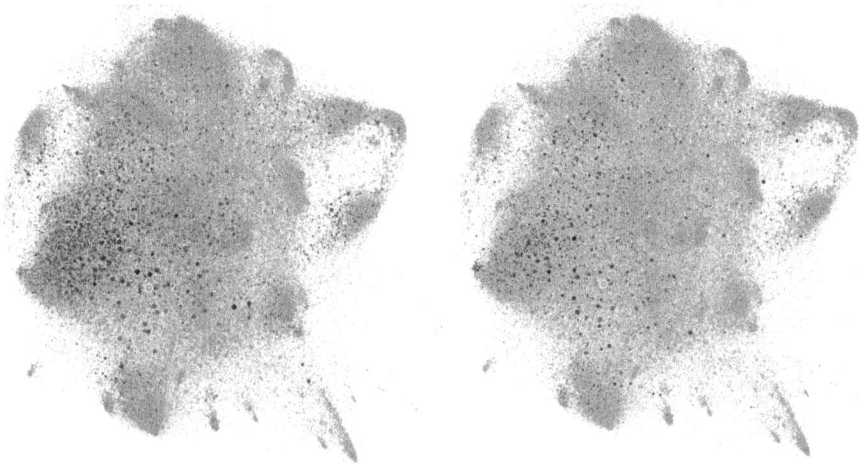

*Figure 8.5* Sharing of links to ABC News (left) and news.com.au (left) by Australian users

and weaknesses of each of these news organizations across the fields they cover and can be used to inform the further strategic positioning of each site.

Space does not permit us to outline a range of other possibilities for combining existing datasets with the network of follower/followee connections in the Australian Twittersphere—but at the same time, a network map such as this is rarely an end in itself, and rather constitutes a means to an end. In the present case, for example, the visualization of Twitter activity across the network map serves as a device to generate further research questions and challenges: once the different clusters have been identified, for example, it becomes possible to compare and contrast their specific compositions (how inward-looking or externally connected are they; how central are their best-connected nodes?), or to explore differences in the specific Twitter activities of the members of different clusters (do different clusters tweet more or less actively than others; do they prefer different news sources?).

## Beyond hashtags, towards 'big data'

Beyond the map itself, the identification of a large part of the total Australian Twitter population also enables the development of entirely new models of gathering Twitter data, in addition to topic-based, 'hashtag' studies. At least in theory, the database of Australian users that we have gathered would also enable us to track the public communication activities of all (or of a selected subset) of these users, to develop a more heterogeneous understanding of the day-to-day activities, interests, and contributions of Australian Twitter users. This substantially more comprehensive dataset would not need to rely on the topic selection process required to collect hashtagged tweets, and in particular it might cast important new light on the thematic and social dynamics of everyday, 'ordinary' tweeting outside of the limelight of the kinds of public events (elections, uprisings, Olympic Games) framed as significant by the existing news values of the traditional media.

Such even more data-intensive, and arguably also even more data-*driven*, research (which gathers Twitter data at large scale and on an ongoing basis in order to identify and explore activity patterns, ahead of formulating specific hypotheses to be addressed in the research) is possible in principle, but severely hampered in practice by the increasingly restrictive nature of API-based access to Twitter data (see Puschmann and Burgess 2013). While the tracking and capture of hash-tagged tweets remains comparatively trivial and unencumbered, Twitter requires researchers wishing to track more than 5,000 active users at any one time to purchase data access from its commercial reseller Gnip, at volume-dependent costs that are likely to remain unaffordable for publicly funded projects or individual researchers. Truly 'big data' research into the use of Twitter (and similar social media platforms) for the most part remains the realm of commercial market research, thereby limiting the availability of reliable and verifiable information on the diverse roles of such social media platforms in contemporary society (see Burgess and Bruns 2012b). Considering the growing role of social media in public, private, and 'privately public' (Papacharissi 2010; also cf. Schmidt 2011) communication, this lack of researcher access to such important communicative resources is deeply problematic.

However, even if and when such access is available, there remain considerable other challenges in the further development of the digital humanities. First, many of the tools and technologies required to work with such 'big data' resources remain in the early stages of their development, and there is a tendency for the simultaneous development of similar tools in separate research facilities that remain unaware of one another's efforts. Our own research project has chosen to make the research tools we have developed publicly available under Creative Commons licences wherever possible, therefore, and to similarly document our methodologies in significant detail through the project's website, http://mappingonlinepublics.net/. Further, such methodological innovation takes place under precarious conditions, as continuing changes to the affordances and functionality of the Twitter API document: changes to API request and data formats, and changes to the rules and conditions of access, may undermine once promising research approaches at very short notice, and without an opportunity for appeal or renegotiation.

Finally, both the development and the use of such research methodologies and tools also requires a combination of disciplinary expertise that is not readily found amongst humanities researchers, nor developed in mainstream research training. Working with 'big data' necessarily requires a certain degree of mathematical and statistical knowledge—not commonly a strength of media, cultural, and communication studies graduates; social media APIs and the tools to use them also necessitate considerable technical expertise. There is a considerable risk that mathematical and technical tasks are treated as black-box activities that may be delegated to research assistants and developers but are never questioned or problematized; this approach limits the range of interpretive activities that are possible, as well as hindering further methodological and conceptual innovation.

Finally, we are acutely aware of the limitations to our own ability to present a full discussion of our approaches to visualizing the Twitter network maps we have presented above and their implications, not for the straightforward representation of actually existing networked publics, but in fact for the production of new 'calculated publics' (Gillespie 2014). In addition to the choices we have made about the size and composition of the original datasets (such as focusing on the most connected Australian accounts), each visualization involves a substantial number of choices about visualization algorithms and their specific settings. Each of these choices would have produced different versions of the 'calculated public' we are calling 'the Australian Twittersphere', but a detailed critique of these choices would not have been possible in the space of this chapter. Indeed, we have gone dangerously close to treating the data visualization process as a black box, where network data are fed in at one end and a network graph is spat out at the other. Highlighting these limitations at least serves as a reminder of the performativity of digital methods and an acknowledgement that there is far more work to be done as we further develop the intersection of social media and digital humanities via data-driven research methods and practices. Through reflexive critique, ongoing research training, and interdisciplinary engagement we need to continue working at cracking open and reassembling the black boxes that are the very stuff of the 'computational turn' (Berry 2012).

## Note

1. Higher-resolution versions of all graphs in this chapter can be found at http://mappingonlinepublics.net/2014/01/01/repurposing-appendix/.

## Works cited

Berry, David. (2011). 'The Computational Turn: Thinking About the Digital Humanities'. *Culture Machine* 12. Available at: http://www.culturemachine.net/index.php/cm/article/view/440/470.

Berry, David, ed. (2012). *Understanding Digital Humanities*. London: Palgrave Macmillan.

boyd, danah. (2010). 'Social Network Sites as Networked Publics: Affordances, Dynamics, and Implications'. In *Networked Self: Identity, Community, and Culture on Social Network Sites*, ed. Zizi Papacharissi, 39–58. New York: Routledge.

boyd, danah, Scott Golder, and Gilad Lotan. (2010). 'Tweet, Tweet, Retweet: Conversational Aspects of Retweeting on Twitter'. Hawaii International Conference on System Sciences (HICSS-43), 5–8 January 2010, Kauai, Hawaii. Available at: http://www.danah.org/papers/TweetTweetRetweet.pdf.

Bruns, Axel, and Hallvard Moe. (2014). 'Structural Layers of Communication on Twitter'. In *Twitter and Society*, eds. Katrin Weller, Axel Bruns, Jean Burgess, Merja Mahrt, Cornelius Puschmann, 15–28. New York: Peter Lang.

Bruns, Axel, and Jean Burgess. (2011). '#ausvotes: How Twitter Covered the 2010 Australian Federal Election'. *Communication, Politics, and Culture* 44, no. 2: 37–56.

Bruns, Axel, and Stefan Stieglitz. (2012). 'Quantitative Approaches to Comparing Communication Patterns on Twitter'. *Journal of Technology in Human Services* 30, nos. 3–4 (July): 160–85.

Bruns, Axel, and Stefan Stieglitz. (2013). 'Towards More Systematic Twitter Analysis: Metrics for Tweeting Activities'. *International Journal of Social Research Methodology*, 22 January. DOI: 10.1080/13645579.2012.756095.

Bruns, Axel, Jean Burgess, Kate Crawford, and Frances Shaw. (2012). *#qldfloods and @QPSMedia: Crisis Communication on Twitter in the 2011 South East Queensland Floods.* Brisbane: ARC Centre of Excellence for Creative Industries and Innovation. Available at: http://cci.edu.au/floodsreport.pdf.

Bull, Tim. (2010). 'How Many Australian Twitter Users Are There, and Where Are They From?' *Tribalytic blog*, 13 May. Available at: http://blog.tribalytic.com/how-many-australian-twitter – users-are-there-and-where-are-they-from/.

Burgess, Jean, and Axel Bruns. (2012a). '(Not) the Twitter Election: The Dynamics of the #ausvotes Conversation in Relation to the Australian Media Ecology'. *Journalism Practice* 6, no. 3: 384–402. DOI:10.1080/17512786.2012.663610.

Burgess, Jean, and Axel Bruns. (2012b). 'Twitter Archives and the Challenges of "Big Social Data" for Media and Communication Research'. *M/C Journal* 15, no. 5. Available at: http://journal.media-culture.org.au/index.php/mcjournal/article/view/561.

Burns, Alex, and Ben Eltham. (2009). 'Twitter Free Iran: An Evaluation of Twitter's Role in Public Diplomacy and Information Operations in Iran's 2009 Election Crisis'. *Record of the Communications Policy and Research Forum 2009*, Sydney, 298–310.

Christensen, Christian. (2011). 'Twitter Revolutions? Addressing Social Media and Dissent'. *Communication Review* 14, no. 3: 155–57.

Coleman, Stephen. (2006). 'How the Other Half Votes: Big Brother Viewers and the 2005 General Election'. *International Journal of Cultural Studies* 9, no. 4: 457–79. DOI:10.1177/1367877906069895.

Deller, Ruth. (2011). 'Twittering On: Audience Research and Participation Using Twitter'. *Participations* 8, no. 1. Available at: http://www.participations.org/Volume%208/Issue%201/deller.htm.

Dröge, Evelyn, Parinaz Maghferat, Cornelius Puschmann, Julia Verbina, and Katrin Weller. (2011). 'Konferenz-Tweets: Ein Ansatz zur Analyse der Twitter-Kommunikation bei wissenschaftlichen Konferenzen'. *Proceedings of the 12th International Symposium for Information Science*, 9–11 March 2011, Hildesheim. Verlag Werner Hülsbusch. Available at: http://ynada.com/pubs/isi2010.pdf.

Gephi.org. (2012). 'Gephi, an Open Source Graph Visualization and Manipulation Software'. Available at: http://gephi.org/.

Gillespie, Tarleton. (2014). 'The Relevance of Algorithms'. In *Media Technologies*, ed. Tarleton Gillespie, Pablo Boczkowski, and Kirsten Foot. Cambridge, MA: MIT Press.

Harrington, Stephen, Tim Highfield, and Axel Bruns. (2012). 'More Than a Backchannel: Twitter and Television'. In *Audience Interactivity and Participation*, ed. José Manuel Noguera, 13–17. Brussels: COST Action Transforming Audiences, Transforming Societies. Available at: http://www.cost-transforming-audiences.eu/system/files/essays-and-interview-essays-18-06-12.pdf.

Hartley, John. (2009). 'From Cultural Studies to Cultural Science'. *Cultural Science* 2, no. 1. Available at: http://www.cultural-science.org/journal/index.php/culturalscience/article/viewArticle/19/68.

Highfield, Tim, Stephen Harrington, and Axel Bruns. (2013). 'Twitter as a Technology for Audiencing and Fandom: The #Eurovision Phenomenon'. *Information, Communication, and Society*, 3 January. DOI: 10.1080/1369118X.2012.756053.

Jacomy, Mathieu, Sebastien Heymann, Tommaso Venturini, and Mathieu Bastian. (2011). 'ForceAtlas2: A Graph Layout Algorithm for Handy Network Visualization'. Discussion paper, Paris, 29 August. Available at: http://webatlas.fr/tempshare/ForceAtlas2_Paper.pdf.

Larsson, Anders Olof, and Hallvard Moe. (2011). 'Studying Political Microblogging: Twitter Users in the 2010 Swedish Election Campaign'. *New Media and Society* 14, no. 5: 729–47.

Lotan, Gilad, Erhardt Graeff, Mike Ananny, Devin Gaffney, Ian Pearce, and danah boyd. (2011). 'The Revolutions Were Tweeted: Information Flows During the 2011 Tunisian and Egyptian Revolutions'. *International Journal of Communication* 5: 1375–405.

Manovich, Lev. (2012). 'Trending: The Promises and the Challenges of Big Social Data'. In *Debates in the Digital Humanities*, ed. Matthew K. Gold, 460–75. Minneapolis: University of Minnesota Press.

Marwick, Alice. E., and danah boyd. (2011). 'I Tweet Honestly, I Tweet Passionately: Twitter Users, Context Collapse, and the Imagined Audience'. *New Media and Society* 13, no. 1: 114–33.

Mendoza, Marcelo, Barbara Poblete, and Carlos Castillo. (2010). 'Twitter Under Crisis: Can We Trust What We RT?' *First Workshop on Social Media Analytics* (SOMA '10), Washington, D.C.

Palen, Leysia, Kate Starbird, Sarah Vieweg, and Anabda Hughes. (2010). 'Twitter-Based Information Distribution During the 2009 Red River Valley Flood Threat'. *Bulletin of the American Society for Information Science and Technology* 36, no. 5: 13–17.

Papacharissi, Zizi A. (2010). *A Private Sphere: Democracy in a Digital Age*. Cambridge: Polity.

Papacharissi, Zizi A. (2011). 'Conclusion: A Networked Self'. In *A Networked Self: Identity, Community, and Culture on Social Network Sites*, ed. Zizi Papacharissi, 304–18. New York: Routledge.

Puschmann, Cornelius, and Jean Burgess. (2013). 'The Politics of Twitter Data'. *HIIG Discussion Paper Series* 2013–01. Available at: http://dx.doi.org/10.2139/ssrn.2206225.

Schmidt, Jan-Hinrik. (2011). *Das neue Netz: Merkmale, Praktiken und Folgen des Web 2.0*. 2nd ed. Konstanz: UVK.

Stieglitz, Stefan, and Linh Dang-Xuan. (2013). 'Social Media and Political Communication: A Social Media Analytics Framework'. In *Social Network Analysis and Mining* 3, no. 4: 1–15. DOI: 10.1007/s13278-012-0079-3.

Twitter. (2012a). 'Olympic (and Twitter) Records'. *Twitter Blog*, 12 August. Available at: http://blog.twitter.com/2012/08/olympic-and-twitter-records.html.

Twitter. (2012b). 'GET Users/lookup'. *Twitter Developers*. Available at: https://dev.twitter.com/docs/api/1.1/get/users/lookup.

Weller, Katrin, Evelyn Dröge, and Cornelius Puschmann. (2011). 'Citation Analysis in Twitter: Approaches for Defining and Measuring Information Flows Within Tweets During Scientific Conferences'. First Workshop on Making Sense of Microposts, #MSM2011, Heraklion, 30 May 2011. Available at: http://files.ynada.com/papers/msm2011.pdf.

Wilken, Rowan. (2013). 'Twitter and Geographical Location'. In *Twitter and Society*, eds. Katrin Weller, Axel Bruns, Jean Burgess, Merja Mahrt, Cornelius Puschmann, 155–68. New York: Peter Lang.

# 9

# iResearch

## What Do Smartphones Tell Us about the Digital Human?

*Mark Coté*

> I don't believe society understands what happens when everything is available, knowable, and recorded by everyone all the time.
>
> —Eric Schmidt, in Jenkins 2010

When Google CEO Eric Schmidt reflected on the explosion of big data and its far-reaching implications, humanity was collectively generating about 6.8 exabytes of data (6.8 quintillion bytes) every two days. Only eight years before, it took more than one year for that much data to be produced—five exabytes in all of 2002. This big-data explosion continues apace; through to 2020, the International Data Corporation predicts a 50-fold increase in data generation, reaching 40 zettabytes (40,000 exabytes) annually, or five terabytes for each person on the planet (Gantz and Reinsel 2011).

Such staggering numbers are difficult to comprehend, and we face a monumental task of understanding what it means to live in the age of big data. Here I delimit the focus and concentrate on what can be called big social data (BSD) as opposed to big data.[1] Such a focus omits much of the data produced, which is strictly machine-to-machine—that is, sourced from industrial and domestic sensor networks, big science projects like the Large Hadron Collider, and financial markets—and concentrates on metadata and symbolic content that people generate in their everyday lives through new mediated cultural and communicative practices. BSD delineates the social and cultural realm of data: every time we go online, every smartphone interaction, every app we use, and all our clicks and purchases. BSD also includes machine-to-machine data, but only in the form of the metadata that mobile devices continuously generate, tracing the who, where, and when of the 'digital human'.

The scope of BSD remains enormous: two million people search on Google at any given second; Facebook processes ten terabytes of posts, likes, and photos a day; Twitter, seven terabytes of tweets; and in the United States alone, there are 6.1 trillion text messages a day (Hunt 2013). Social media corporations, advertisers, business, and governments are all studying the social production of data intently, seeking new profits and the improved delivery of service. BSD is also reconfiguring the life of its producer, what I call the digital human.[2] This figure lives predominantly in an assemblage with the smartphone, is increasingly ubiquitously connected, and accesses and produces data while in quotidian motion and at rest. In short, BSD is an important new source of born-digital material and offers privileged insight into contemporary cultural heritage.

I propose that digital humanities is a cognate discipline for the study of BSD. For example, witness the Prosopography of Anglo-Saxon England (PASE) and its large database on recorded inhabitants of early medieval England; or the Proceedings of the Old Bailey, notable as the largest database of non-elite people ever published; or myriad projects using crowdsourcing and other forms of scholarly data mining. Further, from its beginnings in humanities computing, the discipline has long established the interdependence of tools and the production of knowledge. BSD is mined and aggregated, producing information—knowledge—that 'pings' back to us, increasingly enabling and constraining how we can live. Yet most of that transpires in the proprietary environment of private enterprise or the security state. There is a pressing need, however, for critical scholarly inquiry. My research problem is less about the epistemic impact of tools on knowledge production and more about the ontological impact on being qua digital being—thus, the aforementioned digital human, which can be a contemporary object of study for the digital humanities. To paraphrase Andrew Prescott (2012) paraphrasing Patrick Juola (2008), the smartphone can act as a 'killer app' here, and be deployed as an innovative tool for theorizing and understanding the rapidly changing condition of the digital human under BSD.

I proceed first by outlining my movement as a media theorist into the digital humanities through a collaborative process of 'building things' with the Victoria e-Research Strategic Initiative (VeRSI). Here I emphasize the transformative effects of such collaborations. As a media theorist, the tools I used were all conceptual, and thus I regarded the smartphone as an object of study for theoretical inquiry. A very different research vision emerges in a collaborative environment replete with technical and infrastructural support. Therein, the smartphone shifted from being a mere object of study to a research tool. Thus, I describe how we developed the Proof of Concept. I then suggest how such digital humanities research can uniquely facilitate the conceptualization of the digital human and critical scholarship on BSD.

## iResearch: The smartphone from object of study to research tool

BSD and the digital human can be situated in a broader trend dating back to the rise of business computation, more flexible and globally diffused production, and the spread of the productive zones of capital into everyday life. The waxing importance of cultural work is a key element of that computational-cultural diffusion, what Lazzarato called 'immaterial labour' (1996). This concept signals the growing importance of cultural content across production and consumption, in practices not traditionally thought of as work: 'defining and fixing cultural and artistic standards, fashions, tastes, consumer norms, and, more strategically, public opinion' (1996, 2). The Internet was nascent when Lazzarato developed this concept, but he emphasized dynamics that became central to social media and the generation of BSD, namely social relationships, the integration of communication, and enlargement of productive cooperation. In short, he outlined how activities that were once solely cultural became a source of profit, and, as such, a form of work. When social media was becoming popular, Jennifer Pybus and I deployed immaterial labour to frame the conflation of media consumption and production therein, rendering it 'immaterial labour 2.0' to highlight the media environment of the distributed network and new cultural practices that produced digital subjectivities (Coté and Pybus 2007, 2011). These are the core born-digital practices of user-generated content, and their affective and communicative relations comprised not only important new cultural practices but also a source of value for emerging new media corporations.

With the rise of the smartphone, my research focused on mobility, location, and information and the increase in user-generated content across mobile platforms. I found it challenging to adequately theorize this new assemblage, its attendant data flows, and its transformative effects on the increasingly digital human. This mobile diffusion of the aforementioned cultural, communicative, and cooperative capacities is indicative of how enmeshed our lives are becoming with the new information economy, including the way we live with our smartphones and other mobile touch-screen devices. One might say this new intersection of the human and digital tools is predicated on a *syntax,* a concept developed by the late French paleoanthropologist Andre Leroi-Gourhan to denote the human's deeply recursive and constitutive relationship with technology: 'This operating syntax is suggested by memory and comes into being as [an extra-discursive] product of the brain and the physical environment' (1993, 114). In other words, just as all native speakers know syntax without formal study or even comprehensive understanding, similarly we quickly develop a syntactic relationship with technology. This point is worth developing, as it indicates what is so opportune and necessary about the digital humanities, at least from this trajectory of media theory. Leroi-Gourhan uses the term 'technics' to denote how our gestures and tools are organized in the operational sequence of a veritable syntax. Further, he hypothesizes that the structural complexity of symbolic production and language corresponds to the level of contemporaneous technics. Whereas technology denotes instrumentality, technics offers a richer concept for the digital humanities. With technics, the syntax of gesture and artefact is constitutively related to symbolic production, and thus always imbricated at the core of the humanities. This paradigm offers exciting opportunities for understanding the structural complexity of the digital human and its cultural forms. Following it requires a methodological engagement with the technics of BSD that generate this new kind of born-digital material, a task ill suited to media studies alone.

It was truly serendipitous, then, that a chance opportunity arose for me to collaborate with my then-university's associate director of e-research, Lyle Winton, and, in turn, gain infrastructural and technical support for research from VeRSI. Two things should be noted here. The support I was offered was modest. VeRSI is an Australian consortium serving the state of Victoria, and as such my access was limited, given that its services are shared among seven different universities and two government bodies. Further, mine was an exploratory project with only modest internal funding, further truncating available support. Nonetheless, there was a shared enthusiasm and desire to explore the possibilities of smartphones as a research tool, especially given that my VeRSI collaborators typically work on big science projects, making us all neophytes regarding smartphones and app development. Methodologically, this was a true and shared pedagogical opportunity. These factors put us on the modest fringe of the digital humanities, especially in relation to other projects examining mobile new media and big data—for example, the Lev Manovich Software Studies initiative, handsomely supported by the Mellon Foundation, or the Queensland University of Technology's ARC Centre of Excellence for Creative Industries and Innovation's Media Ecologies and Methodological Innovation project.

My VeRSI collaborators—Jared Winton, Gary Ruben, Greg Long, and Kieran Spear—provided ongoing researcher-driven support for the mobile application development project plan, dubbed 'iResearch'. We were fully aware that the smartphone was already being used as a research tool—in commercial ethnography, for example; via crowdsourcing apps for mobile focus groups like dscout; or in qualitative research platforms like ethos, Revelation, and Qualvu. Academic researchers are also increasingly turning to mobile apps for field research ranging from archaeology to community health. We, however, wanted to crack into the born-digital material of symbolic content and its related metadata, which remain largely locked in a proprietary environment. Thus we used markers of mobility, location, and information as coordinates for gathering data on how people used their smartphones to access and produce information through social media apps. In turn, we developed a Proof of Concept, and I address here the challenges faced in bringing it to fruition. Our inquiry began with a series of practical considerations, the most important being a question of scale.

BSD is defined as the metadata and symbolic content we produce in our everyday lives, primarily with our mobile devices, although also with laptops and desktops. The unprecedentedly massive scale means that a more rigorous and comprehensive engagement with BSD could easily scale up to a larger research environment—for example, running MapReduce in a Hadoop cluster. Our initial inquiry, however, was only seeking to establish a Proof of Concept and demonstrate an ability to gather and store some of the born-digital material of BSD. Such research requires ethics approval. While this does not necessarily require anonymization, researchers must be cognizant that strategies for protection notwithstanding, forensic analysis could reveal user identity.[3] For the time being, we kept in mind the concise and cogent point made by danah boyd and Kate Crawford: 'Just because it is accessible doesn't make it ethical' (2012, 671). Finally comes the practical point of the accessibility of data, a question that depends upon the platform we chose. While we sought a single solution for both iPhones and Androids, we quickly realized that was simply not a shorter-term possibility.

Androids and iPhones, which comprise 91 per cent of all smartphones, use different operating systems (International Data Corporation 2013). Key differences between these competing operating systems impact the kinds of tools and apps that can be developed. The iPhone uses the iOS mobile operating system, functioning on a closed source model and proprietary software. The software development kit has been available since 2007, and many consumer apps are available. The app development process, however, is highly centralized. All third-party native applications must be sanctioned by Apple and are only accessible through its App Store. These conditions in no way preclude researchers from following this path. It is, however, more time-consuming, more expensive, and less flexible, and there is no guarantee whatsoever of academic freedom. Judging by recent developments, the outcomes are quite to the contrary. For example, Drone+, an app developed by a New York University graduate student, used available data on US drone strikes in Pakistan, Somalia, and Yemen overlaid on an interactive map and would send push notification for each new drone strike. The app, however, was thrice rejected by Apple due to 'objectionable content', and because it was 'not useful or entertaining enough' (Wingfield 2012). This rejection stands as a warning to the difficulties academic researchers might face if they want to develop a research app for the iPhone that might in any way be construed as critical.

Facing this closed, tightly controlled, and highly proprietary environment, we used publicly available apps in a workaround solution. The first step was to utilize a virtual private network (VPN), which enables remote users—as smartphones do—to securely connect to the Internet via a private network. Through a simple set of instructions, users could reconfigure their phone settings and establish the VPN connection in two clicks. This 'virtual connection' means the mobile device communicates via a VPN server to connect with the Internet and the destination, such as Facebook or Twitter. The research benefit is that the VPN channels all network traffic through a central controlled environment. There we could log the IP address of the smartphone, identifying the user as well as the destination IP address and the time of communication. Open-source software like Snort or tcpdump allowed us to identify specific users through VPN log-in information and correlate the data. In short, this solution passively gathers data on the user, the social media used, and time of use.

What remained was gathering location information for iPhone users. Again, there was an existing solution. We used OpenPaths.cc, a free mobile app that tracks the movement of your phone, visualizes user movement on an interactive map, provides a secure data locker for location information, and allows that raw data to be downloaded in a variety of formats (JSON, CSV, or KML). My VeRSI colleagues wrote software using Ruby script to correlate user data from OpenPaths with that from the VPN. The result is a dataset comprising user ID, time, location, and social media used, which offers many opportunities for mining and analysis. The major plus of this approach is that the components are free. Use of a VPN with a large research cohort, however, could prove to be very expensive. As well, VPN connectivity is limited unless you use proprietary software, as smartphone battery-saving features automatically disconnect after a short period of inactivity, requiring users to constantly reconnect. In our test run, we found that even the two clicks needed were often an insurmountable barrier, so users were only intermittently connected, and the data gathered was partial. Finally, the OpenPaths location information is not always reliably finely granulated, and thus is of inconsistent accuracy.

The Android operating system holds a 75 per cent market share compared to Apple's 15 per cent (International Data Corporation 2012). Owned by Google, it is Linux-based, with open source code and permissive licensing, meaning it can be fully modified and is inherently open to app development. For this operating system we were able to modify an existing one, the Android OS Monitor, that captured data on the user, the social media app deployed, and time. The Android OS Monitor lists all TCP connections, identifies the app making them without requiring root privileges, and allows available sensor information to be logged. Ruben and Spear modified the app to obtain location information and log the sensor and location data, producing a dataset similar to that of the iPhone. One clear benefit is that the app can run persistently in the background. Another benefit is that it did not require users to regularly log on, and as a result was far more consistent in data gathering, making it a more reliable research tool. For both operating systems, then, we were able to successfully develop a rudimentary but fully functional research tool for gathering elemental BSD on mobile social media use.

My VeRSI colleagues emphasized the trade-offs inherent in following either a customized solution or in repurposing an existing one. A custom solution enables more closely calibrated and efficient monitoring of the desired data, yet carries the ongoing burden of support for the different software. Repurposing existing software requires less ongoing support, but it may not behave in an optimum way and may demand further resources for combining and transforming the data. The latter approach also depends upon open source software, from which we benefited greatly, and without which we would have faced prohibitive costs. VeRSI shares a commitment to open research; as such, the code and solutions we developed are all available to any interested researchers, which is in stark contrast to commercial research apps. The aforementioned ethos app is designed not for academics but for corporations that want to better understand how their brand fits into consumers' lives, capturing data via video, pictures, audio, and text. It is designed thus not for scholarly inquiry but for corporate '[d]ialogues that are instantaneous and rich, and will change the way large organizations interact with their consumers and employees' (Murphy 2011).

I cite this quotation to highlight a primary challenge with BSD: moving its research, analysis, and understanding beyond direct market application. This parallels a more general challenge faced by the digital humanities as identified by Alan Liu, namely 'the post-industrial paradigm of knowledge work' (2012, 10). In this paradigm I would include the pressures that scholars face when researching in a primarily proprietary environment. The depth and breadth of proprietary barriers was a singular finding of our Proof of Concept. The myriad practical workaround solutions required for any sustained research focus on BSD by digital humanists will, however, provide what Liu calls 'a critical awareness of the larger social, economic and cultural issues at stake' (2012, 11). Further, the unprecedented depth and breadth of BSD necessitates multiple projects engaging an array of humanist scholars from media and communication studies to cultural studies to history, among others. I have suggested the smartphone as but one innovative research tool to be deployed as part of this task. Regardless, BSD and the digital human offer commodious opportunities for doing theory, as this assemblage of the human and technology is cohered in unprecedented complexity and through previously unknown computational power. To conclude, I outline a particular theoretical paradigm that my aforementioned collaboration helped me to clarify, and that I am pursuing.

## From the digital humanities to the digital human

Early advancements using technology for critical inquiry into the possibilities of a knowing subject and the general conditions of knowledge under BSD are well under way. The comprehensive platform-focused research on Twitter, for example, at the Media Ecologies and Methodological Innovation initiative (see Bruns and Burgess in this volume) is particularly notable. First, it helps substantiate the claim made over a decade ago by Lev Manovich that the database is *the* cultural form of the twenty-first century (2001). Second, it is a forward-looking example of the kind of media-specific analysis of texts called for by Hayles (2005), and one clearly in the realm of media, as opposed to literary studies.[4] While BSD is eminently suitable for myriad forms of narrative inquiry and textual analysis— after all, data mining proceeds on semantic relationality and keywords—it can also help us radically rethink the very concept of mediation and its attendant assemblages. This rethink, in part, answers the recent calls of many digital humanists for a greater focus on mediation in a broadly situated 'Digital Humanities 2.0' (Berry 2011; Davidson 2008; McPherson 2009; Schnapp and Presner 2013). BSD, if framed via mediation, enables the contemporary parameters of the human and technology to be reckoned, in turn repositioning the digital humanities more in line with the practices of BSD, and better able to engage in significant theoretical advancements vis-à-vis the human. I propose doing so by first emphasizing the materiality of BSD—the kinds of data of which it is composed, its computational environment, and the algorithmic practices through which it is processed (Coté 2014). This approach accounts for the materialities of nonhuman bodies and objects to which we are related, and the technical transmission and processes of culture and life. BSD, then, is a matrix through which we can parse contemporary assemblages of the human–nonhuman. In short, as an object of study, BSD can be framed as a medium, what Mitchell and Hansen call 'the notion of a form of life, of a general environment for living—for thinking, perceiving, sensing, feeling— as such' (2010, xii). Studying BSD using the technologies that constitute it offers conceptual insights into the possibilities for the digital human to 'know thyself'.

The second step is to rethink the condition of the human itself, in addition to the materiality of its mediation. Protracted cross-disciplinary debates have taken place over the possibilities and conditions of the human. For many, the posthuman is now a preferred trope (Wolfe 2010). This reconceptualization reflects the myriad unsettling of the 'human': biological, through genetic intervention; poststructural/postmodern, through symbolic decentring and a relational, not universal, verity; and technological, in becoming cyborgs that are both/and dystopian/utopian. I situate the digital human as a nuanced differential of the posthuman to further unsettle the notion that there ever was a normative human outside a constitutive relation with technology. BSD, then, can be understood as an important and active material element among the assemblage of nonhuman forces with which our lives, labour, and culture unfold. This conceptual framing of the digital human can be assisted by an emerging genealogy of feminist theory, a useful trajectory of new materialism that shifts questions of embodiment to that of nonhuman 'agential matter' (Barad 2003) in a 'prosthetic culture' comprising a complex web of technologically mediated social relations (Braidotti 2006). To be clear, this is not the humanism of the transcendental, a priori knowing subject and normative conditions for knowledge. Instead, a new materialist medium theory denotes complex and recursive relations, and as such the question is not what technology does to the a priori human but how it helps make us human.

The digital human, then, denotes an historically grounded medium specificity, directly challenging any a priori or transcendental human nature. Further, the digital human can be doubly articulated for the digital humanities. First, it indicates a methodological covalence in the BSD database, from the epistemic inquiries of innovative textual analysis to ontological reflections on a mediated environment for life. Second, it conceptually links my project to a paradigm established by Leroi-Gourhan that positions the human as always already in a constitutive relationship with technology. Elsewhere I have written extensively on this theoretical paradigm as it relates to the human and technology (Coté 2010, 2012). More recently, Frabetti (2011) has linked it to a rethinking of the digital humanities, primarily in temporal terms. Here I attempt to concisely explicate Leroi-Gourhan's concept of originary technicity, steeped as it has been through the work of a number of interlocutors (Derrida 1976; Beardsworth 1996; Stiegler 1998). Schematically, it means that human speciation occurred in a deeply recursive relationship with technology. This startling claim, that we have only ever been human in an assemblage with technology, undermines much of Western metaphysics, which from Plato on has insisted on a strict separation of the natural human and artificial technology.[5] Further—and this is a point of particular relevance to the digital humanities—not only is the human an inherently prosthetic being; tools also function as a storehouse of memory. The human, then, becomes human through the exteriorization of memory, stored in technical objects, from the most rudimentary lithic industry to writing to 1s and 0s. Stiegler (1998) stresses this point: memory, formerly limited to living mnemonic support, is for evermore accumulated and preserved in technics. In my reading, memory and technics constitute the enduring foci of the digital humanities.

Memory and technics, then, form the mutable crucible of humanity and represent the intersection through which culture emerges. Such a paradigm productively repositions the digital humanities for a rich examination of the born-digital material of BSD. As Frabetti asks, 'Have not the humanities always been concerned with technology?' (2011). This underpins my turn to the digital humanities for making critical inquiries into the digital human, for example, on the new syntax of BSD, in an environment that is distributed, ubiquitous, mobile, information rich, simultaneously local and global, and highly proprietary. The smartphone is a key tool in this environment, facilitating mediated cultural practices of ubiquitous connectivity, acting as a main vector for the generation of data, and passively recording that memory as it is exteriorized. Finally, the BSD we generate is not only of unprecedented size, it is mobile and motile.

Data motility is one way to emphasize the new generative capacities of the complex materialities of BSD, the environment of the digital human. Motility, from Aristotle to Hegel to Heidegger, has marked *the* ontological baseline for being. The BSD we generate can be categorized as motile. Cloud[6] security analysts use the term 'motility' to describe the movement of data that occurs in a manner outside direct administrator knowledge or consent. Human-made algorithms still ultimately dictate the movement of BSD in these complex environments of external storage, yet it nonetheless provides an evocative trope. Motility, for example, can denote the cultural and economic flow of the BSD. Once we click or tap 'send', the BSD we generate forever moves beyond our control, from the database of one company to another. In short, BSD is literally motile in cloud storage—materially so as it is aggregated and reaggregated, driven by algorithms and autonomous software agents, and proprietarily so, controlled by digital media corporations such as Facebook and Google.

The smartphone, then, can function as an important research tool[7] providing both epistemological and ontological insight into the digital human. BSD is a key source of born-digital material that largely moves autonomously of our control, locally and globally, through dispersed networks of mostly proprietary datasets. Yet while the data we generate moves autonomously, it remains deeply recursive, constantly 'pinging' back, enabling us in some ways and constraining us in others. BSD, then, acts as a cipher of the digital human, a born-digital material that provides innovative opportunities for the digital humanities. Opportunities abound to theorize and collaborate on building things in order to cultivate a broad array of interdisciplinary reflections on BSD and the digital human 'about and through the digital in community' (Rockwell 2009 [2004]).

## Notes

1. Lev Manovich (2011) also used the term 'Big Social Data'.
2. This should not be read as a mere variation of the 'posthuman' as used by Katherine Hayles and others, insofar as it challenges the notion of a normative 'human' that could be chronologically 'posted'. By using the single-word modifier 'digital' I mean to emphasize the iterability of the human. In short, I posit a human who was not once 'natural' and later modified by technology, but as human qua human, always already in a constitutive relationship with technology.
3. Industry standards and privacy laws apply to social media corporations or other businesses that mine, aggregate, and analyze BSD, and as such, anonymization is the norm. Yet the very parameters of digital anonymity are in flux. For example, enterprises generate increasing financial value in the market analysis of BSD—that is, in making precise connections between specific people and their myriad digital traces. These traces, in turn, come back to us in myriad ways, be it through targeted online ads or a security flag,

enabling and constraining our agency. As such, the very notion of anonymity for the digital human needs further study.

4. Hayles has argued against Manovich's claim to the cultural preeminence of the database, while agreeing to its importance. My intent is simply to emphasize that the rise of BSD will add further cultural import to the database.

5. Space precludes a detailed discussion of episteme-techne, the distinction from Greek antiquity of theory and practice. Yet it is relevant, not only because it identifies a key fault line and source of disciplinary anxiety, but because that binary distinction is effaced by originary technicity. Researching the digital human within that paradigm offers the digital humanities an opportunity to theorize through the deployment of techne. Indeed, the words of Jean Luc Nancy—'techne is the know-how to obtain from nature what it does not offer of itself' (Barison and Ross 2004)—hint at an ontologically rich disciplinary vein waiting to be explored. In other words, to paraphrase Stiegler (1998), humanities knowledge qua knowledge is necessarily constituted and organized instrumentally.

6. The cloud is a term commonly used across enterprise computing and refers to the external storage of data. Its relevance here is to indicate an architecture of data storage that is increasingly external to the platforms, apps, and digital enterprises through which data is generated. As such, it is indicative of the commercial storage environment of BSD.

7. I am pursuing further research on BSD in the Department of Digital Humanities at King's College London through a multiyear AHRC-funded grant with Tobias Blanke, Giles Greenway, and Jennifer Pybus, in partnership with youth coders from Young Rewired State. See http://big-social-data.net/ and https://twitter.com/AHRC_BSD.

## References

Barad, Karen. (2003). 'Posthumanist Performativity: Toward an Understanding of How Matter Comes to Matter'. *Signs* 28, no. 3 (Spring): 801–31.

Barison, David, and Daniel Ross. (2004). *The Ister*. Icarus Films.

Beardsworth, Richard. (1996). *Derrida and the Political*. New York: Routledge.

Berry, David. (2011). 'The Computational Turn: Thinking about the Digital Humanities'. *Culture Machine* 12. Available at: http://www.culturemachine.net/index.php/cm/article/viewArticle/440.

boyd, danah, and Kate Crawford. (2012). 'Critical Questions for Big Data: Provocations for a Cultural, Technological, and Scholarly Phenomenon'. *Information, Communication, and Society* 15, no. 5: 662–79.

Braidotti, Rosi. (2006). *Transpositions: On Nomadic Ethics*. Cambridge: Polity Press.

Coté, Mark. (2010). 'Technics and the Human Sensorium: Rethinking Media Theory Through the Body'. *Theory and Event* 13, no. 4. Available at: https://muse.jhu.edu/journals/theory_and_event/summary/v013/13.4.cote.html.

Coté, Mark. (2012). 'The Pre-Historic Turn? Networked New Media, Mobility and the Body'. In *The International Companions to Media Studies: Media Studies Futures*, ed. Kelly Gates, 171–94. Oxford: Blackwell.

Coté, Mark. (2014). 'Data Motility: The Materiality of Big Social Data'. *Cultural Studies Review* 20, no. 1. Forthcoming.

Coté, Mark, and Jennifer Pybus. (2007). 'Learning to Immaterial Labour 2.0: MySpace and Social Networks'. *Ephemera* 7, no. 1: 88–106.

Coté, Mark, and Jennifer Pybus. (2011). 'Social Networks: Erziehung zur immateriellen arbeit 2.0'. In *Generation Facebook: Über das lebem im social net*, ed. Theo Rohle and Oliver Leistert, 51–74. Bielefeld: Transcript Verlag.

Davidson, N. Cathy. (2008). 'Humanities 2.0: Promise, Perils, Predictions'. *Publications of the Modern Language Association of America* 123, no. 3: 707–17.

Derrida, Jacques. (1976). *Of Grammatology*. Baltimore: Johns Hopkins University Press.

Frabetti, Federica. (2011). 'Rethinking the Digital Humanities in the Context of Originary Technicity'. *Culture Machine* 12. Available at: http://www.culturemachine.net/index.php/cm/article/view/431/461.

Gantz, John, and David Reinsel. (2011). 'The Digital Universe Decade: Are You Ready?' *International Data Corporation*. Available at: http://www.emc.com.

Hayles, N. Katherine. (2005). *My Mother Was a Computer: Digital Subjects and Literary Texts*. Chicago: University of Chicago Press.

Hunt, Ira. (2013). 'The CIA's Grand Challenge with Big Data'. *GigaOm Structure Data Conference*, New York City, 21 March. Available at: http://www.sisense.com.

International Data Corporation. (2012). 'Android Marks Fourth Anniversary since Launch with 75.0% Market Share in Third Quarter'. *International Data Corporation*, 1 November, Available at: http://www.idc.com.

International Data Corporation. (2013). 'Android and iOS Combine for 91.1% of the Worldwide Smartphone OS Market in 4Q12 and 87.6% for the Year'. *International Data Corporation*, 14 February. Available at: http://www.idc.com.

Jenkins, W. Holman. (2010). 'Google and the Search for the Future'. *Wall Street Journal*, 14 August. Available at: http://online.wsj.com.

Juola, Patrick. (2008). 'Killer Applications in Digital Humanities'. *Literary and Linguistic Computing* 23, no. 1: 73–83.

Lazzarato, Maurizio. (1996). 'Immaterial Labour'. In *Radical Thought in Italy: A Potential Politics*, ed. Paolo Virno and Michael Hardt, 133–47. Minneapolis: University of Minnesota Press.

Leroi-Gourhan, Andre. (1993). *Gesture and Speech*. Cambridge, MA: MIT Press.

Liu, Alan. (2012). 'The State of the Digital Humanities: A Report and a Critique'. *Arts and Humanities in Higher Education* 11, nos. 1–2: 8–41.

Manovich, Lev. (2001). *The Language of New Media*. Cambridge, MA: MIT Press.

Manovich, Lev. (2011). 'Trending: The Promises and the Challenges of Big Social Data'. Available at: http://www.manovich.net.

McPherson, Tara. (2009). 'Introduction: Media Studies and the Digital Humanities'. *Cinema Journal* 48, no. 2 (Winter): 119–23.

Mitchell, W. J. T., and Mark B. N. Hansen. (2010). *Critical Terms for Media Studies*. Chicago: University of Chicago Press.

Murphy, David. (2011). 'Ethnography Goes Mobile'. *Mobile Marketing*, 10 March. Available at: http://mobilemarketingmagazine.com.

Prescott, Andrew. (2012). 'Consumers, Creators, or Commentators? Problems of Audience and Mission in the Digital Humanities'. *Arts and Humanities in Higher Education* 11, nos. 1–2 (February–April): 61–75.

Rockwell, Geoffrey. (2004). 'Humanities Computing Challenges'. *Theoreti.ca*, 31 August. Available at: http://theoreti.ca/.

Schnapp, Jeffrey, and Todd Presner. (2013). 'Digital Humanities Manifesto 2.0'. 26 February. Available at: http://www.humanitiesblast.com/manifesto/Manifesto_V2.pdf.

Stiegler, Bernard. (1998). *Technics and Time, 1: The Fault of Epimetheus*. Stanford: Stanford University Press.

Wingfield, Nick. (2012). 'Apple Rejects App Tracking Drone Strikes'. *New York Times*, 30 August. Available at: http://bits.blogs.nytimes.com.

Wolfe, Cary. (2010). *What Is Posthumanism?* Minneapolis: University of Minnesota Press.

# 10

## Screenshots as Virtual Photography

### Cybernetics, Remediation, and Affect

*Christopher Moore*

Screenshots are a ubiquitous form of visual communication online and off. They are common across the Web, in print and televisual media, where such images are required to provide evidence of screen activity. Critical analysis of screenshots as digital tools and media objects has rarely been attempted in media studies and the digital humanities, but these disciplines offer powerful and complimentary means for examining the assumptions embedded in their form and function. In this chapter I couple the investigation of screenshots as a convergence of old and new media technologies with the emerging processes for data analysis and network visualization. I seek to augment the hermeneutic and phenomenological interpretation of screenshots by drawing on the new tools for gathering quantitative information and mapping patterns of their circulation online. I take digital game screenshots as the primary subject of inquiry and consider them as a form of virtual photography, examining the role of cybernetics, remediation, and affect in their production and distribution. This study employs the open source network visualization tool NodeXL to expand the theoretical and qualitative investigation by graphing the deployment of game screenshots across two social media sites, Twitter and Flickr. The results presented here demonstrate details of Flickr screenshot tagging practices and the use of screenshots in Twitter profile images as two examples of participation in networked digital game cultures and the individual expression of online persona.

Screenshots play important and unacknowledged roles in the methods of mapping, graphing, and visualizing, as well as the general communication of research. They are transparent digital tools and media objects (Svensson 2009), outside the small percentage of technologies described by Rieder and Röhle (2012, 69) as those recognized in the 'narrow sense of "heuristic" procedure'. Critical examination of screenshots and their uses is important to the digital humanities as the layers of software and hardware that mediate every stage of knowledge production can and do structure the research that is produced within the field (Berry 2012). An inquiry into screenshots is an opportunity to participate in the 'unification of foundational concepts' proposed by Liu (2011, 11) in his sketch of the primary concerns within the field. Foregrounding the analysis of large datasets, databases, and digital collections, Liu seeks to 'recover a "logic" in technology (or techno-logic) continuous with media logic' (2011, 12). By considering the materiality and spectacle of screenshots, the approach is influenced by Liu's vision of the study of media that expands to incorporate subjects and objects in a complex array of contestation and complementary actions. Screenshots are an excellent example: as digital tools they diminish permanence in exchange for malleability and performativity. As media objects they can be dynamically traced across the networks of their dissemination and require a reevaluation of the axioms of cultural production that considers texts independently of experience.

The argument proposed here is that screenshots are a form of virtual photography and can be understood in terms of their cybernetic, affective, and remediatory capacities. The critical analysis is expanded by drawing on the tools of visualization to chart the patterns of these phenomena as they are employed in the online performance of the self and the iteration of persona across digital and networked environments.[1] As a preliminary example, consider the network visualization of search results for digital images tagged with the term 'screenshot' on the image-sharing site Flickr graphed in Figure 10.1 using the open source NodeXL application. To make the graph clearer, the number of visible points, called 'nodes' or 'vertices', is reduced by hiding outlier results that do not share many tags with other images. Vertex pairs are connected by 'edges', shown in Figure 10.1 as long thin lines, indicating images that share a common tag. The graph is plotted using the Harel-Koren Fast Multiscale algorithm, which distributes the nodes according to a force-directed model automating the layout in an 'aesthetically pleasing' manner (Harel and Koren 2001, 8). The results are clustered into regions of proximity according to the Clauset Newman Moore algorithm, which automatically identifies communities of use. The intergroup edges are merged into

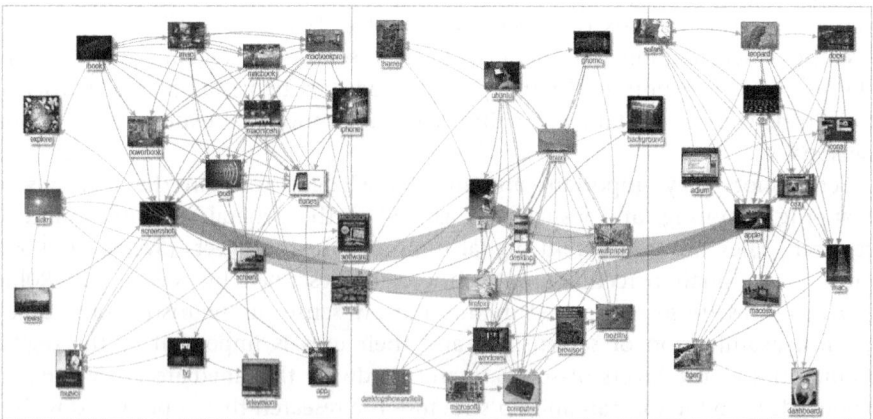

*Figure 10.1*   Network overview of the Flickr tag search 'screenshot'

the thick grey lines to reduce the visual clutter of the image and assist in revealing the broader contexts for those images tagged in conjunction with the term 'screenshot'.

The graph reveals a tag network, with three clusters, or communities, of tags applied to images occupied with the hardware of personal computers (PCs), mobile and portable devices, and software, especially Internet browsers and operating systems. One reason for the common association with operating systems is the ubiquity of screenshot functions; all versions of Microsoft's Windows can 'capture' an image of the screen with the 'Prt Scn' button found standard on most desktop keyboards. On PCs, intermediary software is required to make the transition from the cached information to digital object with the use of image-editing software such as Microsoft's MS Paint. The current Apple operating system, OS X, uses a trio of keys pressed to record an image file directly to the desktop. The elimination of the two-step process and the direct integration of the OS X version of image-managing software iPhoto with Flickr helps to account for the increased frequency of Apple-related results overall.

Capturing screenshots from Apple's iOS devices is achieved by simultaneously pressing the 'power' and 'home' buttons, literally inverting the act of mobile digital photography. The popularity of screenshots originating from mobile devices has increased with the availability of apps, including its Flickr, Facebook, and Twitter integration. Flickr is an important online repository for digital images, but the site's relationship to the everyday practice of photography, argues Murray (2008), is in part its association with other media, websites, and social networks. Flickr acts as a resource to collect and curate displays of photographs, and serves as an archive of content for blogs and other websites. Flickr functions as an interstitial connection between images and the habits of users across sites including Facebook, Twitter, Tumblr, Pinterest, and many others. As Murray suggests, removed from its rarefied authority of mimesis, Flickr contributes to the sense of photography as an everyday, transitory practice rather than a rarefied pursuit. Flickr is at the center of a 'communal aesthetic' that actively overwrites the private/public, amateur/professional, fixed/malleable binary distinctions between analogue and digital photography. It signals 'a definitive shift in our temporal relationship with the everyday image … that has helped alter the way that we construct narratives about ourselves and the world around us' (Murray 2008, 151). Photographs, screenshots, and tags are all bound up in social performativity of the image shared online, and they are not constrained by categorical thinking or the subcultural boundaries of prior media forms (Lee and Wellman 2012).

One of my concerns for this chapter is the question of how to effectively navigate the path between the 'closeness' of critical reading and the 'distance' of Moretti's (2000) algorithmic analysis. Moretti's close/distant dualism positions the tools, if not the philosophies, of critical reading in the humanities to be insufficient to the task of analysis on a global scale. Liu considers scale as a constituent concept for the digital humanities, one that opens up new investigations into the kinds of humanistic phenomena that only appear at a 'distance'. He also identifies the problems of scale and the human 'bottleneck' in the balance between equation and expertise, where the use of algorithmic and computational methods must also stand with the rigours of philosophical scouring and the quality control of scholarship (Liu 2012, 20–21).

This investigation rallies to Hayles's observation that the 'troops march together: tools with ideas' (2012, 30). The function of the theories and concepts offered here is to consider how they suggest strategies for incorporating new applications for the analysis of the network assemblages and the techno-social features of digital media objects. Screenshots of games and play are particularly useful as they are heavily circulated online and frequently involved in complex expressions of networked identity. Network visualizations assist in connecting the close and distant, rendering significant elements of a phenomenon under examination more apparent than others, but there is a reductive character to the algorithmic cartography necessary to produce graphs with significant argumentative impact (Rieder and Röhle 2012). The selection processes involved in producing the visualization create a technological frame to position the critical analysis of screenshots and their movement across networks in meaningful ways in order to develop viable interpretations. The techniques of mapping and analysing connections in and between networks provide a range of contemporary and historical perspectives that together with critical theory can develop explanations of the structural formations, transmissions, and transformations of mediated objects, tools, users, emotions, experiences, and the networks themselves (Emirbayer and Goodwin 1994).

Currently there is a rise in the number of dynamic tools for producing aesthetically impressive graphs. Gephi is among the best known of these, a sophisticated network visualization application built by the French nonprofit Gephi Consortium. Described by its user community as the 'Photoshop for graphs', Gephi is remarkably powerful (Gephi 2013), but not all images need to be 'Photoshopped' in order to communicate effectively. The open source software NodeXL was selected for this research in order to produce simple and effective graphs. The application produces visualizations that assist in making sense of screenshot tagging practices on Flickr and help explore their role in the production of gamer persona through Twitter profiles. NodeXL is an acronym for Network Overview, Discovery, and Exploration; it is a freely available, open source plug-in for Microsoft Excel created by the Social Media Research Foundation. Chief social scientist for the foundation March Smith describes the goal of NodeXL as to be the Internet browser or MSPaint of network analysis and visualization (Smith 2012). The group's stated aim is to reduce the time spent with the software before obtaining useful graphs that can assist in the interpretation of complex network patterns. The primary consideration for selecting NodeXL was the basic Excel database literacy needed to produce revealing graphs and the availability of accessible guides for beginners in social network analysis to conduct innovative and revealing research using the software (Hansen et al. 2011). The visualizations produced assist the critical analysis of key concepts involved, but the graphs are not definitive datasets. They are snapshots capturing a moment in time, recursively also screenshots themselves—virtual photographs of the network in operation.

## Virtual photography

Video game screenshots reveal important intersections in the relationships between the software and hardware of computers, screens, cinema and photography, linking the static image to the dynamic 'live' sensory experience. To use Sobchack's (1999) metaphor, screenshots are the material salvage, the 'flotsam and jetsam' that result from play and the participation in digital games cultures. As with photographs, screenshots are echoes—footprints and traces of connected moments, combining personal memories with communal narratives, documentary evidence, and a collective mass-mediated past. Through the act of 'reverential framing' of photography, screenshots form 'reliquaries' as gamers preserve and celebrate themselves and events in action; they become 'the fragment, the souvenir, the talisman, the exotic', and cross over from common, digital, and 'ephemeral' object to 'rarest heirloom' in a single post, share, or favourite (Sobchack 1999).

Poremba's (2007) study of screenshots considers photography as a dominant archaeological heuristic and invokes a history of the image within the potential for game play to push the boundaries of the photographic aesthetic. This approach can be expanded with attention to the computational components of screenshots ensconced in the personal and creative expression of online identity management. The screenshot is a mimetic recording of the screen that is not entirely bounded within its frame of visual representation, but part of the new media history and 'social operating system' of networked individuals (Lee and Wellman 2012). The characteristics of computational devices and screens recorded by screenshots produce a particular phenomenological understanding, the type Sobchack (1999) considers to be embedded in the context of the engagement with and within the image.

Video game screenshots captured as a result of the proceedings of play demonstrate a powerful capacity to modulate an affective sense of time and space (Ok 2012). They work in a fashion comparable to Sobchack's (1999) example of the photographic image ensnaring a viewer in 'compelling emptiness'. Foucault's account of images that are made up of recognizable objects but produce 'an essential empty void' similarly describes the subject within the frame as being 'elided' (Foucault 1966/2012, 18). The representation freed from its foundation offers a pure experience in itself, slipping beyond the referent signs on which the simulation is based. Science fiction dystopias, fantasy vistas, isometric projections, hypermasculinist military engagements, and all other imaginary game worlds can be recorded in screenshots, and yet the resulting images contain more than the mimetic reproduction of the virtual setting. They are also representative of an instance of the physical and embodied encounter between player and game, the hardware and software of the machine and controlling body, and the person in front of the screen and behind the frame.

## Game screenshots: Persona and remediation

Collections of game screenshots make useful case studies for analysing the participatory elements of online cultures and their distribution across social media profiles and websites. Gamers rely on screenshots and other direct and indirect products of play including status updates, hashtags, scores, achievements, save games, and online profiles to assemble their social connections and curate their cultural experiences. Sharing screenshots is an everyday communication practice in digital games cultures, and players have come to rely on them in ways that promote specialized visual literacies and tacit knowledge requirements (Reiger 2010). Making full sense of game screenshots necessitates familiarity with the norms, skills, and politics of play. The games industry relies heavily on these literacies as they use screenshots to communicate the future sensations of games in development. Screenshots are prominent in marketing and promotional practices, which support the cycles of production and further encourage the use of screenshots to participate in the wider circulation of games-related 'paratexts' (Grey 2010).

Screenshots are a recording of emphatic events coming into 'being', which Sobchack (1999) argues is delivered by film and cinema in a much closer act of real-time 'becoming' than by the static images of photography. Cubitt (2000), however, proposes that the mobile and remote transactions between users and digital technologies disrupts the notion of equivocation between the 'run time' of the cinematic and a synchronous 'real time' of the audience. He argues that the orders of mechanical and human occurrence of time often represented as stable and whole in cinema are disunited and dispersed in new ways by digital media (Cubit 2000). Game screenshots intensify this dispersal as the digital mediation of time, space, and objects further disrupts the notion of the image as a claim to a 'real' referent point. Distributed across social networks and the Web, game screenshots both connect and disjoint the context of play and the 'run time' of the game narratives and events. The image documents the experience, and comes into being through play, but fragments notions of authenticity and the actuality of experience.

Put towards the performance of identity, virtual photography expands what can be thought of as play, as the textual components of the game are simultaneously foregrounded in the image and put to more complex uses. Sobchack (1999) writes of Andre Bazin's 'myth of total cinema', citing cinema as a legacy 'primary cultural interface' for the computational and the screen—the 'mythic teleology' of cinema that is extended in the virtual at the same time it is endlessly cannibalized in the 'face of transformation' as a perpetually remediated cinematic convention in digital games. Following Sobchack (1999), the 'poetic and phenomenological power' of screenshots can be considered as explicitly linked to the relationships between the material qualities of the digital images and the 'memorial' potential of their objectivity that exist as fragments of personal experience, assembled as emblems of a past and a presence that is too large to be enclosed in the representational alone. This interplay can be directly observed in the circulation of screenshots via Flickr and other social media sites, where tagging, sharing, embedding, and liking practices become part of the act of remixing play into the networked identity performance of a gamer persona.

Gamers use screenshots to 'point to their own presence as the poignant and precious "visible landmarks" of an unseen, lost, and incomprehensible field of experience' (Sobchack 1999). Profile images are a clear example of this, and most game-related social networks, such as Xbox Live and the PC digital distribution platform, Steam, require players to add images to their profiles (often called avatars). These images are as much a part of the player's identity, or persona, as their in-game names or characters. Few individuals include digital photographs of their physical selves, relying instead on images from popular culture and screenshots that speak to a much broader concept of the self as a mediated, cultural, and social being. Similar to the user profile pictures on Facebook, these images become associated with the actions, messages, chats, status updates, and posts of the individual, enabling those identifying as gamers to produce themselves in specific ways. These players assemble links to particular games, genres, or types of popular culture as they collate their online personae. The social networking components of Steam, Flickr, Twitter, Facebook, and Reddit invite players to display screenshot collections directly, so that others can validate and reward their investment with votes, favourites, or comments. Flickr enables the sharing and embedding of images in other sites, creating vast and intricate matrices of networked connections and image-related hyperlinking practices.

New technologies and innovations that remediate the photographic past and acquire by convergence the capacity to create and disseminate screenshots gain an extensive mobility and digital flexibility. Each successive generation of these technologies evolves to cover more geographic and socially networked distance than its predecessor (Liu 2011). Remediation (Bolter and Grusin 1999) of the photographic, cinematic, and televisual intersect in the production of game screenshots, which is symptomatic of the resulting shift in the materiality of images to the digital, generating novel layers for the cultural history of textuality (Cranny-Francis 2005). Examples of the remediation involved in virtualized photographic practices can be observed in the visualization of the Flickr images tagged in conjunction with the term 'SecondLife' in Figure 10.2. Second Life is not a game per se, but a virtual world in which users can build digital objects, such as houses and vehicles as well as personal fashion items for avatars, including moveable hair or behavioural 'scripts' for different walking styles.

The Second Life Flickr group was chosen because it is one of the most populated game-themed groups on the site, with 16,068 members and 440,104 individual image items at the time of writing. The high number of tags associated with a framing of the photographic aesthetics is evident in the graph. A concentration of terms connected to the tag 'photography', including 'landscape', 'light', 'art', 'pose', and 'portrait', occurs in the top right cluster. These terms are used to assemble a persona of the virtual photographer on Flickr and in the virtual world by remediating the notion of the professional. The connections to tags in the other clusters, particularly those relating to gender, socializing, modelling, and relationships, emphasizes the art and practice of virtual photography within Second Life and the performance of identity beyond the simulation.

Remediation is an important concept when dealing with the virtual photography of games and simulations, but it is not a simple transliteration. Producing images capable of signification and affective responses, screenshots can make us feel, even if we don't possess the exact visual literacies or specific game knowledge of how to 'read' them. There is a remediation at the level of the software repurposing the cinematic and aesthetic conventions, such as lens flare, in the visual spectacle of the simulation. It is through the opportunities for self-expression produced in the experience of play and shared across networks that the game world itself is remediated as images that become part of the individual's persona.

The composition of screenshots is part of the performance of self, but these choices are just as important as the social media functions, such as tag use and sharing practices, which offer a different, nonproximal claim to a notion of the real. This sense of performance can be observed in Figure 10.2 as tags connecting screenshots with terms related to the body, and particularly the face, including eyes, hair, and skin colour, and tags associated with gender performance, including notions of femininity and transgender identity play. These images and tagging practices are not only representational; they are affective and cybernetic in their incorporation of the physical and the virtual in their enactment. Game screenshots enable different types of persona enunciations by making use of the new actuality of events recorded in the images capturing the creative assemblages of games and play.

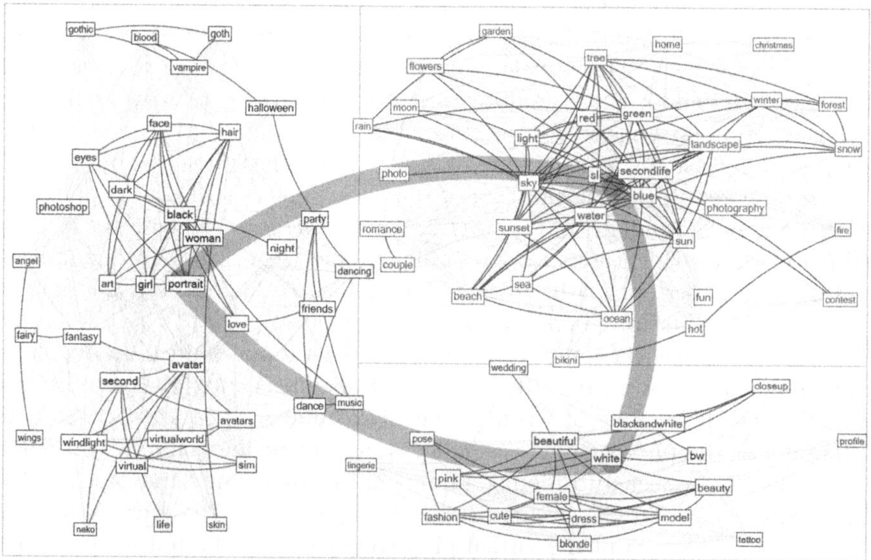

*Figure 10.2*   Network overview of the tag 'secondlife' on Flickr

The digital realities of screenshots are the results of layers of algorithms and hardware configurations, cybernetic interfaces, and player choices. The cybernetic dimensions are worth considering in terms of Poremba's adoption of Sontag's (1977) tourist photographic 'frame'. Poremba regards screenshots as familiar photographic processes that validate a specific construction of a reality of the subject in the act of documenting the personal response to a publicly ritualized space. Sontag (1977) saw photography as a means for gaining power over the subject. Virtual photography is therefore capable of producing dynamic sensations and powerful reactions to the digital object rendered in the moment of interaction between human and machine, code and performance. Images captured from game environments are enlivened through the image's distribution, alteration, and annotation as part of networked communication and the player's socially mediated reality.

Examples of the tourist frame in action can be found in screenshots from prominent Massively Multiplayer Online Roleplaying Games (MMORPGs), including *Guild Wars*, *Star Wars: The Old Republic*, and *World of Warcraft* shared via Flickr. The tags connected to the term 'Warcraft', mapped in Figure 10.3, reveal a considerable degree of crossover between images taken in the game and other participatory games-culture phenomena (Raessens 2005). Tourist photos of in-game locations share common tags with the highly ritualized experiences of game 'expos', conventions, and other popular public events. A prime example is Blizzcon, the annual showcase run by the *World of Warcraft* developer and publisher, Blizzard. The convention includes employee panels and presentations, player competitions, exhibits of new technologies and game features, as well as the unveiling of new content.

The network graph in Figure 10.3 reveals a high occurrence of tags related to 'cosplay', where players wear costumes of favourite game characters. This positions the virtual photography of in-game events alongside more customary tourist photography, at events like Blizzcon. In both locations the players are adorned as their in-game character, performing that identity through ritualized photography as well as the sharing and tagging of the image. In a broader sense there is also an interesting transition between the online and offline forms of play experiences, and between the digital camera and the screenshot as a means for recording them. Both are an enactment of power over the source text, a remediation of the representational elements of the game texts, and both are a performativity that occurs via Flickr as a socially networked expression of the self and engagement in the larger social sphere of the game's culture.

## Cybernetics and affect

The 'gameness' of virtualized photography is emphasized by Poremba's (2007) consideration of the game screenshot as remediation at the intersection of photography, art, and play. As a result, the player contributes directly to the 'post-photographic aesthetic' of the screenshot (Poremba's 2007, 57). Many publishers promote their games with terms like 'immersion' and 'realism' alongside claims

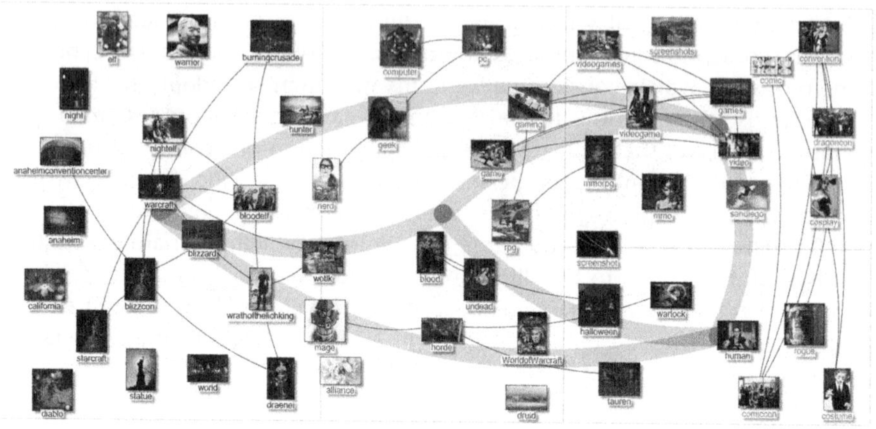

*Figure 10.3*   Network visualization of the tag 'worldofwarcraft'

to technical sophistication and the other 'features' designed to 'mask poesis as mimesis' (Rentfrow 2008). Bolter and Grusin's (1999) concept of remediation integrates Derrida's (1981) account of mimesis and imitation, which considers 'true' mimesis as the relationship between two producing subjects and not between two uniquely objective properties. Derrida's reading of a 'true mimesis', argues Melberg (1995), condemns the concept of 'imitation while elevating creativity'. This point suggests that screenshots composed around a phenomenological and cybernetic encounter are a creative response to the affective sensation that results from play.

One of the more difficult concepts to convey via a network visualization is Brian Massumi's (2002) account of affect, which I have described elsewhere as a phenomenon linking elements of game design, player experience, and the expression of gamer personae (Moore 2010, 2011, 2012). Following Derrida's critique of Kant's aesthetics, Wilson (2007) argues that the imposition of a logical framework on a subjective or affective response, such as a representational analysis of a game screenshot, risks completely effacing the role of the raw affect in communication that is not always logical. Wilson claims affect as an inalienable feature of aesthetic response, one that may not be completely observed on the surface, but in the ripples of its wake as it passes. As game screenshots move easily across the Web and social networks, their roles as visual records of embodied experience create connections and traces of affective resonances that may be possible to visualize graphically.

The role of affect in games connects the will to action and the capacity for self-expression through the products of play to the fleeting episodes articulated in the participatory practices of gamer culture and identity relations, especially those between audiences and texts, economies and lives, power and politics. The body's relationship to the digital, through the embodied interfaces of computers, such as keyboards and mice, video game console controllers or the haptic screens of mobile devices, invigorates the personal and creative expression of the screenshot as a highly gestural action—much like the quick casual 'snap' or digital 'pic', compared to the more planned and posed image of the tourist photo.

It is easy to write out the body in the play of games; as with the stereotypes of gamers the body is framed as something forgotten or neglected. Arguments over media effects, violence, and player aggression typically consider the body only in terms of an apparatus to be stress-tested for various responses to stimuli, and not something that fuels creativity, participation, and sociality. The player's body and its role in the construction of digital objects like screenshots is often effaced and yet it is an equal partner in the sensations of experience, framing of the image, and the meanings generated, as much as the screen and other hardware. The eyes and the head, the hands and the arms, the body in its seat—all work in conjunction with controllers, interfaces, memory units, and operating systems in a materiality, mediation, identity, and performance of play.

Affect can be accounted for in the screenshot's integration of the player's perspective through the recording of the screen in a confrontation between a remediated past and digital present. There is a nostalgia embedded in screenshot practices for the formal limitations of media technologies, one that shapes characteristic technical features, such as the satisfying whirring and metallic click of the digital audio file emitted from Apple devices. This aligns the senses to the experience and echoes of embodied manual and mechanical tasks of analogue camera history, one that many users will only be familiar with in an indirect sense, if at all. Games and operating systems often provide similar audio feedback and other sensorial cues to accompany the taking of screenshots.

Consider these events more generally; when composing a screenshot the computer screen acts as a virtualized camera. The software and hardware assembly simulates the lens and viewfinder as one; while the digital image object is intangible at one level as code, it is also recorded to physical memory and therefore has a material component. Screenshots capture a moment of human–machine interaction from the user's perspective, recording a singular instance of cybernetic operation. The process converges and remediates multiple media functions as it translates the physical encounter of the body's interface with the computer and screen into a digital image object. The representational qualities of screenshots alone do not convey all the affective channels of play, but they do contribute to our sense and reading of feedback amplification as 'communicational' media. Tomkins's (1962) taxonomy of affect considered the face, the voice, and the body to be primary sites of mimetic communication and affect transmission. Screenshot images similarly function as sites of affect amplification, magnification, and contagion (Gibbs 2001), which the player communicates through Flickr archives, Steam profile pictures, Facebook updates, or screenshot-reliant memes on Tumblr or Reddit. The capacity to remediate and produce affective responses is important for understanding notions of the real and new accounts of cybernetic embodiment and digitally networked identity performances.

The study of media in the absence of cybernetics is 'scarcely conceivable', argues Hayles (2010). Cybernetics is the interpretation of the mind and body in computational terms; it produces specifically mediated experiences that are partly constructed in code and materials of the technology, and partly in the psychology and physiology of the biological through real-time events. The implications of the co-construction of cybernetics and media have important consequences for the study of images and their role in the production of the self online:

> The material and technological levels of computational media correspond to cybernetic artifacts, while the semiotic level is routinely understood as information flows, and the social contexts involve myriad feedback loops between humans and computers that continue to reconfigure social, economic, and technological conditions for people throughout the world.
>
> (Hayles 2010, np)

Considering the body as media, argues Hayles, is as much a cybernetic move as considering computers as media. The computational mediation of the digital in cybernetics is located in 'complex, networked, adaptive, and co-evolving environments through which information and data are pervasively flowing, a move catalyzed by the rapid development of ubiquitous technologies and mixed realities system' (Hayles 2010, np). The cybernetic world powerfully shapes understanding of the materiality and meaning of the digital, but the danger of the cybernetic accounts, argues Cohen (2012), is the premature foreclosure on theories of the body.

One visualization of the connection between screenshot, game, machine, and body emerged in Figure 10.4, a mapping of the tags connected to the term 'FPS', an acronym for first-person shooter games. The network overview of the Flickr FPS tags reveals anticipated associations between major video game franchises, including Activision's *Call of Duty* games, Electronic Arts's *Crysis*, id Software's *Quake*, and Valve's *Left4Dead*, all prominent in the FPS genre. In this graph the vertex size indicates the popularity of the tag: the larger vertex labels, the more frequent the use. In the second and third clusters, however, there are some surprising terms, including the Nikon-camera related tags and the 'streetart', 'finstreetart', and 'helsinki' tags. These connections are explained by a manual Flickr image tag search, which reveals that 'FPS' is also a heavily photographed street art 'tag' (a scrawled pseudonym in the graffiti sense) in Finland.

The crossover goes further, as the camera model used for the images with street art tags is also used to photograph PC, Xbox, and PlayStation games at the mass local area network (LAN) gaming events held in stadiums in Helsinki and across Finland. The photographs and screenshots from these LANs capture the amazing temporary cybernetic interactions between humans and computers in networks that occur for days at a time in giant physical assemblies. The congruencies of these tags in their overlapping uses also suggests a further complication to the notion of virtual photography, as the digital cameras record

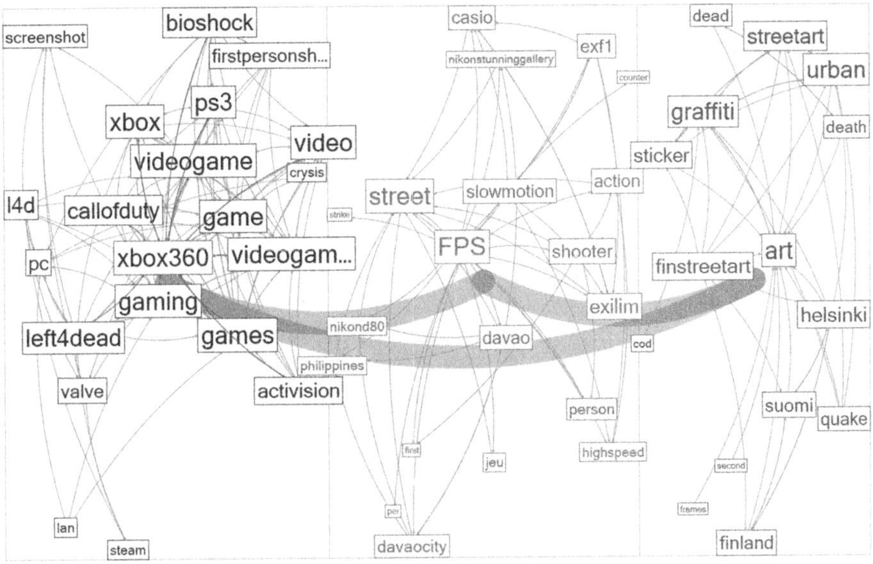

*Figure 10.4*   Network visualization of the Flickr tag 'FPS'

the ritualized relationship between the video game consoles, their screen displays, and the bodies of the players. The digital photographs and screenshots of the annual LAN events capture the cyberneticism of humans at play; some gamers are hunched over screens concentrating fiercely, some are slumped across keyboards sleeping, and others pose in front of giant TVs with console controllers in hand. The distinction between the types of images loses coherence as both are mediated extensions of the cybernetic confluence of bodies and machines, within the specific time and place, and the graph reminds us that it is also important to consider these phenomena together, no matter how random, removed, or alien they may first appear.

Phenomenologically, cybernetic interfaces prepare the body's mediated circumstance for the social shaping of the network (Cohen 2012). Parallel logic in the science of human cognition and the turn to embodiment in critical theory, for Cohen, models the relationship between the physical and conceptual:

> The primacy of embodied perceptions requires rejection of both the conventional distinction between absolute truth and ephemeral experience, on the one hand, and deconstructionist claims about the arbitrariness of purportedly natural categories, on the other.
>
> (Cohen 2012, 7)

One option is to consider screenshots as object and subject formations, digital versions of what Michel Serres (1982) describes as the 'quasi-object'. This concept conveys a sense of the complex nature of the relationship between subjects, their environments, and the designation of a subject by an object, one that in its absence would deny the status (Serres 1982, 225).

Serres gives the example of children playing games that require a button, rock, coin, or gesture, not unlike the 'tag' that marks the player as 'it'. Serres's account of the world as networks of relationships in which objects play constituent roles in the experience of embodiment enables us to consider the processes through which tags and screenshots are used to convey the subject's capacity for feeling, thinking, and producing itself. The game screenshot, and its Flickr tags, designate the subject as a 'gamer' and much more. The screenshot conveys the cybernetic and affective capacities of a moment of play, while the aesthetic framing of the image capturing the simulation in that instance communicates the representational elements of the game. The FPS street art wall graffiti, the FPS screenshot tag, and the tags connected to the LAN events in Figure 10.4 are as much part-objects and part-subject formations as the characters and other identity choices within the game environments.

One of the limitations of using NodeXL is the inability to easily map the movement of the images between different sites, to observe where the images are circulated and how they are reframed at these various locations. For example, many of the images from my Flickr screenshot collection have found their way across the Web in blogs and news media sites as I make them available using a Creative Commons license and use Google image search to track the filenames. Finding new ways to map this movement of digital image objects would assist in overcoming the tendency to deal with games and the products of their play as isolated phenomena.

The Flickr contact network in Figure 10.5 displays the 'buddy icon' of my own profile on the site, which is taken from a popular screenshot (one that attracted many views and favourites). This image designates my Flickr identity and gamer persona at the center of the left cluster. The cluster visualizes the network of Flickr 'contacts' with whom I have had conversations around their photos and mine. The cluster to the right is my family and friends network connected to the 'family' Flickr account I use to store and share personal images. Grey icons with simple pixel lines for eyes and mouth are those accounts without buddy icon images. The groups to the lower right indicate clusters of contacts who have commented on mine and other users' images in the network. The different types of image used in the 'buddy icons' clearly designate a broad range of associations and identities; some are recognizably gamers, others are noncommittal, some are abstract, but each one contributes to an individual persona.

Another way to consider this persona formation is with the graph in Figure 10.6, which maps the ego network for the Flickr users who contributed the most screenshots to the Flickr photo group 'Game Screenshots'. The size of the 'buddy icons' vertices are mapped according to the number of submitted photos; those posting more screenshots have larger profile images. A trend emerges in the cluster in the top right corner, which is dominated by icons formed from Second Life avatar screenshots. The avatars are not simply an identity performed in the virtual world, but part object, part subject formations as screenshots that move their user's identity outside of the experience of the simulation and into the network.

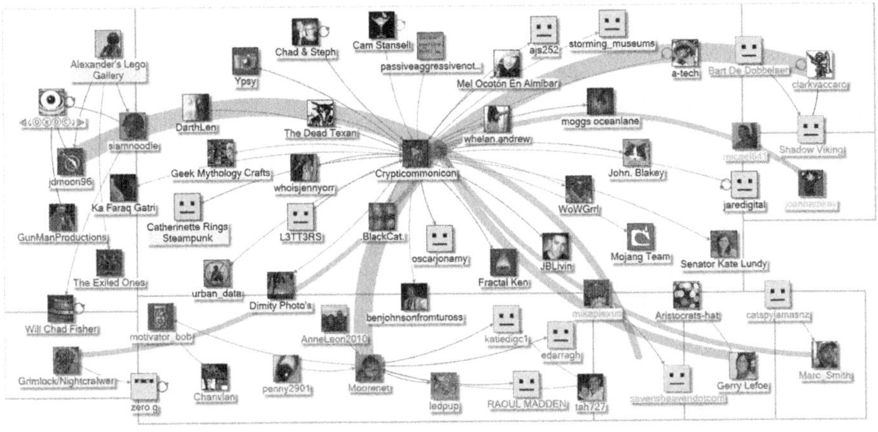

*Figure 10.5*   Author's ego network of Flickr contacts

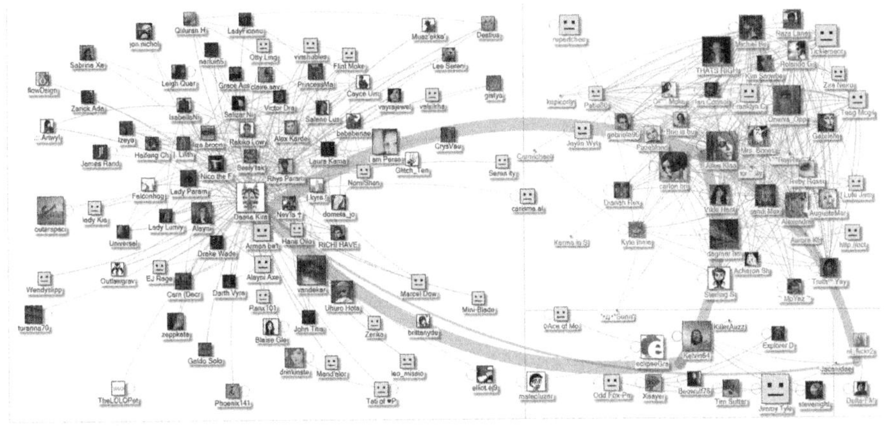

*Figure 10.6*   Network of connections of the most prolific poster in the 'game screenshots' Flickr user group

One way to perform the analysis of persona traversal across multiple sites is to examine the overlap between the profile images of users on both Flickr and Twitter. An example of this circulation and the movement of the screenshot as identity performance can be considered in Figure 10.7, with the visualization of the Australian education technologist specializing in Second Life and *Minecraft*, 'Jokay'. Jokay operates educational activities in both virtual worlds, including primary-school-age programmes and support in *Minecraft*. The graph is a visualization of the core group of Flickr users in the contact list and users who have commented on images in Jokay's collection. The overall number of nodes has been reduced to show only those with very strong social ties and clustered to indicate users that focus comments and contacts within those groups. Those nodes with higher numbers of

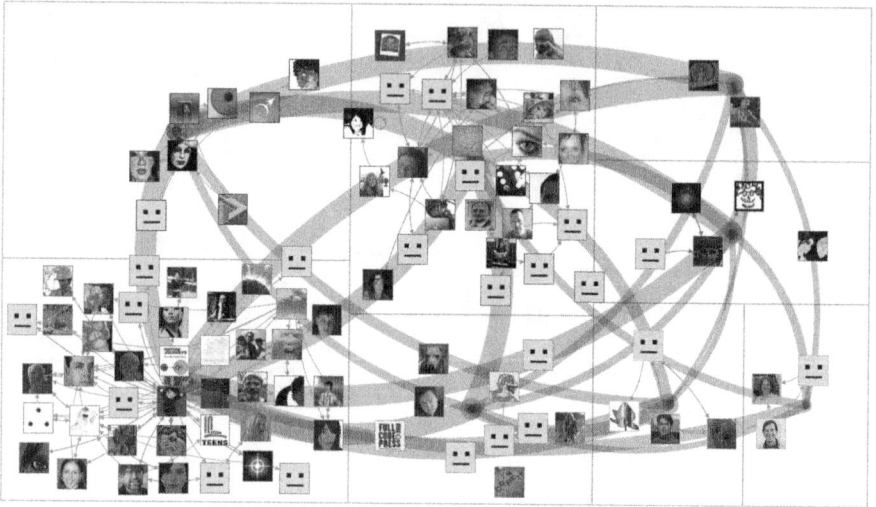

*Figure 10.7* Visualization of the Flickr user Jokay's ego network of contacts and images commenters

connections suggest individuals with important social roles or personal influence in this community of Flickr members.

The high degree of 'buddy icons' with Second Life avatars indicates a strong grouping of Second Life users. Second Life has a much more established presence on Flickr, with an older user group. There are no tags associated with the term *Minecraft* on Flickr, although there are many untagged *Minecraft* screenshots, suggesting that the typically younger-aged *Minecraft* players do not frequently participant in the Flickr folksonomy. Flickr does not feature many *Minecraft* images, but the game has an active following on Reddit, with a popular 'subreddit' forum devoted to the game, which features hundreds of screenshots submitted to the site daily.

Figure 10.8 is a visualization of the Twitter contacts or 'followers' for Jokay, and Figure 10.9 is the lower-center cluster enlarged and mapped to a grid formation. Here we observe a similar pattern to the Flickr users who use Second Life avatar screenshots in the 'buddy icons' and in Twitter profile images (often called 'avis'). There are clear groups of Second Life users who employ screenshots of their virtual-world avatars in both their Twitter and Flickr profiles (many use the same image), producing a consistency to their personae between the game and the social networks of both sites. Together these visualizations reveal the movement of screenshots and avatars as digital object and subject formations in the production of a persona across multiple social media sites, networks, and practices.

## Conclusion

The subject and object formations made possible by virtual photography provide new orientations for thinking about the cybernetic, remediatory, affective,

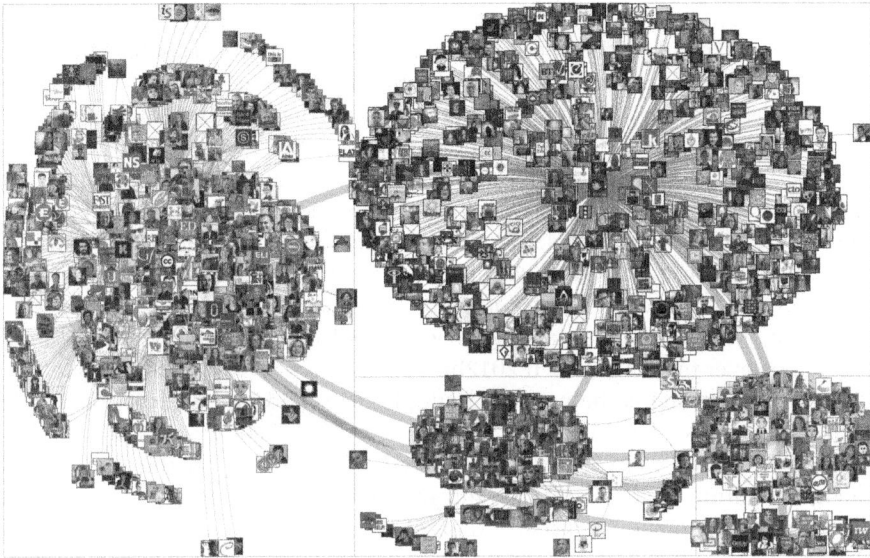

*Figure 10.8*   Twitter network overview of user 'Jokay'

*Figure 10.9*   Zoomed view of the lower-center cluster of Figure 10.8

and networked qualities of online personae. The question remains: How best to develop and expand on the opportunities for investigation and analysis presented in this chapter? More formal and systematic network analysis will improve the methodology, and Lev Manovich's Cultural Analytics and the Software Studies Initiative (2009, 2012b) provides opportunities for the analysis of large datasets of images, employing automated and algorithmic visualization techniques and innovative display technologies to generate numerical and visual descriptions of complete image sets (Manovich 2012b). Manovich frames the examination of the new iterations of interfaces with dynamic 'software performances' (Manovich 2012a, 3) and the core effects of social changes and technological progress by tracking the movement of digital globalized cultures through their image collections over time (Manovich 2012b).

Manovich highlights the need for multiple maps and cartographies of the cultural landscapes of large datasets. No one singular visualization is able to fully encapsulate digital network culture and reveal the totality of the territories of emerging cultural fields. Extensive and multiple mapping attempts are required to appreciate the obvious diversity. Maps of cultural landscapes, argues Manovich (2012b), reveal fuzzy and overlapping clusters rather than discrete categories or rigid boundaries. Cultural analytics will be of use in developing the approach presented in this chapter to draw on the properties of large collections of screenshots and multiple iterations of NodeXL-style sociograms to consider changes in composition, use, and circulation of these images over time. This approach could be applied to other forms of cultural production and online personae to produce culturagrams, moving the study from gamers to fans, sports stars, celebrities, and the performance of other professional identities, such as academic and politician. The usefulness of open source and free software programs designed for sophisticated algorithmic analysis with accessible visualization techniques, including Gephi, NodeXL, and others, will make it more feasible to experiment in this field and to contribute meaningful and original research.

## Notes

1. See Barbour (2013), Barbour and Marshall (2012), and Marshall (2010; 2013) for further accounts of the development of online personae and Moore (2010; 2011) with regard to the gamer persona.

## Works cited

Barbour, Kim. (2013). 'Hiding in Plain Sight: Street Artists Online'. *Journal of Media and Communication* 5, no. 1: 86–96.

Barbour, Kim, and David Marshall. (2012). 'The Academic Online: Constructing Persona Through the World Wide Web'. *First Monday* 17, nos. 9–3. Available at: http://firstmonday.org.

Berry, David. (2012). 'Introduction: Understanding the Digital Humanities'. In *Understanding Digital Humanities*, ed. David M. Berry, 1–20. New York: Palgrave Macmillan.

Bolter, Jay David, and Richard Grusin. (1999). *Remediation: Understanding New Media*. Cambridge, MA: MIT Press.

Cohen, Julie. (2012). *Configuring the Networked Self*. New Haven: Yale University Press.

Cranny-Francis, Anne. (2005). *Multimedia: Texts and Contexts*. London: Sage.

Cubitt, Sean. (2000). 'Cybertime: Ontologies of Digital Perception'. *Society for Cinema Studies*, Chicago, March. Available at: http://dtl.unimelb.edu.au.

Derrida, Jacques. (1981). 'Economimesis'. *Diacritics* 11, no. 6: 2–25.

Emirbayer, Mustafa, and Jeff Goodwin. (1994). 'Network Analysis, Culture and the Problem of Agency'. *American Journal of Sociology* 99, no. 6: 1411–54.

Foucault, Michel. (1966/2012). *The Order of Things: An Archeology of the Human Sciences*. London: Routledge.

Gephi. (2013). *Gephi Consortium*. Available at: https://gephi.org/.

Gibbs, Anna. (2001). 'Contagious Feelings: Pauline Hans and the Epidemiology of Affect'. *Australian Humanities Review* 24. Available at: http://www.australianhumanitiesreview.org/archive/Issue-December-2001/gibbs.html.

Grey, J. (2010). *Show Sold Separately: Promos, Spoilers and Other Media Paratexts*. New York: New York University Press.

Hansen, Derek L., Ben Shneiderman, and Marc A. Smith. (2011). *Analyzing Social Media Networks with NodeXL: Insights from a Connected World*. Burlington, MA: Morgan Kauffman.

Harel, David, and Yehuda Koren. (2001). 'A Fast Multi-Scale Method for Drawing Large Graphs'. Available at: http://www.wisdom.weizmann.ac.il.

Hayles, Katherine. (2010). 'Cybernetics'. In *Critical Terms for Media Studies*, ed. W. J. T. Mitchel and Mark Hansen. Kindle ed. Chicago: University of Chicago Press.

Hayles, N. Katherine. (2012). *How We Think: Digital Media and Contemporary Technogenesis*. Chicago: University of Chicago Press.

Lee, Rainie, and Barry Wellman. (2012). *Networked: The New Social Operating System*. Kindle ed. Cambridge, MA: MIT Press.

Liu, Alan. (2011). 'Friending the Past: The Sense of History and Social Computing'. *New Literary History* 42, no. 1: 1–30.

Liu, Alan. (2012). 'The State of the Digital Humanities: A Report and a Critique'. *Arts and Humanities in Higher Education* 11, no. 8: 8–41.

Manovich, Lev. (2009). 'Cultural Analytics: Visualising Cultural Patterns in the Era of "More Media"'. *Domus* (Spring). Available at: https://docs.google.com/viewer?url=http%3A%2F%2Fsoftwarestudies.com%2Fcultural_analytics%2FManovich_DOMUS.doc.

Manovich, Lev. (2012a). 'How to Follow Software Users'. *Softwarestudies.com*, March. Available at: https://docs.google.com/viewer?url=http%3A%2F%2Fwww.softwarestudies.com%2Fcultural_analytics%2FManovich.How_to_Follow_Software_Users.doc.

Manovich, Lev. (2012b). 'How to Compare One Million Images?' In *Understanding Digital Humanities*, ed. David M. Berry, 249–98. New York: Palgrave Macmillan.

Marshall, P. D. (2010). 'Persona Studies: The Proliferation of the Public Self'. Opening Public Lecture, Celebrity News: An Oxymoron, international conference, Geneva, Switzerland: University of Geneva, 15 September.

Marshall, P. D. (2013). 'Persona Studies: Mapping the Proliferation of the Public Self'. *Journalism*, 2 June. Available at: http://jou.sagepub.com/content/early/2013/05/28/1464884913488720.abstract.

Massumi, Brian. (2002). *Parables for the Virtual: Movement, Affect, Sensation*. Durham, NC: Duke University Press.

Melberg, Arne. (1995). *Theories of Mimesis*. Cambridge: Cambridge University Press.

Moore, Christopher. (2010). 'Hats of Affect: A Study of Affect, Achievements and Hats in Team Fortress 2'. *Game Studies* 11, no. 1. Available at: http://gamestudies.org/1101/articles/moore.

Moore, Christopher. (2011). 'The Magic Circle and the Mobility of Play'. *Convergence* 17, no. 4: 373–87.

Moore, Christopher. (2012). 'Invigorating Play: The Role of Affect in Online Multiplayer FPS Game'. In *Guns, Grenades, and Grunts: First-Person Shooter Games*, ed. Gerald A. Voorhees, Josh Call, and Katie Whitlock, 341–63. London: Continuum.

Moretti, Franco. (2000). 'Conjectures on World Literature'. *New Left Review* 1, Jan/Feb 54–68.

Murray, Susan. (2008). 'Digital Images, Photo-Sharing, and Our Shifting Notions of Everyday Aesthetics'. *Journal of Visual Culture* 7, no. 2: 147–63.

Ok, HyeRoung. (2012). 'Cinema in Your Hand, Cinema on the Street: The Aesthetics of Korean Cinema'. *Public*, no. 40: 109–17.

Poremba, Cindy. (2007). 'Point and Shoot: Remediating Photography in Gamespace'. *Games and Culture* 2, no. 1: 49–58.

Raessens, Joost. (2005). 'Computer Games as Participatory Media Culture'. In *Handbook of Computer Games Studies*, ed. J. Raessens and J. Goldstein, 373–88. Cambridge, MA: MIT Press.

Reiger, Oya. Y. (2010). 'Framing Digital Humanities: The Role of New Media in Humanities Scholarship'. *First Monday* 15, no. 10, 4 October. Available at: http://firstmonday.org/htbin/cgiwrap/bin/ojs/index.php/fm/article/view/3198/2628 >.

Rentfrow, Daphnée. (2008). 'S(t)imulating War: From Early Films to Military Games'. In *Computer Games as a Sociocultural Phenomenon: Games Without Frontiers, War Without Tears*, ed. Andreas Jahn-Sudmann and Ralf Stockmann, 87–98. New York: Palgrave Macmillan.

Rieder, Bernhard, and Thoe Röhle. (2012). 'Digital Methods: Five Challenges'. In *Understanding Digital Humanities*, ed. David M. Berry, 67–84. New York: Palgrave Macmillan.

Serres, Michel. (1982). *The Parasite*. Trans. L. Schehr. Minneapolis: University of Minnesota Press.

Smith, Marc. A. (2012). 'Charting Collections of Connections with Maps and Measures'. *Media X Stanford*. Available at: http://www.youtube.com/watch?v=VwVvQhhLUqc.

Sobchack, Vivian. (1999). 'Nostalgia for a Digital Object: Regrets on the Quickening of QuickTime'. *Millennium Film Journal* 34. Available at: http://www.mfj-online.org/journalPages/MFJ34/VivianSobchack.html.

Sontag, Susan. (1977). *On Photography*. London: Penguin.

Svensson, Patrick. (2009). 'Humanities Computing as Digital Humanities'. *Digital Humanities Quarterly* 3, no. 3. Available at: http://digitalhumanities.org/dhq/vol/3/3/000065/000065.html.

Tomkins, Silvan. (1962). *Affect Imagery Consciousness*. Volume 1. *The Positive Affects*. London: Tavistock.

Wilson, Ross. (2007). *Subjective Universality in Kant's Aesthetics*. Berne: Peter Lang.

# Part III
# Critical Curation

# 11
# Rethinking Collections

*Julia Flanders*

For humanists working in the digital research environment, digital collections are a common and familiar formation. In important ways they shape the conditions of our work just as physical collections—libraries, archives, museums—have created and shaped the conditions of knowledge work over the past few centuries. Because of their resemblance to (and in many cases their basis in) physical collections, it may be difficult for us to recognize the novelty of digital collections and the distinctive epistemological conditions under which they present themselves to us. In this chapter I attempt to scrutinize those conditions and bring them to visibility.

To illustrate this novelty very briefly at the outset, consider what happens to our understanding of a 'collection' when its constituent items are no longer the primary unit of meaning. The Google n-grams viewer (https://books.google.com/ngrams) offers a view of the Google Books collection not as a set of texts, but as a set of word groups that can be filtered by time and language. The viewer models for us an approach to collections in which discovering specific textual items within an aggregation is less interesting than discovering trends, subgroupings, patterns. Whereas in a traditional collection the metadata is chiefly significant to us as a way of locating the specific item we seek, in the digital collection we must attach much greater significance to what Carole Palmer calls 'contextual mass': the density and interconnectedness of the collection with respect to a specific theme or research agenda, through which the collection can show us patterns that are both relevant and informationally significant. In order to understand what is distinctive about digital collections, we must look more deeply at both their origins and their conditions of operation.

In the late 1980s and early 1990s the culturally prominent form of digital textuality was not the collection but the hypertext. For early theorists like Andries van Dam, Jay David Bolter, Michael Grusin, and George Landow, the significance of the electronic text rested in its protean malleability and readerliness, its openness to rewriting and to shared authorship. In the world of hypertext, the singularity of the individual text was understood to intersect with the plurality of the hypertextual world through the link: an authored gesture of connectedness that operates rhetorically to carry the reader from one textual locus to another along a reading path.[1] This decentred, rhizomatic structure was understood as the basis for a radical rethinking of textuality and its politics:

> Electronic linking... has radical effects upon our experience of author, text, and work, revealing that many of our most cherished, most commonplace, ideas and attitudes towards literary production are the result of the particular technology of information and cultural memory.... We can be sure that a new era of computerized textuality has begun; but what it will be like we are just beginning to imagine.
>
> (Delaney and Landow 1990, 6–7)

The structural logic of the digital collection, coming into prominence simultaneously but within a quite different research community, instead situates the electronic text within an apparatus of management and authority that tends towards aggregation. The individual item is contextualized within the plurality of the collection through metadata and through the collection's search and navigational apparatus: mechanisms that do not arise as part of the rhetoric of the individual text but rather are constituted as informational layers that may operate independently of any single text. The data standards and digital methods through which this kind of contextualization could take place are those of the digital archive and the digital library: initiatives like the Text Encoding Initiative (TEI), which was begun in 1987 to provide a shared language for representing metadata and transcriptions of primary sources, and the Encoded Archival Description (EAD), which followed soon after as a language for representing archival finding aids in digital form. These and similar research efforts provided the underlying data standards for an entire new research infrastructure of digital editions, digital archives, digital corpora, digitized special collections, and digital 'projects' whose common element—now more visible than ever in the era of large-scale data—was the way they managed and exposed large numbers of texts.

A thought experiment in the first version of the TEI Guidelines (version P1, circulated in 1990) suggests the nature of the shift taking place, from a digital research ecology oriented around individualized relationships between single texts and single scholars to one oriented around the collection. The guidelines offer a scenario in which a scholar of Sanskrit is transcribing a dictionary:

> Suppose that Dr. X has spent two months at his word processor, typing out the text of a Sanskrit dictionary.... Dr. X soon starts to get letters from colleagues who have heard what he has done, and who want copies of the dictionary on disk. Glad to oblige, Dr. X sends out several copies of his work to his grateful colleagues, only to find himself deluged with queries: 'What is the key to the transliteration scheme you have used?' 'You appear to have omitted many Buddhist terms. Was this deliberate? What was your criterion?'... Inevitably, Dr. Y sends Dr. X a disk containing a modified version of the file, in which she has corrected a number of typing errors, and has tagged all the infinitives. Dr. X copies Dr. Y's file onto his hard disk, accidentally overwriting one copy of his own version, and getting into a muddle about which is which. And so on.

How can this situation be controlled?

Clearly it would have saved a lot of wasted time on all sides if Dr. X had included the sort of information he is being asked for as part of the header of his text file in the first place, and if there had been a well-defined place for Dr. Y to record the nature of her modifications.

(Text Encoding Initiative 1990, 5.1.1)

This scenario provides the impetus and use case for information systems like the metadata represented in the TEI header by proposing several things about digitally mediated research. First, it projects a shift from a comparatively inefficient peer-to-peer geometry—in which each scholar communicates directly with all other relevant colleagues and where the distribution of scholarly research materials follows the same path—to a comparatively efficient hub-and-spokes publication model in which data is distributed 'blind' and digitized in anticipation of generalized usage. Second, the scenario posits a resulting need for a formal apparatus of documentation that can operate effectively in this distribution environment. Third, the scenario makes the assumption that research materials will be reused, and by extension that one's research materials are not created for oneself but for others, both present and future. Fourth, the scenario argues that the modelling of the data should follow a set of commonly accepted standards ('a well-defined place') to facilitate this kind of interscholar communication and sharing. The scenario, in other words, establishes the need for not only the TEI Guidelines themselves (considered as a language) but also for the entire apparatus of systems like the TEI as a domain of social and communicative practices.

What would become even clearer with the advent of the Web is how strongly these practices are predicated on the management of research materials through collections. Indeed, the TEI arose at a moment when (and from the fact that) texts began to be distributed in a new way. Once digital texts are created for reuse, the texts themselves start to be considered as infrastructure, one that thus merits development and funding on a large scale, through aggregations organized under a common approach.

The term 'collection' carries a range of meanings that help to locate and bound the concept of the 'digital collection'—and also to historicize it. If we note that a digital collection may arise as a representation of a physical collection—a library collection, a museum collection—we also thereby open a question: To what extent is the digital collection governed (perhaps vestigially) by the same logic of physical proximity, by the kinds of managerial regimes that make physical collections possible, by attention to specific local collection agendas? In other words, how does the digital collection inherit or re-echo constraints that its virtual status should enable it to transcend? Similarly, the digitization of a physical collection is predicated on the emergence of a standard set of methods, on the ability to repeat the act of digitization in a consistent manner across the multiple items that constitute the collection. This standardization in turn speaks not only of technologies that facilitate this repetition, but also of a broadly shared agenda to perform the work: an apparatus of investigation, agreement, 'best practice' that makes the effort intelligible and legitimates it within the institutional setting.

Again, from another angle: We could also define the 'collection' by observing the way it operates through a certain kind of user interface and usage model. We recognize a set of recurring features: the home page or splash screen with its description and navigational options, the invitations to 'Browse' and 'Search', the consistent page design that reminds us that our navigations are taking place within a single informational space. For collections to which access is limited, the collection's home page or navigational entry point is also the means through which authentication can take place. The collection in this sense occupies a 'product' space that has taken shape within the 20 years since the advent of the Web: texts bundled together as a unit that can be conveniently sold, distributed, and used. And even collections that are open access find this paradigm beneficial for the ways it establishes identity and hence permits the assignment of responsibility, credit, and authenticity—the other coin of the realm.

The digital collection in practice goes by many other names that associate it with a more or less specific set of scholarly practices. The proper names of collections are full of these terms: 'Archive', 'Edition', 'Project', 'Collection'.[2] By identifying a genre or a set of scholarly practices through this nomenclature, we are also saying something about our own intentions—or about deliberately holding intentions in abeyance. This identification, too, is historically situated: the 'digital archive' and 'digital edition' emerge as genres through a dialogue about the shaping role of scholarship in constructing the collection and organizing it towards a specific interpretive end or set of research goals, a specific kind of epistemic outcome. By contrast, 'collections' and 'projects' choose to say something instead about work, foregrounding the organizational structure or the topic rather than the treatment of the texts.

However, this varied terminology suggests more systematic differentiation than is really present. These formations now constitute a familiar genre of scholarly digital activity that has also begotten a familiar genre of grant proposal, a familiar formation of workflow and staff, a familiar set of tools. Collections, in the sense that I use the term here, are thus an extraordinarily common way we fund and organize and interact with digital scholarly resources, a great deal of the time. As a result they have taken on a certain self-evidence: we recognize and use the genre without questioning its terms. In the process of this routinization, certain questions have become invisible: How are collections constituted and held together? How do curated collections differ from just-in-time, user-generated, or dynamic collections? How do *we constitute* a collection? In the activity of rethinking that I propose here, I am asking that we examine the work that collections (and in particular digital collections) do for us and how they do it.

## What constitutes a 'collection'?

We now understand a collection as a predominantly *informational* construct, rather than an effect of physical proximity. But if the capacity to virtually aggregate physically distant objects now seems commonplace, it is worth returning to the moment when it was striking and novel—treating the novelty not as an effect of naiveté but as a form of alertness. In a 1996 article on the beginnings of the Rossetti Archive, Jerome McGann describes in considerable detail how that collection constructs the relationship between the data, the interface, and the reader's activities at a time when the Web was very new and the 'browser' was an unfamiliar tool:

> We are constructing software filters that permit the database to generate on-the-fly organizations of the database information....The filters select fields of information from the database and organize them for presentation....The hypermedia structure of the Web then becomes an instrument for organizing further complex searches and comparative studies of the archive's materials.
>
> (McGann 1996, 153)

*   *   *

> Note that in all this structure there is no 'copytext' or 'basic text' or 'reading text'. Every textual document is readable; the student makes the choice, not the editor or the archive's compiler. The latter will of course provide informed commentary—his or her own or others'.... This commentary is not designed to promote any particular approach to the study of the documents, however, but simply to lay out what is known about them, and hence to supply students with information that promotes informed judgments and decisions.
>
> (McGann 1996, 155)

McGann here within the span of a single train of thought comments both on the actual organization of the data—directories and subdirectories, the flow of information from the data files to the web browser, the 'vertical organization of the hypertext structure' (McGann 1996, 154), the role of schemas—and also on the intellectual organizing principle underlying the archive. He is asking in effect how the act of reading (which is also editing) will be constrained within a matrix of possible narratives enabled by the materials and data structures at hand. The crucial methodological decentralization taking place here, the displacement of the 'editor' or 'compiler' in favour of 'students', is being effected by the collection's structure, by its data model.

McGann approaches the account of this collection by assuming that nothing about it is either self-evident or irrelevant. The writing, which to a twenty-first-century reader accustomed to digital seamlessness seems to dwell excessively on details that lie below the threshold of importance (like talking about the exhibit cases in the museum), reveals already an interest in the *architecture*, the *collected-ness* of the archive: in short, the internal logic and workings that cause this thing to hold together both intellectually and technically. Notably, he also assumes that those two organizing principles have everything to do with one another. As he put it elsewhere later on: 'understanding the structure of digital space requires a disciplined aesthetic intelligence' (McGann 2004, xi).

McGann here is doing several things that are very interesting for this analysis. First, he is taking the scholarly edition—a genre that originally looked as if it was organized around a single thing: a 'work' (in the terms established by the Functional Requirements for Bibliographic Records)[3]—and reconceiving it as a collection. He thereby establishes a fundamentally contextual ('social') method-ology of reading around an emerging technology-as-genre. Second, he posits a 'philosophical urgency' (1996, 148) as a motivating force behind the design: an urgency 'toward scholarly editions that can incorporate as much facsimile material as possible into their analytic apparatus', thus moving towards a method-ological inclusiveness or accommodation. This inclusiveness points towards a liberation from an artificial dichotomy between documentary and critical edito-rial approaches. Finally, he is approaching the design of a collection by considering the standards of intellectual adequacy it must meet, the expressive satisfaction it must afford the editor as an expression of textual knowledge. The 'philosophi-cal urgency' he names here arises outside of the digital space; indeed, it has been present all along, evident in the editorial rift he describes. However, it exercises a shaping force upon the collection: for McGann, the shape and size of the digital space designed for the Rossetti Archive has everything to do with a specific set of textual questions. In other words, he is seeking something more nuanced and pre-cise than simple unboundedness or a simple freedom from the constraints of the print book. The space of the digital archive is scoped and bounded by the editorial problem it is designed to address.

Another essay in the same volume suggests a different kind of philosophical urgency—in this case, the urgency of a logic of informational yearning. Simon Gatrell's 'Electronic Hardy' gives a detailed specification of an electronic edition of Thomas Hardy's fiction, in which the space of the digital edition (imagined as potentially limitless) authorizes a fantasy of informational abundance and intel-lectual satisfaction. Gatrell offers us an array of possible materials to include: page images, watermarks, bindings, unpublished documents, printer's archives, visual and auditory reproductions of works of literature and music from which Hardy borrows, images of locales, even (whimsically, as a kind of limit case) the sound of the wind in Hardy's Wessex trees. The difficulty of drawing a line around what 'belongs' in this space—a boundary between the relevant and the irrelevant—calls into question the possibility of defining the edition as a bounded space at all. Almost as if to recuperate that space, the CD-ROM (on which the edition was to be published) serves as a kind of artificial boundary that imposes an arbitrary lim-itation of capacity and forecloses the discussion before it can become more than a thought experiment.

Putting these two cases side by side, we can pose already a set of important ques-tions. First, how do the boundedness and internal cohesion of a collection help to define its intellectual purpose? What happens, particularly in the digital realm, if we think of those bounds as intellectually enabling and as having to do with genre rather than imposed by limitations on technology or resources? Is Google

Books an environment with an intellectual purpose, or does the trajectory that takes us from 'text' to 'edition' and thence to 'oeuvre', to 'genre', 'period', and 'topic' ultimately bring us simply to 'totality'—at which point we are both everywhere and nowhere? Another way of asking these questions is to ask how the modelling of the collection—that is, the set of parameters by which its boundedness and internal cohesion are precisely determined—helps to define and reflect its intellectual purposes. Once we have identified the possibility of a 'philosophical urgency' motivating the design of a collection, we are also in a position to attribute agency to this urgency: Who experiences it? For whom does this urgency produce a set of responsibilities, and what are they? For whom is the collection modelled?

## What are we modelling in a collection?

One way of coming at these questions is to inventory the informational regions where modelling takes place. An obvious place is metadata *about* the collection: for instance, information about the forms of agency through which the collection comes into being, such as authorship, creation, sponsorship, and data curation practices. Similarly, we typically represent information about the design of the collection qua collection: selection criteria, representational practices (transcription practices, interface design, encoding methods, etc.). We might also include here the ways in which we represent the identity, boundaries, and contents of the individual items themselves through their representation as specific data objects with item-specific metadata.

In a subtler way, we also model collections through explicit interconnections between items, or between the collection and a set of related resources. These may take the form of cross-references, links between multiple witnesses or versions, relationships between different expressions of the same work, links to common data sources such as glossaries or gazetteers, or shared systems of annotations. What this modelling establishes (by both its exclusions and its inclusions) is a common intellectual regime for the collection, a frame of reference or informational horizon within which it operates. For example, a collection that resolves geographic references to a modern mapping service creates a very different set of interpretive and analytical possibilities from one that uses a georeferenced map contemporary with the collection's contents.

If we shift our attention to metamodels, we encounter ways of representing the *shape* of the collection through systems of constraint such as schemas, data typing, database field definitions, and the like. Systems like these can tell us (and can allow us to control) how varied the collection's information structures and descriptive vocabularies are, and precisely where the collection's items most differ from or resemble one another.

Finally, through the collection interface, we also model the reader's epistemological relationship to the collection: What can the collection assume about what the reader knows? A table of contents assumes a level of familiarity with individual titles: when I see the thing I want, I will recognize it. A search interface, on the other hand, assumes a knowledge (or a set of expected parameters) about the significant features of the text that will permit it to be retrieved. 'Recognition' and 'discovery' interfaces both work from the same kinds of aggregated item-level phenomena: metadata like author, genre, date, and subject. But in addition to these explicit facts worn on its sleeve, the collection may also provide a view of internal or implicit phenomena through which we perceive or discover its subtler contours. These phenomena are commonalities and patterns that emerge from the collection itself by inspection through tools like data mining or text analysis: for instance, the distribution of specific parts of speech within a linguistic corpus, or the set of 'topics' that emerges as an effect of vocabulary distribution in topic analysis. As with a contour map, when we set a threshold of visibility or granularity in a certain place, we see a profile emerge that seems to identify a 'feature' or a set of 'features': a genre, a repeated rhetorical pattern, an authorial style. But these will change their shape and even their perceptibility as a function of how the data is modelled and how it is inspected.

The complex distribution of agency that becomes evident in these different kinds of modelling sheds a different light on McGann's 'philosophical urgency'. The design parameters that he outlines in such detail, and that are so carefully aimed at achieving a radical editorial outcome, constitute a form of conscious modelling that we can now understand as only a small part of the collection's actual informational shape. The commonalities and patterns the collection reveals to us at the intersection of its interface and our inquiry are unforeseeable, in large degree, by the collection's designers, although shaped by their choices. Another way to say this is that these commonalities or associations are not simply 'there' to be found, waiting for us in some literal sense through the modelling work of the collection's creators: they are assembled and constituted, both through activities of inquiry and also through the ideological systems that create the conditions of perceptibility, the sense of what can be thought.

Steve Ramsay starts an article entitled 'The Hermeneutics of Screwing Around' with the premise that the collection is necessary. It serves, in effect, as a useful model or miniature of the world that we can use as its surrogate. The features of the 'collection' that are familiar to us (for instance the search and browse interface, the connection between the 'result' and the fuller context where it occurs) all serve to shuttle us between the convenient epitome and the fuller reality that we ultimately would love to master if we had infinite time. Ramsay points out, however, that while this shuttling is often structured (by collection interfaces) as if it were laden with specific intention and driven by specific questions, in fact it is often (more productively) motivated by what he calls 'the hermeneutics of screwing around':

> The second way goes like this: I walk into the library and wander around in a state of insouciant boredom. I like music, so I head over to the music section. I pick up a book on American rock music and start flipping through it . . . .
>
> This is called browsing, and it's a completely different activity [from searching]. Here, I don't know what I'm looking for, really. I just have a bundle of 'interests'

and proclivities. I'm not really trying to find 'a path through culture'. I'm really just screwing around....

'Can I help you?' 'No, I'm just browsing.' Translation: 'I just got here! How can you help me find what I'm looking for when (a) I don't know what's here and (b) I don't know what I'm looking for?' The sales clerk, of course, doesn't need a translation.

(Ramsay 2010)

Ramsay contrasts this approach with the always doomed strategy of mastery, the attempt to find 'an ordered path through culture' that will approximate what we imagine to be the truth about that culture: in other words, what we would know about culture if we could see every point in the cultural matrix at the same level of detail as we can see the one we are currently scrutinizing.

If we take Ramsay's point seriously, it has some interesting implications for our understanding of the collection. 'Searching' produces a contingent, negotiated, just-in-time, dynamically derived 'collection' that responds to a specific question or wish. Searching infers the presence of an answer from a set of markers for that answer (i.e., search terms, metadata fields). The kind of 'screwing around' or 'browsing' that Ramsay describes (*exploring* rather than *searching*) can be guided and shaped (and made more fruitful) by the associative logic underlying the collection itself. Thus browsing in a record store is different from browsing in a grocery store or a library or a used book store or an attic. To a certain extent, for the browsing reader, the collection itself (its collectedness) acts as a proxy or substitute for the intentionality of the 'search'. Once we understand this, we can articulate a more nuanced sense of the 'search': not as a request by the reader for a specific set of things, but rather a request that the collection reveal its modelling to us: that it offer us (to use Mitchell Whitelaw's terms[4]) an interface that is 'generous' rather than 'stingy'). Instead of playing a guessing game with the passive-aggressive collection, we would much prefer to be able to ask the collection to show us its hand in a helpful way; we would like to understand how the collection is modelled, understand what meaningful categories are represented in it, so that we can explore with some intelligence. We want the collection to throw its data out like patterns of sparks, like magnetic fields that we can use to learn our way through it.

Our exploration of that data might happen through a good collection interface, with tools that reflect the collection's own internal modelling: maps, timelines, spatial visualizations. But it might also happen through data mining, as in Ramsay's discussion, or by further extension through access to an API (Application Programming Interface) that gives us direct access to the modelling of the collection at the deepest level. The algorithms through which we explore are themselves *collection models* insofar as they successfully model language structures, identification of named entities, rhetorical features, and so forth.

## What is the cultural significance of collections?

Let me conclude by thinking about collections from another angle: one that brings us back to questions of agency and design in an attempt to understand the cultural significance of collections. In 'Sidney's Technology', Alan Liu (2008) examines the modelling of literary history, and in a tantalizingly brief and suggestive passage at the very end he juxtaposes two different modelling regimes: the *network* and the *patchwork*. He has not developed this juxtaposition further, but we can make some useful extrapolations from his starting point. We can understand the network as a flow of information via interconnection, a perpetual ongoing contextualization through which literary histories 'manage and socialise representations of literature' (204). The patchwork by contrast is understood as an assemblage; the metaphoric resonance of 'patchwork' implies a suturing together of things that were previously unrelated, though it assumes they are commensurable, can be accommodated to one another (for instance, all textiles). While the network models things that we stipulate are 'there to be modelled', so to speak (in other words, that have a kind of prior connectability), the patchwork asserts juxtapositions by main force, through a violent, highly crafted assemblage. Patchwork assumes that collectability does not arise from the natural properties of objects but from our will to collect.

How does this help us think about collections? What would it mean to 'collect' under the sign of patchwork quilting rather than under the sign of the network? For one thing, it turns our attention *from* the phenomenon of the collection itself (its 'thereness') *to* the animating method—the 'technique' in Alan Liu's terms—through which the collection comes into being: in effect, it asks us to think about the collection as an *activity* rather than a self-evident *thing* or a set. A network connects pre-existing informational nodes that are assumed to be commensurable, intertranslatable: in literal terms, a network (technically) constitutes and is underpinned by a set of agreements about communication and linking protocols. You have to be on the network—you have to be addressable—in order *to be addressed*.

A collection operating under the sign of (or within the terms of) the network is one that assumes from the start that the connections are there to be discovered, marked, connected to. It proceeds in an optimistic and progressive spirit, an assumption that is analogous to what Liu elsewhere calls 'the blind spot on the page' in web design, the space of the feed or the query: in interface terms, the protocol or algorithm for invoking the content via a uniform set of parameters from an already known set of available data feeds or fields. A patchwork or mosaic, on the other hand, connects pre-existing informational nodes while acknowledging them to be *incommensurable:* taken from different semantic spaces, from different contexts of purposiveness and original utility, not automatically the right size and shape. It reshapes information spaces and connects them by doing the work of that connection: making them fit, accommodating their oddities to a new design. A collection operating under the sign of patchwork quilting, we might imagine (we can't imagine it otherwise) will be cobbled together, ad hoc, 'hacked' as Liu puts it (2002): marked as unsatisfactory from a viewpoint of extensible, maintainable design. It will also bear and acknowledge the visible marks of its own madeness.

The digital humanities has something of a divided allegiance here. 'Madeness' is an appealing concept in a discipline that has embraced the 'maker culture' and that has a sustained engagement with media specificity and materiality.[5] At the same time, the digital humanities has a deep investment in the emerging seamlessness of what Liu calls the 'network': the increasing harmonization of data standards and vocabularies, and linking protocols, towards an ever more complete commensurability. We avow the possibility, the necessity, the desirability of this network as a mode of operation and a design principle, and we desire earnestly that our data can approach this state of total commensurability. Yet we are at the same time aware of the friction, the edge cases, the material that can't be thought, the data that can't be brought under rule: the inconvenient postscript, the writing up the side of the page, the book with a title page in its middle, the nonrectilinear book. We treat these cases as exceptions that prove, rather than test, the rule: we nod to them ('It's an imperfect world') but we treat them as noise rather than as signal; we deny that they are the meaning of the system. The patchwork collection would be a way, perhaps, of admitting to the internal friction and representing exceptionality, rather than conformance to type, as the interesting case.

The ongoing debate within the TEI community about interoperability is an important example in this context: it is essentially an argument about how much the exceptional case should be representable. Each of the collections I work with has its frictional case, of which I will offer just one example. The Women Writers Project's symptomatic exception, interestingly enough, is a text called 'A Patchwork Screen for the Ladies', which exhibits what the TEI world familiarly calls the Sheherezade Problem in a peculiarly acute form. It consists of a set of nested stories grouped within a framing narrative; it thus violates the TEI's paradigmatic understanding of document structure and for a time was genuinely unencodable until the creation of a new element (the 'floating text') to represent this peculiar kind of structure. So this patchwork text serves as a marker—by its difference—of the textual assumptions that underpin standard ideas of book design and that carry over into the design of major representational systems like the TEI: it captures the friction within the system rather than smoothing it over.

If the patchwork collection thus acknowledges its manufactured quality, then it can also help us understand the collection as both expressing and supporting analysis. It expresses, through its internal modelling, the theories of genre, textuality, and so forth that shape the information being offered. To return to Steve Ramsay's browsing scenario, this would be the equivalent of a sign declaring whether the collection is a whole foods cooperative with grains in big bins, or a convenience store where we'll find neatly boxed packets of flavoured oatmeal. And the patchwork collection supports analysis, through that same explicitness and transparency, by permitting a distinctively important kind of intellectual transaction: not the all-sufficiency of traditional scholarly product that seeks to say everything itself, and not the passivity of the library that seeks only to 'support' and be 'raw', but a give and take, a negotiation of meaning that reminds us that scholarly inquiry is always a transaction involving agency on both ends.

## Notes

1. See, for instance, Bolter 1991/2001; Landow 1992/1997. For a more critical view, see Moulthrop 1994.
2. Some examples by way of illustration: the Walt Whitman Archive, the Rossetti Archive, the Willa Cather Archive, the Herman Melville Electronic Library: A Critical Archive, the Dickinson Electronic Archives, the William Blake Archive, the Piers Plowman Electronic Archive, the Canterbury Tales Project, the Women Writers Project, and the Victorian Women Writers Project.
3. The Functional Requirements for Bibliographic Records (FRBR) define four primary entities representing levels at which bibliographic records may represent bibliographic objects: work, expression, manifestation, and item. The 'work' level is the authorial idea distinct from any realization through language or material instantiation.
4. I am grateful to Katherine Bode for drawing my attention to this important connection.
5. Matthew Kirschenbaum's work on 'forensic' and 'formal' materiality is also crucial here: that distinction and the way it is enacted at a technical level is an important instance of the friction I am describing here. See Kirschenbaum 2012.

## Works cited

Bolter, Jay David. (1991/2001). *Writing Space: The Computer, Hypertext, and the History of Writing*; 2nd ed.: *Writing Space: Computers, Hypertext, and the Remediation of Print*. Mahwah, NJ: Lawrence Erlbaum Associates.

Gatrell, Simon. (1996). 'Electronic Hardy'. In *The Literary Text in the Digital Age*, ed. Richard Finneran, 185–92. Ann Arbor: University of Michigan Press.

Kirschenbaum, Matthew. (2012). *Mechanisms: New Media and the Forensic Imagination*. Cambridge, MA: MIT Press.

Landow, George. (1992/1997). *Hypertext: The Convergence of Contemporary Critical Theory and Technology*; reprinted as *Hypertext 2.0: The Convergence of Contemporary Critical Theory and Technology*. Baltimore: Johns Hopkins University Press.

Liu, Alan. (2002). 'The Art of Extraction: Toward a Cultural History and Aesthetics of XML and Database-Driven Web Sites'. Text of a paper delivered at the Interfacing Knowledge conference, University of California, Santa Barbara, March. Available at: http://dc-mrg.english.ucsb.edu/conference/2002/documents/Alan_Liu_Art_of_Extraction.html.

Liu, Alan. (2008). 'Sidney's Technology'. In *Local Transcendence: Essay on Postmodern Historicism and the Database*, 187–206. Chicago: University of Chicago Press.

McGann, Jerome J. (1996). 'The Rossetti Archive and Image-Based Electronic Editing'. In *The Literary Text in the Digital Age*, ed. Richard Finneran, 145–83. Ann Arbor: University of Michigan Press.

McGann, Jerome J. (2004). *Radiant Textuality: Literature After the World Wide Web*. London: Palgrave Macmillan.

Moulthrop, Stuart. (1994). 'Rhizome and Resistance: Hypertext and the Dreams of a New Culture'. In *Hyper/Text/Theory*, ed. George Landow, 299–322. Baltimore: Johns Hopkins University Press.

Ramsay, Stephen. (2010). 'The Hermeneutics of Screwing Around; or What You Do with a Million Books'. Text of a paper delivered at Brown University, April. Available at: http://www.playingwithhistory.com.

*Text Encoding Initiative P1 Guidelines for the Encoding and Interchange of Machine Readable Texts*. (1990). Draft Version 1.1, 1 November. Available at: http://www.tei-c.org/Vault/GL/teip1.tar.gz.

# 12
# Methods and Canons

## An Interdisciplinary Excursion

*Katherine Bode and Tara Murphy*

A growing number of data-rich analyses of literature and literary culture—variously described as 'distant reading' (Moretti 2005), 'algorithmic criticism' (Ramsay 2008), 'macroanalysis' (Jockers 2013), and 'new empiricism' (Bode and Dixon 2009)—have in the last decade significantly transformed literary studies. This international trend is strongly reflected in Australian literary studies, where there have been multiple quantitative analyses of borrowing records (Dolin 2004, 2006; Lamond 2012; Lamond and Reid 2009), book sales (Davis 2007; Zwar 2012a, 2012b), newspaper reviews (Thomson and Dale 2009), and bibliographic data (Bode 2010, 2012a, 2012b; Carter 2007; Ensor 2008, 2009; Nile and Ensor 2009). As important as this work has been for reconceptualizing the object and scope of literary studies, its credibility and progress as a whole is inhibited by the fact that many of these authors provide little detailed discussion of the processes involved in creating, curating, and analysing their data sources. Even less rarely do they publish these sources. While there are exceptions,[1] such lack of access to data is true of the most high-profile work in this field—including Jockers's and Moretti's influential monographs—and prevents other scholars from investigating, extending, and potentially challenging these authors' findings and arguments.

This situation cannot be blamed on traditional publishing conventions. Not only are there now humanities journals that enable and encourage this activity—not least of all, digital humanities journals such as *Literary and Linguistic Computing* and *Digital Humanities Quarterly*—but any researcher capable of producing and analysing data in the first place can easily release this data online, and refer or link to it in any publication, print or digital.[2] The situation instead arises from the complex relationship of literary studies and methodology. Perhaps more than any other discipline, literary critics routinely occlude methodology, such that a 'close reading' of, for instance, sexuality in the works of Shakespeare and Marlowe is presented as a clear and apparent object of study without reference to the selections, and gradual accretion of evidence and patterns, that led to the identification and conceptualization of this topic. More pointedly, those areas of literary studies—such as bibliography and scholarly editing—that focus explicitly on methodology have, in the last half century, been separated from and regarded as ancillary to the more high-profile and esteemed work of literary criticism and theory (McGann 2004, 409).

Arguably, the history of computational literary studies compounds this perception of methodologically explicit literary research as marginal and inferior, further diminishing the willingness of literary scholars in digital humanities to discuss and—by publishing their data—demonstrate their methodology. As Stephen Ramsay argues, part of the reason why traditional forms of humanities computing, such as computational stylistics, have been ignored by mainstream literary scholars is that their focus on method is bound up in a narrow, positivist scientific paradigm where 'the accumulation of verified, falsifiable facts' is the point of the exercise and the only 'basis for interpretive judgment' (2008). This approach is not only theoretically naïve but, existing at odds with the hermeneutics of most literary criticism, does not address and advance the concerns of that field. In the shift from humanities computing to digital humanities, and the forging of new historical, interpretive, and expansive approaches to literary data, there is a sense in which the detailed attention to methodology that characterizes computational stylistics has been sloughed off as part of an embarrassing history of scientific positivism.

While methodological openness and access to data are necessary for digital and data-rich literary scholarship to progress and gain credibility, it would be entirely counterproductive if this was the only focus; the field also needs to fulfil the requirements of all humanities research: of presenting arguments, providing insights, and advancing new understandings. This paper presents one model for integrating these aspects of research that draws explicitly on our interdisciplinary collaboration between a literary scholar and an astrophysicist to adapt for digital humanities a common form of publishing in astronomy. Key to research in this scientific field are articles that announce the release of new data; describe the processes, decisions, and selections underpinning the creation and exploration of this data; and present initial analyses and findings.[3] Other astronomers are able to assess how the data has been collected, defined, and analysed: if they agree with this process and its outcomes, they can use the data in their own research, citing the original paper so that they do not need to go into the same level of detail about the data; if they disagree, they can challenge the findings and offer alternative interpretations. Importantly, such articles also provide a means of recognizing and rewarding the important and time-consuming work of gathering, processing, and investigating large amounts of data, and in this respect could help to address a difficult problem in the digital humanities—the lack of reward for creating, implementing, and maintaining digital collections and resources[4]—that has itself contributed to minimal publication of data sources in this field.

Following this model, in this chapter we announce a new resource for humanities research: four datasets regarding critical attention to Australian novelists.[5] The first part of this chapter describes the processes by which we gathered data from AustLit[6]—an online bibliography of works on and about Australian literature—and checked, cleaned, and analysed these datasets to identify their limitations and potential. The second part uses these datasets to explore canon formation in this national literary field, as well as related issues of cultural value of interest to the humanities broadly. Far from reasserting the narrow scientific positivism that Ramsay criticizes in computational stylistics, the view of data in this chapter—and indeed, despite the perceptions of some humanities scholars, across the sciences—is as an outcome of multiple decisions, and based on arguments, not certainties, regarding degrees of reliability, bias, and purpose. Our point in this chapter is not only to combine the presentation of important research findings and questions with explicit discussion of methodology and publication of datasets; it is to highlight that these supposedly technical issues are themselves inherently critical and theoretical, and they cannot be separated off from the arguments they underpin. By describing our journey from the original conceptualization of the project to the types of questioning we ultimately believe these datasets can support, we demonstrate that data-rich research requires not comprehensiveness or completeness, but a clear understanding of data characteristics and parameters.

## Methods

Created in 1999, AustLit merged a number of existing specialist datasets and bibliographies and has since involved well over a hundred individual researchers, supplementing and updating records of works of and about Australian literature. The database now contains almost a million records and aims 'to be the definitive virtual research environment and information source for Australian literary, print, and narrative culture scholars, students, and the public'.[7] Indeed, due to the work of many individuals, the long-standing investment of government and institutional funding, and the relatively recent origins of Australian literature, AustLit is the most comprehensive online bibliography of a national literature currently available. In this respect, it offers a valuable test case for future quantitative work with a range of digital bibliographies not currently at this stage of development. At the same time, the data in AustLit is not perfect or complete; AustLit also warns that its data is not sufficient for statistical analysis. We return to these two points in detail.

Our collaboration began as an attempt to explore 'The Critical Careers of Australian Novelists', with respect to publication, reception, and reputation. AustLit lists 'works by' and 'works about' each Australian author in the database. Approximately half of all Australian authors with novels published from 1900 to 2006 (the period we consider) have no 'works about'. Even so, 'works about' are by far the most extensive component of the database. Among these, articles in newspapers, literary magazines and academic journals, and books and book chapters predominate, but other forms include bibliographies and collections, correspondence, dissertations, literary responses and screen adaptations, and multimedia and websites.[8] When we started the project, we were interested in whether different relationships between novel publication and critical reception exist for particular groups of novelists: for instance, do authors who receive no critical attention tend to write in particular genres, or at particular times; do men and women novelists tend to accrue critical attention at different rates; is there a particular trajectory of critical reception (for instance, immediate attention or the gradual accrual of critical acclaim) more likely to lead to an established and long-standing prominence in the critical arena (in other words, how might canonical literary reputations develop)? We hoped that analysis of large numbers of reviews of authors' works would produce patterns representative of particular relations to the literary field and its processes of reputation building.

AustLit is designed, and predominantly used, for finding information about particular authors or texts. Its guided search function enables searching of particular literary forms, date ranges, genres, and so on, and up to 1,000 results can be displayed and extracted as tagged text; but there is presently no facility to explore the database using a general query language. The impossibility of directly querying AustLit, and the volume of data on critical works, meant that to perform this study we had to automatically extract the data by writing code that performed, much more quickly than is manually possible, the searches supported by AustLit (entering each author's name, requesting 'works about' them, then going to each of those works to gather the bibliographical data). This process occurred in February 2007, using a list of novelists that excluded 'non-AustLit' authors,[9] and yielded a dataset with characteristics shown in Table 12.1.

As with any manually created resource, some entries in AustLit contain inconsistencies—such as the same information entered in different ways or under different headings[10]—that present difficulties for automatic extraction. To check that our extraction process did not introduce errors, we conducted a number of tests, including randomly selecting subsamples of authors and works and manually comparing their attributes with AustLit's online records and producing diagnostic plots to map the dataset to identify outliers. Outliers often reveal errors in the data, but if not erroneous, they can indicate exceptional or interesting cases. An example diagnostic plot is Figure 12.1, which displays authors according to the

*Table 12.1*   Properties of the dataset extracted from AustLit

| | | |
|---|---|---|
| Total Number of Authors | 11,305 | |
| Authors with ≥ 1 novels | 5,837 | |
| Authors with ≥ 1 poems | 5,463 | |
| Authors with ≥ 1 short stories | 1,527 | |
| Total Number of Novels | 19,671 | |
| Total Number of 'Works About' | 92,250 | |
| Review | 47,067 | (51%) |
| Criticism | 18,164 | (20%) |
| Biography | 9,186 | (10%) |
| Column | 7,630 | (8%) |
| Interview | 2,088 | (2%) |
| Uncategorized | 1,820 | (2%) |
| Autobiography | 1,492 | (2%) |
| Correspondence | 1,256 | (1%) |
| Other[11] | 3,547 | (4%) |

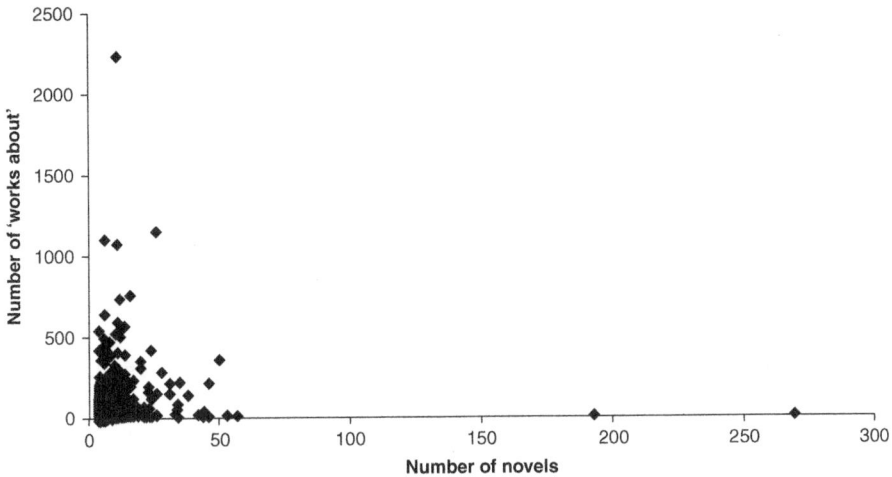

*Figure 12.1* Australian novelists—number of novels written and number of 'works about'

number of novels written versus the number of 'works about' received.[12] By repeating these diagnostic procedures, we improved our system to the point where we were confident that the extraction process had not distorted the dataset.

From there, we turned to assessing the nature and reliability of our extracted data. As might be expected with a database designed for individual searches, AustLit's descriptions of its data are not helpful in determining the types of quantitative analysis it can support. Describing the ongoing work 'to correct unevenness and gaps in bibliographic coverage', AustLit states that 'until this process is complete, some AustLit data is insufficiently comprehensive to be used for statistical analyses'.[13] Even where the database attempts to provide detail, information about the scope and content of AustLit's 'works about' Australian authors and texts is frustratingly vague. Noting that its 'coverage is stronger in some areas than in others', AustLit continues, 'Periodical and newspaper literature, for example, is much more comprehensively covered from 1988 than for earlier years. Some specialist areas are rich and virtually complete, while others continue to evolve. Coverage of the nation's major newspapers is extensive but not exhaustive.'[14] While this reference to 1988 proved useful in our analysis, as we will show, for the most part these descriptions—no time frame for completion of the process of correction; vague references to 'some' and 'other' areas—offer no useful overview of content and scope for defining the parameters for quantitative analyses.

While on the surface AustLit is simply warning researchers of possible gaps in its records, at a deeper level its reference to a future where these problems will no longer exist implies the possibility of perfect and complete data, and identifies such perfection and completeness as a precondition of quantitative analysis. The simple, practical consideration of the inevitable lag between the ongoing publication of works of and about Australian literature and their inclusion in AustLit precludes this imagined future ever arriving. More importantly, ontologically, it is impossible for any dataset of Australian literature to be complete and correct. As is acknowledged elsewhere in AustLit, '[t]he definition of "Australian" and "Literature" moves according to current debates and changing reading, teaching and research patterns'.[15] Instead of a situation where AustLit approaches and eventually attains a reflection of the 'real world' of Australian literature, the database is engaged in an ongoing process of representing and constructing that category. Where AustLit can develop a set of parameters to define, for instance, an 'Australian author'—including, at present, such considerations as where they were born, where they spent their formative years, and the content of their fiction[16]—this category is inevitably dependent on a current set of interpretations and thus will change as the Australian literary field is continually redefined.

Rather than awaiting perfect data, our aim and challenge were to define a 'static' dataset suitable for analysis from a changing and evolving database; in this respect, characterizing the data is key. More broadly, such characterization is increasingly important for humanities research because of the growing interest in data-rich analysis of major datasets (such as Google Books, Gale's Nineteenth Century Collections Online, the National Library of Australia's Trove Database, the British Library's Newspaper Archive) that were not specifically created to enable quantitative analysis.[17] One important—and somewhat limiting—characteristic of our datasets arises from the definitions we employed in our process of extraction. We defined an Australian novelist as any 'Australian' author in AustLit who had written at least one novel. As a result, our data is linked to the author, not the novel, and thus cannot indicate titles that received more attention than others. This definition also means that authors are present in the dataset who have written a novel or novels, but who are primarily known—and who received the majority, if not the totality, of critical attention recorded in AustLit—for other literary genres, such as poetry or plays. In other words, these authors we defined as Australian novelists by one set of parameters would not be defined as Australian novelists within literary critical discussion broadly.

To minimize the number of authors in this category, we removed from our datasets authors who had written only one novel. While this step improved the overall focus of the data, it also introduced bias (a dataset absent of first-time authors and excluding one writer in particular, Helen Darville, who received substantial attention—much of it negative—in relation to a single novel[18]). This bias we justified by our interest in tracking the careers of authors; in this respect, novelists with only one title cannot usefully be compared to authors with multiple novels. Note that the introduction of bias—while never an aim of quantitative analysis—is only a travesty if data is perceived as truth or fact. Acknowledging, instead, that all data is value-laden and culturally produced changes the goal from eliminating bias to identifying, and either attempting to accommodate, or make an argument for, the types of bias that inhere in data.

As part of the process of characterizing our datasets—to assess the types of analysis and questioning they can support and enable—we created a series of plots for Australian novelists showing the titles they published in relation to the critical commentary they received. Figure 12.2 shows these results for Katharine Susannah

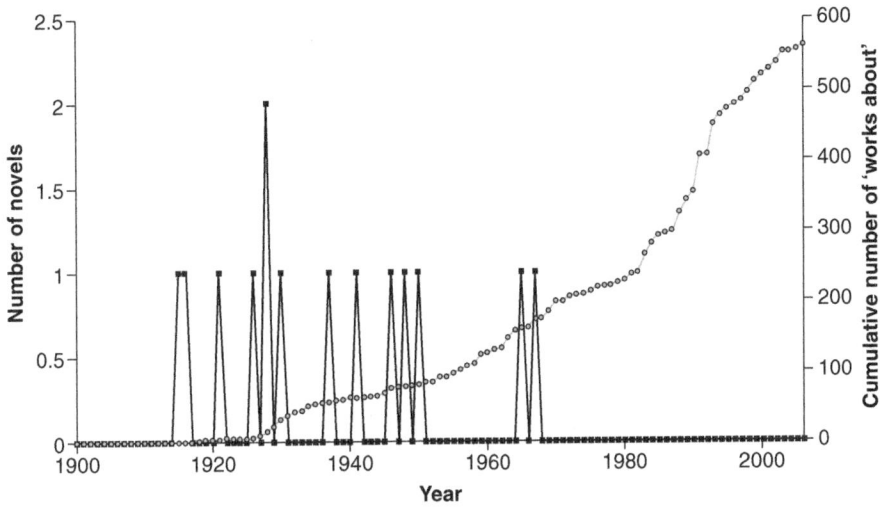

*Figure 12.2*  Katharine Susannah Prichard: number of novels by and 'works about', 1900–2006

Prichard (1883–1969), a politically active Australian journalist and renowned novelist, with the left-hand axis measuring the number of novels published, the right-hand axis the cumulative number of 'works about' Prichard, and the x-axis the years of both types of publication.

According to the results displayed in this graph, Prichard received some critical attention for her first three or four novels, but this attention significantly accelerated in the late 1920s, following the publication of *Working Bullocks*, *Coonardoo*, and *The Wild Oats of Han*. Two further stages of accelerated growth in critical attention follow: first, from the late 1950s to the early 1970s, during which time she published only one novel; and second, from the early 1980s to the mid-2000s, after Prichard's death. In the 1980s and 1990s, approximately the same number of 'works about' Prichard was published as in the previous seven decades. One could easily imagine a whole article exploring these different phases and the factors contributing to the posthumous growth in Prichard's reputation: Is this an ongoing effect of second-wave feminism, a consequence of the more general vogue for anthologizing earlier Australian authors, or something else (for instance, the professionalization of criticism as 'research' in universities in the 1980s, and of research as a key performance indicator in these institutions)?

While the idea of such an article is exciting, comparison of these results for Prichard with the overall number of 'works about' extracted, shown in Figure 12.3, raises questions about the reliability of this type of analysis. Figure 12.3 shows the same stages of growth in critical attention overall—in the 1920s and 1930s, in the 1960s, and in the 1980s and 1990s—as Figure 12.2 shows for Prichard.[19] The correspondence between these periods of growth raises the possibility that 'trends' in critical attention to Prichard could actually reflect broader shifts in AustLit's

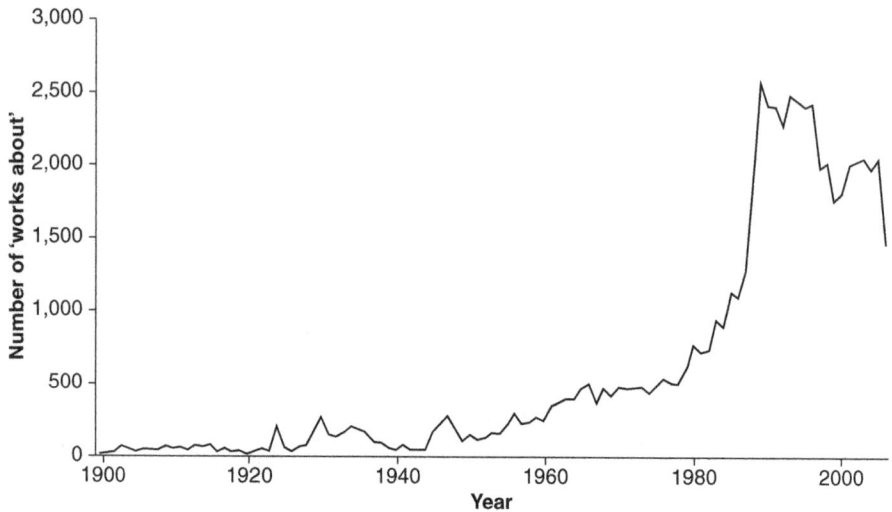

*Figure 12.3*  Total number of 'works about'

indexing process. Comparison with other authors does not resolve this issue: the same pattern could indicate the relative comprehensiveness of AustLit at particular times, similarities in the critical reputations of those authors, or increased attention to Australian literature broadly; differences could signal dissimilarities in the critical reputations of authors or different degrees of focus, from AustLit, on those individuals. More broadly, the growth in critical attention to Prichard, in these three periods and overall, correspond with what David Carter identifies as three periods of nation-oriented expansion of critical attention to Australian literature: 'intellectual nationalism' in the 1920s and 1930s; institutionalization and professionalization in the 1950s and 1960s; and 'neo-nationalism' in the 1980s and 1990s (2000). There is simply not enough information, from these graphs and AustLit's account of its scope and content, to determine the significance of these numerical results. Proposing that these trends are reliable because they correlate with the accepted history of Australian literary criticism runs the risk of confirmation bias (of accepting the interpretation that confirms existing, and strongly held, beliefs). These beliefs could equally have shaped the collection of data, with indexing inadvertently focused on those periods when 'works about' Australian novelists are perceived to be highest (a process known as selection bias).

Further analysis, however, suggests that indexing has not been overly skewed by such selection bias or by the more comprehensive attention to periodical and newspaper records after 1988 (the only specific information AustLit provides regarding content and scope). Figure 12.4 represents the number of authors per decade who were ranked in the top ten for critical attention each year (a number that must be between ten—if the same ten authors shared the top ten positions each year—and 100—if the top ten authors were different each year).[20] If either of the effects described above occurred, we would expect to see a greater range of authors in the periods aligned with the expansion of literary criticism—the 1920s

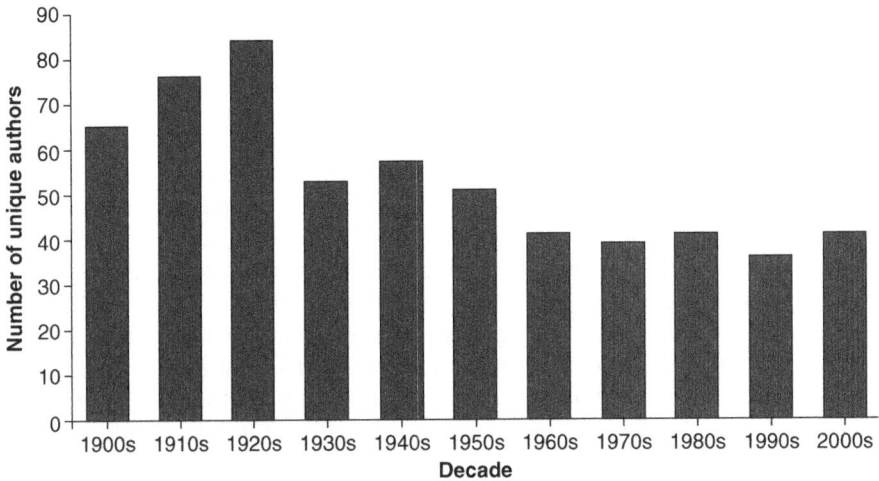

*Figure 12.4* Number of unique authors in the yearly top ten for 'works about', per decade

and 1930s, the 1960s, and the 1980s and 1990s—and a more limited range at other times. As Figure 12.4 shows, this pattern does not occur; instead, there is an overall decline, from the 1920s, in the number of unique authors in the top ten for critical attention.

While we believe the data has not been significantly skewed by our extraction process or by AustLit's indexing practices, and we can thus offer a reliable basis for analysis of trends over time, it should not be understood as either a complete or a random sample of critical attention to Australian novelists. It seems likely the data will have some bias towards well-known authors, so any comparison of those at the top of the critical hierarchy with those lower in the rankings should be conducted with full awareness of this probability. In particular, given the lack of detail from AustLit regarding scope and content, questions relying on numerical accuracy, including those across a range of authors—for instance, the percentage of novelists who were the subject of two 'works about'—cannot usefully be asked. For those seeking information about individual authors or to compare particular careers, AustLit will be the best resource, supplemented by intensive checking of records to ensure that all 'works about' are discovered.

The four datasets we have produced—and which provide the basis for the second part of this paper—include the number of overall 'works about' received by Australian novelists from 1900 to 2006, as well as the number of 'works about' in the three categories of publication from 1950 to 2006: newspapers, academic journals and literary magazines.[21]

## Canons

The process of literary reputation making has been explored by Pierre Bourdieu, in his groundbreaking sociological work on the literary field (1983, 1996), and by scholars in both literary studies and empirical literary studies.[22] Although Bourdieu is frequently cited as a reference point for this latter group, unlike Bourdieu—who focuses on the 'struggle' among multiple groups, institutions, and individuals in the literary field—researchers in empirical literary studies are generally united in their censure of literary criticism as an activity that does not and cannot do what it supposedly claims to do: gauge literary quality and assign authors positions in a hierarchy on that basis. According to Marc Verboord, lacking a 'clear theoretical and empirical grounding'—and especially without 'unequivocal standard[s] to measure literary quality'—literary criticism is 'methodologically unsustainable' (2003, 259). Similarly, C. J. Van Rees contends that, 'most of the critical tenets on a writer's work are defective insofar as they fail to be empirically testable', and as a result, literary critics 'lack the capacity of ascertaining the intrinsic quality of a work of art' (1987, 275, 276). Such statements clearly demonstrate the same uncritical positivism, theoretical naivety, and misunderstanding of the hermeneutics of literary criticism that Ramsay identifies in computational stylistics, and show why these studies have had no effect on mainstream literary criticism's discussion of reputation.

These features of their approach also underpin the erroneous view of empirical literary scholars that the findings of their studies—that factors external to the text affect the likelihood of an author receiving critical attention[23]—challenge the very grounds of literary criticism. In fact, while the Romantic ideal of the author as solitary genius remains an influence in literary criticism, it would be difficult to find a literary scholar who did not recognize that value judgements are at least partly culturally produced—that is, the product of social, economic, national, institutional, and professional interests. Indeed, although empirical literary scholars are apparently unaware of them, one of the things that literary critical analyses of reputations—which generally take the form of critical studies of particular authors, including Nathaniel Hawthorne (Thompkins 1983) and, in the Australian context, Peter Carey (Turner 1993), Helen Garner (Darcy 1999), Patrick White (During 1996), and Tim Winton (Dixon 2005)[24]—demonstrate so well is how various institutional, political, economic, and social factors contribute, at different times and in different ways, to the construction and discussion of these authors.

Our analysis of critical attention to Australian novelists aims to do something different from either group. Like the literary critics, we accept that literary reputations are the outcome of complex, ongoing processes involving multiple factors. However, while the potential certainly is present in the data to identify and explore the hierarchical valuation of particular authors, we are concerned instead with literary reputation in the aggregate. Like empirical literary scholars, we take a data-rich approach, but we are not interested in measuring the extent to which different factors—of ability, personal and institutional affiliation, and history and culture—contribute to the reputations of novelists; nor do we intend this study to disprove literary critical assessments. Instead, we explore broad trends in the critical field, including changes in the distribution of critical attention over time and in the relationship between different forms of literary criticism, as well as the role of gender in these shifts. The results we discuss in what follows, in other words, are as much concerned with the historiography of Australian literary criticism as with the reputations of authors in that field.

One widely accepted trend in literary criticism since the late 1960s and 1970s—motivated, in particular, by identity-based political movements such as Marxism, feminism, and postcolonialism—is the widening of the literary canon, with the traditional great author revealed as a white man and forced to cede ground to a range of other groups and perspectives. Given this well-established trajectory, the results in Figure 12.4 are surprising, as they show an overall decline, in each decade since the mid-twentieth century, in the number of unique authors who are ranked in the yearly top ten for critical attention. Quite in contrast to the view that the canon is expanding, this result suggests—in relation to Australian novelists at least—a narrowing of critical attention. For example, in the 1990s, only 36 authors appeared in the yearly top ten across the decade, compared with 84 in the 1920s.

Figure 12.5 provides a useful context for, and explanation of, this seemingly contradictory trend. This graph shows the proportion of critical attention accorded to the top ten authors per decade,[25] revealing an overall decline from the mid-twentieth century to the 2000s (notwithstanding a slight increase in the 1960s and 1970s). In other words, despite greater agreement on the most important Australian novelists as the century progressed (see Figure 12.4), critical attention spread to an increasingly large group of authors. Taken together, the results in these two graphs suggest growing critical confidence, with increasing agreement on the best authors signifying consensus on what constitutes a 'good' or 'great' Australian novel, at the same time as the spread of critical attention signals confidence in the overall quality—and worthiness for critical attention—of the range of novelists.

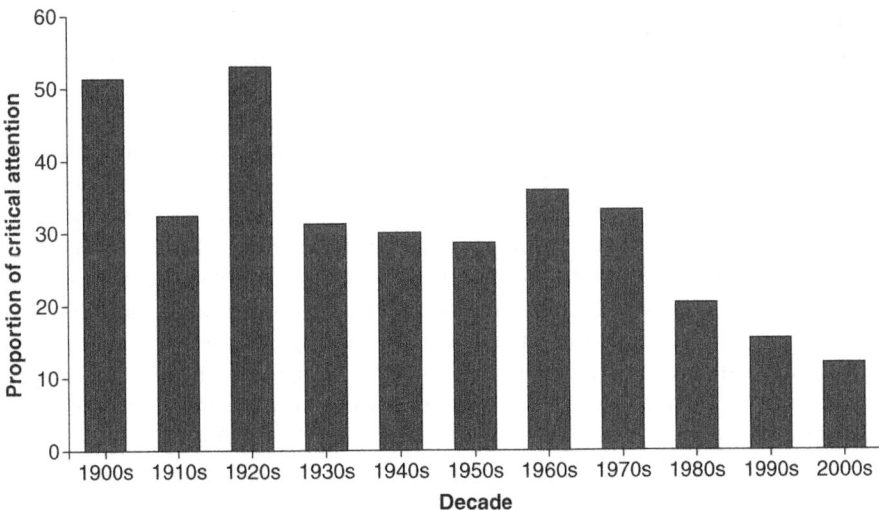

*Figure 12.5*   Proportion of critical attention to top ten authors, per decade

*Table 12.2*  Proportion of critical attention to top ten authors, per decade

| Decade | Overall % | Newspapers % | Academic Journals % |
| --- | --- | --- | --- |
| 1950s | 29 | 45 | 33 |
| 1960s | 36 | 36 | 36 |
| 1970s | 33 | 40 | 39 |
| 1980s | 20 | 28 | 34 |
| 1990s | 15 | 30 | 32 |
| 2000s | 12 | 25 | 32 |

A different picture of this confidence emerges if we consider particular categories of criticism: specifically, academic journals and newspapers. In both cases, the concentration of critical attention to the top ten authors is greater than for overall results, especially from the 1970s, as Table 12.2 shows. While we might expect academic criticism to be more focused on a select group of novelists than overall criticism, it is interesting that this relatively concentrated focus also occurs in newspapers, where publishers compete—commercially, not simply at the level of cultural value—to have their authors featured. Bourdieu's description of the function of critical pronouncements—'Every critic declares not only his judgment of the work but also his claim to the right to talk about it and judge it' (1983, 317)—suggests a reason for the relative concentration of critical attention in both areas. To maintain a reputation and capacity to offer opinions, a critic cannot afford for his or her judgement to differ, repeatedly, from the group: that is, from the consensus about what is good literature. In the worlds of newspaper and academic criticism, where having the right to judge brings a range of professional and social rewards, it makes sense that critical consensus would be relatively strong.

While the consensus within academic and newspaper criticism is relatively high, there is declining agreement, between the two areas, on the authors most worthy of discussion. Figure 12.6 depicts the proportion of Australian novelists who appear in the top 50 for both academic and newspaper discussion from the 1950s, and shows—with the exception of the 1980s—a marked decline in this crossover to the 2000s. Whereas 63 per cent of Australian novelists in the top 50 for academic and newspaper criticism appear in both categories in the 1950s, by the 2000s this figure falls to 21 per cent. The exception of the 1980s provides a framework for explaining the broader trend. Following a decade of intensive cultural nationalist funding, and centring on Australia's 1988 bicentenary, the decade of the 1980s is widely recognized as an exception period in Australian cultural history, when a broad set of concerns—regarding feminism, Aboriginal land rights, multiculturalism, and national identity—animated both public discussion and academic discourse, and were expressed with particular force and impact in Australian fiction, especially novels (Davis 2009; McPhee 2001).

The fact that the 1980s are recognized as exceptional—specifically in the connection that occurred between academic and public discussion of literature—tallies with Graeme Turner's description of a broader international shift in the public sphere since the 1960s, marked by the growing alienation of

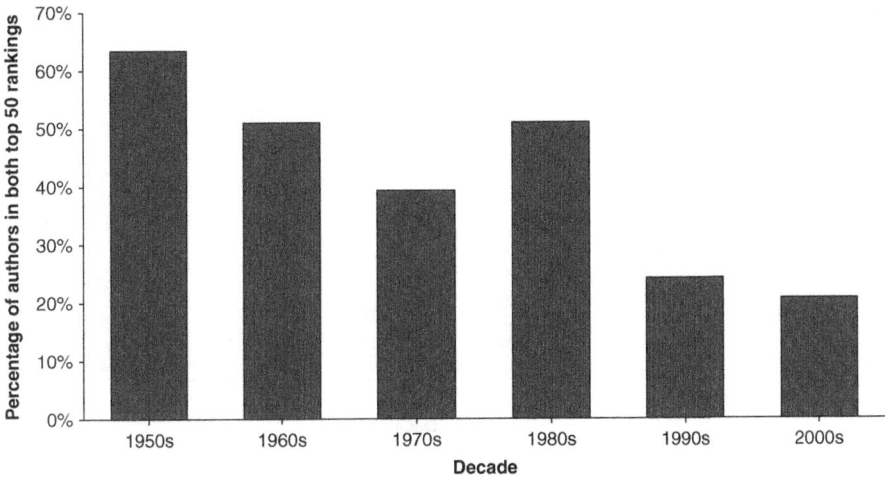

*Figure 12.6* Proportion of authors who feature in the top 50 for both academic and newspaper criticism, 1950–2006

'the academic study of literature . . . from the language of public debate' (1999, 9). In this light, the results displayed in Figure 12.6 provide an interesting perspective on what we have called a trend of growing confidence in pronouncements about Australian literature. Although academic critics may increasingly agree on the Australian novelists who are worthy of discussion, the distance of these pronouncements from public discussion—brought into focus by the very small readership of academic journals compared to newspapers—suggests the cultural authority exercised by this academic agreement, and its weight in directing broader public discussion, has significantly declined.

We conclude by touching briefly upon a trend—in gender—that highlights one important consequence of this separation of academic and newspaper discussion of Australian literature. Figures 12.7 and 12.8 show the proportion of women among the top ten, 20, and 50 ranked authors per decade in academic journals and newspapers, respectively. The fact that approximately half of the top ten and 20 most-discussed Australian novelists in academic journals in the 1990s and 2000s are women suggests that the feminist deconstruction of the canon continues to influence conceptions of literature in this area.

In newspaper criticism, by contrast, only 10 to 20 per cent of authors in the top ten and 20 rankings in these two decades are women. The significant difference in gender trends in the canon (or canons) of Australian literature suggests that the equation of great author and man has recently reasserted itself—indeed, has become more trenchant than in the 1950s and 1960s—in the public sphere.[26] To avoid losing the progress that feminist critics made in challenging male-oriented definitions and valuations of literature requires, as a necessary first step, a reengagement of academic critics in public discussion of Australian literature.

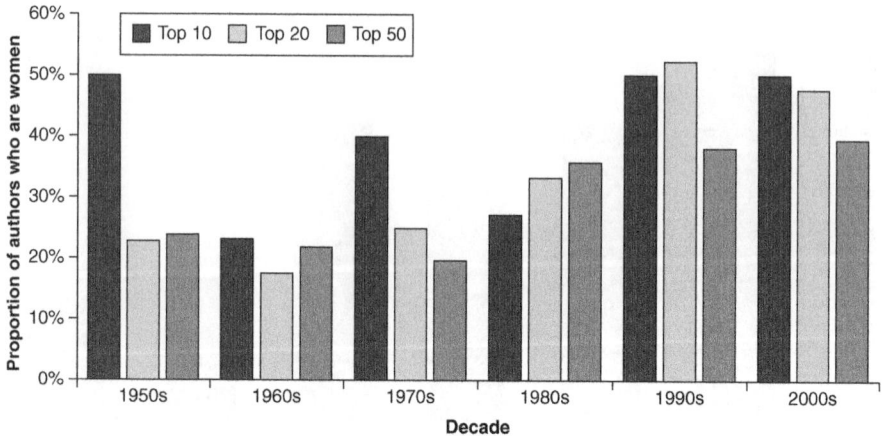

*Figure 12.7*  Proportion of women authors in the top ten, 20, and 50 for academic attention, 1950s–2000s

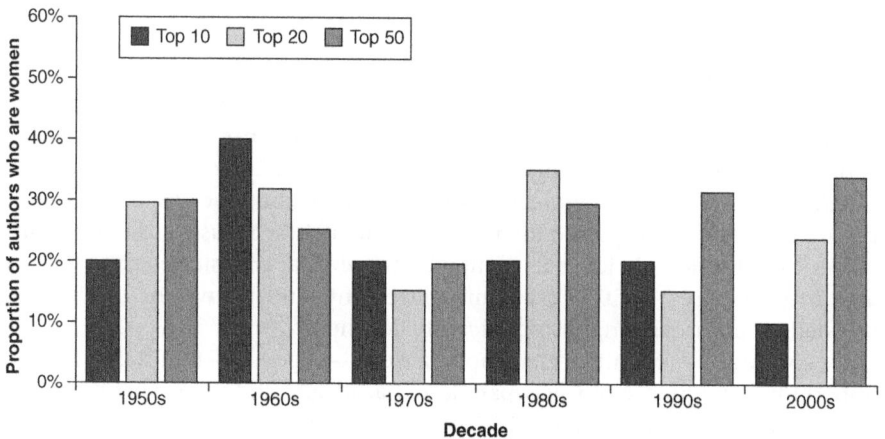

*Figure 12.8*  Proportion of women authors in the top ten, 20, and 50 for newspaper attention, 1950s–2000s

All of these interpretations of the data are contestable; indeed, they can be contested through further exploration of the datasets we have published. A major aim of this paper has been to encourage and enable such contestation and future analysis by providing characterized and reliable data for researchers to use. The work of gathering, checking, and analysing this data to understand the types of questioning it can enable and support is a significant task, requiring expertise that is increasingly located in digital humanities. Drawing on the practice in astronomy of formally publishing datasets, this chapter presents an approach that enables this technical and methodological work to be used and recognized by the wider scholarly community, while contributing to the broader humanities endeavour of raising new questions, offering new knowledge, and contributing to public debate. Ultimately, the technical and methodological cannot be separated from the critical and theoretical. Characterizing—that is, considering the epistemological implications—of data is an explicitly theoretical and critical process. Equally, humanities research that draws upon digital resources and data requires deep understanding of the methodological processes and decisions underpinning those constructs. Of necessity, digital humanities must be an arena where these two fundamentally intertwined aspects of digital and data-rich research are combined and balanced.

## Notes

1. The datasets underpinning *Reading by Numbers*, by Katherine Bode, are available at http://www.austlit.edu.au/austlit/page/5962221.
2. The fact that only one of the five existing Stanford Literary Lab pamphlets includes access to data, despite all being published online, shows that this lack of openness about data is more than an effect of publishing strictures.
3. For example, the data release papers for the massive Sloan Digital Sky Survey underpinned a decade of scientific work. They have provided the basis for hundreds of scientific papers and been cited many thousands of times (see Stoughton et al. 2002).
4. This topic was discussed in respect to tenure in a special issue of the *Journal of Digital Humanities* (see, for example, Cavanagh 2012; Nowviskie 2012).
5. http://katherinebode.wordpress.com/articles-chapters/methods-and-canons-data/
6. AustLit, www.austlit.edu.au.
7. AustLit, 'About AustLit', http://www.austlit.edu.au. For a detailed history of AustLit, see Hetherington 2005.
8. The number of 'works about' an author does not indicate different levels of critical attention: one instance is recorded whether the author is the subject of an entire monograph or critical essay, or is just mentioned in passing in a newspaper article or academic review. While collapsing one type of variation in the critical field, the data captures the essence of literary reputation better than, say, a word count, because it brings into sharp relief—indeed, amplifies—the presence of those authors who emerge as reference points for critical discussion.
9. 'Non-AustLit' are usually well-known writers (such as George Eliot, Harriet Beecher Stowe, and Charles Dickens) included in AustLit because they are deemed to have profoundly influenced particular Australian authors. The list of authors used in this automatic extraction process also excluded non-Australian authors in the 'banned books' AustLit subset, which lists works censored in Australia.
10. For example, a pseudonym is indicated by 'Writing name for' as well as 'Used as a writing name by'.
11. 'Other' incorporates 23 categories of publication, each with less than 1 per cent of total 'works about', including prose, obituaries, poetry, essays, theses, and bibliographies.
12. Each point on the plot is a single author, and only authors with four or more novels are shown. The majority of authors are clustered in the bottom left, with a moderate number of novels and critical works. The extreme points in the graph are pulp fiction author Grover Marshall on the far right (with 683 published novels and three 'works about'), and literary fiction author David Malouf on the upper left (with six novels and 1,103 'works about').
13. AustLit, 'About Scope', http://www.austlit.edu.au.
14. AustLit, 'About Books', http://www.austlit.edu.au.
15. AustLit, 'About Scope'.
16. AustLit, 'Inclusion Criteria for Authors', http://www.austlit.edu.au.

17. For discussion of the difficulties involved in using the Google Books archive and its Ngram viewer, see Cohen 2010; Jockers 2010.
18. As AustLit explains, '*The Hand that Signed the Paper* purported to be a family history based on oral testimony, relating a family's role in Jewish concentration camps' (AustLit, 'Darville, Helen', http://www.austlit.edu.au). The book won a number of prestigious awards—including the Vogel Prize, the Australian Literature Society Gold Medal, and the Miles Franklin Award—and provoked enormous controversy when Darville's actual background was revealed.
19. Figure 12.3 is also one of the diagnostic plots we used to explore and test the process of extraction and the resulting dataset. The obvious peak in 'works about' in 1924—which might indicate an error or a focus by a specialist dataset—actually relates to the publication of *The Boy in the Bush* by D. H. Lawrence and M. L. Skinner. Due to Lawrence's international fame, this work attracted considerable critical attention in Australia and elsewhere.
20. This number could actually be greater than 100 if more than ten authors were in the top ten in any year (for instance, if tenth place was shared by two or more authors receiving the same amount of critical attention). The nature of the data produces some bias in the results: because there was much less critical attention to Australian novelists early in the twentieth century, multiple authors were more likely to tie on the number of critical works. By decade, the average number of authors in the yearly top ten is: 1900s, 12.9; 1910s, 15.4; 1920s, 16.9; 1930s, 12.4; 1940s, 11.9; 1950s, 12.3; 1960s, 10.7; 1970s, 10.8; 1980s, 10.4; 1990s, 10.1; 2000s, 10.6.
21. The names of these files, respectively, are: 'Critical Attention to Australian Novelists Overall, 1900 to 2006', 'Critical Attention to Australian Novelists in Newspapers, 1950 to 2006', 'Critical Attention to Australian Novelists in Academic (Peer-Reviewed) Journals, 1950 to 2006', and 'Critical Attention to Australian Novelists in Literary Magazines, 1950 to 2006'. Periodicals were manually categorized. Academic journals were identified retrospectively, based on those that employed peer review in 2007. These datasets are available at http://www.austlit.edu.au/austlit/page/5962221.
22. This field comprises predominantly sociologists and psychologists who use empirical methods to investigate aspects of literary culture, including reception and audience studies (see, for example, Janssen and van Dijk 1998; Zyngier et al. 2008).
23. For instance, research in empirical literary studies shows that critically acclaimed authors are more likely to have pursued academic studies in literature and be members of writers' organizations (Gerhards and Anheier 1989); that critics are more likely to pay attention to authors who have already received critical recognition (Verdaasdonk 1987, 238–39) or are involved in public roles besides writing (Janssen 1998); and that the reputation of an author's publishing house is often decisive in determining which authors will gain critical attention (Nooy 1991, 509–10; Van Rees and Vermunt 1996; Janssen 1997; Nooy 2002).
24. An exception to these studies in literary criticism of individual authors is David Damrosch's analysis of what he terms the 'hypercanon', 'countercanon', and 'shadow canon' of Romantic British and world literature (2006).
25. In three decades, there were more than ten authors in the top ten: in the 1900s and 1910s, 11 authors were in the top ten; in the 1960s, there were 12.
26. For a detailed discussion of the relationship between gender trends in newspaper and academic criticism and the feminist movement, see Bode 2012a, 131–67.

## Works cited

Bode, Katherine. (2009). 'Resourceful Reading: A New Empiricism in the Digital Age?' In *Resourceful Reading: The New Empiricism, eResearch, and Australian Literary Culture*, ed. Katherine Bode and Robert Dixon, 1–27. Sydney: University of Sydney Press.

Bode, Katherine. (2010). 'Publishing and Australian Literature: Crisis, Decline, or Transformation?' *Cultural Studies Review* 16, no. 2: 24–48.

Bode, Katherine. (2012a). *Reading by Numbers: Recalibrating the Literary Field*. London: Anthem Press.

Bode, Katherine. (2012b). ' "Sidelines" and Tradelines: Publishing the Australian Novel, 1860 to 1899'. *Book History* 15: 93–122.

Bourdieu, Pierre. (1983). 'The Field of Cultural Production, or: the Economic World Reversed'. *Poetics* 12, nos. 4–5: 311–56.

Bourdieu, Pierre. (1996). *The Rules of Art: Genesis and Structure of the Literary Field*. Trans. Susan Emanuel. Stanford: Stanford University Press.

Carter, David. (2000). 'Critics, Writers, Intellectuals: Australian Literature and Its Criticism'. In *The Cambridge Companion to Australian Literature*, ed. Elizabeth Webby, 258–93. Cambridge: Cambridge University Press.

Carter, David. (2007). 'Boom, Bust, or Business as Usual? Literary Fiction Publishing'. In *Making Books: Contemporary Australian Publishing*, ed. David Carter and Anne Galligan, 231–46. St Lucia: University of Queensland Press.

Cavanagh, Sheila. (2012). 'Living in a Digital World: Rethinking Peer Review, Collaboration, and Open Access'. *Journal of Digital Humanities* 1, no. 4. Available at: http://journalofdigitalhumanities.org.

Cohen, Dan. (2012). 'Initial Thoughts on the Google Books Ngram Viewer and Datasets'. Available at: http://www.dancohen.org.

Damrosch, David. (2006). 'World Literature in a Postcanonical, Hypercanonical Age'. In *Comparative Literature in an Age of Globalization*, ed. Haun Saussy, 43–53. Baltimore: John Hopkins University Press.

Darcy, Cath. (1999). 'What's in a Name? Helen Garner and the Power of the Author in the Public Domain'. In *Australian Literature and the Public Sphere*, ed. Alison Bartlett, Robert Dixon, and Christopher Lee, 44–50. Toowoomba: Association for the Study of Australian Literature.

Davis, Mark. (2007). 'The Decline of the Literary Paradigm in Australian Publishing'. In *Making Books: Contemporary Australian Publishing*, ed. David Carter and Anne Galligan, 116–31. St Lucia: University of Queensland Press.

Davis, Mark. (2009). 'Making Aboriginal History: The Cultural Mission in Australian Book Publishing and the Publication of Henry Reynolds's *The Other Side of the Frontier*'. In *Resourceful Reading: The New Empiricism, eResearch, and Australian Literary Culture*, ed. Katherine Bode and Robert Dixon, 176–93. Sydney: University of Sydney Press.

Dixon, Robert. (2005). 'Tim Winton, *Cloudstreet*, and the Field of Australian Literature'. *Westerly* 50 (November): 240–60.

Dolin, Tim. (2004). 'The Secret Reading Life of Us'. In *Readers, Writers, Publishers: Essays and Poems*, ed. Brian Matthews, 115–33. Canberra: Australian Academy of the Humanities.

Dolin, Tim. (2006). 'First Steps Toward a History of the Mid-Victorian Novel in Colonial Australia'. *Australian Literary Studies* 32, no. 3: 273–93.

During, Simon. (1996). *Patrick White*. Melbourne: Oxford University Press.

Ensor, Jason. (2008). 'Reprints, International Markets, and Local Literary Taste: New Empiricism and Australian Literature'. *Journal of the Association for the Study of Australian Literature*. Special Issue: 'The Colonial Present': 198–218.

Ensor, Jason. (2009). 'Is a Picture Worth 10,175 Australian Novels?' In *Resourceful Reading: The New Empiricism, eResearch, and Australian Literary Culture*, ed. Katherine Bode and Robert Dixon, 240–73. Sydney: Sydney University Press.

Gerhards, Jurgen, and Helmut K. Anheier. (1989). 'The Literary Field: An Empirical Investigation of Bourdieu's Sociology of Art'. *International Sociology* 4, no. 2: 131–46.

Hetherington, Carol. (2005). 'AustLit: A Resource for Print Culture Research'. *Journal of Publishing* 1 (October): 115–27.

Janssen, Susanne. (1997). 'Reviewing as Social Practice: Institutional Constraints on Critics' Attention for Contemporary Fiction'. *Poetics* 24, no. 5: 275–97.

Janssen, Susanne. (1998). 'Side-Roads to Success: The Effect of Sideline Activities on the Status of Writers'. *Poetics* 25, no. 5: 265–80.

Janssen, Susanne, and Nel van Dijk, eds. (1998). *The Empirical Study of Literature: Its Development and Future*. Rotterdam: Barjesteh van Waalwijk van Doorn & Co's Uitgeversmaatschappij.

Jockers, Matthew. L. (2010). 'Unigrams, and Bigrams, and Trigrams, Oh My'. Available at: http://www.matthewjockers.net.

Jockers, Matthew. L. (2013). *Macroanalysis: Digital Methods and Literary History*. Champaign: University of Illinois Press.

Lamond, Julieanne. (2012). 'Communities of Readers: Australian Reading History and Library Loan Records'. In *Republics of Letters: Literary Communities in Australia*, ed. Peter Kirkpatrick and Robert Dixon, 27–38. Sydney: Sydney University Press.

Lamond, Julieanne, and Mark Reid. (2009). 'Squinting at a Sea of Dots: Visualising Australian Readerships Using Statistical Machine Learning'. In *Resourceful Reading: The New Empiricism, eResearch, and Australian Literary Culture*, ed. Katherine Bode and Robert Dixon, 223–39. Sydney: Sydney University Press.

McGann, Jerome. (2004). 'A Note on the Current State of Humanities Scholarship'. *Critical Inquiry* 30, no. 2: 409–13.

McPhee, Hilary. (2001). *Other People's Words*. Sydney: Picador.

Moretti, Franco. (2005). *Graphs, Maps, Trees: Abstract Models for Literary History*. London: Verso.

Nile, Richard, and Jason Ensor. (2009). 'The Novel, the Implicated Reader, and Australian Literary Cultures, 1950–2008'. In *The Cambridge History of Australian Literature*, ed. Peter Pierce, 517–48. Melbourne: Cambridge University Press.

Nooy, Wouter de. (1991). 'Social Networks and Classification in Literature'. *Poetics* 20, no. 6: 507–37.

Nooy, Wouter de. (2002). 'The Dynamics of Artistic Prestige'. *Poetics* 30, no. 3: 147–67.

Nowviskie, Bethany. (2012). 'Evaluating Collaborative Digital Scholarship (or, Where Credit Is Due)'. *Journal of Digital Humanities* 1, no. 4. Available at: http://journalofdigitalhumanities.org.

Ramsay, Stephen. (2008). 'Algorithmic Criticism'. In *A Companion to Digital Literary Studies*, ed. Susan Schreibman and Ray Siemens. Oxford: Blackwell. Available at: http://www.digitalhumanities.org.

Stoughton, Chris, Robert. H. Lupton, Mariangela Bernardi, Michael. R. Blanton, et al. (2002). 'Sloan Digital Sky Survey: Early Data Release'. *Astronomical Journal* 123, no. 1: 485–548.

Thompkins, Jane. (1983). *Sensational Designs: The Cultural Work of American Fiction, 1790–1860*. New York: Oxford University Press.

Thomson, Robert, and Leigh Dale. (2009). 'Books in Selected Australian Newspapers, December 1930'. In *Resourceful Reading: The New Empiricism, eResearch, and Australian Literary Culture*, ed. Katherine Bode and Robert Dixon, 119–41. Sydney: Sydney University Press.

Turner, Graeme. (1993). 'Nationalising the Author: The Celebrity of Peter Carey'. *Australian Literary Studies* 16, no. 2: 131–39.

Turner, Graeme. (1999). 'Australian Literature and the Public Sphere'. In *Australian Literature and the Public Sphere*, ed. Alison Bartlett, Robert Dixon and Christopher Lee, 1–12. Toowoomba: Association for the Study of Australian Literature.

Van Rees, C. J. (1987). 'How Reviewers Reach Consensus on the Value of Literary Works'. *Poetics* 16, nos. 3–4: 275–94.

Van Rees, C. J., and Jeroen Vermunt. (1996). 'Event History Analysis of Authors' Reputation: Effects of Critics' Attention on Debutants' Careers'. *Poetics* 23, no. 5: 317–33.

Verboord, Marc. (2003). 'Classification of Authors by Literary Prestige'. *Poetics* 31, nos. 3–4: 259–81.

Verdaasdonk, H. (1987). 'Effects of Acquired Readership and Reviewers' Attention on the Sales of New Literary Works'. *Poetics* 16, nos. 3–4: 237–53.

Zwar, Jan. (2012a). 'More than Michael Moore: Contemporary Australian Book Reading Patterns and the Wars on Iraq and Afghanistan'. *Publishing Research Quarterly* 28, no. 4: 325–39.

Zwar, Jan. (2012b). 'What Were We Buying? Non-Fiction and Narrative Non-Fiction Sales Patterns in the 2000s'. *Journal of the Association for the Study of Australian Literature* 12, no. 3: 1–27. Available at: http://www.nla.gov.au.

Zyngier, Sonia, Marisa Bortolussi, Anna Chesnokova, and Jan Aurache, eds. (2008). *Directions in Empirical Literary Studies*. Amsterdam: John Benjamins.

# 13
# Reading the Text, Walking the Terrain, Following the Map

## Do We See the Same Landscape?

*Øyvind Eide*

How do we know where we are? When I navigate my way through an unknown landscape with the help of a map, keeping the synchronization between me as a moving body in the landscape and the spot on the map representing my current position is of key importance. Sometimes I come to a sudden realization: I am not where I think I am. The route I have been following through the landscape has a different representation on the map from the one I thought it had. This could be expressed as, 'I thought I knew where I was, but it turned out I was wrong'. And if I have no clue as to where the spot I am occupying is on the map—that is, what place on the map represents the place in the landscape where I am—I would say, 'I am lost'.

The map I use to find my way is there in the landscape with me—it has to be in order to be used for navigation. But it is also outside the landscape, representing it. When I point at the map saying, 'Here I am', I make a claim about my location in the landscape represented by the map. This is different from the claim made if I point to somewhere on a page of text describing a landscape claiming, 'Here I am'. The latter would usually be taken as a reference to where I am in reading the text, rather than a claim of where I am in an external reality referred to by the text.

Maps and texts refer differently to the landscape. I claim in this chapter that not only do we express the same knowledge about landscapes in different ways in the two media, but also that the knowledge that can be expressed using each of the two media differs. This claim is supported by research presented in the next section, where I review a series of modelling experiments in which differences between texts and maps were studied in detail. The study was made through a computer-assisted close reading of one specific text. I then show how the differences are linked to the way we relate to the landscape and outline the connections to media comparisons in general; each medium can mediate only certain aspects of a total reality. I conclude by looking briefly into one of the most important aspects of the ongoing digital spatial turn,[1] namely, the use of maps and texts in integrated geocommunication systems.

## Experimental evidence

Neither the text nor the map is the landscape we experience directly. Further, they are distinct from the landscape in different ways. How can these differences be investigated using the digital humanities tool of experimental modelling?[2] To investigate this I based my modelling experiments on a collection of documents from the 1740s used in the border negotiations between Denmark (including Norway) and Sweden (including Finland) leading up to the border treaty of 1751, printed as Schnitler (1962).[3] The documents were written in Danish, which was also the written language used for Norwegian dialects at the time.

In Scandinavia in the mid-eighteenth century, common people were seen as an important source of information in the resolution of boundary disputes. This perception was linked to the two main principles behind the establishment of the border—topography and possession—and how they were understood at the time.[4] The topographical principle stated that the border should follow the highest mountain ridge. The principle of possession was based on tax subjects; the area of a country was the area possessed by the subjects of the country's sovereign. This point was problematic, however, as much of the border area was inhabited by seminomadic Sami reindeer herders who used land on both sides of what was later to become the border and paid taxes to both the Swedish and the Danish kings.

The resolution of the boundary disputes included input from the local population: officials travelled the area and conducted court investigations, questioning the common people—Norwegian, Swedish, Sami, and Finnish farmers as well as Sami reindeer herders—about their perceptions of the border location as well as their general knowledge of the area. Schnitler's protocols include these court proceedings, together with older written sources, as well as summaries written by Schnitler himself.

The modelling experiments were performed in a stepwise formalization process inspired by the concept of deformation found in McGann (2001), using a computer program developed for the task.[5] The first step established statements close to the textual way of expressing spatial understanding, whereas the latter steps established increasingly 'maplike' statements. The statements, in the form of triples, rephrased expressions in the source text. If the text said 'place A is east of place B', then three things were included in the model: two place references, A and B, and a link between them, which is the statement that A is east of B. The modelling was in line with conceptual analysis as used in the development of ontologies such as CIDOC-CRM (Doerr 2003).

The statements of the model are rather simple. However, by putting a number of them together, a more complex structure is established. The model created this way was used in four case studies where experiments were run on parts of the source text modelled in great detail. Each of the statements went through the formalization steps as shown in the example in Table 13.1. This process showed how information had to be added and taken away in order to reach the goal, which was to express the statements in the form of maps.

*Table 13.1*   Example of stepwise formalization from text to vector data

| Text | Primary model | Formalised model | Vector data |
|---|---|---|---|
| Some ¼ mile East of A is B | Some ¼ mile Direction: east | 2 kilometres Direction: 90° | A = (0,0) B = (2000,0) |

There is no single correct interpretation of the fact that A is east of B in the spatial language used in maps. The semantic potential of 'east' includes not only straight east, but also grades of north-east and south-east. Looking into the longer history of spatial expressions in Norwegian, we can see how Holtsmark (1961) describes the Nordic medieval system in which a direction includes the area around the angle. Old Norse used a system of eight directions. In line with this system, east can be taken to represent the span from 67½° to 112½°. This system was used in Norway in the eighteenth century, also doubled to a system of 16, which is still used in the Norwegian language today.

A topographical map, however, expresses one direction only. When we make the map, not only *can* we choose one interpretation of this geographical relationship at the cost of losing all the other possible ones, but we actually *have to* make such a choice. One could, of course, draw a sector on the map showing a possible interpretation of east of a specific place. This would, however, introduce an area of possible location for a place, which is normally a well-defined object on topographical maps. In addition, the span representing the possible location conveyed by the sector drawn on the map would still remain a different expression from the textual one. The figure on the map would have lost some underspecification compared to the textual expression. The width of the sector remains open in the text; east can be more or less than 45° wide, whereas it must be specified on the map.

In the experiments, comparable differences were found for distances between places. Other types of relationships between places were even less specified in the text, such as the claim that a place is between two other places. Such underspecification was found not only in descriptions of the relationships between places, but also in the spatial descriptions of each place. In two of the case studies, fewer than 10 per cent of the places mentioned in the text had been given measurements of either length or width (Eide 2013)—and none of the places' forms were described to a level where they could be drawn unambiguously based on the description alone.

What I call 'underspecification' here is relative to the task at hand; the text is underspecified relative to what is needed to create a map based on the text only. If the task was to express the spatial understanding read from the text on a preexisting map—for instance, one of Schnitler's own maps—it may be the case that the text is only underspecified in a limited number of cases, if at all. The same can be said of the description of the places: if the description and the place name suffice to locate the place on the map, the place description is not underspecified in reference to the task at hand.

The cases of underspecification are examples in which the text provides too little information; it does not say what we need to know in order to make the map. We can still make maps based on such a text, but not one single definite map; rather, significantly different maps that each conform to the text can be made. Thus, the exact spatial expression found in the text cannot be represented as a map. When textual expressions are anchored to pre-existing maps, a large number of choices are made en bloc.

In some cases the text provides too much information to make one single map. One example is a sequence of Schnitler's aggregation where he explains how two groups of witnesses claim that a border mark is located on either one or another mountain (Schnitler 1962, 174). The two mountains are presented on his list of border mountains with an 'or' between the two names. The information expressed by the word 'or' cannot be expressed on one single static map image in any other way than using a textual disjunction to explain the situation. On a dynamic map, changes over time may be used to express disjunction.

Other situations push the limits of the map even further. While the text may use expressions such as, 'there are no neighbouring farmers, before eight miles to the west' (Schnitler 1962, 142),[6] this is hard to express on a map. Blankness on a map would seem logical, but blankness does not convey 'no farms', but rather 'nothing of interest'. Farms could be there even where the map is blank. In order to make the lack of a symbol signify no farms, one needs to add every single farm to the map and inform the map users through a text about this completeness. However, that would not work in the case of a map made to represent this text, for the text does not describe all farms. So there would be no way of telling if a spot on the map had no farm symbol because the text found farms in the area unimportant and did not mention them, or because the text said explicitly 'no farms'. The only way to express it would be through a textual description on or connected to the map, thus creating a hybrid document—a geocommunication system.

## Texts, maps, and landscape

When we compare the problems discussed above with the third corner of the triad established in the introduction—namely, the landscape itself—we see how the text and the map alike are underspecified in the sense that they can never express everything about the landscape. However, if we look at the landscape as a space of travel for people with certain knowledge, then both the text and the map may be well specified. As long as the text or the map gives you enough information to understand where the places mentioned are located, then it is sufficiently specified for the task.

Texts and maps as representations of a landscape can be seen as two opposites, as in the discussion above. If we look at their semiotic systems they are indeed quite different. Texts have nothing resembling the indexical grid lines of a map.[7] Written texts and maps both exist as documents, but their systems of reference differ. They are complementary; a textual document can easily include a map, and maps generally include short texts.

Studies of US university students show that route descriptions in texts specify quite similarly what drawings of the same routes do (Tversky and Lee 1999). The drawings in question are graphical figures of the way to go, but the distances and the angles of turns represent the landscape differently from the way a topographical map would. A turn to the right tends to be drawn as a sharp angle, different from a topographical map, where the actual angles in the landscape would be reproduced. The route figures look more like metro network maps; what is represented is quite similar to textual expressions such as 'turn right,' which does not indicate the accurate angle of the turn either. The topographical map claims an accurate specific angle as a consequence of the map genre, whereas metro maps or route description figures make no such claims.

The growth in map production in Europe in early modern times affected also the two Scandinavian powers, Denmark and Sweden, often in connection with military needs and territorial claims (Woodward 2007, 1792–95), and maps and charts were used for navigation by the army and seafarers, for instance. But I have found no evidence for the use of maps for navigation among Sami people or other people of the lower classes in the border areas between Denmark-Norway and Sweden-Finland in the eighteenth century. It is impossible to completely rule out use of ephemeral maps, of course. But no remains of paper or vellum maps used for navigation, and no evidence in the sources for such use, indicates that their use must have been limited at best. Schnitler knew the area quite well, having worked there for more than two decades, and there is no evidence he used maps in the interviews with his more than 100 witnesses from the lower classes. He received a map from only one source, a priest.

In the Sami tradition, symbolic representations that to our modern eyes would look like maps were well known. The ritual drums, as well as the layout of the interior of a Sami tent or turf hut, are seen as maps of selected parts and aspects of the world (Mathisen 1991). But this had little or nothing to do with wayfinding in the physical landscape. The only known use even remotely close to navigation is for making hunting decisions (Keski-Säntti 2003).

But even if paper maps were not used, what about cognitive maps? One theory holds that humans, as well as other species—including rats—carry cognitive maps in their heads, maps that are representations of the world they live in. When Tolman (1948) used 'map' for what we have in our heads, this was based on a functional similarity; his aim was to argue against a simple stimulus–response interpretation of rats' ability to find the way. Gibson, however, criticizes the idea of cognitive maps as confusion between categorically different things:

> The getting of a bird's-eye view is helpful in becoming oriented, and the explorer will look down from a high place if possible. Homing pigeons are better at orientation than we are. But orientation to goals behind the walls, beyond the trees, and over the hill is not just a looking-down-on, and it is certainly not the having of a map, not even a 'cognitive' map supposed to exist in the mind instead of on paper. A map is a useful artifact when the hiker is

lost, but it is a mistake to confuse the artifact with the psychological state the artifact promotes.

(Gibson 1986, 199)

The map as a document is categorically different from the landscape—not only because the map is scaled and created by humans, but also because maps are used differently from the way the landscape is used. The wayfinder is inside the landscape. When one looks at a map to find out where one is (on the map), one is physically outside the map, but conceptually in the map. Thus one is outside the landscape looking down at it with a bird's-eye view. One moves through a landscape, whereas one is outside the map (Ingold 2000, 227–34). This also has consequences for our sensorial system. We mainly move the eyes while looking at the map, but we are embodied creatures, constantly moving the full eye-head-body system, when travelling through the landscape. Documents and landscapes both relate to practice, but they do so in different ways.

In an interview at the *Brain Science Podcast*, Nicolelis clarified his view on the use of 'map' when describing the brain's spatial systems:[8]

> I don't even use the word 'maps' anymore. 'Maps' gives us an impression of a static 2D or 3D; and that's the reason they were used, actually. When Penfield first described them in humans, and Sherrington, in animals, I think this was actually the intent: to show that there was a static, carved-in-stone representation of the world. But I think that, once this revolution comes–in neuroscience, I mean–the word 'maps' is going to disappear; because they carry too much baggage with them.
>
> I like to talk about dynamic representations, or dynamic models. That's what I think the brain is doing: the brain is creating; continuously creating and updating.
>
> (Nicolelis 2011, 21)

The idea of the cognitive map was developed as an 'as-if' concept. If we see the brain as carrying a cognitive map, how far can we get in understanding how the brain works? I believe we have reached the end of that road—that more useful metaphors can be found to describe the wayfinding and navigation systems of the brain. The use of conceptual modelling of textual information can play a role in clarifying these new metaphors. Such modelling is central to the digital component of the research I describe in this chapter.

Texts and maps are sign systems, whereas the landscape is not; rather, the landscape only becomes a sign system when we make it one (Basso 1996). The landscape itself is outside the map, and also outside the text. Wayfinding is done by employing a combination of words, body, brain, senses, landscape, fellow creatures, and, quite recently, also maps. The ways in which it is done vary significantly. We can actively engage in finding the way. We can discourse with our fellow travellers, use maps, remember a route description told to us earlier, or make an inner argument: 'If I go this way, then I will find that valley, which will take me to the lake.'

However, much evidence points towards another possible method of finding our way: we can do it without thinking in words, by 'just knowing' where to go, as seen in cultures where people have perfected dead reckoning (Levinson 2003, 5). We can find the way 'without thinking', that is, in an automatized way, without consciously remembering it afterwards (Tuan 1975, 207). I aim to see how the use of maps is a special case, as is the use of an oral or written text. We may have a map with us, or we may have memorized a map image. We may have a textual route description with us, or remember such a description, possibly as a song or a chant. It could be a memorized series of highly descriptive place names. Some cultures use tone patterns in expressions referring to places, so that musical expressions become part of a place name.[9]

The landscape, again, is something different from both maps and texts. The landscape has a physical presence independent of observers, but the landscape we have access to is encultured. We have names for features, both at type level and at particular level. In my experience, maps, especially topographical maps and the like, tend to focus attention on the landscape as a physical structure with all rivers, contour lines, and roads denoted. Texts tend to open more up for the human experience of the landscape.[10] My understanding based on personal communication with Sami people falls well in with the claim made by Keski-Säntti:

> [The Chukchi's] method of spatial depiction is comparable to what we learn from a number of sources about the spatial depictions of the Inuit in the Arctic: instead of drawing a map, both the Chukchi and the Inuit describe their surroundings and their journeys orally. These often-repeated descriptions include place-names and details of the shape of the landscape and of memorable landmarks.
>
> (Keski-Säntti 2003, 120)

In this way, the map expresses the actual physical layout of the landscape more clearly; thus, we must be told that maps lie (Monmonier 1996), but not that texts lie.

## Intermediality

Maps and texts alike fall short in representing the landscape as the total reality available to our experiences. No media expression can capture everything we experience while moving around in a landscape. Further, texts and maps are able to capture different aspects of this reality, as would other media such as music or theatre. 'Every medium has the capacity of mediating only certain aspects of the total reality' (Elleström 2010, 24), as we saw above: a text can say 'east', whereas a grid-based map must express exact geometric relationships between places. This causes differences in how the aspects of reality presented by a text and a map are experienced.[11] These differences not only apply to *how* things are expressed but also influence *what* is said. The messages presented to Schnitler by the witnesses were more than the medium in which they were expressed, but they were clearly influenced by the medium. If a witness had been asked to draw a scaled map, different aspects would have been presented.

So we have three different things: a landscape offering itself to our senses, and two different ways of expressing our understanding, feeling, and sense of the landscape. Two different texts will express different aspects of that reality. So will two different maps. Even two different readings of the same text or the same map will be different. Because a text includes points of contact that depend on an understanding reader in order to be realized, and because these points of contact cannot at the level of meaning be disconnected from the reading instance, and because each and every reading and reading instance is unique, the text cannot be the same in two readings. That is, the text is not self-identical (McGann 2001, 188–89). But the differences between expressions adhering to the different semiotic systems of maps and texts operate at another level.

In a certain sense, all media expressions are intermedial (Arvidson, Askander, Bruhn, and Führer 2007, 13–14), but many expressions are close to being single-media expressions—for instance, Schnitler's texts and his maps. Combining such expressions creates combined utterances with a more outspoken intermediality. Combining maps and oral or written texts, and possibly other media as well, constitutes a case of geocommunication (Brodersen 2008). Geocommunication is commonly used in modern digital map systems. Google's route services is a well-known example in which maps, images, and texts are combined to advise the user how to find the way to a certain place.

But geocommunication is not new. When a person uses a map as the background for describing a past, future, or ongoing journey, a situation of geocommunication is created, combining the map with an oral text to produce an ephemeral intermedial document. The court sessions documented by Schnitler were likely to have been geocommunication situations in which oral text, gesture, and possibly even maps were used to convey a story. This story was then taken down by the scribe as a textual document. What can be seen as a translation from oral to written can also be seen as a translation from a kind of geocommunicative staging, where the landscape itself was used as an affordance in the process of telling a story.

Some of the many choices being made in court were free choices in the sense that one can choose to mention a mountain—or not. One also has to make choices based on the medium used, as seen above: when the text says 'east', it includes an openness that cannot survive on the map—the mapmaker has to choose the exact geometrical angle between two places. On the other hand, the scribe could not choose to include the specific odour in a valley in his text, he could only include a description of that smell—this was not a free choice. But the fact that no such descriptions are included was a free choice.

The main role of digital modelling experiments in my research is to find the details that are needed to establish a larger picture of media understanding. The algorithmic processing of text is different from the meaning-seeking reading of humans. I use the stupid explicitness of the computer to get to the core of things. The strength of unknowing, decontextualized computers is similar to the problems of situatedness and embodiment in artificial intelligence research, as Pfeifer and Scheier discuss (1999, 71–73), seen from the other side. What is problematic in artificial intelligence becomes an asset in my work (McGann 2001, 190–91). Digital humanities exploits the fact that computers are less goal-oriented than we are, less framed in sympathetic exchanges with desire for meaning, so they can help us find other readings than the ones we see. All humanists know that media are different. Modelling experiments can tell us how these differences play out at the micro level. In order to understand the meaning of the micro level differences, however, the digital may not be of much help; humanists may rather need to work with different disciplines within the humanities as well as beyond: history, linguistics, psychology, anthropology, neuroscience, geography, and cartography, to mention just a few relevant to the work at hand.

The landscape we envisage when we know it only from a text is different from the landscape we know from another text, from a map, or from travelling the landscape. These differences are systematic. Two texts have the potential to present the same impression, and two maps have a similar potential. But as shown in the examples above, trying to transfer a message conveyed by a text onto a map expression is fruitless. The textual message simply cannot be presented as a map, and the fullness of the landscape is ungraspable in either medium.

It is naive to believe that what a text can express about a landscape can be transferred to a map-based expression without significant loss of meaning. But it is similarly naive to believe that adding a map to a text, or a text to map, will not create a richer story. This richer story may not be truer, but it tells the reader more. It is often the case that the reader will experience a loss in freedom as a result; in the case of historical texts, such a loss in freedom is often seen as a gain in knowledge, but not always. A map can manipulate. Still, the necessary tension between the text and the map, the fact that they convey different parts of the full reality, opens up a space for conflicting stories that the clever creator of the expression can use, and that can assist the aware reader in gaining deeper understanding. In my opinion, this is digital mapping's most important role as a critical tool.

To make the one and only map of a text would imply that one could capture the one and only stable text, which is not possible. As we saw above, a text is not self-identical. One can only make a map of one or several readings of a text; the map is a model expressing one or several interpretations. This is the case no matter if the text is a paragraph or a million books. When digital humanities methods are used to create detailed models of short texts, modelling becomes a microscope and the subjectivity of the map model is obvious. However, the subjectivity of the map may be harder to see when one is mapping thousands or millions of books. Modelling in close and distant reading are both useful digital humanities practices, but they focus on different perspectives. The users of distant-reading binoculars may be well advised to pay attention to what the microscope users do, and perhaps to look into the microscope of digital close reading from time to time. In addition, we who use the microscope can learn from looking through the binoculars to see a larger picture.

## Notes

1. The spatial turn is discussed in several places in Bodenhamer et al. (2010), most explicitly in Ayers's article.
2. The experiments summarized below were part of my PhD research. For more detailed coverage of the experiments, see Eide (2013). The full description can be found in the thesis (Eide 2012). They were based on the well-established method of modelling in digital humanities (McCarty 2005).
3. For details on the source text, the printed edition, and the process of digitizing it, see Eide and Sveum (1998).
4. For more details, see Schnitler (1962, XIII–XXXIII) and Sámi Instituhtta (1989).
5. On the digital sources in general and the computer program used in the analysis, see http://www.oeide.no/dg/dp/ (visited on 22 February 2013).
6. Translated from the Danish by the author.
7. Some examples question this; see, for example, Squire (2011). These are rare, however, and are not considered here.
8. Miguel Nicolelis is a medical professor of neuroscience and founder of Duke University's Center for Neuroengineering.
9. This is how the Sami *joik* may refer to places (Tirén 1942). Collignon (2006) gives a good example of the use of a complex system of place names (or rather named relations between point of observation and the observed place) among the Inuinnat, another Arctic culture.
10. One example is that First Nation map surveys are based on the telling of stories from which information is extracted and put on a map (Tobias 2009).
11. Such differences were already pinpointed in Greek antiquity (Eide 2014).

## Works cited

Arvidson, Jens, Mikael Askander, Jørgen Bruhn, and Heidrun Führer. (2007). 'Editor's Fore-word'. In *Changing Borders: Contemporary Positions in Intermediality*, ed. Jens Arvidson, Mikael Askander, Jørgen Bruhn, and Heidrun Führer, 13–16. Lund: Intermedia Studies Press.

Basso, Keith H. (1996). *Wisdom Sits in Places: Landscape and Language Among the Western Apache*. Albuquerque: University of New Mexico Press.

Bodenhamer, David J., John Corrigan, and Trevor M. Harris, eds. (2010). *The Spatial Humanities: GIS and the Future of Humanities Scholarship*. Bloomington: Indiana University Press.

Brodersen, Lars. (2008). *Geo-Communication and Information Design*. Fredrikshavn: Tankegang.

Collignon, B. (2006). *Knowing Places: The Inuinnait, Landscapes, and the Environment*. Edmonton: CCI Press.

Doerr, Martin. (2003). 'The Cidoc Conceptual Reference Module: An Ontological Approach to Semantic Interoperability of Metadata'. *AI Magazine* 24, no. 3: 75–92.

Eide, Øyvind. (2012). 'The Area Told as a Story. An Inquiry into the Relationship Between Verbal and Map-Based Expressions of Geographical Information'. PhD dissertation, King's College London.

Eide, Øyvind. (2013). 'Why Maps Are Silent When Texts Can Speak: Detecting Media Differences Through Conceptual Modelling'. *Proceedings of the 26th International Cartographic Conference: ICC 2013*, Dresden, 25–30 August. Available at: http://www.icc2013.org/_contxt/_medien/_upload/_proceeding/31_proceeding.pdf (visited on 26 January 2014).

Eide, Øyvind. (2014). 'Verbal Expressions of Geographical Information'. In *New Worlds out of Old Texts: Developing Techniques for the Spatial Analysis of Ancient Narratives,* ed. Elton Barker, Stefan Bouzarovski, Chris Pelling, and Leif Isaksen. Oxford: Oxford University Press. Forthcoming.

Eide, Øyvind, and Tor Sveum. (1998). *Dokumentasjonsprosjektet ved Universitetsbiblioteket i Tromsø. Rapport.* Tromsø: Universitetet i Tromsø, Tromsø museum.

Elleström, Lars. (2010). 'The Modalities of Media: A Model for Understanding Intermedial Relations'. In *Media Borders, Multimodality and Intermediality,* ed. Lars Elleström, 11–48. Basingstoke: Palgrave Macmillan.

Gibson, James. J. (1986). *The Ecological Approach to Visual Perception.* Hillsdale, NJ: Lawrence Erlbaum.

Holtsmark, A. (1961). 'Himmelstrøk og -retninger'. In *Kulturhistorisk leksikon for nordisk middelalder fra vikingtid til reformasjonstid. VI. Gästning-hovedgård,* ed. F. Hødnebø, 566–68. Oslo: Gyldendal.

Ingold, Tim. (2000). *The Perception of the Environment: Essays in Livelihood, Dwelling, and Skill.* Abingdon: Routledge.

Keski-Säntti, J., U. Lehtonen, P. Sivonen, and V. Vuolanto. (2003). 'The Drum as Map: Western Knowledge Systems and Northern Indigenous Map Making'. *Imago Mundi: The International Journal for the History of Cartography* 55, no. 1: 120–25.

Levinson, Stephen C. (2003). *Space in Language and Cognition: Explorations in Cognitive Diversity.* Cambridge: Cambridge University Press.

Mathisen, Hans Ragnar. (1991). 'Samiske Kart'. In *Sámi Kulturmuittut: Báikenammačoaggima Giehtagirji,* ed. Hans Ragnar Mathisen, 41–55. Romsa: Keviselie forlag.

McCarty, Willard. (2005). *Humanities Computing.* Basingstoke: Palgrave Macmillan.

McGann, Jerome J. (2001). *Radiant Textuality: Literature After the World Wide Web.* New York: Palgrave Macmillan.

Monmonier, Mark. (1996). *How to Lie With Maps.* 2nd ed. Chicago: University of Chicago Press.

Nicolelis, Miguel. (2011). 'Interview with Miguel Nicolelis, MD, PhD, Author of Beyond Boundaries: The New Neuroscience of Connecting Brains with Machines—and How It Will Change Our Lives'. Interview by Ginger Campbell. *Brain Science Podcast* 79. Available at: http://brainsciencepodcast.com/bsp/miguel-nicolelis-md-phd-bsp-79.html (visited on 26 January 2014).

Pfeifer, R., and C. Scheier. (1999). *Understanding Intelligence.* Cambridge, MA: MIT Press.

Sámi Instituhtta. (1989). *Lappcodicillen av 1751: Var det samernas Magna Charta?* Guovdageaidnu: Sámi instituhtta.

Schnitler, Peter. (1962). *Major Peter Schnitlers Grenseeksaminasjonsprotokoller 1742–1745.* Vol. 1. Oslo: Norsk historisk kjeldeskrift-institutt.

Squire, M. (2011). *The Iliad in a Nutshell: Visualizing Epic on the Tabulae Iliacae.* Oxford: Oxford University Press.

Tirén, Karl. (1942). *Die Lappische Volksmusik. Aufzeichnungen von Juoikos-Melodien bei den Schwedischen Lappen.* Stockholm: Gebers.

Tobias, T. N. (2009). *Living Proof: The Essential Data-Collection Guide for Indigenous Use-and-Occupancy Map Survey.* Vancouver: Ecotrust Canada and Union of British Columbia Indian Chiefs.

Tolman, E. C. (1948). 'Cognitive Maps in Rats and Men'. *Psychological Review* 55, no. 4: 189–208.

Tuan, Yi-Fu. (1975). 'Images and Mental Maps'. *Annals of the Association of American Geographers* 65, no. 2: 205–13.

Tversky, Barbara, and Paul U. Lee. (1999). 'Pictorial and Verbal Tools for Conveying Routes'. In *Spatial Information Theory: Cognitive and Computational Foundations of Geographical Information Science: International Conference Cosit '99, Stade, Germany, 25–29 August: Proceedings*, ed. Christian Freksa and David M. Mark, 51–64. Berlin: Springer-Verlag.

Woodward, D., ed. (2007). *Cartography in the European Renaissance*. Volume 3, *The History of Cartography*. Chicago: University of Chicago Press.

# 14

# Doing the Sheep Good

## Facilitating Engagement in Digital Humanities and Creative Arts Research

*Deb Verhoeven*

> But metaphor is never innocent. It orients research and fixes results.
>
> Derrida 1980, 17

In the mid-1960s, with support from the National Science Foundation, Sol Worth (a communications scholar and documentary filmmaker) and John Adair (an anthropologist) took the unprecedented step of providing movie cameras to the Navajo community they were studying. This act is now regarded as one of the pivotal moments in the development of visual anthropology and more specifically the emergence of 'participant visual media research'. Worth and Adair hoped to glean new insights into Navajo culture through formal and thematic analyses of the films produced by members of the Pine Springs Reservation community. From the specific representations made, they expected to deduce defining cultural differences between themselves and the community under scrutiny.

Senior members of the community, in particular Sam Yazzie, were not entirely convinced by the proposed exercise and questioned Worth and Adair in some detail:

> After some thought, Sam turned to Worth and through the interpreter asked, 'Will making movies do the sheep any harm?' Worth was happy to explain that as far as he knew no harm would befall the sheep if movies were made in the community.
>
> Sam thought for a few seconds, and looking straight at Worth asked, 'Will it do them any good?' Worth was forced to reply that as far as he knew it wouldn't do the sheep any good.
>
> Sam looked at us both and said...
>
> 'Then why make movies?'
>
> (Worth and Adair 1972, 4)

Reflecting on this exchange, Worth and Adair credit Yazzie's enquiry with an unwitting metaphorical dimension, presuming that his real anxiety was not the sheep but the Navajo community and 'how the new method of communication that we were to teach his people could help the Navajo. How would making films support their values and their way of life?' (Worth and Adair 1972, 6). In contrast to their prosaic depiction of Yazzie's concern for community uplift, they propose their own theoretical and analytic ambitions: teaching a small group the skills of filmmaking in order to 'get away from an examination of man as an object and try to learn more about him as a subject' (Worth and Adair 1972, 26). For Worth and Adair the community cameras were a methodological ploy designed to create the ideal circumstances through which the ethnographers could critically assess the Navajo's creative facility with a new media technology.

Elsewhere I have written about the failure of the two anthropologists to concede agency for the nonhuman in this exchange (Verhoeven 2006). But what also remains unexplored in Worth and Adair's evaluation of this encounter is Sam Yazzie's deeper questioning of agency in research activities. By asking whether the filmmaking will harm or help the sheep, Yazzie suggests he is aware that the proposed ethnographic experiment is a metonymy for the research process itself. At the heart of his ovine enquiry is a question about whether the technology offered to the Navajo community (which pointedly includes sheep) might also provide opportunities for a co-production—whether the cameras might prove, for example, to be a diagnostic tool for the Navajo rather than simply an innovative exercise in content provision for the entertainment and advancement of the anthropologists.

Like Yazzie, this essay is also concerned with questions of inclusion and participation in the scholarly use of technologies, with the changing alignments of agency and the nonhuman made possible in contemporary research practices. In particular it explores the use of databases in academic research—the production, organization, and communication of data—and their consequences for the configuration and character of recent humanities and creative arts scholarship. Databases are a constitutive feature of modern scholarship and its administration, yet are still developing as objects of scholarly interest in their own right. The resulting emergence of political, practical, and philosophical questions about databases (around agency and automation, or privacy and transparency, for example) parallel growing public, commercial, academic, and government reliance on databases across a full range of social phenomena. Specifically, how and what do research databases 'do'? What positions might databases assume in the production of knowledge? How have changes to the nature of data itself also changed databases and their roles? How do debates about databases implicate our own practices as digital humanities and creative arts scholars? I explore these questions in detail through two case studies that exemplify some of the ways in which digital research technologies might bear on the practices of contemporary research scholarship (and vice versa).

## Introduction

And such is the flood that even things that might have done good lose all their goodness.

Erasmus, *Adages* 2.1.1

Familiar accounts of information behaviour reach for easy metaphor. We live, it is said, in an age of information overflow (Gleick 2011). Information arrives torrentially and ceaselessly. Data courses without care through contemporary culture, simultaneously lifting us from the shallows of our former existence and drowning everything in the depths of insignificance. Shouldering aside the shaky structures of previous knowledge architectures, data overwhelms meaning in its wake. This pervasive story of data's relentless ascent is rendered in the style of the classics, as an apocalyptic 'deluge myth' of destruction and rebirth.

Databases, we might then infer, are the product of diluvian times. In an age of data inundation, databases are designed to harness, channel, and sometimes hinder the flow of information. They are conduits and strainers in the face of unreserved turbulence. Like weirs and levees, they attempt to govern the behaviour of information, enabling flow but limiting the damaging aspects of a current too strong. Databases render the flooded rivers of data navigable as well as facilitating the measurement of their waters. In their efforts, databases can also produce an impact on surrounding ecologies, creating downstream problems and accumulating collections of redundant or unwanted debris.

In quantitative terms alone, the metaphor of flooding, certainly as we have experienced it, may not be enough to even begin to describe the rising tide of the dataverse. In a recent study, the IDC predicted there will be some 40 zettabytes of data by 2020 (IDC 2012). By comparison, there are only 1.3 zettalitres of water stored in all the earth's oceans (National Oceanic and Atmospheric Association 2014). And the metaphor has further limitations. In this hydrologic economy of information, data is accorded an *a priori* status in which human effort is directed to acts of 'external forcing', to the (ultimately futile) imposition of boundary conditions (such as databases). Perhaps we might better aim to think about databases as operating in a type of socio-hydrology (Di Baldassarre et al. 2013), as a dynamic co-evolution of the interaction between humans and information systems. In this view, information is no longer autonomous. Instead, we recognize the ways we have opened up, the ways we think and live beyond data, as we also live with data. This alternative account of information inundation has implications that swell beyond the banks of singular research queries, washing away at the edges of disciplinary jurisdictions and the bulwarks of institutional authority in the academy, the state, and industry.

Saying that databases have proved to be especially useful for digital humanities and creative arts scholars across a wide range of research disciplines is almost glib. By organizing and structuring information, databases expand our capacity to comprehend and compare social and cultural phenomena in ways hitherto unimaginable. *But databases are not (just) a system for ideas. They are also an idea for a system.* As Kenneth M. Price points out:

> A database is not an undifferentiated sea of information out of which structure emerges. Argument is always there from the beginning in how those constructing a database choose to categorize information—the initial understanding of the materials governs how more fine-grained views will appear

because of the way the objects of attention are shaped by divisions and subdivisions within the database. The process of database creation is not neutral, nor should it be.

(Price 2009)

The creation of databases requires considerable work; even off-the-shelf systems that encourage us to take the work of databases for granted rely on expertise, discipline, coordination, and large-scale resources to establish their infrastructure. Databases both result from and produce acts of communication and agency whose meaning and functions cannot be reduced to a narrow instrumentality. Databases are productions, and they are also productive and generative. For example, databases produce reactions; they intervene in the worlds they describe and propose. And databases both produce and certify knowledge. They also define (and redefine), through processes of simplification, classification, comparison, inference, and calculation, the relationship between those who evaluate and those who are evaluated. Technologies alone do not produce 'social good' any more than they produce social 'goods'. That is to say, databases don't just describe cultural information. Databases are cultural information, shaped by our organizational and scholarly needs and in turn shaping them. Constantly.

Constantly, because as the nature of data changes, so too does the nature of data collection and organization, and then so too do our strategies as scholars. The volume, velocity, and variety of contemporary data, for example, have changed the way databases operate. In the past it might have made sense to 'contain' data inside a database in order to 'clean' (normalize) and curate (give schematic structure to) information. Now, especially since the advent of 'the Internet of things', data arrives in clusters with predefined identity and versioning. Consequently there is a shift from targeted, discrete forms of information collection to always-on, ubiquitous, rapidly expanding, and accelerating data collection, which has resulted in significant changes to our understandings of information processing. New database formats such as NoSQL (not only SQL) and object-oriented databases, for example, have emerged to deal with this new type of data behaviour and rest on new theoretical organizing principles such as Identity and Versions, Attribution, Inferences, and Inheritances (in both the technical sense and also in the sense that any new theory of data must include precursor database taxonomies and technologies).

Some of these observations of the generative nature of databases have been taken up in emerging areas of study, such as critical code studies (Mackenzie 2006; Kitchin and Dodge 2011), software studies (Manovich 2001; Azuma 2009; Fuller 2008), platform studies (Montfort and Bogost 2009; Jones and Thiruvathukal 2012; Maher 2012), and other areas of the digital humanities (Folsom 2007; Hayles 2012; Liu 2008). This chapter complements these studies by specifically asking how established research behaviours such as authorizing, legislating, interpreting, and agenda setting are being challenged, unfolded, and reinvented by the technological and social changes brought about by new forms of digital media, including databases.

With this question in mind, Martin Weller's exploratory account of new forms of digital scholarship makes a case for four alternative 'scholarly functions' to the standard Boyer model of scholarship based on discovery, application, integration, and teaching. Weller proposes instead the key activities of engagement, experimentation, reflection, and sharing (Weller 2011). This essay presents two case studies in order to reflect on aspects of best practice for 'engagement' in digital humanities and creative arts research. Several key features are explored through these two case studies, including the ways digital humanities and creative arts scholars might:

1. *Span and expand (disciplinary) spaces* in ways that go further than the adoption of modular research practices, such as assembling scalable interdisciplinary academic teams to focus on problem-oriented projects, and instead invite us to consider research engagement in the broadest sense. For instance, to date very little critical debate has taken place about those cultural research methods that exist outside the academy and how powerful these might be in scholarly research. As Mike Savage suggests, we now have an opportunity, 'to broaden our repertoire and recognise the changing stakes involved in the circuits of "knowing capitalism"' (Savage 2009, 249).

2. *Emphasize making and maintaining relations,* both in terms of the data we work with and our sociality as academics (and not just with other academics). Carolyn Ellis reminds us that academic prosociality needs to go beyond interdisciplinarity. For Ellis, this means researchers who exercise a 'relational ethics' value and respect the connection between themselves and the people they study, and also between researchers and the communities in which they live and work (Ellis 2007, 4).

3. *Work at circumventing intermediaries* both by directly opening access to information to those outside the academy, and emphasizing high levels of transparency in academic practice. Thomas Osborne's powerful reconfiguration of the contemporary academic as a 'mediator' (Osborne 2004), responsible for progressing and moving knowledge between institutions, is tested by an emerging research ecology that gives both the public and scholars direct access to one another's ideas. But now we can equally imagine what the role of an academic 'disintermediator' might look like—producing opportunities for just-in-time knowledge via generous discovery interfaces, for example, or adopting the use of iterative project management tools that facilitate open processes of adjustment and improvement to multiple research stakeholders.

4. *Share and make available processes, materials, and knowledge* whilst being mindful of their meaning and value as a potential contribution for further research discovery, retrieval, exchange, reuse, and preservation. This includes understanding that our own digital traces, our successes and failures as we develop our research, are also retrievable and analysable.

5. *Commit to co-producing contents, technologies, infrastructures,* and *analyses* by recognizing how digital and social media platforms have altered traditional modes of production, including those of scholarly researchers themselves. In

this sense, 'engagement' means more than ensuring that the outcomes of our knowledge add value beyond our specific domains by improving access for others, including those outside the academy, to make use of it. Equally it also means creating research that is specifically designed to enable the co-production of knowledge with nonacademic groups through a commitment to multimodal knowledge. This could involve working in modes that are not necessarily written, for example (Bryson 2004). David Beer has considered how this gesture, coupled with changes in the behaviour of data itself, could prompt the profound rethinking of our understanding of the centrality of human agency in research: 'This is to technologise our research practices in a way that was not previously possible, in so doing it moves some more of the analytical processes of . . . research into the hands of machines' (Beer 2012).

The following two case studies are offered as partial explorations of these emerging principles of digital research practice. Whilst they describe vastly different registers of digital humanities and creative arts research, they share a mutual commitment to reflecting and following up on the changing relationship between scholarly researchers and their many stakeholders.

## Case study 1

### The Humanities Networked Infrastructure (HuNI) Project: Ontologies from Below

The Humanities Networked Infrastructure (HuNI) project (http://huni.net.au) is a major new infrastructure service for humanities researchers in Australia developed by a consortium of 13 institutions. HuNI ingests and aggregates data from a total of 31 different Australian datasets that cover a wide range of disciplines in the humanities and creative arts, including literature, biography, performing and visual arts, media studies, and linguistics. Through its use and development of innovative technologies and techniques, the HuNI project proposes some large questions, far beyond the specific queries of participating researchers: how, for example, might the opportunities presented by an unprecedented proliferation of networked data also challenge the unspoken assumptions and ordinary practices of conventional humanities research? Underlying the HuNI initiative is the recognition that cultural data is not economically, culturally, or socially insular, and in order to explore its dimensions fully, researchers need to collaborate across disciplines, institutions, and social locations. If we understand humanities research problems as comprising interdependent networks of institutional, social, and commercial practices, then new kinds of 'evidence', and new ways of organizing, accessing, and presenting this evidence, are critical for our enquiries.

To this end, HuNI provides a number of online research capabilities for humanities researchers to discover and work with the large-scale aggregation of data derived from different research domains and initially developed to solve different research questions. These capabilities enable researchers to create, save, and publish selections of data from HuNI; to analyse and manipulate the data; and to export the data for reuse in external environments. The tasks that users can carry out in HuNI include searching and browsing the aggregated data, constructing private or shared virtual collections of HuNI data, exporting virtual collections for external analysis, and enhancing external databases for publishing into HuNI.

One of the most interesting and innovative features of HuNI, however, is the way it enables researchers to link entities within the HuNI aggregate through socially curated assertions. Using this feature, researchers are able to make statements about relationships between entities represented in the aggregated data. If, for example, they search the data aggregate and identify two entities in their result set that are related in some way, they can add a link between the two records and describe the nature of the relationship. The linking statement may be drawn from a suggested vocabulary of relationships, or the researcher may simply use free text. This feature also allows a researcher to assert that two entities are not related, in recognition that this kind of statement is also a key characteristic of humanities research.

To help visualize these social links, each entity has its own network graph, showing up to six degrees of separation, resulting in an expanding network of dynamic connections. These 'social linking' assertions are visible in the HuNI data aggregate. They may also appear in virtual collections assembled and published by individual users of the HuNI Virtual Laboratory. In this way, the 'social linking' of data forms the basis for researchers to create as well as browse network graphs within the HuNI Lab.

Crucially, the provenance of all these 'social linking' statements is also captured, enabling subsequent researchers to see who made each assertion. HuNI users can annotate these socially produced links with their own comments and assessments. Additionally, HuNI is an aggregate with a relationship to its own history. Researchers can trace how records (including the links between them) have changed over time. This capability recognizes that humanities research involves the mutual study of conceptual and temporal relationships. In other words, our research not only involves making connections between entities; it also involves assessing variations in cultural flow and network relationships through time. Each HuNI record is time-stamped, meaning that although researchers will always see the current view of a record, alongside its related records and assertions, they will also have the option to view how the record has changed since it was first harvested. The provenance information for each record, together with any curated assertions, is captured so that researchers can see when the records were harvested and by whom. A link to the originating data record at source is also provided in the user interface.

The capacity for HuNI users to assert data relationships in their own terms, in what we might call 'vernacular linking', is a central feature of the HuNI virtual laboratory. Instead of relying on a predetermined mapping to a detailed ontology, we are relying on researchers and community users to establish most of the connections within the heterogeneous data aggregate. This enables HuNI to capture the different disciplinary perspectives of users, rather than trying to fit all the data into a single normative framework. It also acknowledges the productive differences that both define and link specific domains through a form of generative knowledge transfer. The opportunity to socially link data allows HuNI to encourage its users to share their knowledge and research findings in the form of specific assertions, and to discuss or debate these statements with each other.

This technology was developed in consideration of the need to balance the disciplinary imperatives for specific vocabularies and data structures with designing a service that is explicitly intended to transcend disciplinary boundaries and link related data effectively and meaningfully. Socially linked data as proposed by HuNI questions the use of standardized ontologies across a large-scale aggregation of heterogeneous humanities data. It suggests that 'linked open data' might equally be explored through 'open linking' as much as the more conventional emphasis on 'open data'. Paul Walk (2009) has very usefully summarized the various permutations of 'linked open data' as

- Data can be *open*, while **not** being *linked*
- Data can be *linked*, while **not** being *open*
- Data which is both *open* **and** *linked* is increasingly viable
- The *Semantic Web* can only function with data which is both *open* **and** *linked* [emphases in original]

To this summary HuNI might add,

- Linking can be open, while data is not.
- Linking and data can both be open.
- Linking that is both open and treated as data (time-stamped and retrievable) is increasingly viable.
- The Semantic Web is more meaningful with frameworks in which both data and linking is open.

The ontological frameworks that sit behind linked open data typically exist in *a priori* structures and are open to the kinds of criticisms that are frequently directed at humanities information and knowledge management strategies. Humanities data is heterogeneous, complex, inconsistent, interpretive, and frequently qualified. Ontologies 'make sense' of what might appear like flux through processes of agreed normalization and simplification. Ontologies are required for automated reasoning and typically rely on agreed common vocabularies and shared understandings of the semantic and conceptual structure of a domain. As Burrows and Verhoeven have noted (2014), in this context ontologies are limited in their ability to grapple with:

- *Variations in terminology*. The same concept or phenomenon may be described using different terms by different researchers, let alone by the wider community.
- *Vagueness of terminology*. The same term may be capable of referring to different concepts or phenomena, depending on the context.

- *Historical change*. The understanding of a knowledge domain is likely to have changed dramatically over time, along with the vocabulary and values used. Ontologies do not usually have a temporal dimension.
- *Multilingualism*. Much humanities research involves languages other than English, either for the subject of the research or for the research discourse itself. Most ontologies, on the other hand, use a standardized (and often quite formal) version of the English language.
- *Interdisciplinarity*. There is an obvious tension between (and even within) humanities disciplines in their terminology, methodologies, and intellectual models.

HuNI asks, why can't we have 'fluid ontologies' (Srinivasan and Huang 2005) that are not predefined but emergent and adaptive? What would it look like to enable ontologies to be co-created 'from below', to give ontologies a vernacular dimension? Can links themselves (and not just the data they connect) be more open? Do user-generated ontologies also open new lines of enquiry about how different communities make sense of the world?

This proposition is different from the vision painted by Clay Shirky in his advocacy for 'distributed classification'. An outspoken critic of both institutionally regulated data collection and its publication in formats to which members of the public have very little access, Shirky instead encourages information strategies such as collaborative tagging, folksonomies, distributed classification, or ethnoclassification so that information users are enabled to create and aggregate their own metadata. But for Shirky these strategies are oriented to the same end, a (differently produced) version of information harmonization. For example, in his essay 'Ontology Is Overrated' (2005), Shirky argues that 'flipping' ontologies from a 'top-down' view of the world to one that is generated from the 'bottom up' will ultimately produce a new and more valid form of consensus rather than HuNI's recognition of multiple and sometimes discordant information stakeholders.

Vernacular ontologies such as that enabled by HuNI, on the other hand, incorporate a 'data ethics' that realizes that the quest for increasing standardization and alignment can be an intrusion, at the same time acknowledging that ontological relativism is equally distracting. Vernacular ontologies perform ethically insofar as the orthodox information management quest for coordination is replaced by cooperation; they accommodate instead the multiplication of difference and the social production-through-linking of other realities and experiences of the world. Vernacular ontologies champion the potential of open, participatory and collaborative linked data practices to produce new possibilities, for both knowledge and for linked data itself. Socially linked data opens the researcher to the associative. It asks, for instance, is it possible to organize information along expressive or ephemeral coordinates?

HuNI's 'social linking' brings to the fore the prosociality of databases—not only as artefacts of human action, imagination, ambition, and accomplishment (and failure), but in terms of bringing into prominence the ethical implications and possibilities of databases. Recent years have seen the rapid development of social networking technologies (Baym and boyd 2012). While considerable investigation of the sociological and communication aspects of social networking has taken place, less attention has been paid to the potential for social networks to catalyse and enable humanities research itself—and even less to the larger question of what scholarship itself might mean in a digital ecosystem where sociality (rather than traditional systems for assessing academic merit) affords research opportunity and success. An implicit outcome of HuNI's focus on socially linked data is that it also draws attention to our own relationships in research, and not only amongst our scholarly selves; it recognizes that a genuine commitment to open linking reveals and recasts the relationship between researchers and the public in terms that are larger than the conventional practices of 'crowdsourcing' content.

## Case study 2

### Songification: Enhancing Opportunities for Multimodal Knowledge

'Songification' is a method for enhancing auditory data that arose from work with The Ultimate Gig Guide (TUGG) database application (http://tugg.me). TUGG maps the Australian music industry at the level of individual performances from the mid-1960s. TUGG was specifically developed to better understand the flow of live music culture, through revealing the itineraries of bands, the socio-spatial location of music performances, and the various factors that have a role in the sustainability of music venues.

To capture band itineraries, the TUGG application represents a band's gigs spatially on a Google map (what we like to call a form of 'gigography'). But the scale of travel between venues is difficult to view in these maps—bands might play a sequence of gigs in the inner city and then move far afield to a country venue. For example, it is almost impossible to see the intricacies of adjacent movements around the city of Melbourne in the same map as a gig in the rural location of Colac (about 150 kilometres away) without losing a great deal of the detail. And because the Google maps are static, we cannot see the sequential order of a band's gigs either.

To better represent these fluctuations of spatial scale and temporal sequence— and to 'repatriate' our research more meaningfully to the music community itself—we decided to try 'sonifying' our data (Hermann 2011). In particular, we were motivated by the idea of 'thinking through' our research in formats that make the most sense to the communities and industries we were studying. We didn't want our research to be released as a fully formed, *a posteriori* afterthought to other academics only—any more than we want to just 'deliver' our results to the musicians and fans we think will be interested in TUGG. Avoiding this typical division between academics as agents (generating analysis) and nonacademic communities as the objects of research (generating content) meant ensuring that our research is undertaken in multimodal ways—acknowledging that although academics might enjoy written texts for developing and communicating their thinking, other communities might prefer to think visually or aurally.

The process of sonification was fairly straightforward and involved calculating the relative distance of gig venues from a central location, translating these figures into frequencies, transposing these into a frequency range that was recognizable to the human ear, and then translating these pro-rated frequencies into the nearest note in a C-major scale. The inharmonious result, however, defeated the idea that the sonified data could be easily shared. We then decided to take steps to enhance the sonifications, to enable clearer pattern detection and to honour the musical provenance of the data.

Songification entails an elaboration of the method by which sonification realizes data in the form of auditory values. By further transforming our research data into music, we created an improved experience for discerning the relations and rhythms in the data, demonstrating how enhanced auditory data design provides both a medium for aural intuition and an inclusive, 'vernacular' opportunity for nonprofessional research participation. It was also an opportunity to create some unique music by literally playing (with) the data.

We wrote backing tracks in the style of the bands we were studying and then added the itinerary data sequence as a lead guitar riff. Each gig/note was played in the succession in which it was originally performed—by date. The length or duration of each note was set to the number of days between one gig and the next gig. The longer the delay between gigs, the longer the note. The culmination of this process was a live performance by the TUGG team (all of whom play an instrument) of live performance data at the eResearch Australasia conference in 2013 (see Verhoeven 2013).

The songification method was specifically developed with an expanded view of what might constitute 'open data'. In this context, exposing and enabling data sharing and reuse meant more than simply providing opportunities to make the data exportable into other data formats. As is typical in many data-driven projects, the TUGG research outcomes were available for public feedback online, but were presented in complex graphs and tables and were consequently inaccessible to the communities under study. Instead we were intent on re-presenting the data in forms and formats that made the most sense to the communities it described—in this case, the music industry.

The unprecedented opportunities presented by cultural data projects like TUGG, then, are that they lead not only to innovative methods for studying and understanding the creative industries and creative labour, but conversely, they enable us to simultaneously understand the creative potential of digital humanities research itself. And it changes the 'ordering of things' in other ways too, requiring a change of temporality—knowledge is always in process—not *a priori nor a posteriori*.

The specific point of a methodology like songification is to enable the live music community to engage with and contribute to our analysis as we develop it. We want them to be involved in helping us along with our analysis, to be much more than the passive recipients of our thinking. Songification is the instantiation of a belief that research itself is always in beta mode—that what is important is not the end result of a purely scholarly exercise but that the research that truly matters is inevitably iterative, multimodal, recursive, and co-created.

The TUGG researchers, for instance, developed diverse modes of participation and roles in the project that involved working with and through different media and information technologies—as researchers, performers, creators, audiences, and community members. From the outset, the TUGG research team included information managers, music industry analysts, IT developers, and geospatial scientists. We moved from one (or more) modes of action to another, depending on the aim of (and our role in) different activities (information manager/bass player/analyst). This form of modular research practice exceeds Biagioli's (2009) description of specialized interdisciplinary collaborations occurring in a limited temporal window and instead expands on our own capacity to simultaneously undertake multimodal roles. We were (non)academics, concurrently both the subjects and objects of our research undertaking, in chorus with the live music communities whose data we were studying/performing.

Songification explicitly recognizes the role of the media in shaping research, not just communicating it. The very act of playing the data as music had unexpected repercussions for our relationship to the research field—throwing even more significance onto the collaborative nature of large data-driven projects, emphasizing our ability to (really) listen, providing a (creative) medium for drawing together disparate ideas, and exercising our facility to focus on the present and the future simultaneously, to name a few. But even more curiously, playing the data/music has produced an affective response for some of our audiences, an unexpected feature of the project that remains to be further explored.

The development of songification was intended to be more than just an exercise in 'epistemic egalitarianism'. It opened new avenues for information and participation that also created opportunities for diversification of data analysis and associated research practices. The project began by recognizing that media producers and media scholars could both traverse the same pathways for discovery, development, discussion, and dissemination. What it had not anticipated was how productively the roles of media producer and scholar might themselves be entwined. The project also proposes further questions. How then might creative industry studies itself be rethought in a networked world where personal and professional identities so intimately overlap?

## Conclusion

> I wanted so much to write the story of the ocean. But what and where was the structure? I was, as they say, *all at sea*.
>
> Winchester 2010, 24

The two case studies outlined in this chapter are interdisciplinary projects that were in part intended to elicit a reflection on the broader role of academics in society, which itself should not be seen as homogeneous but as composed of diverse (yet interlinked) interests and viewpoints. They were founded in the belief that there is value in reducing insularity in cultural and creative arts research—that an arm's-length critical distance is not always the most reliable way to grasp something. Their operative view of openness and engagement is not restricted to the distribution of information but importantly also incorporates the formation of knowledge. And they recognize the value of the disaggregated cultural analysis that can be found outside the academy in places ranging from multinational corporations such as Google to the informal genealogies produced at the local library. In so doing, they aim to create new practices and politics of knowledge through digital scholarship—not just at the level of collection but at the level of analysis.

In the socio-hydrologic description of data inundation, that some digitally adept scholars might see themselves as latter-day Noahs is not surprising—building defensive arks to safeguard select and unique cultural collections, for example. Buried in here is a subsurface discourse of the 'Digital Humanities as Noachian', populated by 'saviour academics' returning the humanities to a time of prelapsarian order and structure. But data inundation can also have the effect of lifting our research imagination beyond familiar workflows into unfathomed waters. Here the digital humanities charts potential opportunities for rethinking our disciplines and for adjusting the course of our conduct in order to realize the challenge that databases present for the authority, influence, and purpose of the academic humanities.

Both HuNI and songification propose the digital creation of a social research ecology, made up of overlapping technologies, places, organizations, agents, concepts, and workflows. The effect of these intricate entanglements is to extend the scope of our scholarship at the same time as decentring it. For example, an emphasis on the ways that digital research produces new relations (and therefore also new forms of relationality) has a direct bearing on the production of our own digital scholarly selves. As David Beer and Mark Taylor (2013) suggest, engaged digital research initiatives ultimately mean

> looking beyond the academy to see how 'ordinary people' are playing with the data themselves, how interns of companies are using it to understand and visualise their 'customers', to see what computer scientists and the like are producing with the data, to see what artists and others are creating with it.

In other words, as truly engaged academics, we don't just learn from the data itself but also from the way that data is used and reused. An academic humility is at the heart of engagement-led digital scholarship, an acknowledgement that the ontological primacy of our own academic agency has (always) been dispersed and that the slipstreams of co-production cast their own currents.

Whilst this essay is explicitly about databases and the economies of engagement they afford—how they inflect what we do as digital scholars, how we do it, and whom we do it with—it is less obviously an essay about our thinking. Working with databases has repercussions for the course of our thoughts, appending to the intended use of the technologies in our research a recognition of the range of meanings made possible by these same technologies. As Sam Yazzie suggested in the example at the beginning of this paper, we might take pause to include the sheep as part of our thinking, to think of 'sheep' (or even like a sheep) without succumbing to the recommendations of metaphor. By acknowledging nonhuman frameworks of what is meaningful, we may come close to Yazzie's aspiration for 'doing the sheep good'.

The case studies outlined in this chapter illustrate the benefits of an expanded and inclusive view of digital humanities and creative arts research; in which computation and communication, method and media, in combination enable us to explore the larger question of how we can work with technologies to co-produce, represent, analyze, convey and exchange knowledge. They suggest this exchange in the broadest sense—beyond the domestic diversions of academic interdisciplinarity. The key issue confronting the digital humanities is not the (largely self-defined) differences between academics but the perceived difference between academics as a whole and the community (both of which include the nonhuman). These case studies are a timely reflection on how our practices have lent weight to these perceptions and how an expanded and inclusive digital humanities and creative arts effort might redress them.

## Acknowledgements

I would like to acknowledge the contributions of a number of people who have played a role in aspects of this paper: Thanks are due to the two anonymous reviewers whose acute assessments lent welcome improvements. The concept of 'socially linked data' was developed by the HuNI team, in particular the technical lead, Marco la Rosa, in conjunction with the HuNI Project Director (Deb Verhoeven); HuNI project manager, Alex Hawker; the HuNI semantic lead, Anne Cregan; and the HuNI product owner, Toby Burrows. Songification was elaborated by the author in collaboration with Alwyn Davidson, James Verhoeven, Alex Gionfriddo, and Peter Gravestock. Sound and video files relating to Songification can be found at http://kinomatics.com/songification/.

## References

Azuma, Hiroki. (2009). *Otaku*. Minneapolis: University of Minnesota Press.
Baym, Nancy K., and danah boyd. (2012). 'Socially Mediated Publicness: An Introduction'. *Journal of Broadcasting and Electronic Media* 56, no. 3 (September): 320–29.
Beer, David. (2012). 'Using Social Media Data Aggregators to do Social Research'. *Sociological Research Online* 17, no. 3 (August). Available at: http://www.socresonline.org.uk/17/3/10.html.
Beer, David, and Mark Taylor. (2013). 'The Hidden Dimensions of the Musical Field and the Potential of the New Social Data'. *Sociological Research Online* 18, no. 2 (May). Available at: http://www.socresonline.org.uk/18/2/14.html.
Biagioli, Mario. (2009). 'Postdisciplinary Liaisons: Science Studies and the Humanities'. *Critical Inquiry* 35, no. 4 (Summer): 816–35.
Bryson, John. (2004). 'What to Do When Stakeholders Matter'. *Public Management Review* 6, no. 1: 21–53.
Burrows, Toby, and Deb Verhoeven. (2014). 'Deploying Ontologies in the Humanities and Creative Arts'. Presentation at Expanding Horizons: Digital Humanities Australasia, University of Western Australia, 19 March.

Derrida, Jacques. (1980). *Writing and Difference*. Chicago: University of Chicago Press.

Di Baldassarre, G., A. Viglione, G. Carr, L. Kuil, J. L. Salinas, and G. Blöschl. (2013). 'Socio-Hydrology: Conceptualising Human-Flood Interactions'. *Hydrology and Earth Systems Sciences*, no. 17: 3295–303. DOI:10.5194/hess-17-3295-2013.

Ellis, Carolyn. (2007). 'Telling Secrets, Revealing Lives: Relational Ethics in Research with Intimate Others'. *Qualitative Inquiry* 13, no. 1 (January): 3–29.

Folsom, ed. (2007). 'Database as Genre: The Epic Transformation of Archives'. *PMLA* 122, (October): 1571–79.

Fuller, Matthew, ed. (2008). *Software Studies: A Lexicon*. London: MIT Press.

Gleick, James. (2011). *The Information: A History, a Theory, a Flood*. New York: Pantheon Books.

Hayles, N. Katherine. (2012). *How We Think: Digital Media and Contemporary Technogenesis*. Chicago: University of Chicago Press.

Hermann, Thomas, Andy Hunt, and John G. Neuhoff, eds. (2011). *The Sonification Handbook*. Berlin: Logos Publishing House.

IDC. (2012). *Digital Universe Study,* December. Available at: http://www.emc.com.

Jones, Steven E., and George K. Thiruvathukal. (2012). *Codename Revolution: The Nintendo Wii Platform*. Cambridge, MA: MIT Press.

Kitchin, Rob, and Martin Dodge. (2011). *Code/Space: Software and Everyday Life*. Cambridge, MA: MIT Press.

Liu, Alan. (2008). *Local Transcendence: Essays on Postmodern Historicism and the Database*. Chicago: University of Chicago Press.

Mackenzie, Adrian. (2006). *Cutting Code: Software and Sociality*. Oxford: Peter Lang.

Maher, Jimmy. (2012). *The Future Was Here: Commodore Amiga*. Cambridge, MA: MIT Press.

Manovich, Lev. (2001). *The Language of New Media*. Cambridge, MA: MIT Press.

Montfort, Nick, and Ian Bogost. (2009). *Racing the Beam: The Atari Video Computer System*. Cambridge, MA: MIT Press.

National Oceanic and Atmospheric Administration (NOAA). (2014). 'About 96 Percent of Earth's Water Is in the Ocean'. 23 January. Available at: http://oceanservice.noaa.gov.

Osborne, Thomas. (2004). 'On Mediators: Intellectuals and the Ideas Trade in the Knowledge Society'. *Economy and Society* 33 (2004): 430–47.

Price, Kenneth M. (2009). 'Edition, Project, Database, Archive, Thematic Research Collection: What's in a Name?' *Digital Humanities Quarterly* 3, no. 3. Available at: http://www.digitalhumanities.org.

Savage, Mike. (2009). 'Against Epochalism: An Analysis of Conceptions of Change in British Sociology'. *Cultural Sociology* 3, no. 2 (July): 217–38.

Shirky, Clay. (2005). 'Ontology Is Overrated: Categories, Links, and Tags'. Available at: http://www.shirky.com.

Srinivasan, Ramesh, and Jeffrey Huang. (2005). 'Fluid Ontologies for Digital Museums'. *International Journal on Digital Libraries* 5, no. 3 (May): 193–204.

Verhoeven, Deb. (2006). *Sheep and the Australian Cinema*. Melbourne: Melbourne University Press.

Verhoeven, Deb. (2013). 'Turning Gigs into Gigabytes (and Back Again): Songification and Live Music Data'. Available at: http://kinomatics.com.

Walk, Paul. (2009). 'Linked, Open, Semantic?' Available at: http://www.paulwalk.net.

Weller, Martin. (2011). *The Digital Scholar: How Technology Is Transforming Scholarly Practice*. London: Bloomsbury Academic.

Winchester, Simon. (2010). *Atlantic: A Vast Ocean of a Million Stories*. London: Harper Press.

Worth, Sol, and John Adair. (1972). *Through Navajo Eyes: An Exploration in Film Communication and Anthropology*. Bloomington: Indiana University Press.

# 15
# Materialities of Software
## Logistics, Labour, Infrastructure

*Ned Rossiter*

In this chapter I bring digital humanities research into the domain of logistical industries. The primary task of the global logistics industry is to manage the movement of people and things in the interests of communication, transport, and economic efficiencies. The software applications special to logistics visualize and organize these mobilities, producing knowledge about the world in transit. Yet for the most part the enterprise resource planning (ERP) software remains a black box for those not directly using these systems as a matter of routine in their daily work across a range of industries, which include but are not limited to logistical industries. The health care, medical insurance, education, mining, and energy industries, along with retail and service sectors, also adopt ERP systems to manage organizational activities. One key reason for the scarce critical attention to ERP systems is related to the prohibitive price of obtaining proprietary software, which often costs millions of dollars for companies to implement. The aesthetics of ERP software are also notoriously unattractive, and the design is frequently not conducive to ease or pleasure of use.

The result for the digital humanities is that ERP software analysis is limited to IT services and programmers associated with the shipping, warehousing, aviation, rail, and road transport industries, and procurement, human resource, inventory, and supply chain management.[1] As such, logistical software may seem to hold little relevance as an object of study for digital humanities researchers. However, I argue in this chapter that logistics has a broad social reach and impact in terms of how people undertake work. Logistical software functions as a technology of governance and control, measuring the productivity of labour using real-time key performance indicators (KPIs). Central to logistics is the production of new subjectivities of labour. More than any other aspect of logistical industries, this characteristic of logistics software makes it relevant to researchers in digital humanities. Why? Because such techniques of management are finding their way into academic workplace settings, which are undergoing a transformation into what I would term the logistical university (Rossiter 2010, 2014a). The recent rise of MOOCs (massive open online courses) is a logistical operation that will result in the offshoring and outsourcing of knowledge production. As neoliberal capitalism diversifies its modes of accumulation from the debt economy of housing to the extraction of wealth from student debt and global education markets (Anonymous 2012; Lazzarato 2012; Ross 2009, 2014), logistical critique becomes ever more pressing as a political, social, and intellectual undertaking. A focus on logistical media is one line of entry into the development of such a critique.

Methods developed within the digital humanities also have an important role to play in the critique of logistical power. Rather than turn to established humanities methods, or even those developed from within the digital humanities proper, this chapter outlines how the process of devising questions and the problem of method coextensive with research on logistics industries lends digital humanities an occasion to reorient research methods as well as the production of concepts. I explore such possibilities for digital humanities research with reference to the material dimensions of software systems operative within global logistics industries. Particular focus is given to transport and shipping activities undertaken at Port Botany in Sydney in order to highlight the multiplicity of logistical forces exerted upon labour. The development of a digital visualization drawing on data from productivity reports of the port is foregrounded to register the relation between design and research practice with regard to the question of method within digital humanities research. While the aesthetic logic of the visualization is not markedly different from the many visualizations developed in digital humanities, it is nonetheless distinct for the way in which it brings to the fore the practice of method through the process of designing a visualization. In the case of the Port Botany study, the visualization served two key purposes: first, as a methodological device in the practice of transdisciplinary research, and second, as a media form that made visible the pressures on labour within the shipping and transport industries. Both aspects of the visualization enable a critique of logistics, with the visualization providing a kind of substitute interface in the absence of access to the software actually used in logistical industries.

Jangling in the background of this chapter is an interest in developing a theory of logistical media.[2] Forecasted in the work on 'logistical modernities' by urban theorist and military historian Paul Virilio (2006), and elaborated to some extent in the study on gameplay and war simulations by media philosopher Patrick Crogan (2011), the term 'logistical media' is named as such by communication historian and social theorist John Durham Peters (2012, 2013).[3] For Peters, the concept of logistical media 'stresses the infrastructural role of media' (2012, 43). In addition to storage, transmission, and processing systems, I would suggest that the larger study of logistical media might also include attention to how the aesthetic qualities peculiar to the banality of spreadsheets, ERP systems, and software applications have arisen from particular histories in military theatres, cybernetics, infrastructural design, transport, and communications. Given the elusiveness of logistical software as an object of encounter, in this chapter I instead shadow such logistical media with recourse to digital visualizations of logistical operations. I emphasize how the digital visualizations are not just a method of aggregating disparate datasets into a new synthetic form that provides insight into conditions of labour; they also work as a mediating apparatus in terms of the sociality and design of research. In other words, the visualizations mediate the relation between people, organization, and things. Finally, I suggest that the visualizations offer digital humanities an opportunity to extend research into the politics of labour as it meets the logistical force of supply chain governance and technologies of control.

## Digital humanities and the problem of method

The digital humanities is a diverse and emerging field that harbours different kinds of innovation and eclecticism. By and large, however, the digital humanities has been notable for its adherence to traditional research objects and rehashing of old methods following the integration of new forms of computational power within institutional settings. Historical literary texts are digitized to revise assumed economic patterns and social forces. Geographers scan topographic maps to produce information layers and digital elevations that reveal new frontiers for research. Google Earth is traversed to uncover obscure archaeological curiosities in a dirt-free manner. Even cutting-edge research in the field of digital media cultures tends to transpose established humanities and social science methods to conduct ethnographies of Facebook, complex visualizations of networks, and content analyses of the Twittersphere.

To simply import existing methods (surveys, interviews, questionnaires, focus groups) from the humanities and social sciences and then use digital technology as a technique of enhancement is not really sufficient for the invention of new methods situated within computational architectures (*media form*). Methods developed from within media of communication—including graphic design and digital visualization—can assist in understanding, for example, how software architectures operate as key technologies for governing labour within logistical industries. This does not mean producing bar graphs and pie charts using routine applications such as Excel, PowerPoint, or Microsoft Word, nor does it involve undertaking geospatial mapping using Google Earth in order to represent the territorial distribution or location of datasets. Likewise, software used in quantitative research such as SPSS that codes questionnaire data for statistical analysis does little to inform research interested in the ways software itself at once shapes and emerges out of material conditions (social relations, economic forces, cultural dynamics).

Such methods fit largely in what David Berry (2011) and others have identified as the first wave of digital humanities research, with its focus on the digitization of archives and artefacts along with developing infrastructure associated with digital repositories and expanding research agendas.[4] This wave also involved the scramble for funding that consumes much energy in academics, albeit with a high degree of variation across different national settings. The digital humanities presented humanities academics with the occasion to start scratching at the edges of high-stakes funding and infrastructural needs more often commandeered by disciplines in science, technology, engineering, and medicine.

By Jeffrey Schnapp and Todd Presner's account, the so-called second wave of digital humanities is characterized by 'born-digital' methods of analysis and modes of curated knowledge generated from within the media of communication (Schnapp and Presner 2009, cited in Berry 2011). Berry posits an emergent third wave of digital humanities research, which is interested in how software and code set computational parameters to the production of knowledge. Central to such an approach is a critique of the assumption within much humanities research that its organizing concepts and methodological practices are somehow independent of algorithmic architectures or computational cultures. While Berry isn't direct in saying so, the spectre of technological determinism lurks in the background here. After around three decades of research in literary, media, and cultural studies on the agency of audiences, readers, and fan cultures, the pervasiveness of digital media warrants a serious review of how technical systems and computational code format cultural expression and social practices. A further step would examine how the integration of digital technology into economic and social life is transforming neurological processes and biological systems.[5]

Another key line of investigation attending Berry's call for a 'computational turn' would include a taxonomy and political economy of software applications and the cultures of code operative within institutional settings across the world. Such an undertaking might begin a critique of the extent to which knowledge production and the management of university routines and their economies are formatted in ways specific to computational regimes of communication. A project of this order is certainly beyond my scope here, but I think it is nonetheless worth registering as relevant to future research within digital humanities. Needless to say, I present aspects of such an undertaking in this chapter, namely an interest in how economies of code broaden the question of method and production of concepts beyond what is normally assumed of digital humanities research.

Cutting-edge digital humanities research requires an invention of methods developed through the use of digital media technologies. Methods situated within media of communication—including graphic design, game development, and digital visualization—can assist in understanding how the rules special to 'algorithmic architectures' structure the organization and analysis of data (see Terzidis 2006). Algorithmic architectures are computational systems of governance that hold a variable relation between the mathematical execution of code and an 'external' environment defined through arrangements of data (see Parisi 2012). The capacity of algorithmic architectures to organize and analyse data on labour productivity in real-time, for instance, means they function as technologies for governing labour within logistical industries. Moreover, they constitute a key site of intervention for digital humanities research interested in the relation between knowledge, power, and computational systems.

In order to invent methods that could actually use logistical data in an analytical sense, the development of a video game will be an important component of a current project that tracks Chinese-led globalization through infrastructure (Rossiter 2014a). Our interest is to identify new regimes of global governance that arise from logistical operations and the coordination of supply chains. Building on earlier collective research undertaken during the Transit Labour project, which I discuss in more detail below, the Logistical Worlds project focuses on the operation of zones, corridors, and concessions prompted by logistical industries in

Piraeus (Greece), Kolkata (India), and Valparaíso (Chile).[6] The video game, provisionally titled *Logistical Worlds*, extends the premise of digital visualizations as a technique of method by collecting data on labour conditions and logistical operations as the condition of play. Whether this takes the form of scraping publicly available data on port activities or user submission of productivity statistics, for instance, is a matter to be decided. As with the digital visualization developed in the Transit Labour project, the concept of the game as a method for generating and arranging data for the purpose of critical analysis is a core precept informing the game's design. The media form of the game also offers the project an idiom of expression through which to produce counter-imaginaries of what anthropologist Anna Tsing (2009) terms 'supply chain capitalism' while providing a conceit for data collection through the act of play.

## Big data, disciplinarity, and the absence of critique

The emergent field of digital humanities has sought to develop digital tools such as geographical information systems (GIS), simulation, data mining, and network analysis to assist the humanities and social sciences in an attempt to formulate new research questions and techniques of analysis. More often these tools take the form of software applications able to 'capture, manage and process' large datasets, or what computer scientists and industry refer to as 'big data' (Manovich 2011a). This may include transactional data such as web searches and mobile phone records, along with digital books, newspapers, statistics, photographs, music, interviews, and their supporting information architecture of tags, traces, and comments.

There is a concept-free zeal about the capacity for digital methods to verify some kind of hitherto unobtainable empirical truth.[7] In part, this stems from a fidelity in the correlation between data, its referent, and the material world. In the database economy derived from content management systems, ERP software, and social network media cultures, data has indeed become the new empiric. Displacing earlier analogue methods such as focus groups, phone surveys, and questionnaires designed to measure audience taste and consumer behaviours, digitally encoded data has a capacity to scale, recombine, and granulate the micro-practices of people, finance, and things in ways to which predigital methods could only aspire.

Needless to say, the frequently assumed empirical dimension of data is better understood in terms of its self-referentiality than its correspondence with an external material world. Once such a claim is accepted, the capacity for data to be modelled in ways that generate what Foucault termed regimes of truth is—at least, I find—less objectionable at a theoretical level. This is not to say that data is without empirical substance, nor is it to valorize analogue objects or offline worlds as imbued with greater materiality or analytical verisimilitude.[8] Rather, the emphasis is to acknowledge the role of protocols, standards, norms, and parameters special to software platforms and their political economy that define the contours of expression through which data is made intelligible. Moreover, when data is understood to operate within, and indeed constitute, regimes of truth, a secondary empirical quality emerges in the shaping of social practices and material conditions in ways not so dissimilar from how policies of various kinds result in forms of action. Think of the rhetorical power of climate modelling, which refers to itself as a technical system while impacting on the economic cost, if not the rate, of greenhouse gas emissions.

In the process of drawing connections within or across datasets, old or existing research objects are remodelled in new ways. Unsurprisingly, business also has a strong interest in devising new techniques for extracting economic value using tools that produce meaning from the process of data recombination and governance. As a report from *The Economist* (2010) put it, the proliferation of data 'makes it possible to do many things that previously could not be done: spot business trends, prevent diseases, combat crime and so on. Managed well, the data can be used to unlock new sources of economic value, provide fresh insights into science and hold governments to account.' That *The Economist* hitches a neoliberal democratic ethos or agenda to the market potential of data management should come as no surprise. While not especially novel or insightful, *The Economist* foresees problems with the rise of big data, including data storage availability and privacy and security issues. The digital humanities could contribute to these debates in ways that address, for example, cultural and social dimensions wrought by the accumulation of big data.

For the digital humanities, the problems presented by digitalization and, to a lesser extent, big data are quite different. With its tendency towards text-based analysis using digital tools (parsing the Shakespeare archive to reveal grammatical variation, for example), the digital humanities is arguably at a formative stage in terms of developing critical methods and concepts that can address cultural, social, and political phenomena and challenges in the world at large (see Craig and Kinney 2009). Alan Liu signals this current impasse with precision in his critique of digital humanities: 'the digital humanities are not ready to take up their full responsibility because the field does not yet possess an adequate critical awareness of the larger social, economic, and cultural issues at stake' (2012, 11). It is almost as though nothing happened after New Criticism in literary theory and positivism in the social sciences. Broadly speaking, there seems to be a studious avoidance of inventing digital research methods outside disciplinary comfort zones. Nor is there any substantive academic engagement with the politics of data as it intersects with labour and life. Critical studies involved in research on virtual work or digital labour tend to reduce the experience and condition of labour to people working in the cultural and media industries, rather than identify how diverse sectors of the economy and society are affected—often in conflictual yet mutually constitutive ways—by the expansion of information economies and their attendant technologies.[9]

Referring to the absence of canonical figures in the digital humanities compared to those generated within the early years of cultural studies, Andrew Prescott is quite scathing in his characterization of the field: 'the focus of much digital humanities work has been on the creation of online projects anchored in conventional subjects' (2012, 72). While Prescott's desire for a canon seems to linger as a form of nostalgia for the days when cultural and media studies 'branch[ed] out into new fields in the way the work of (say) Hoggart did' (72), it is not something he sees as necessary or even possible for the digital humanities. Indeed, whether the orientation of research in digital humanities, irrespective of its substance, has the capacity to produce canonical works is doubtful. Projects situated within or alongside digital humanities are largely conducted independently of each other as a result of their diverse global and geocultural distribution. As a consequence, a certain disciplinary, institutional, and geocultural fragmentation ensues that does not lend itself to the production of disciplinary canons. At the very least, canon formation requires both a distillation and articulation of shared ideas and energies across a broad range of inquiries. One might also debate the need or relevance for a shared theoretical point of reference in order to advance conceptual apparatuses and methodological practices. But this is less Prescott's point. More urgent for Prescott is the need within digital humanities to give attention to theorizing and critical reflection with reference to digital technologies and objects of research.

At the level of disciplinarity, the digital humanities often finds itself set against institutional structures that corral projects into disciplinary silos. In a similar vein, Liu argues that 'the underlying issue is disciplinary identity not of the digital humanities but of the humanities themselves' (2013, 410). More straight-forwardly, disciplines have disciplinary interests irrespective of whether they have undertaken a computational turn. Art historians probe computationally generated patterns in visual archives, linguists develop speech analysis tools, literary scholars build databases to survey the history of book industries, mediaevalists reconstruct the Middle Ages through digital cartographies. As a consequence, new research questions are often posed in terms of how to tackle larger-scale datasets rather than address a material world unscored by complex problems.

The work on digital methods by sociologist Noortje Marres (2012) is emblem-atic of such an approach. With an interest in how 'natively digital' research tools 'take advantage of the analytic and empirical capacities that are "embedded in online media" ' (151), Marres's advocacy of digital methods contrasts with those developed in the digital visualization of Port Botany discussed below. In focus-ing on the empirics of data as it is generated through algorithmic operations of search tools such as Issue Crawler, the analysis of political issues, discourses, and actors become displaced from the material conditions from which they arise (see Kanngieser, Neilson, and Rossiter 2014). As it turns out, 'method as interven-tion' for Marres is a fairly exclusive online undertaking no matter that it might involve a 'redistribution of research' and 'transfer' of knowledge among diverse actors (see also Rogers 2013). Search data and its visualization become the uni-verse of critique. The subject of labour is divided between humans and technology in the practice of method but not the interface between politics, economy, sub-jects, and objects, and the material and technical conditions from which they emerge.

In the social science and humanities disciplines undertaking transnational and transcultural research using digital methods for collecting and sampling large-scale datasets, there is a tendency for analyses to formulate a universal system of questions to ensure maximum consistency in generating usable data. In adopting such methodological and analytical approaches, the disparity between the particularities of the object of study and the abstraction of knowledge becomes even further amplified than might be the case in, for example, more traditional methods of practice in anthropological fieldwork. Alternatively, abstraction itself becomes the object of study, which is the direction taken in Franco Moretti's quantitative method of 'distant reading' of literary history (see Bode 2012, 9).

An additional and rarely addressed problem can arise with projects international in scope that place a priority on modelling, visualizing, aggregating, and analysing large datasets. The underlying method within many 'global' approaches to comparative research in media, social, and cultural research often seeks to integrate and make uniform data that is nonassimilable due to protocological conflicts, parametric irregularities, qualitative differences, and the like. In doing so, such approaches reproduce some of the central assumptions of area studies—namely, that the study of geocultural difference is predicated on equivalent systems of measure that demonstrate difference in terms of self-contained areas or territories and civilizational continuities often conforming to the borders of the nation state. Yet it is a mistake to suppose that cultural variation can be distinguished in terms of national cultures, at least in any exclusive sense. In the case of transnational research on logistics industries (and, more broadly, any research project taking a global perspective), digital methods of comparative research need to be alert to the asymmetrical composition of datasets on transport and communication industries and labour performance, which upsets any desire for equivalent units consistent across time and space that might provide the basis for comparison.

The challenge is not about integrating historical or archival data into ever larger sets but involves working across variable, uneven, and often incomplete datasets. Here the fantasy of logistical industries of creating interoperability through protocols of electronic data interchange (EDI) and ERP software platforms hits its limits. Designed to track the movement of people and things, EDI and ERP architectures are intended to function as real-time registrations of labour productivity and the efficiency of distribution systems. Yet these technologies of optimization frequently rub up against any number of disruptions in the form of labour struggles, infrastructural damage, software glitches, supply chain problems, and so forth. This discrepancy between the calculus of the plan and the world as it happens suggests that the most interesting sites to study are those where interoperability breaks down and methods of organization external to logistics' software routines are instituted in an attempt to smooth out the transfer of data and material goods (Neilson 2014).

Technologies of logistical governance external to software architectures may include border regimes such as special economic zones (SEZs), territorial concessions, and trade corridors. They may also manifest as juridical power in the form of labour laws or extra-state forms of governance, such as manufacturing and industrial design standards, communication protocols, and the politics of affect as it modulates the diagram or relations special to subjectivity. Borders, in short, proliferate, multiply, and at times overlap (Mezzadra and Neilson 2013). Clearly, studying such an expanse of governmental techniques is beyond my scope in this chapter. But the techniques are important to note by way of signalling that the digital is not as ubiquitous as is often claimed or assumed. And this has implications for the design of methods within digital humanities; chief among these is an 'invention of new knowledge practices and methods that intervene in the world' (Neilson 2014, 79).

## Positioning logistical media theory

A study of logistical media begins to address some of these issues. With its attention to flexibility, contingency, control, and coordination, logistical media critique opens the relation between economies of data and the remodelling of labour and life. In terms of disciplinary orientation, logistical media theory does not yet exist. It is a theory whose status has yet to coalesce into a sustained analytical and methodological body of research and knowledge. For the purpose of sketching some contours of influence, I would suggest that logistical media theory is informed by the fields of network cultures, software studies, critical organization studies, Canadian communications research, and German media theory in addition to anthropological and historical research on infrastructure. Given the focus on digital methods in this chapter, I limit my comments here to the relation between logistical media critique and software studies.

The programme of cultural analytics, headed by Lev Manovich (2011a) and his Software Studies Initiative at the University of California–San Diego, summarizes its project in ways that essentially transpose already existing techniques rather than invent new methods per se: 'Today sciences, business, governments and other agencies rely on computer-based analysis and visualization of large datasets and data flows. They employ statistical data analysis, data mining, information visualization, scientific visualization, visual analytics, and simulation. We propose to begin systematically applying these techniques to contemporary cultural data' (Manovich 2011b, 2013).

By contrast, a study of software within the global logistics industries prompts the question of method with regard to how to research the relation between software and the management of labour; the role of logistics infrastructure and the reconfiguration of urban, rural, and geopolitical spaces; and the production of new regimes of knowledge within an organizational paradigm. Software systems operative within global logistics industries such as SAP or Oracle generate protocols and standards that shape social, economic, and cross-institutional relations within and beyond the global logistics industries. How such governing forces and material conditions are captured and made intelligible through the use of digitally modified data is, in part, the challenge of method.

Forms of pattern recognition beyond the basic data hold relevance for how the emergent paradigms of digital humanities and software studies analyse the massive volume of big data generated by digital transactions and user-consumer practices online. Big data analysis of habits of consumption is interesting for commercial entities, but not particularly exciting for social and political analysis of network ecologies. How to ascertain a relation between data, materiality, and subjectivity is a problem little addressed by either digital humanities or software studies.[10] What would the critical practice of digital humanities research consist of in the study of big data? How might such practices be designed on transnational scales involving networks of collaborative constitution? What are some of the particular problems surrounding the politics of depletion that come to bear both in the method of digital humanities research and the datasets under scrutiny? Where is the dirt that unravels the pretence of smooth-world systems so common within industry, IT, and state discourses around global economies and their supply chains? And can disruption be understood as a political tension and form of conflictual constitution?

Within cybernetics, 'noise' is a force of ambivalence, interference, and disruption, refusing easy incorporation within prevailing regimes of measure. Constituent forms of subjectivity and the ontology of things often subsist as noise. Undetected, without identity, and seemingly beyond control, noise is the 'difference which makes a difference' (Bateson 1972). Digital humanities research would do well to diagram the relations of force and transformation operative within ecologies of noise populated by unruly subjects, persistent objects, and algorithmic cultures. A form of critique is required that is not simply an extension of classical political economy into the realm of digital labour, as exemplified by the work of Christian Fuchs (2008, 2014). Logistical media theory is one possible alternative that brings method and critique together in ways sufficient to the task of examining how algorithmic capitalism shapes the experience and condition of labour.

## Data, method, labour

In elaborating digital methods developed out of logistical operations, I refer to the Transit Labour project, which examined how circuits of labour are reshaping the contours of regions while coming up against, testing, and transforming a multiplicity of borders.[11] Our work around digital methods builds upon international research we have been conducting on labour, logistics, and the production of subjectivity in Shanghai, Kolkata, and Sydney. After an initial interest in labour in the cultural industries, we quickly realized how labour mobilities that condition the possibility of cultural labour cannot be reduced to the cultural sector alone. Indeed, we found that logistics is key to forms of 'differential inclusion' such as SEZs, land acquisition policies, residential permits, software protocols, and manufacturing standards (see Mezzadra and Neilson 2013). Along with cultural and social borders, these kinds of devices or apparatuses that modulate inclusion and movement within logistical industries also function to govern labour and supply chains in the informational economies.

The political challenge for research on logistics is to devise techniques and strategies that operate both within and outside the territory of control exerted by logistics technologies and their software algorithms. I emphasize the need for politically inflected research here for the obvious reason that technology and software shape how practices of knowledge production are organized and how labour is governed. And I register such research as a challenge due to the difficulty, among others, of producing—let alone even identifying—counter-logistical worlds. Needless to say, researchers can make a start. The study of how databases, supply chain software, GPS, Voice Picking, and RFID technologies affect work in the logistics industries contributes to a politicized conception of humanities and social research (see Kanngieser 2013). Furthermore, the incorporation of digital methods into critical research on logistics can facilitate and inform the politics of data, which I would suggest is also a politics of labour and life, borders and movement, knowledge production and infrastructural implementation.

Relevant here for the development of digital methods is the question of how labour performativity is incorporated into the computational design of visualizations as distinct from decision-making undertaken by machines. Given that the body of labour is at the centre of logistical calculations of productivity and efficiency, it is also the least visible for those not directly working within logistical industries or involved in developing and implementing parameters for supply chain software. Thus, one of the key reasons why a critical study of logistics is going to devise quite different computational and design methods than, say, Manovich's program on cultural analytics has to do with the difficulty of obtaining datasets due to commercial confidentiality agreements along with the politically sensitive nature of some of this data. Statistics on labour productivity are especially protected across the institutional spectrum in the case of Australia's ports, which have been marked by industrial dispute between the MUA (Maritime Union of Australia) and stevedoring companies in recent years (to say nothing of the long history of struggles). In the formal, high-end sectors of the logistics industries, it is particularly difficult to research the actual software used to oversee supply chains and measure labour performativity in real-time. One reason is prohibitively expensive proprietary licenses that enclose the computational operations of logistical firms, coupled with the highly guarded ways in which companies and authorities regulate access to this software and the data it generates. As a result, other processes and techniques of computational research are required in order to model logistical worlds, foregrounding the labour dimension of 'supply chain capitalism'.

Based on publicly available datasets published in *Waterline* reports from the Australian government's Department of Infrastructure and Transport, the pilot study we conducted on logistics operations at Port Botany in Sydney aimed to digitally visualize the relations between container loading/unloading times, truck turnaround times, and the pressures that come to bear upon labour productivity and efficiency.[12] These government reports provide statistics on a set of parameters designed to measure wharfside productivity (loading and unloading of containers) and landside performance (truck turnaround times upon entering and exiting the port). The report's statistics are compiled from data supplied by port authorities (Sydney Ports) and stevedoring companies (DP World, Patricks) operating around the country. While the reports provide a range of productivity indicators, they do not provide data on labour performance even though they indicate that 'elapsed labour time' was one of the measures used to calculate the vessel working rate (or number of containers handled per hour). Sydney Ports and the Department of Planning and Infrastructure have been unable to provide us with figures on labour performance, and we are looking into other possible organizations such as transport unions that might open these datasets for our analysis. Container loading and unloading times, and indeed truck turnaround times, can therefore be read as a substitute for labour productivity (see Figure 15.1).

Unsurprisingly, the genre of the reports is unable to register the various tensions that underlie performance measures that seek to smooth over glitches between the movement of trucks throughout the port area and the unloading of containers from ships (Hepworth 2013). Port authorities attempt to regulate traffic problems landside through the use of RFID vehicle tracking and online 'vehicle booking slots' (VBS), which determine when a truck enters the port and the time it has to be serviced by the stevedore and exit without incurring penalty. Following the introduction of VBS at Port Botany in 1999, Katie Hepworth (2013) notes, 'the VBS became the site of intervention by the ports authority into the operations of its leaseholders, DP World and Patrick Stevedores; the slot became the means of reorganizing the operators' relationships with various terminal users.' Yet it also resulted in conflicts between data systems through governance methods quite different from data transaction protocols (EDI, ERP, and so on). Extra booking slots

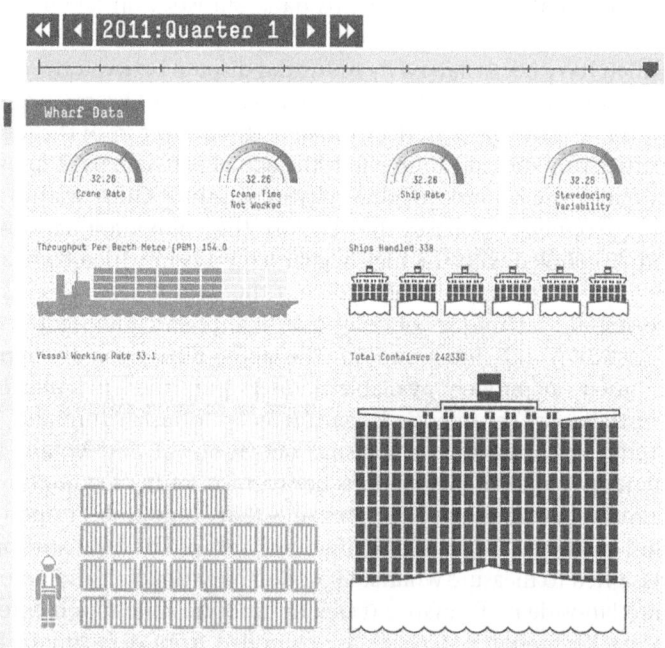

*Figure 15.1*    Port Botany wharf data visualization
*Notes*: Design: Kernow Craig; research: Katie Hepworth; visual analytics programming: Quang Vinh Nyugen; concept: Brett Neilson and Ned Rossiter.
*Source*: http://transitlabour.asia/documentation/.

would be made available online for trucks during periods when the port was less busy, for example, or warehouses able to receive goods may not have been operating while containers were being loaded on the wharf. Traffic congestion across the urban road network intervenes as another contingency unable to be accommodated within the circumscribed universe of the vehicle booking slot system. Time and space, in other words, upset interoperability in multiple ways.

Through the more traditional humanities and social science method of conducting interviews and site research, the Port Botany research identified data sources usually not subject to critical digital humanities analysis. Much data on logistics industries is frequently not publicly accessible on websites. The Port Botany project showed that datasets often only become known about in the instance of discussion with informants. Data on the impact of technology on labour practices and conditions, for example, is something many unions collect for the purpose of internal analysis. And typical of more anthropological modes of investigation, we found that unions are willing to make that data available to university researchers once a relationship of trust has been established. Along with productivity figures obtained from publicly accessible government and industry reports, such data on workplace productivity can then serve as analytical parameters in the digital visualizations of logistical operations.

A recent technology report noted that 'data must be broken out of silos in order to be mined, and the organization must learn how to communicate and interpret the results of analysis' (Dumbill 2012). With most high-end logistical software systems only available through prohibitively expensive proprietary licenses, the Port Botany project sought to remodel publicly and commercially available datasets as digital visualizations that assist in the analysis of logistics, infrastructure, and labour. In this respect, a key outcome of this study involved understanding that 'The art and practice of visualizing data is becoming ever more important in bridging the human–computer gap to mediate analytical insight in a meaningful way' (Dumbill 2012). The central analytical framework for designing and interpreting the digital visualizations consists of translating the data (for example, on labour productivity, container movements, truck turnaround times in ports, supply chain volumes, and so on) with a view to understanding how the combination of infrastructure and algorithmic architectures function as technologies that govern logistical labour. The digital visualizations effect their own algorithmic architecture (or rules of code) distinct from those available through proprietary licenses. Obviously the visualizations are not software applications that coordinate supply chains; rather, the digital visualizations begin to offer an analytical medium through which to register the interrelations between logistical infrastructure, algorithmic rules, labour practices, and supply chain assemblages.

To be clear, the animated digital visualizations that the Transit Labour project developed in collaboration with colleagues in computer science and design do not profess to represent in any veridical manner the conditions and experiences of labour. Nor do they assume to be particularly innovative at the level of design, method, or concept when compared to other visualizations of temporality in digital humanities projects. Rather, the visualizations make a claim for research on the politics of labour within the field of digital humanities. Again, such research can be distinguished from work done on virtual or digital labour, which, like the digital sociology of Marres and others, takes the online world as its milieu of action at the expense of studying how online worlds or digital apparatuses and the methods we bring to them are entangled with material conditions of possibility. In contrast to such approaches, the visualizations indicate a diagram of relations special to logistical operations at Port Botany and, more generally, to logistical worlds. Simple as it may seem, to chart a ten-year period of truck turnaround times and loading and unloading times at Port Botany begins to make visible some of the forces around labour productivity (see Figure 15.2). Moreover, the visualization begins to suggest that logistics is substantially removed from the all-pervasive smooth-world fantasy upheld by industry, government, and the IT sector in which complex operations move across a seamless continuum of control and order. Logistical operations are better understood as event processes underscored by conflict, dispute, glitches, and contingency.

Here, we can think about the waterfront disputes heating up in Australia and New Zealand, where labour flexibility and demands for increasing productivity are key issues in concert with managerial drives for enhanced automation technologies. An announcement by Patrick in 2012 explains that the 44 AutoStrads (automated straddles not requiring human operation) ordered for delivery at

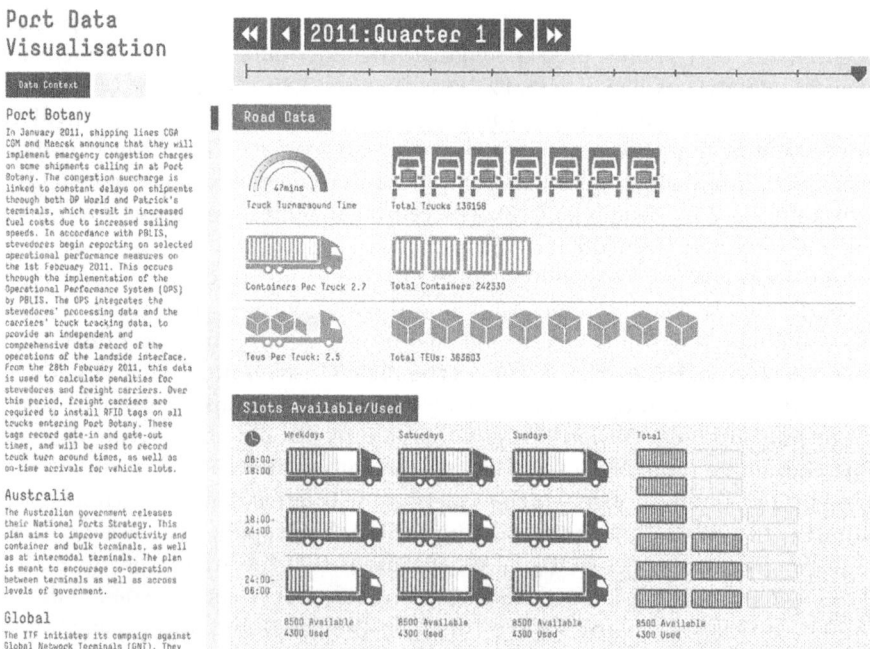

*Figure 15.2*  Port Botany road data visualization
*Source*: http://transitlabour.asia/documentation/.

Port Botany in 2013–14 'will operate unmanned, using radar and laser guidance technology to navigate the straddles around the yard, moving and stacking containers from the quay line into the holding yards, onto vehicles and back to the quay cranes with pinpoint accuracy of better than 2cm' (Patrick 2012). Automation thus presents an index of industrial dispute as maritime labour confronts stevedores such as Patrick (whose container ports were acquired by Asciano in 2007 following a restructure of Toll Holdings), DP World, and Hutchinson, which are all set to increase productivity rates across the country's container terminals through unmanned straddle carriers. While efficiency gains are the prime motivation behind such technological upgrading, an obvious cost occurs in terms of labour redundancies. Labour on Sydney's ports, in short, is set to be transformed in terms of new modes of work following the introduction of automation.

Another example of the centrality of labour to logistics can be drawn from Occupy Oakland, which concentrated on port blockades in an attempt to disrupt global supply chains of capital accumulation.[13] As with many disputes, there are frequently internal lines of division. In this case, the tactic of port blockades ran afoul of local unions and at least some of their members, who claimed that the occupation resulted in workers and their families suffering economic hardship due to loss of income. We could also see this as an interesting contest over the right to intervene by different organizational forms. Back to the national setting in Australia: the 1988 waterfront dispute was the iconic strike of the Howard-era government and took a defining toll across many other areas of labour in Australia, shaping the form of the current resource-driven economy (fly-in-fly-out workers, offshoring of labour within both the mining industry and more recently across a range of service industries on the eastern seaboard of the country).

The remarkable thing about logistics is its capacity to incorporate these sorts of disruptions within ever expanding parameters through the rubric of 'fault tolerance'. While labour struggles, infrastructural breakdowns, supply chain blockages, natural disasters, and so forth may have significant effects, they also prompt logistics to reorient shipping routes, relocate warehouses and factories, search for economic zones with more favourable labour regulations and better tax incentives, and so on. Contingency, in short, conditions the reproduction of logistics.[14] This flexible dynamic of absorbing disturbances to produce new regimes of coordination and control lends a high degree of temporariness and partiality to attempts to diagram logistical relations through the design of visualizations.

The digital visualizations produced in the Transit Labour project point to the undulations and irregularities of seemingly mechanical functions that can be better understood when situated in broader economic and political contexts that encompass local, national, regional, and global scales. The transdisciplinary practice of collectively producing the visualizations corresponds with Willard McCarty's notion of the 'model' and 'modelling', which he understands as 'the process seen in and by means of a developing product, not the definitive achievement' (2005, 22). At the level of method, Transit Labour's visualizations operate as models by feeding back into a research process and constellation of practices, prompting a revision of research questions and pointing to institutional settings and relevant experts for follow-up engagements that may well take the form of more traditional humanities research methods such as interviews, discussions, and site visits.

The visualizations also signal that data aesthetics has a central role to play in devising suitable methods for research projects that cut across the otherwise smooth relation assumed between labour, software, infrastructure, and economic growth. Data aesthetics bring critique together with design in the invention of method. Or as Liu writes, 'Seeing design in data is a method for knowing meaning in the digital humanities' (2013, 416). At stake, I would suggest, is not only the development of novel methods shaped by the social-technical dynamics of digital media but the constitution of subjectivity itself. Since software and technology are transforming how we do work, there is an opportunity here to alter the parameters and thus topological horizons of machine intelligence and its increasing governance of labour and life.

## Politics of parameters

Digital humanities is in danger of becoming stuck at the level of the digitalization of existing archive material, producing visualizations of these and other so-called big data. By shifting the object of research beyond traditional areas of study (literary archives, datasets of artworks and museum collections, etc.), digital humanities research becomes relevant to broader social and political concerns that place great emphasis upon economic activities and associated infrastructure. Digital methods can address political issues and the routines and institutions that sit between people and states, labour and capital, borders and subjectivity. Digital humanities research at the current conjuncture might decide to investigate how circuits of capital connect with the constituent force of labour, life, and things, shaping the production of time, space, and economy in a variety of ways. With an interest in making visible the new subjectivities of logistics and the politics of parameters, I have positioned research on logistical media and 'supply chain capitalism' within the digital humanities, not the social sciences.

In the age of big data, everything and anything is or has the capacity to become digitally encoded. Datasets are everywhere, residing as a standing reserve awaiting incorporation as topological parameters into analytical models and capital expropriation. As Paul Edwards notes, 'Parameterization illustrates the interaction of computational friction with the limits of human knowledge' (2010, 338). Within a topological horizon, the politics of parameters amounts to a battle around epistemological and social legitimacy in the form of measure. Parameters are also a matter of protocols, which Alexander Galloway understands as 'the technology of organization and control operating in distributed networks' (2006, 317). Parameters and protocols are both rules that govern systems. If a person, thing, or phenomenon is without rule or measure, it might just as well not exist. In assembling datasets, selection is predicated on the poverty of excess, which is data gone to waste. This, at least, is the doxa of a logistical worldview where everything is about accountability, efficiency, and productivity calibrated in systems of real time. Data produces and is accompanied by other forms of waste, forms more insidious than the economist's 'wasted opportunity'.

The social production of value and the algorithmic mining of data seem the last frontiers of economic extraction. But so often we're talking about a social milieu and informational economy that is profoundly abstracted from the multiple informal economies and geocultural settings engaged in secondary forms of value extraction. A substantial portion of the latter are associated with economies of electronic waste, with the Global South structurally and historically consigned the role of manufacturing and later dispersion of discarded ICTs and consumer electronics. Both the production and dismantling of e-waste exposes 'workers and ecosystems to a morass of toxic components' (Maxwell and Miller 2012, 3). With Internet transmissions long ago exceeding measure, and annual increments in computational power ensuring planned obsolescence, analytical capacity and consumer desire both become destined to their own forms of obsolescence. Jennifer Gabrys writes, 'Obsolescence is not so much innovation in reverse as it is the ongoing maintenance of a sense of technological development' (2011, 116). On the sidelines of speed, digital humanities research might seem left pondering the disaster as a programme beyond control.

## Notes

I would like to thank Katherine Bode, Mark Coté, Alan Liu, and Brett Neilson for their suggestions for revision and comments on an earlier draft of this paper. Thanks also to Bob Land for his careful copy-editing work prior to manuscript submission.

1. The work of David Golumbia (2009) is one notable exception. He sets out a critique of spreadsheets and ERP systems in the chapter 'Computationalism, Striation and Cultural Authority'. Golumbia gives special attention to the health-care sector and its adoption of customer relationship management (CRM) software developed by ERP vendors such as SAP, Oracle, and Microsoft, among others. While aspects of his critique and analysis are relevant to an analysis of ERP systems in logistical industries, Golumbia does not focus on the relationship between software and labour, nor does he raise the question of method as a research practice informed by ERP systems as an architecture whose abstract presence prompts the need for alternative visualizations that begin to register the relation between software, labour, and research methods.
2. I have made an initial outline of logistical media theory in Rossiter (forthcoming 2014b).
3. I take the term 'logistical modernities' from Benjamin Bratton's introduction to the 2006 edition of Virilio's *Speed and Politics*.
4. This essay was reprinted in a slightly modified form in Berry 2012. See also Evans and Rees 2012.
5. There is, indeed, a growing body of research interested in the relation between technology and neurological processes. At the more populist end, a very crude form of technological determinism pervades the claims made by the likes of neurologist Susan Greenfield (2008) in her various writings, including *ID: The Quest for Identity in the 21st Century*, and technology commentator Nicholas Carr's *The Shallows: What the Internet Is Doing to Our Brains* (2010). Such psychologically driven accounts can be offset by more critical and technically astute studies such as Anna Munster's *An Aesthesia of Networks: Conjunctive Experience in Art and Technology* (2013) and N. Katherine Hayles's *How We Think: Digital Media and Contemporary Technogenesis* (2012). For an

overview of literature related to the 'neurological turn' in Internet criticism, see also Lovink 2010.
6. Logistical Worlds: Infrastructure, Software, Labour, http://logisticalworlds.org.
7. For literary studies critiques of this position, see McCarty 2008. See also Bode 2012. For a critique of the empirics of big data, see boyd and Crawford 2012.
8. Thanks to Mark Coté for pushing this line of thought further.
9. See, for example, Hesmondhalgh and Baker 2011; Deuze 2007; and Scholz 2013. I would emphasize that I consider all the above titles fine studies and do not exempt myself from this criticism, having contributed in the past to various debates around creative and digital labour. Since around 2006–07, it has nonetheless become clear to me that an account of the constitutive outside of cultural industries in the form of migrant workers and informal economies such as electronic waste industries highlights the conditions of possibility for cultural economies.
10. Some notable exceptions include Matthew Kirschenbaum's (2008) research on 'forensic materiality', Anne Balsamo's (2011) pedagogical experiments and design research on 'technological imagination', and N. Katherine Hayles's (2012) study of 'technogenesis'.
11. Transit Labour: Circuits, Regions, Borders, http://transitlabour.asia. Primary researchers project funded by the Australian Research Council (2009–12) included Brett Neilson, Sandro Mezzadra, Ranabir Samaddar, Anja Kanngieser, Katie Hepworth, Ishita Dey, and myself.
12. The digital visualizations produced for the Transit Labour study of Port Botany can be found at http://transitlabour.asia/documentation.
13. Occupy Oakland, http://occupyoakland.org.
14. In this respect, logistics shares with neoliberalism the capacity to incorporate crises. As Philip Mirowski (2013, 53) notes, 'Crises is the preferred field of action for neoliberals, since that offers more latitude for [the] introduction of bold experimental "reforms" that only precipitate further crises down the road.'

## Works cited

Anonymous. (2012). *The Debt Resistors' Operations Manual: A Project of Strike Debt/Occupy. Wall Street*, New York, September. Available at: http://www.scribd.com.
Balsamo, Anne. (2011). *Designing Culture: The Technological Imagination at Work*. Durham, NC: Duke University Press.
Bateson, Gregory. (1972). *Steps to an Ecology of Mind*. New York: Ballantine Books.
Berry, David M. (2011). 'The Computational Turn: Thinking About the Digital Humanities'. *Culture Machine* 12: 1–22. Available at: http://culturemachine.net.
Berry, David M., ed. (2012). *Understanding the Digital Humanities*. Basingstoke: Palgrave Macmillan.
Bode, Katherine. (2012). *Reading by Numbers: Recalibrating the Literary Field*. London: Anthem Press.
boyd, danah, and Kate Crawford. (2012). 'Critical Questions for Big Data: Provocations for a Cultural, Technological, and Scholarly Phenomenon'. *Information, Communication, and Society* 15, no. 5: 662–79.
Bratton, Benjamin H. (2006). 'Logistics of Habitable Circulation'. In Paul Virilio, *Speed and Politics*, trans. Marc Polizzotti, 7–25. Los Angeles: Semiotext(e).
Carr, Nicholas. (2010). *The Shallows: What the Internet Is Doing to Our Brains*. New York: W. W. Norton.
Craig, Hugh, and Arthur F. Kinney, eds. (2009). *Shakespeare, Computers, and the Mystery of Authorship*. Cambridge: Cambridge University Press.
Crogan, Patrick. (2011). *Gameplay Mode: War, Simulation, and Technoculture*. Minneapolis: University of Minnesota Press.
Deuze, Mark. (2007). *Media Work*. Cambridge: Polity.

Dumbill, Edd. (2012). 'What Is Big Data? An Introduction to the Big Data Landscape'. *O'Reilly Radar*, 19 January. Available at: http://radar.oreilly.com.

The Economist. (2010). 'Data, Data Everywhere (interview with Kenneth Cukier)'. 25 February. Available at: http://www.economist.com.

Edwards, Paul N. (2010). *A Vast Machine: Computer Models, Climate Data, and the Politics of Global Warming*. Cambridge, MA: MIT Press.

Evans, Leighton, and Sian Rees. (2012). 'An Interpretation of Digital Humanities'. In *Understanding the Digital Humanities*, ed. David M. Berry, 21–41. Basingstoke: Palgrave Macmillan.

Fuchs, Christian. (2008). *Internet and Society: Social Theory in the Information Age*. New York: Routledge.

Fuchs, Christian. (2014). *Digital Labour and Karl Marx*. New York: Routledge.

Gabrys, Jennifer. (2011). *Digital Rubbish: A Natural History of Electronics*. Ann Arbor: University of Michigan Press.

Galloway, Alexander R. (2006). 'Protocol'. *Theory, Culture, and Society* 23, nos 2–3: 317–20.

Golumbia, David. (2009). *The Cultural Logic of Computation*. Cambridge, MA: Harvard University Press.

Greenfield, Susan. (2008). *ID: The Quest for Identity in the 21st Century*. London: Sceptre.

Hayles, N. Katherine. (2012). *How We Think: Digital Media and Contemporary Technogenesis*. Chicago: University of Chicago Press.

Hepworth, Katie. (2013). 'Enacting Logistical Geographies'. Unpublished paper.

Hesmondhalgh, David, and Sarah Baker. (2011). *Creative Labour: Media Work in Three Cultural Industries*. Oxon: Routledge.

Kanngieser, Anja. (2013). 'Tracking and Tracing: Geographies of Logistical Governance and Labouring Bodies'. *Environment and Planning D: Society and Space* 31, no. 4: 594–610.

Kanngieser, Anja, Brett Neilson, and Ned Rossiter. (2014). 'What is a Research Platform? Mapping Methods, Mobilities, and Subjectivities'. *Media, Culture, and Society* 36, no. 3: 302–18.

Kirschenbaum, Matthew G. (2008). *Mechanisms: New Media and the Forensic Imagination*. Cambridge, MA: MIT Press.

Lazzarato, Maurizio. (2012). *The Making of Indebted Man: An Essay on the Neoliberal Condition*. Trans. Joshua David Jordan. Los Angeles: Semiotext(e).

Liu, Alan. (2012). 'The State of the Digital Humanities: A Report and a Critique'. *Arts & Humanities in Higher Education* 11, nos 1–2: 8–41.

Liu, Alan. (2013). 'The Meaning of the Digital Humanities'. *PMLA* 126, no. 2: 409–23.

Lovink, Geert. (2010). 'MyBrain.net: The Colonization of Real-Time and Other Trends in Web2.0'. *Eurozine*, 18 March. Available at: http://www.eurozine.com.

Manovich, Lev. (2011a). 'Trending: The Promises and the Challenges of Big Social Data'. Available at: http://www.manovich.net.

Manovich, Lev. (2011b). 'Cultural Analytics: Visualizing Cultural Patterns in the Era of "More Media"'. Available at: http://www.manovich.net.

Manovich, Lev. (2013). *Software Takes Command*. New York: Bloomsbury Academic.

Marres, Noortje. (2012). 'The Redistribution of Methods: On Intervention in Digital Social Research Broadly Conceived'. *Sociological Review* 60: 139–65.

Maxwell, Richard, and Toby Miller. (2012). *Greening the Media*. New York: Oxford University Press.

McCarty, Willard. (2005). *Humanities Computing*. Basingstoke: Palgrave Macmillan.

McCarty, Willard. (2008). 'Knowing: Modeling in Literary Studies'. In *A Companion to Digital Literary Studies*, ed. Susan Schreibman and Ray Siemens. Oxford: Blackwell. Available at: http://www.digitalhumanities.org.

Mezzadra, Sandro, and Brett Neilson. (2013). *Border as Method, or, the Multiplication of Labor*. Durham, NC: Duke University Press.

Mirowski, Philip. (2013). *Never Let a Serious Crisis Go to Waste: How Neoliberalism Survived the Financial Meltdown*. London: Verso.

Munster, Anna. (2013). *An Aesthesia of Networks: Conjunctive Experience in Art and Technology*. Cambridge, MA: MIT Press.

Neilson, Brett. (2014). 'Beyond Kulturkritik: Along the Supply Chain of Contemporary Capitalism'. *Culture Unbound: Journal of Current Cultural Research* 6: 77–93. Available at: http://www.cultureunbound.ep.liu.se.

Parisi, Luciana. (2012). 'Algorithmic Architecture'. In *Depletion Design: A Glossary of Network Ecologies*, ed. Carolin Wiedemann and Soenke Zehle, 7–10. Amsterdam: XMLab and the Institute for Network Cultures.

Patrick. (2012). 'Asciano Signs Contract for Automated Straddles for Port Botany'. 3 September. Available at: http://www.patrick.com.au.

Peters, John Durham. (2013). 'Calendar, Clock, Tower'. In *Deus in Machina: Religion, Technology, and the Things in Between*, ed. Jeremy Stolow, 25–42. New York: Fordham University Press.

Peters, John Durham, with Jeremy Packer. (2012). 'Becoming Mollusk: A Conversation with John Durham Peters about Media, Materiality, and Matters of History'. In *Communication Matters: Materialist Approaches to Media, Mobility and Networks*, ed. Jeremy Packer and Stephen B. Crofts Wiley, 35–50. New York: Routledge.

Prescott, Andrew. (2012). 'Consumers, Creators, or Commentators? Problems of Audience and Mission in the Digital Humanities'. *Arts and Humanities in Higher Education* 11, nos 1–2: 61–75.

Rogers, Richard. (2013). *Digital Methods*. Cambridge, MA: MIT Press.

Ross, Andrew. (2009). 'The Rise of the Global University'. In *Nice Work If You Can Get It: Life and Labor in Precarious Times*, 189–205. New York: New York University Press.

Ross, Andrew. (2014). *Creditocracy and the Case for Debt Refusal*. New York: OR Books.

Rossiter, Ned. (2010). 'The Informational University, the Uneven Distribution of Expertise and the Racialisation of Labour'. *Edu-Factory Journal* Zero Issue (January). Available at: http://www.edu-factory.org/wp/wp-content/uploads/2010/10/edufactory-journal-0.pdf.

Rossiter, Ned. (2014a). 'Logistical Worlds'. *Cultural Studies Review* 20, no. 1: 53–76.

Rossiter, Ned. (2014b). 'Locative Media as Logistical Media: Situating Infrastructure and the Governance of Labor in Supply-Chain Capitalism'. In *Locative Media*, ed. Gerard Goggin and Rowan Wilken. New York: Routledge (forthcoming).

Schnapp, Jeffrey, and Todd Presner. (2009). 'The Digital Humanities Manifesto 2.0'. Available at: http://www.humanitiesblast.com.

Scholz, Trebor, ed. (2013). *Digital Labor: The Internet as Playground and Factory*. New York: Routledge.

Terzidis, Kostas. (2006). *Algorithmic Architecture*. Oxford: Architectural Press.

Tsing, Anna. (2009). 'Supply Chains and the Human Condition'. *Rethinking Marxism* 21, no. 2: 148–76.

Virilio, Paul. (2006). *Speed and Politics*. Trans. Marc Polizzotti. Los Angeles: Semiotext(e).

# Part IV
# Research Futures

Part I

# 16
## Digital Humanities
### Is Bigger, Better?

*Peter Robinson*

The history of what we now call 'digital humanities' is brief. The term itself is little over a decade old, replacing the earlier 'humanities computing', only in currency from the 1960s.[1] The novelty of the concept is such that the scope of the term 'digital humanities' is very much the subject of debate. Is it a discipline? Or is it a collection of people who consider themselves part of a community—and how is that community defined? But we can agree on this: digital humanities, whatever it is, is much bigger than it was some 30 years ago, and there are many more digital humanists (whatever they are) than there were 30 years ago. Key to the growth of the digital humanities in the last two decades has been the flourishing and well-funded existence of digital humanities centres, predominantly in North America and Europe. Yet, it did not, and does not, have to be that way. I argue in this chapter that this foundation of the growth in the digital humanities in comparatively few centres was the product of a set of circumstances specific to the needs and possibilities of the time. I argue further that, two decades on, the landscape has altered so radically that we now face a different set of imperatives and possibilities. The model of digital humanities centres nourished by substantial funding has served us well, but (at the least) requires radical adaptation to meet the challenges now pressing on us.

Humanities computing two decades ago was not just much smaller than digital humanities is now: it was rather different. The prevailing model of humanities computing through the 1980s and early 1990s was an individual academic sitting at a computer terminal, usually on a mainframe computer, making his or her own electronic texts, writing computer programs to explore the texts he or she had made. Sometimes the scholar had access to an early optical character reading system; sometimes grant funding was available. Most frequently the scholarly output of this research was an article, published in *Literary and Linguistic Computing* or *Computers and the Humanities*. Sometimes, the scholar deposited the electronic work files in the Oxford Text Archive, specifically created for this purpose. More rarely, the scholar worked with an existing academic publisher to publish formally in electronic form. A prime instance of this was the Wittgenstein Archive, published (after a long gestation) by Oxford University Press. In a few notable cases, publishers actually took the initiative in undertaking digital humanities projects.

An outstanding instance was the creation by Chadwyck-Healy of the English Poetry Full-Text Database (and numerous other enterprises), now published by ProQuest as part of Literature Online; another was the work by Oxford University Press on the Oxford English Dictionary family, culminating (after several decades of experiment) in the fully online OED.

Two aspects of humanities computing, as it was around 1990, differ markedly from digital humanities, as it is around 2013: funding and centres. For the first, in the United Kingdom, in the years before the creation of the Arts and Humanities Research Board (in 1998) there was very little funding for any kind of humanities research, digital or otherwise. The result was that humanities computing research was typically done by individuals, in the time they could steal for themselves from other activities. For the second, in the absence of funding, what centres there were lived on enthusiasm and scraps. Indeed, in those times (1985) there were just a handful of centres of consequence supporting computing and the humanities. An observer might have reasonably concluded that the route for growth in this emergent area did not lie primarily, or even substantially, through the establishment of centres. In those days, much (or even most) of what we now call digital humanities research was initiated by individual scholars, working with what help they could find. Then as now, effective research in the digital realm required more than one person. In several significant cases, and particularly for large multischolar projects, the key help to the scholar came not from a digital humanities centre but from a publisher. In the absence of funding and the established infrastructure that digital humanities centres now provide, the publisher often provided key enabling resources not otherwise available to the scholars. This worked particularly well for me, as Cambridge University Press gave crucial support to the Canterbury Tales Project from 1992 on.[2] According to this model, support for the research came from two sources: first, that traditionally offered by universities for research, in the form of time and other resources given to faculty; second, the money paid by people who bought the publications.

Much is attractive about this formulation, not least that the marketplace of publishers might support individual scholarly enterprises that funding agencies might not.[3] But this model did not survive. The level of sales for the electronic publications Cambridge achieved with my help in this period was not enough to sustain the model, and from 1998 on, Cambridge wound down the experiment. This model did not just fail at Cambridge—it failed everywhere, as traditional publishers struggled to come to terms with the arrival of the Web. Oxford UP had already started withdrawing from the electronic marketplace in the early 1990s, as it closed down its Oxford Electronic Publishing division. In the same period, Michigan University Press closed down its own foray into academic digital publishing, as did a range of commercial publishers, including Dorling Kindersley, HarperCollins, Penguin, and the Borders chain.[4]

Rather than publishers playing a key role in the growth of digital humanities, with funding agencies and support centres having a lesser place, the last two decades have seen a complete reversal. The growth in the digital humanities we have seen since 1990 has been founded in, sustained by, crucially dependent on, and coeval with the growth in digital humanities centres over the same period. centerNet (http://digitalhumanities.org/centernet/) counts more than 200 digital humanities centres worldwide. Some of these centres are substantial, the equivalent of a well-established university department.[5] One may measure the influence and reach of digital humanities centres in other ways. The 'peak' organization of the digital humanities is the Alliance of Digital Humanities Organizations (www .adho.org): over half of the people listed on the Steering Committee page (http://www.adho.org/administration/steering) are based within digital humanities centres. The same is true of the Text Encoding Initiative consortium, where over half of the board of directors and the council are based within digital humanities centres (one notes, too, the overlap in membership between the two bodies).

Indeed, the growth in digital humanities in the last decades could not have occurred without the growth in digital humanities centres; the two fed off, and fed, each other—for two reasons. The first is the increasingly complex interaction between computing and the humanities, especially after the advent of the Web opened up so many possibilities—and, simultaneously, raised the bar for what was acceptable in terms of data presentation and dissemination. The second reason concerns the impact of funding agencies. While the normal output of humanities computing work was an article, with publication in electronic form (if it happened at all) usually taking the form of deposit of the data files in the Oxford Text Archive or somewhere similar, after the Web everyone (in principle) could publish beautifully, effectively, and for free over the Internet. But preparing materials for the Web meant mastering a whole new range of skills. It also required access to servers, to systems that would maintain the servers and the data on them. These tasks were vastly complicated as it became clear that text—the lifeblood of the humanities— required elaborate preparation, in the form of encoding, for electronic use. This had been foreseen even before the invention of the Web, with the foundation of the Text Encoding Initiative in 1987, which developed a set of guidelines for encoding humanities texts in Standard Generalized Markup Language (SGML). The lingua franca of the Web, HTML, was itself a simplified derivative of SGML, but distant enough from the TEI's far more complex and rich vocabulary for publication on the Web of TEI-encoded materials to be a major task. As Web publication became more and more sophisticated, and scholarly projects became increasingly ambitious, technical needs grew so complex as to require whole teams of software engineers, database analysts, and interface experts. As an example, almost at random: the King's College Jane Austen manuscripts website lists in its Technical Introduction (http://www.janeausten.ac.uk/edition/technical.html) XML, the TEI, ODD, Photoshop, Zoomify, METS, ImageMagick, ExifTool, XSLT, Python, XHTML, jQuery, Ajax Solr, Apache Solr, Apache Lucene, Apache Cocoon, and Django. A single person is not likely to have mastery of all these technologies, and the Project Team page lists six people as members of the Technical Research Team, in addition to a technical research associate and a technical director. Not so much a village as a small city.

No single scholar, not even a group of scholars, could ever reasonably expect to be expert in all these areas, as well as on the research subject itself. The only way to create these projects was through a collaboration between the subject expert and technical experts. Further, the unique nature of each project meant that the collaboration had to be ongoing and close, beginning right at the project's first conception or very soon after, collaborating in writing funding proposals, devising protocols for data capture and manipulation, specifying and testing interfaces and functionalities, all the way to publication and beyond, typically extending over years of work. One might fairly call this the King's College model: though every digital humanities centre followed this model, with minor variations, King's adopted it explicitly and followed it through more thoroughly and in more projects over a wider range of materials than anywhere else.[6] It is obviously efficient to bring all these people together in a centre (or something like it), to give continuing organizational and other support. Then one centre can support many different projects, with obvious attractions for funding agencies—with more funding in turn enabling the centre to grow, and becoming even more effective at winning funding, in a virtuous circle of which university administrators dream.

Here, the second factor I identify as instrumental in the growth of digital humanities centres comes into play: the impact of funding agencies. We have seen, over the two decades from 1990 on, a great increase in the amount of third-party funding for humanities research.[7] Some of this has come from the creation of new funding agencies (such as the Arts and Humanities Research Council in the United Kingdom, and the European Research Council), some from increased funding in existing agencies. Within this increase, the share of funding going to projects with a substantial digital element—a category that did not exist before 1990—has far outpaced the overall growth of funding. Digital projects promise democratization of scholarship; they enable scholarship in areas and of types never before known; they make headlines. Funding agencies have been quick to respond, both by funding many projects with a digital element and by setting up programs directly addressing digital methodologies.[8] Digital humanities centres, typically located within established universities with premier research pedigrees, were perfectly placed to appeal to funding agencies looking for good places to invest their digital research dollars. Unsurprisingly, too, once a centre shows that it makes good use of the funding, agencies are likely to return to it: one notes, for example, the recurrent support by the Mellon Foundation for projects at the University of Virginia and Oxford University.

The faith of funding agencies in digital humanities centres, and the willingness of universities and other institutions to establish them, has been thoroughly vindicated. The last two decades have brought extraordinary things to us all. First, we have had the projects themselves: scores of them, worldwide, offering (again and again) access to outstanding scholarship and to resources otherwise inaccessible. Collectively and individually, they have redefined what is possible. Second, we have the tools and methods developed for and by these many projects. Foremost among these are the Text Encoding Initiative guidelines: first formalized in 1993 (in the publication of the 'P3' version), then developed, transformed, and refined by an expanding community to their current shape. By providing a fundamental language for the creation of textual materials in electronic form, they underpin research in the digital medium right across the humanities. Third, and perhaps most significantly, we now have communities of digital humanists in almost every humanities discipline. They speak to each other across discipline boundaries; they see what has been done, and their enthusiasm and eagerness to do more is palpable whenever and wherever they meet—in traditional academic conferences, in the burgeoning informal 'THATcamps' ('The Humanities and Technology' camps), everywhere. The eruption of so many people working and thinking differently within traditional humanities disciplines is itself transforming the academy.

Of course, over this period not all work in the digital humanities, and not even all extraordinary work, has happened within digital humanities centres. But a great proportion of it has—and even when it has not been done physically within a centre, often a centre or centres stand close by.[9] Beyond any doubt, the growth we have seen in the digital humanities would not have occurred without the parallel growth in digital humanities centres; further, the key role of digital humanities centres determined how that growth occurred.

This, then, is where we are now: we have a history of remarkable success and growth, and digital humanities centres are the key to that history. We face today a quite different set of circumstances to those prevailing in 1990. At that time very few books, and almost no manuscripts and art images, had been digitized. Now, there are millions of books, tens of thousands of manuscripts, and countless images, in digital form. Already in 1990, academics and students commonly used word-processing programs and email, but hardly anyone published anything in digital form. Now, there are over a billion people actively using Facebook each month.[10] Twenty-something years ago, one could have accommodated all the people who might have called themselves 'digital humanists' (if the term had existed) in a small room; now there are hundreds, even thousands, of digital humanists.

The circumstances are different; the challenges are different, too. Then, we had to show that digital methods really can offer something new and valuable, and we had to develop the techniques to make these new and valuable things. This was a task for a few people, working very closely together with great intensity and concentration. We did these things: we were the classic 'early adopters'.[11] Now we have millions of digital objects to address, as the whole body of world knowledge and culture is translated into digital form. Now we have in the Internet a medium that unites communication, collaboration, and publication into an instantaneous and fluid whole. In a moment, we can see what someone else has created, we can add to it, publish it—and in turn, another person can see, add, publish. And 'anyone' is anyone with a computer, anyone with a mobile phone—more than a billion people. We are no longer pioneers for a few. The whole world is turning digital, and we are part of it.

But what part? This challenge is on a far different scale. We have millions of books and other digital objects to examine, read, annotate, link with others, correct, explore. Through the rise of crowdsourcing—or, better, the citizen scholar movement—we may have tens of thousands, hundreds of thousands, millions, of people to do these things. Even within universities, we may reasonably expect that in an age when anyone can write a blog post or make a Facebook page, then any scholar who can do good scholarship should be able to do that scholarship in digital form. Twenty years ago the task was for a few people to work out what could be done and do it. Now we know that the digital medium is accessible to anyone, and that many more people can contribute than ever before—everyone, even. But how do we make this happen?

Clearly, what we have done in the last decades, with the foundation of digital humanities in a few well-resourced centres, will not suffice, or even come close. The answer is not, and cannot be, that we just need more centres, which will train more people, who will do more projects, who will go on to create yet more centres, and train more people, until the whole world has what a very few of us now have. The resources simply are not available. The flourishing of digital humanities centres has been predicated on what is, in historical terms, a flood of third-party funding. But the US National Endowment for the Humanities, the British Arts and Humanities Research Council, and the European Union can provide only so much funding. Indeed, the concentration of so much funding in a few centres has already led to a perception that digital humanities is (the dreaded word) 'elitist', the property of just a few major universities with access to lavish funding. There is at least as much evidence of a backlash against this model as there is evidence of enthusiasm for the creation of yet more centres.[12] But even in these few major universities, these centres would not have existed without outside funding. So far, this outside funding has enabled the creation of perhaps a few score significant digital humanities centres (defining 'significant' in a shorthand way, of a centre having at least one scholar employed full-time on an academic contract and at least one technical expert also employed full-time, generally accompanied by multiple staff on short-term contracts). Yet there are some 20,000 universities in the world.[13] At the current rate of progress, even if there were sufficient funding, it would take centuries to set up digital humanities centres in even half of these. The limits of outside funding mandate that within universities, libraries, and other cultural institutions, a local digital humanities centre must be funded by the institution itself. Yet most (if not all) digital humanities centres in a university are dependent on a continuing flow of project-based funding by outside agencies, and many were founded explicitly on the premise that outside funding would flow in.[14] My own university is typical. The University of Saskatchewan supports a 'Digital Resource Center' in the College of Arts and Science. This centre has a single full-time staff member, who is not, however, on a regular academic contract; it has at present a single full-time programmer, funded by an outside grant, and a few students working part-time on faculty research projects. Even this modest support is far more than many, or most, universities can manage. Dedicated digital humanities centres are expensive.

One answer to the problem might be that rather than creating more centres, we might create new scholarly infrastructures, which might then offer solutions on a scale commensurate with the challenges we offer. The last years have seen several moves in this direction. In 2006 a report entitled 'Our Cultural Commonwealth', prepared by a commission on cyberinfrastructure appointed by the American Council of Learned Societies, outlined a series of recommendations: substantial investment in infrastructure, support for open access and interoperability, establishment of national centres.[15] These were consciously 'top-down': the report assumed that initiative would flow from the top, which would set strategic priorities (using the report as a starting point), and then send funding towards those priorities. At least three large initiatives have sought to follow this top-down model: the Mellon-funded Project Bamboo and the EU-funded Dariah and Clarin projects.[16] All three chart a similar course: multiple meetings of multiple working groups to identify the needs of stakeholders (scholars, librarians, everyone); then (presumably) a series of actions to satisfy those needs. The following, from the Dariah site http://www.dariah.eu/index.php?option=com_content&view=article& id=3&Itemid=114, is typical of the rhetoric of these enterprises:

> The grand vision for DARIAH is to facilitate long-term access to, and use of, all European Arts and Humanities (A + H) digital research data. The DARIAH infrastructure will be a connected network of people, information, tools, and methodologies for investigating, exploring and supporting work across the broad spectrum of the digital humanities. The core strategy of DARIAH is to bring together national, regional, and local endeavours to form a cooperative infrastructure where complementarities and new challenges are clearly identified and acted upon

So far the achievement of these projects falls somewhat short of their ambition. It is difficult to think of a single piece of software, a single tool, even a single digital research object that has come into existence as a result of these rather massive projects. The most visible output of these projects appears to be the directory of digital research tools maintained on the Bamboo DiRT site (http://dirt .projectbamboo.org/). This directory is useful certainly, but hardly groundbreaking.

There is no question that these projects see very clearly the challenge and the possibilities I outline above, as we reshape what we do in a world where so much data, and so many tools, are digital. The 2006 'Our Cultural Commonwealth' report expresses it with particular clarity:

> The online world is a new cultural commonwealth in which knowledge, learning, and discovery can flourish. (2)

> \*    \*    \*

> A cyberinfrastructure for humanities and social sciences must encourage interactions between the expert and the amateur, the creative artist and the scholar, the teacher and the student. (11)

However, these projects all have this characteristic in common: they look at the challenge from the point of view of the government agency, the library, the university, the scholarly association. Let us look at the challenge from the other end of the telescope, as it were: from the point of view of the individual scholar and citizen. Rather than ask, 'what do we, as administrators and leaders, think the individual scholar and citizen needs; what can we make to provide it?' let us ask, 'What do I, as an individual scholar and citizen, need; what might give me what I need?' As a mediaevalist I can read various mediaeval manuscripts; I can transcribe them; I can identify people, places, and events mentioned in them. Further, many of the manuscripts I am interested in are already on the Web, in facsimile form, and often in transcribed form. I want to be able to transcribe them afresh, or to correct existing transcripts, or enrich them in various ways; to identify other versions of the same text in other manuscripts, or in printed editions from various periods; to label people, places, events, and other matters in the manuscripts.

There are now millions of digitized books and manuscripts on the Web. What I want to do as a mediaevalist is what hundreds, thousands, tens of thousands of people may want to do across the whole field of recorded human knowledge. Yet the average mediaevalist, the average scholar, the average reader cannot do these things. Certainly, he or she can transcribe a manuscript page into a wiki or blog page, or use one of many online transcription tools, but the transcription will be 'plain text' (or HTML at best). To connect it to other versions of the text; to include information about people, places, and events; just to connect the transcription to the original manuscript require complex encodings. Also, how can our scholar make sure that the transcription and all that intellectual effort can be found by other people and will be available to others for years to come? To take a single example, not from mediaeval studies: I might be sufficiently interested in Jane Austen's *Pride and Prejudice* to look for a digitized copy of its first printing, by Thomas Egerton in London in 1813. WorldCat will show me the records of many copies, including (on 3 March 2013) some 14 dating from 1813. But it appears that none of these records link to a freely available digitized copy of the 1813 edition: most link to 'eBooks on demand,' which offers to make a PDF copy for me for five euros, plus 0.36 cents a page. Cheap enough—yet I am sure there must already be a free digitized copy out there somewhere. And indeed, there is. Because I know that Egerton was the publisher, I can go to http://www.archive.org/details/texts and search for 'Pride and Prejudice Egerton', and there it is: Oxford and Duke Universities both have digitized copies and put these online (albeit incomplete: Oxford only has the first volume, Duke the first two). However, there is no way for me to link this information back to the WorldCat catalogue entry. Further, I notice that the 1813 text is available in archive.org, captured by some form of automatic process. A glance through it shows that it is completely unstructured and full of errors ('mudi as she lyul: always been' for 'much as she had always been' on page two of the Oxford copy). I might want to correct these errors and provide some useful structure to the text (dividing into chapters; distinguishing page numbers, catchwords, and running heads from the text), but where would I put this work so that others could have it in a useful form?

In digital humanities, as we now have it, the answer is depressingly familiar. You need either to master a forbidding range of skills and tools, or form an alliance with someone or some group that has access to them. For most scholars, for nearly all readers, neither is possible. We are back where we were in the 1980s: the individual who wants to do useful work in the digital medium has to scratch about to find the resources to do it. Indeed, we are worse off. We now have a huge mass of digitized material at our fingertips. We could add to this, enrich it, provide links, add information, correct errors—yet, we cannot. We are spectators who could be players.

It does not have to be this way. The Web 2.0 world we live in is defined as the Web where every reader is also a writer. We have in vast collaborative social applications such as Facebook webs of complex and interrelated information, so structured as to allow highly sophisticated presentations of relationships among people to shape themselves as people make pages. I can make a Facebook page and have it instantly seen by thousands of people. Facebook can work out who might be my friends and bombard me with helpful hints as to who I might add to my friends list. In another key, the bottom right of my Facebook screen is populated with advertisements, generated by cunning software that figures out (by means I choose not to contemplate too closely) what language classes, holidays, or medications I might be interested in. A Facebook page sits in a complex web of relationships, its apparent simplicity masking deeply interlinked layers. It should be as easy to make, say, a transcript of a page of a mediaeval manuscript as it is to make a Facebook page, and our transcript should be at least as capable of rich communication as is the Facebook page.

From these thoughts, we can make out an agenda for the digital humanities that works at the level of the individual scholar and reader, and for the individual scholar and reader. I see three interlocking requirements as the foundation for this agenda: tools, rights, and access.

Concerning tools, I have already indicated that the tools we need must permit any scholar or any reader with useful knowledge to contribute to do so. This does not mean that everyone can write anything they like anywhere: we can conceive a fine-grained set of permissions erected around areas of data, analogous to those that Facebook and other social media have developed. It does mean that there should be many more opportunities available for scholars and readers to contribute, and for many more kinds of data, than are currently available. We now have massive collections of digital data available: the ten million volumes available in the HATHI Trust (http://www.hathitrust.org/) and the four million on www.archive.org. Greg Crane asks, 'How do we read a million books?' The answer is to use a million people, each with the ability to add what they glean from their reading. In Facebook and other social media we have models of online communities; we have in crowdsourcing many instances of cooperative knowledge creation. We have—in the advances of the last decades in text encoding, in software tools, in metadata—the building blocks we need. It is beginning to happen, with landmark projects such as 'Transcribe Bentham' and the ferment of activity around citizen transcription tools (for example, the blog at http://manuscripttranscription.blogspot.ca/) showing what can be done. As yet, the levels of encoding and metadata supported by these pioneering efforts are not adequate for all the uses we might imagine, and questions about authority, quality control, and sustainability remain unanswered. There is much to be done, as we seek ways to weave together the independent efforts of every reader and every scholar.

Concerning rights, the second requirement, the underlying questions are as follows: What is to happen to all this material, made by so many people? Who is to control it, and to what ends? The first impulse is to think, *I have made a transcription* (for example); *it is mine; I want to control what happens to it, what uses are made of it, how it is changed.* Following this model I should restrict all uses to those I explicitly approve and assert a traditional copyright licence over my work. At the same time I want other people to see it, to use it in their own work, to build on it. Following this model I should adopt some form of Creative Commons unrestricted licence. Which model should prevail? In the context of the Web written by everyone, for everyone, the advantages of the second are overwhelming. First is what one might call a moral argument. The only reason I am able to contribute valuable scholarly work to the Web is because so many others have made so much freely available. For me to use what others have given freely to make something that I choose to restrict (for whatever reason) is, at the least, churlish. Moreover, it is short-sighted. The best way to be sure that my work endures is to allow others to cite it, to absorb it into their own work, to build new work on it, then hand it on to others. Of course, I want others to know what I did, and I would like other people to be able to recover exactly what I did and see how it endures (or not) in the reworkings of others. The Creative Commons Attribution Share-Alike licence, combined with storage of all the various versions of my work, and that of others, in efficient version control systems achieves these ends.

Accordingly, I advocate that all community-driven and community-enabled work on the Web should be not only Attribution but also Share-Alike. By specifying Share-Alike, we are authorizing the making of derivative works: anyone may add to, elaborate, refine, and build on what we have done, as long as they share what they have done as freely as we have. The more derivatives there are from my work, the more it thrives. I advocate, too, that we do not impose the 'noncommercial' restriction. We scholars consider ourselves high-minded and above the merely commercial: hence, the noncommercial restriction feels like a validation, not a restriction. Besides, we think that if anyone should be making money out of what we have done, we should have some say in it. However, the experience of recent years has shown, decisively, the problems with the noncommercial restriction: see the excellent summary at http://www.kuro5hin.org/story/2005/9/11/16331/0655 ('Creative Commons—NC Licenses Considered Harmful'). Work covered by this licence is incompatible with the vast and growing body of free materials; it will disable even uses that any scholar would allow (for example, preventing it from appearing on a page that contains advertising of any kind); it creates anomalies in every direction. (Is Cambridge University Press 'commercial'? Is something paid for by a grant from a commercial company 'noncommercial'?). And in lamentable cases, scholars may use the noncommercial restriction to prevent people they do not like from republishing their work, simply by declaring that they suspect a commercial motive. The noncommercial licence may be a weasely way of pretending to give open access (after all, commercial publishers are not people) while not actually doing so. A further reason for permitting commercial agencies to have access to our data is that we want (or should want) commercial agencies to take what we make and distribute it. The skill of publishers is to know the market and how to tailor publications to the market. If our work finds new audiences through a publisher, excellent; and if the publisher makes money from it, then the publisher has an incentive to keep it available to others. Indeed, releasing work from any restrictions concerning copying and republishing will itself go far towards sustaining it into the digital future.

Concerning access, we have become familiar over the years with the refrain, 'digital research project X, made with Y dollars from funder Z, will remain freely available to all on a website, maintained by institution A', typically accompanied by homiletic utterances concerning the future-proof qualities of TEI encoding. The problem is that in almost every case the expensively gathered data are accessible only through the interface created for that website. Further, very often what is made available is not the original XML encoding but an HTML derivative of it, which is often little better than a plain-text file. Each such site is an island, entire to itself. The data are sealed within the site, and you can do with them only what the interface lets you do: often, even Google and other search engines are kept out of the site. This is out of step (to put it mildly) with the Wiki-like world of dynamic knowledge creation I have sketched in the last pages, with masses of separate information pieces, made by many people working independently, reconfiguring themselves continually into new landscapes of knowledge. The transcription I make of this page of this manuscript, containing the text of this work, should link to images of that page, other texts of this work, annotations, editions, and other resources, through something much more secure than the happenstance of a Google search. Real access means that all these discrete pieces of information can be discovered, retrieved, searched, manipulated, displayed, and republished by automatic means. This means not just freeing the data from any one interface: it means so structuring the data, so enriching it with metadata, that interfaces can be built for it with maximal ease and convenience. We have several working models for this. The Z39.50 protocol, created by libraries to allow access to one another's databases and now extended by many other protocols coming from the digital library and institutional repository communities, already does this for massive numbers of library catalogue entries and—increasingly—for born-digital objects. Outside the academic world, the Web abounds with instances of huge libraries of information pieces being accumulated into multiple—and indeed competing—interfaces. What Google Maps and TripAdviser do for hotels and restaurants, what Orbitz and SkyScanner and Expedia do for airline schedules, we could do for books, manuscripts, texts, knowledge. It is ironic that the commercial world appears much better at sharing data from multiple sources than we in the academic world. It follows, from what I have advocated about permitting commercial entities to reuse research data, that we should expect that commercial entities will actively create their own interfaces to all these research data. Again, we should welcome this. Indeed, if this permits independent publishers to return to the digital realm, and offer scholarship a voice it has nearly lost in the last decades, that would be an excellent outcome.

Here is my dream: I am sitting at home and I discover that a new manuscript of Wyatt's 'They Flee from Me' has been discovered in the Bodleian Library, and a digital image of it is available online. So I make a transcription of it and put it on the Web. While I am making this transcription, someone on the other side of the world is reading a version of the poem online. A little flag pops up in the browser: 'I see you are reading Wyatt's "They Flee from Me". A new manuscript has just been discovered of this poem. Click here to see it.' The reader follows the link, looks at the manuscript image on the Bodleian website. And while that reader is looking at the image, I send my transcript to the Web: a few milliseconds later, a flag pops up on the Bodleian page, saying, 'A transcription of this text is now available. Click here to see it.' So our reader does, spotting a mistake in my transcript. The reader corrects it, and the next reader to look at this site will see the corrected version of my transcript. Along the way, digital library systems all around the world capture the image, my transcript, and the correction to it, and store it so that they will be available forever after, as long as our civilization survives; interface systems all around the world register the existence of this new manuscript and transcription—and in time, all the annotations people might provide—and offer links to it. All automatically, all without any intervention by me or my corrector. We do the scholarship; everything else is done for us.[17]

The right tools, employed to create and use properly free and smart data that shape themselves to the task at hand: we have ample precedents for these in other areas of the Web. Within our own domain, we have huge and increasing quantities of data; we have a growing community of scholars dedicated to advancing scholarship through the digital medium; we have scholars in every discipline with expertise to contribute, and beyond the academy, everyone who puzzles over a text, an image, a fragment of knowledge. There is work here, too—plenty of work—for existing digital humanities centres. We do need infrastructure to support this new world. We do need the tools I have sketched for individual scholars, and much more besides. We need centres and other key groups to take the lead on advocating real open access: that is, adopting the Creative Commons Attribution Share-Alike licence without the noncommercial restriction, and restructuring and enriching their data so that they can be used independently of any one interface. Up until now, digital humanities centres and other leaders have been slow to do any of these things, being rather too ready both to agree to restrictive licences and to lock their data in their own interfaces. One can understand that for centres dependent on continuing funding, exclusive management of valuable research data is a significant card in the game: but the more it is played, the more damage that card does.[18] Funders, too, have a responsibility: they have been too willing to acquiesce to the claims of institutions and individuals to the ownership of digital research materials.

'Bigger' is never 'better' of itself. Indeed, one could reasonably argue that in the digital humanities, 'smaller' is better: we need fewer (or no) grand, all-embracing solutions and more tools that empower the individual. Data, like politics, is local, living in the hands of the individual. We have many individuals, everywhere, with the will to explore and tell others what they have found. We can unlock all that energy, all that commitment, to make not a broader digital humanities, but a better humanities. Where the great advances of the last decades in the digital humanities were grounded in relatively few centres and projects, I believe that over the next two decades, the focus in our field will move from a few high-profile projects, in a few well-funded institutions, to empowering every scholar and every reader in the creation and enrichment of research materials over the Web. If this happens, what we now term 'digital humanities' will be far larger than it currently is. Indeed, the prefix 'digital', in this context, will be redundant, once so much of the humanities is digital. One can expect that there will continue to be specialists, working on particularly demanding and trailblazing projects at the leading edge of the intersection between the humanities and information technology. Ironically, the relationship between what they do and the humanities in general may look more like humanities computing as it was in the 1980s and 1990s. Sometimes, we have to go back to go forward.[19]

## Notes

1. For definitions of 'digital humanities', see Gold 2012, particularly Kirschenbaum 2012. For the history of humanities computing, see Hockey 2004.
2. Thus the Oxford support for the Wittgenstein project; so, too, the support given by Collins for the Cobuild Project (the Collins Birmingham University International Language Database) from 1980 on, and by a consortium of publishers for the British National Corpus from 1991 (and, of course, the various Chadwyck-Healey enterprises). For the British National Corpus, see http://www.natcorp.ox.ac.uk/corpus/index .xml?ID=creation. For my own work on the Canterbury Tales Project, the support of Cambridge University Press from 1992 to 2000 was critical. Fuller perspectives on humanities computing in that period can be gained from Julianne Nyhan's interviews with Harold Short and others published in *Digital Humanities Quarterly* (Nyhan 2012) and from the surveys by Susan Hockey (1980, 2004) and Ian Lancashire (1988, 1991). Instances of scholars working in the manner described can be gleaned from the issues of *Literary and Linguistic Computing* and *Computers and the Humanities* and (with some difficulty) from the holdings contributed to the Oxford Text Archive in those years. The work done by David Robey in those years is exemplary: he created a database of Italian mediaeval and Renaissance poetry that was deposited with the OTA (http://ota.ahds.ac .uk/desc/2455), and published a book drawing on this database (Robey 2000).
3. As indeed happened in the instance of Martin Foys's *Digital Edition of the Bayeux Tapestry*, discussed in Peter Robinson 2013, 94–95, 100.
4. See Robinson and Taylor 1998.
5. For example, the Department of Digital Humanities at King's College London (19 active projects as of 22 February 2013, another 74 completed, and some £17 million in research funding since 2000); the department has around 40 staff, including three professors.
6. Accordingly, the Festschrift for Harold Short, the director of the King's College Centre for Computing in the Humanities (which became the Department of Digital Humanities) was appropriately titled *Collaborative Research in the Digital Humanities* (edited by Willard McCarty and Marilyn Deegan [Ashgate 2012]). See, too, Short's remarks in an interview with Julianne Nyhan: 'It has to be true of any kind of collaborative research, the collaboration has got to be fundamental or it's not gonna work. Everybody has got to understand that the other person has something to contribute' (Nyhan 2012).

7. By 'third party', I mean funding that comes neither directly from the individual researcher nor his or her immediate employer (usually, a university): hence, a national or international government or private agency.

8. To name a few: numerous programs within the European Union Framework series, such as eContentPlus (2005–08) and the current Europeana digital library project; the UK's Arts and Humanities Research Council's current 'Digital Transformations in the Arts and Humanities' theme; the Office of Digital Humanities within the US National Endowment for the Humanities.

9. For example, while the Codex Sinaiticus project (http://www.codexsinaiticus.org/en/) was not the work of a single digital humanities centre, the collaboration of two centres (ITSEE, Birmingham; the Göttingen Digitization Centre) was critical, and several key personnel had previously worked at digital humanities centres and would do so again (for example, Juan Garcés at the British Library during the project, previously at King's, then at Göttingen).

10. Facebook Inc. fourth-quarter and full-year results 2012, reported at http://investor.fb .com/releasedetail.cfm?ReleaseID=736911 on 30 January 2013. The exact figure given is 1.06 billion 'monthly active users', over half accessing Facebook on mobile devices.

11. Everett Rogers (1962) is credited with creating the term 'early adopter'.

12. See Pannapacker 2013: 'A persistent criticism of the digital-humanities movement is that it is elitist and exclusive because it requires the resources of a major university (faculty, infrastructure, money).' Other voices sceptical about various current aspects of the digital humanities (though not specifically focused on the dominance of centres) include Stanley Fish (2012a, 2012b) and the blogs of Ian Bogost (for example, on the corporate move in online learning, http://www.bogost.com/blog/the_walled_kindergarten .shtml) and Andrew Prescott (http://digitalriffs.blogspot.com/; his discussion of Willard McCarty's 2013 Busa lecture is particularly inspiring).

13. http://www.webometrics.info/index.html.

14. King's College London may—in time—prove the exception to this rule, should the transformation of the Centre for Computing in the Humanities into a Department of Digital Humanities, sitting alongside traditional academic departments and seeking to sustain itself by traditional course teaching, be successful.

15. http://www.acls.org/programs/Default.aspx?id=644 gives the background to the commission; the report is at http://www.acls.org/uploadedFiles/Publications/Programs/ Our_Cultural_Commonwealth.pdf. The commission Chair was John Unsworth.

16. Dariah (http://www.dariah.eu/): 'The mission of DARIAH is to enhance and support digitally-enabled research across the humanities and arts. DARIAH aims to develop and maintain an infrastructure in support of ICT-based research practices'; CLARIN (http:// www.clarin.eu/): 'CLARIN is committed to establish an integrated and interoperable research infrastructure of language resources and its technology. It aims at lifting the current fragmentation, offering a stable, persistent, accessible and extendable infrastructure and therefore enabling eHumanities'; BAMBOO (http://www.projectbamboo .org/): 'Project Bamboo is building applications and shared infrastructure for humanities research.'

17. Several projects are already working in a loose coalition to achieve parts (at least) of this vision: thus, the Textual Communities Project that I lead (www.textualcommunities .usask.ca), the Aust-ESE project at the University of Queensland (http://www.itee.uq .edu.au/eresearch/projects/austese/), the Open Annotation Collaboration (http://www .openannotation.org/), and the EU InterEdition project (http://www.interedition.eu/).

18. For example, in the week of 5 March 2013 I surveyed 77 research projects listed as having produced some form of output on the King's College London Department of Digital Humanities website. Of these 77, 47 had some form of digital data output. Almost half of these 47—23—specified no copyright policy. One may presume that, in those cases, a blanket statement (usually '© 2011 King's College London') somewhere on the project site claims the full protection of rights asserted by standard intellectual property law.

In 21 cases, the project specified some form of restrictive licence. This statement, from the Jonathan Swift Archive, is typical: 'All material is made available free of charge for individual, non-commercial use only, provided this publication is acknowledged' (http://jonathanswiftarchive.org.uk/about/copyright.html). In some cases, extra restrictions are specified: thus, the Jane Austen Manuscripts, http://www.janeausten.ac.uk/edition/citation-policy.html, forbids derivative works ('You may not alter, transform, or build upon it'), asserts Kathryn Sutherland's moral right 'to be recognized as author and editor of aspects of this work', permits 'non-commercial' use only and, for good measure, declares, 'All other use is prohibited without the express written consent of the editor. Any requests to use the work in a way not covered by this permission should be directed to the editor.' Just three projects permit unrestricted access as recommended in this article, and also permit the source XML to be downloaded: the three projects relating to ancient inscriptions associated with Charlotte Roueché and Gabriel Bodard.

19. A point made by Susan Hockey in an email to me: 'What will they do when everything is digital?' (24 February 2013).

## Works cited

Fish, Stanley. (2012a). 'The Digital Humanities and the Transcending of Mortality'. *New York Times*, 1 September.

Fish, Stanley. (2012b). 'Mind Your P's and B's: The Digital Humanities and Interpretation'. *New York Times*, 23 January.

Gold, Matthew, ed. (2012). *Debates in the Digital Humanities*. Minneapolis and London: University of Minneapolis Press.

Hockey, Susan. (1980). *A Guide to Computer Applications in the Humanities*. Oxford: Oxford University Press.

Hockey, Susan. (2004). 'History of Humanities Computing'. In *Companion to Digital Humanities*, ed. Susan Schreibman, Ray Siemens, and John Unsworth, 3–19. Oxford: Blackwell.

Kirschenbaum, Matt. (2011). 'What Is Digital Humanities and What's It Doing in English Departments?' Available at: http://mkirschenbaum.files.wordpress.com/2011/01/kirschenbaum_ade150.pdf.

Lancashire, Ian. (1988, 1991). *Humanities Computing Yearbooks for 1988 and 1989–90*. Oxford: Oxford University Press.

Nyhan, Julianne. (2012). 'Collaboration Must Be Fundamental or It's Not Going to Work: an Oral History Conversation Between Harold Short and Julianne Nyhan'. *Digital Humanities Quarterly* 6, no. 3. Available at: http://www.digitalhumanities.org/dhq/vol/6/3/000133/000133.html.

Pannapacker, William. (2013). 'Stop Calling It Digital Humanities'. *Chronicle of Higher Education*, 18 February. Available at: http://chronicle.com/article/Stop-Calling-It-Digital/137325/.

Robey, David. (2000). *Sound and Structure in Dante's 'Divine Comedy'*. Oxford: Oxford University Press.

Robinson, Peter. (2013). 'The History of Scholarly Digital Editions, plc'. In *Papers of the Bibliographical Society of Canada*. Special issue, *What Is the History of (Electronic) Books?* ed. Geoffrey Little, 83–104.

Robinson, Peter, and Kevin Taylor. (1998). 'Publishing an Electronic Textual Edition: The Case of The Wife of Bath's Prologue on CD-ROM'. *Computers and the Humanities* 32: 271–84.

Rogers, Everett. (1962). *Diffusion of Innovations*. New York: Free Press.

# 17
# Margins, Mainstreams and the Mission of Digital Humanities

*Paul Turnbull*

I must confess that I am sometimes of two minds about digital humanities. The scholarly and public benefits of humanists using computational and information technologies are obvious. But so, too, is the continuing marginal status of digital work in the mainstream of humanities disciplines. In this chapter I offer some reflections on the predicament of those of us making substantial use of digital technologies in research and communicating its outcomes, in the course of which I also share some thoughts about what the future might hold.

I do so by first briefly reflecting on the history of historical computing since the mid-1970s and how it has influenced the development of my own interests in digital history. I then turn to consider at some length Patrick Juola and Andrew Prescott's analyses of the causes of digital humanities' continuing neglect by scholars in the mainstream of humanities disciplines. It may seem limiting to narrow the discussion to Juola and Prescott's diagnoses of the condition of digital humanities. However, it seems to me a useful focus as they helpfully identify many of the key issues we need to address in assessing digital humanities' fortunes and future prospects.

Drawing in part on my own experiences in creating online historical resources, I argue that we should not allow our fortunes to be held hostage to disciplinary conservatism but should focus on the development of digital humanities as an intellectually protean 'interdiscipline' that nonetheless strategically and critically engages with colleagues content to pursue conventional, largely print-focus modes of scholarly inquiry and publication. We cannot ignore the mainstream. Indeed, there are compelling reasons to engage with the ideas and ambitions of colleagues employing conventional critical procedures and practices to produce traditional forms of scholarly communication. But neither can we afford to be ruled by mainstream interests and assumptions.

\* \* \*

My earliest experimentation with computing took place at the time of the controversy provoked by *Time on the Cross*, Robert Fogel and Stanley Engerman's two-volume computationally based analysis of the economics of African American slavery (Fogel and Engerman 1974). William G. Thomas recently reminded us how Fogel and Engerman met with extensive and justified criticism for failing to take sufficient account of what slavery meant in human terms for its victims and perpetuators when interpreting the results of computationally based analyses of the day-to-day material conditions of life under slavery. Thomas has also rightly pointed out that, in its aftermath in North America, the controversy legitimated scepticism and disinterest in historical computing (Thomas 2004).

At the time of this controversy, the department in which I was studying was hosting a British Council visit by Peter Laslett. With demographer Tony Wrigley, Laslett founded the Cambridge Group for the History of Population and Social Structure in 1964; at that time he was engaged in computationally based analysis of family life and sexual relations outside of marriage in early modern England (Laslett 1977). We honours students at that time were studying slavery in antebellum America, and after one lecture we were able to ask Laslett whether his computer-based analysis of parish registers and other sources similar to those employed by Fogel and Engerman would likewise discount the significance of individual and collective interpretations of reality.

Laslett had, of course, read *Time on the Cross* and followed its reception. He readily spoke at length with us about what he saw as the strengths and weaknesses of the kinds of large-scale quantitative research projects that computation had made possible (see Laslett 1999). He did so, moreover, with a degree of historiographical sophistication that continues to inform my uses of computer and information techniques in historical research and teaching.

Laslett did not come to computer-based analysis of past lifeways and social structures with formal training in historical demography or economic history. He came with a substantial reputation as a historian of seventeenth-century British political thought (see Locke and Laslett 1960). With Quentin Skinner and J. G. A. Pocock, Laslett was among influential contributors to the development of the so-called Cambridge School of the history of political thought (Pocock 2009).

Laslett carefully explained to us that he, too, was critical of numerous claims by Fogel and Engerman. But he nonetheless believed that there were trends and correlations in their data that required better explanations than the received historiography of slavery offered. Similarly his own work at that time on family and sexuality in seventeenth-century England was guided by the premise that the prime value of computing would be to disclose patterns confirming or challenging assumptions about the social history of the era grounded in explication of contemporary published and private documentary sources (see his contributions to Wachter et al. 1978). In this respect, Laslett's approach to historical computing reflected the influence of the Cambridge School of political thought.[1] It was in harmony with—and perhaps directly influenced by—the views of Michael Oakeshott, the Cambridge conservative philosopher and political theorist. In his final book of essays, *On History* (1983), Oakeshott argued that computer-based analysis could be productively used to 'anatomise an historical situation, to...display the situation as structure composed of correlations'. But, he held, it could do no more than 'suggest interesting questions to pursue' (Oakeshott 1983, 52).

\*   \*   \*

The research projects of the Cambridge Group since the late 1960s have pursued interesting questions, often in collaboration with researchers with cognate interests and expertise employing more traditional modes of historical inquiry. Many new and valuable insights into British social and economic history have thereby been generated. Importantly, the findings of these projects have regularly been reported in leading history journals and published as books that have become essential reading within and often beyond relevant fields. What is more, they have inspired studies of comparable phenomena in continental Europe and other parts of the world.

In this respect, the history of historical computing in British and European universities has differed markedly from what occurred in the United States (Thomas 2004). The controversy over *Time on the Cross* was actually an eruption of antagonism to quantitative historical research that can be traced back to the early 1960s. In 1962, for example, Carl Bridenbaugh, a leading historian of colonial America, used his presidential address to the American Historical Association to decry 'worship at the shrine of that Bitch-goddess, QUANTIFICATION' (Bridenbaugh 1963). Bridenbaugh spoke for many established historians in declaring that the discipline employed 'radically different values and methods' to the social sciences, and that the value of quantitative modes of analysis at best lay in augmenting the findings of historical scholarship squarely focused on the lifeways and thought of individuals (Fischer 1970, 94–95). By the end of the decade, Richard T. Vann, an American historian of religion, could observe, 'Fear of, and animosity toward, quantitative history, is one of the facts of contemporary scholarly life' (Vann 1969, 64).

The causes of this fear and animosity towards quantitative history have yet to be investigated in detail. However, as William Thomas (2004) has shown, many in the mainstream of the discipline objected to quantitative history, alleging that it was crude economic determinism dismissive of the importance of individual agency in history. What is also clear is that critics were disturbed by quantitative projects adapting modes of collaborative research from the natural sciences. Half a century into the age of personal computing, what especially stands out are the fears voiced by North American critics of quantitative history of the 1960s and 1970s that it would consume the lion's share of research funding, while making the discipline more like the natural sciences in that research outcomes would be presented in technical terms understandable only by a handful of specialists. This reasoning seems curious given the greater acceptance of historical computing in British and continental European universities. Possibly it reflects a greater cultural investment by North American academia in the idea of the historian as individual artisan, distilling truths through unconstrained individual exploration of the surviving record of humanity's past experience, and doing so with literary artistry (Vann 1969).

Historically focused computer-based projects were often ambitious in scope, and the costs of data preparation and computing hardware were expensive. They continue to be so in comparison with research driven by questions answerable by more 'craftlike' procedures and practices. However, the fortunes of historical computing from the late 1970s were more influenced by two other factors. One was history absorbing ideas and arguments arising from renewed interest across the humanities in the relations between philosophy and language. A second related factor was mounting dissatisfaction with the trend in social history for research to take the form of fine-grained analysis of localized phenomena.

As I have argued elsewhere (Turnbull 2010), this 'linguistic turn' saw historical computing represented as naive scientism. One of the most influential critics in this respect was Lawrence Stone, best remembered for his work on the cultural history of Britain's elite during the long eighteenth century (Stone 1973, 1977). He spoke to disinterest and doubts about the worth of qualitative methodologies and computational analysis to champion a revival of interest in the essential literary qualities and attributes of history.

In his influential 1979 essay in *Past and Present*, the premier journal for British social history, Stone called for historians to refocus on the centrality of narrative in historical practice, caricaturing practitioners of historical computing as akin to a priestly caste, engaged in building the intellectual equivalent of the pyramids by having 'squads of diligent assistants assemble data, encode it, programme [*sic*] it, and pass through the maw of the computer, all under the autocratic direction of a team-leader' (Stone 1979). Not content with depicting quantitative history as a 'proletarianization' of intellectual labour—with a concomitant loss of focus on the actors individually and collectively making history—Stone was to declare quantitative history to have been an expensive failure. Employing grave and temperate irony reminiscent of Gibbon, Stone lamented,

> It is just those projects that have been the most lavishly funded, the most ambitious in the assembly of vast quantities of data by armies of paid researchers, the most scientifically processed by the very latest in computer technology, the most mathematically sophisticated in presentation, which have so far turned out to be the most disappointing.
>
> (Stone 1979, 12)

This portrayal of the folly and misfortunes of historical computing resonated with many historians who, by the early 1980s, were concerned that it would accelerate what they regarded as social history's already considerable anatomization into microscopic analyses of highly localized phenomena. The degree to which the explanatory contours of key themes in social history were being lost in a mist of fine-grained empirical studies was exaggerated. However, the expansion of history departments during the 1970s generated one or two generations of postgraduate training in social history, which generally takes the form of research for graduate theses and articles analysing localized events and experiences.

The counter-response of several influential historians experienced in quantitative analysis, notably Fernand Braudel and Emmanuel Le Roy Ladurie, was to argue that there was no need to fear this blooming of microstudies: they would provide the empirical foundations for constructing powerful new interpretations of the evolution of economic and social structures with the aid of computing technology (Le Roy Ladurie 1979).

Le Roy Ladurie's championing of computer-based structural analysis gained a sceptical reception (Tulchin 2010). Even Braudel was moved to suggest that his most gifted student overstated computing's potential (Braudel 1980). However, Braudel, while greatly admired, also had his critics. They charged that his ambitious studies of large-scale, long-term patterns and cycles in European history reduced that history 'to a kind of geography that unhistorically separated these larger processes from the influence of specific events and policies of political and military power' (Israel 1983, 63). Some went as far as to speak of his writing 'history without humans' (Dursteler 2010, 68) and exaggeratedly attributed what they saw as his neglect of human agency to his use of computers (Tulchin 2010).[2]

*   *   *

Much of what I now do with digital technology in my research and teaching is influenced by my consciousness of the fortunes of historical computing, and particularly by Laslett and other pioneers of digital history who stressed the importance of using technology to engage in and contribute to ideas and arguments in the wider historical community. Hence I was greatly interested by two related articles—one by Patrick Juola, the other by Andrew Prescott—that address the challenges of connecting digital humanities to the mainstream of humanities scholarship (Juola 2008; Prescott 2011).

Juola's article, which Prescott referred to as 'one of the most challenging and troubling publications of recent years' (Prescott 2011, 61), observes that while humanities scholars are increasingly using digital resources, a small and marginalized digital humanities community continues after 40 years to be largely ignored. He sees this reflected in a lack of participation by 'influential or high-impact scholars', as evidenced by nearly 40 years of conference proceedings and journals in digital humanities attracting very low impact scores and few articles by scholars in leading university departments (Juola 2008, 73–75).

The evolution of historical computing gives cause to be uncertain about the adequacy of this assessment. It seems an occlusive blending of the history of diverse uses of digital technologies in different humanities disciplines over the past 40 years to speak of the failure of 'digital humanities' to yet emerge as a discipline. As far as historians are concerned, I would not disagree that their engagement with digital technologies since the 1960s has been limited and confined to specific fields of historical interest, but historians have had numerous successes in gaining recognition within the mainstream of the discipline by creative use of these technologies, as numerous projects sponsored by the Cambridge Group demonstrate.

One strongly suspects that similar stories can be told about the fortunes of digitally based scholarship in other humanities disciplines.

Still, one is inclined to agree that Juola and Prescott are right in their diagnosis of our predicament in some respects. Speaking from personal experience, the days are long gone since giving papers on my work with digital technologies before senior disciplinary colleagues provoked rehearsals of Lawrence Stone's objections to computationally based historical research—often accompanied by witticisms such as, 'You can't read a computer in the bath'. But as was heard repeatedly at the 2012 inaugural conference of the Australasian Digital Humanities Association, digital scholarship continues to attract meagre attention and little support within established humanities disciplines.

What is not clear to me, however, is that the remedies proposed by Juola and Prescott will help matters much. Prescott cautions us against investing time and energy in the development of digital humanities as a discipline. But much hinges here on what we mean by a discipline, which is not easily specified in the abstract. We can say, however, that disciplines characteristically focus on investigating particular phenomena and generally take institutionalized forms, enabling the production of specialist knowledge and theorizing about those phenomena, which may be quite specific to the discipline—although, importantly, many disciplines do not have a clearly defined research focus nor unifying critical methods or theories.

Digital humanities seems to me best conceived as a discipline in this second sense—as Willard McCarty has called it, an 'interdiscipline' that has little unanimity in the questions it asks of the human condition, or the disciplinary traditions it draws on, beyond a shared conviction that digital tools and technologies might be creatively employed to answer them.

Prescott argues that the fortunes of digital humanities have fared badly in large part because our scholarship has gained little recognition and reward within the mainstream of established disciplines. We have failed to undertake digital projects that address 'large scholarly questions and big intellectual themes capturing the imagination of the mainstream' (Prescott 2011, 64). One is inclined to agree that we should, but not at the expense of exploiting the radical potential value of digital tools and techniques to generate new perspectives on the record of human experience—which may very well arise out of projects that attract little mainstream interest.

Consider Prescott's choice of an exemplary digital humanities project: the *Proceedings of the Old Bailey 1674–1913*, which provides a large corpus of texts relating to the lives of ordinary Britons, together with datasets and analytical tools. No-one can deny that historians and literary scholars are using the *Old Bailey* project to enrich our understanding of numerous aspects of British social and cultural history in new and remarkable ways. Nor can it be denied that the project is an outstanding example of how scholars can capture the interest of a wide and culturally diverse public.

However, the *Old Bailey* project is essentially a digital library, albeit one of immense value, that incorporates useful though conventional tools for analysing the semantic and demographic content of its impressive corpus of texts. It provides rich data well-structured for the asking of large scholarly questions and investigating big intellectual themes. It has taken a great deal of scholarship to create the *Old Bailey*, but the real worth of this and comparable projects will be the scholarship that its users produce.

Prescott observes that 'an academic discipline is only as good or as significant as the scholarship it produces' (Prescott 2011, 64). True enough, but whose judgement do we credit? The presumption in citing the *Old Bailey* as a model project is that the value of digital scholarship must be judged by conventional disciplinary criteria. But the dangers of judging digital scholarly work by traditional criteria are obvious. Experts with remarkable predictive nous can often get it completely wrong. Witness economist Paul Krugman's claim in 1998 that the economic impact of the Internet by 2005 would be no greater than the fax machine (Halpern 2013). It seems on best evidence safe to assume that the focus of governments in the developed economies, in which the overwhelming majority of humanities scholars—digital or otherwise—are located, will, until at least 2030, be on managing the graceful exit of the so-called baby boomers. Government investment in health and services for the aged will severely impact the scale of public research funding. Governments will seek to justify every research dollar they commit in terms of its social relevance. What this almost certainly means is an acceleration in the already marked trend for humanities researchers to address the cultural and historical dimensions of the big problems we face in the twenty-first century: climate change, resource depletion, food and water security—to name three of the most challenging.

The *Old Bailey* and other digital cultural corpora are immensely valuable sources of vicarious knowledge for understanding and addressing the challenges of our global times. But to exploit that value requires the development of tools, services, and intellectual techniques enabling what must almost certainly be collaborative research ventures involving researchers from across the spectra of the humanities, creative arts, and the natural sciences investigating this ever increasing volume of data in innovative and perhaps quite unexpected ways. If the fortunes of digital humanities to date are any guide, it seems highly unlikely that the technology and analytical techniques enabling us to do this work will be developed within conventional disciplinary contexts.

Prescott suggests that another weakness of digital humanities is its supposed failure to engage in creative dialogue with scholars less influenced by the so-called linguistic turn in the humanities. He laments the lack of engagement with the work of Heidegger, Foucault, and Williams on technology and culture by contributors to *Digital Humanities Quarterly*. This would be a just criticism if the arguments in respect of the discursive and material effects of technology put by these three thinkers did not critically inform the design and use of digital tools and techniques for the humanities. For if they did, then the potential of technology to enrich our efforts to interpret the meanings and intentions of past and present human behaviour in diverse contexts could easily be lost to deconstructive questioning of what forms of power relations and disciplining rationalities digital humanities normalizes. However, a quick survey of recent writings beyond *Digital Humanities Quarterly* clearly indicates that digital humanists are drawing on theoretically informed writings by digital practitioners such as Willard McCarty, and gaining inspiration from work such as Stephen Ramsay's playfully experimental 'algorithmic criticism', to engage with the mainstream of humanities scholarship's engagement with philosophical hermeneutics (McCarty 2005; Ramsay 2011).

Prescott's call for digital humanists to connect with the scholarly mainstream echoes the counsel offered over a decade ago by Vernon Orville Burton, a pioneer in historical computing and also one of North America's finest writers of history. Burton stressed that historians had much to gain by acquiring technical expertise and working collaboratively with computer and information scientists, but he warned that they needed to be just as engaged in the arguments and sharing of ideas with disciplinary peers employing more traditional modes of historical inquiry (Burton 2005). Burton knew at first hand how historians and their audiences had been losers because of the antagonism and indifference shown to quantitative history. It led him to argue that the practice of historical computing *within* history departments would best guarantee mutually beneficial dialogue with colleagues pursuing the same or related questions of past phenomena using more traditional investigative procedures.

However, the landscape has changed markedly over the past decade. We have seen remarkable advances in infrastructure and tools enabling qualitative as well as quantitative digital analysis of historical and cultural phenomena. We have also witnessed the increased visibility of digital humanities at the meetings of leading scholarly societies, such as the Modern Language Association and the American Historical Association. What also has important implications for the future of digital humanities is that changes within the academy have made cross-disciplinary conversations more commonplace. Moreover, there is a growing sense that the future of the humanities lies in the direction of engaging with what are publicly agreed to be socially relevant themes. The role for curiosity-driven research by individual scholars still exists; we must do our best to preserve it, as computational analysis is only one way in which we engage with the record of human experience. However, humanities scholars will have stronger incentives to focus on collaborative, interdisciplinary investigation of problems requiring innovative modes of analysing large volumes of digital data.

On a personal note, this has certainly been my experience over the past year with a project I have begun in collaboration with colleagues in several humanities disciplines, computing, and information science centred on data mining and semantic analysis of one of the world's largest online collections of historical data: the National Library of Australia's online Australian newspapers. Briefly, the project, called Paper Miner, aims to enable spatial and temporal analysis of complex cultural phenomena in over ten million digitized pages of Australian newspapers.

Completing a relatively crude but working prototype of the service has only been possible by diverse contributions of expertise and creative thinking from a range of disciplinary perspectives. It would have been impossible to get the project to the point that mainstream colleagues were able to imagine the value of the service, without working at the intersection between technologies and multiple disciplinary interests. In fact, what proved most remarkable was how colleagues with little acquaintance with the critical assumptions and procedures of historical research were responsible for making the service more useful for historians.

This project has confirmed, for me at least, that far more is to be gained by continuing, despite the frustrations, to focus our energies on cultivating an intellectually protean interdiscipline. Also confirmed for me by the positive reactions of fellow historians to the Paper Miner project is that big questions of global concern are increasingly influencing and exercising their minds. In the Australian context, there is clearly a growing receptivity to exploring big themes that require the use of digital tools and techniques.

Turning to Patrick Juola's assessment of the fortunes of digital humanities, one is inclined to question whether he has overstated the degree to which it has suffered neglect in the wider humanities community by conceptualizing digital humanities as a discipline, and measuring its fortunes on criteria traditionally used to measure disciplinary success.

Most historians engaged in computer-based research, for example, would not see journal rankings and impact scores as reliable measures for assessing the state of their art. Much of their reportage and critique of the technical and social informatics dimensions of their work now routinely occurs through Web 2.0 modes of communication—to the point that the future for journals such as *History and Computing*—now the *International Journal of Humanities and Arts Computing*— seems likely to be as archives of peer-endorsed past achievements. Both Juola and Prescott draw attention to what they see as paradoxically the neglect of digital humanities, while scholars in the humanities readily and seamlessly integrate digital tools and online resources into their research and teaching. However, the lesson to be drawn here is that just as word processing, email, and online resources such as JSTOR have become ubiquitous because they enhance conventional scholarly practice, humanists using digital technologies are finding their interests better served by modes of communication beyond the conventional format of the print/electronic scholarly journal.

The more important challenge is to develop the means of judging the quality and impact of digital scholarship in national and international frameworks for assessing research quality. The situation in Australia, for example, is that journal rankings and impact scores formally have no weight in national assessment of research excellence in the humanities. However, the process is still heavily weighted towards print-based publication. Research outcomes in innovative 'born-digital' forms are grossly undervalued, and digital humanists find themselves in the absurd position of gaining greater recognition in the academy by writing articles about using digital technologies rather than by what they actually achieve with the technology.

Where Juola and Prescott diverge is in how digital scholarship can secure equivalent weight. Prescott, as we have seen, calls for digital humanists to engage with the ideas and arguments of scholars in the mainstream. Juola proposes that digital humanists should focus their energies on collaboratively developing 'killer applications'—using the term to mean not only software tools and analytical frameworks but also theories and conceptual approaches enabling scholars in the mainstream to address what they see as significant problems. Juola argues moreover that these applications should be designed to generate interesting findings in incremental stages. Like the 'agile' methodology commonly employed in developing software, the suspension or cessation of iterative development will still leave users with a useful product (Juola 2008).

Juola's call for collaborative development of 'killer applications' for the humanities is attractive by virtue of his recognizing that technological innovations generally succeed when perceived as promising to satisfy widely felt needs and desires. Even so, there are difficulties with the strategy. Juola is aware of the perennial problem of funding, hence his emphasis on the incremental development of applications. However, we need to accept that the global financial crisis has diminished the capacity of national research funding agencies to support the digital humanities; where they have still been able to do so, the outcomes of the investments have proved less beneficial than hoped.

Consider, for example, the US National Endowment for the Humanities (NEH) Digital Humanities Initiative. As Juola rightly observes, its launch in 2006 gave cause for optimism that digital scholarship had won high-level support within the agency. However, the summary report of projects funded between 2007 and 2010 by the initiative's start-up grant programme underscores the point that funding is only part of the solution (NEH 2010). Grantees reported that problems they experienced were overwhelmingly to do with the human dimensions of working with technology. Success hinged on how well they managed the interaction and expectations of project participants, their disciplinary peers, and institutional administrators. They were challenged to develop project management expertise in promoting teamwork and cooperation in meeting realistic milestones. They also learnt the importance of contingency planning for the loss of project participants due to career moves, or changing work tasks as a result of economic difficulties encountered by universities and external institutional research partners.

Also, these start-up awards modestly underwrote projects on the expectation of grantees securing further external funding and institutional support. Most recipients reported winning digital humanities institutional validation and encouragement to continue developing their projects through interinstitutional collaboration and pursuing larger grants. However, grantees reported that moving beyond the start-up phase was difficult. They felt that they were being judged by criteria reflecting the weight that scholarly peers continued to give to books and conventional print-based modes of communication.

I would argue that what all of this confirms is that the success of digital humanities depends on our addressing key cultural and social issues in scholarly practice. One of these issues, as previously mentioned, is the need to advance trust in the intellectual integrity of digital resources. The other is to focus on training digital humanists in the dynamics of collaboration as much as equipping them to exploit the intellectual and creative potential of killer applications.

*   *   *

Will digital humanities be successful to the degree it addresses big intellectual themes rather than technical possibilities? My experiences concerning the reception and use of my own digital work incline me to say yes, but a lot of work remains to be done in terms of cultural change. To give one example: between 1999 and 2004, with the help of a research associate, I created an online edition of the journals of James Cook's momentous first Pacific voyage of 1768–71. The resource provides scholars of eighteenth-century Oceania with the means of easily comparing and contrasting what Cook, Joseph Banks, and the artist Sydney Parkinson recorded in daily journals they kept of occurrences during their time in the Society Islands and their survey of the coasts of New Zealand and Eastern Australia—and how their respective testimony was used in producing the official account of the voyage. This digital version of the journals uses simple hyperlink techniques to enable scholars in the field to ask and formulate answers to important questions (Turnbull 2004).

Scholars of voyaging and eighteenth-century Oceania use this online version of these voyaging journals widely, yet over the past decade only one has formally acknowledged using the resource to undertake comparative analysis of first-hand accounts of Cook's first expedition (Gascoigne 2007). When writing of what they find by using the online versions of these texts, they cite the relevant pages of printed editions.

This point was at first a cause of frustration, especially when seeking institutional recognition of the intellectual investment in building the resource. Before too long, however, frustration was displaced by curiosity. Interviews with colleagues using the resource disclosed that they felt they could not make the same investment of trust that they routinely made, for example, in James Cawte Beaglehole's superb editions of the journals kept respectively by James Cook and Joseph Banks during Cook's first Pacific voyage. Their reluctance made me appreciate the critical importance of infrastructure for digital humanities scholarship.

The obvious point is that the production and interpretation of knowledge is social. It occurs through communally endorsed modes of reasoning and argument, and uses of evidence. Until recently these activities occurred within a complex infrastructure centred on books, journals, and related ancillary forms of printed communication in which authors, editors, publishers, and librarians all contributed to the circulation, reception, and uses of this intellectual labour. This infrastructure has evolved over centuries to have qualities and attributes that more often than not have implicitly inspired trust. Hence we should not be surprised that, while remarkable things have been achieved since the mid-1990s by way of digital scholarly information infrastructure, there should be engrained preferences for the familiar sureties of Gutenberg culture. The rapid acceptance of JSTOR in the scholarly mainstream again comes to mind: it did not exploit the potential of networked digital technologies in any innovative or radical way, but sweetly offered surrogates of familiar, trusted things.

Prescott (2011) charges digital humanities with being preoccupied with technology at the expense of its intellectual possibilities. The charge is not without substance. An embarrassing number of projects over the past two decades have produced tools and services meeting the needs of small constituencies with specialized interests that have proved incapable of adapting to help achieve more widely shared aspirations. There have also been projects creating applications that have gathered dust on the shelf because they were conceived and built with insufficient understanding of the intellectual aspirations they were intended to help scholars achieve.

But where the charge is wide of the mark is in respect of infrastructure. Prescott endorses Jerome McGann's observation that 'the entirety of our cultural inheritance ... [will be] reorganized and re-edited within a digital horizon' (2010, i). Yet he is critical of digital humanists investing in infrastructural initiatives, singling out the Text Encoding Initiative (TEI) as being inwardly focused on preserving 'theological purity ... and debating how many angels may dance on an angle bracket' (Prescott 2011, 67), rather than trying to influence the development of big commercial textual conversion ventures, such as Eighteenth-Century Collections Online and Google Books. Certainly, digital humanists should more actively try to participate in the design of commercial ventures benefiting the humanities as a whole. However, what seem like highly specialized interest developments (Prescott singles out XML markup for Middle Eastern epigraphy) will arguably have as much benefit in the longer term by contributing to the development of techniques for automated historically nuanced translation, as, for example, Ngram analysis of Google Books. Despite its time-consuming and cumbersome development, TEI markup is proving to be of inestimable value when used with commercially developed textual corpora—as is evidenced, for example, by the work of Stephen Pumphrey and his colleagues in realizing the intellectual potential of converting the 128,070 items in the commercially developed Early English Books Online to fully searchable and conceptually analysable TEI-compliant texts (Pumphrey 2012).

We would do well to consider more closely the arguments made by Christine Borgman and Patrik Svensson for humanities' investment in infrastructure. Borgman stresses the critical importance of our having a sociologically informed understanding of infrastructure as made up of not only technical functionalities but also the actors who exploit them and the sociocultural contexts in which they do so (see especially Borgman 2007). Svensson extends the argument to make the crucial point that in building digital infrastructure we need consciously to avoid the 'kind of epistemological conservatism that would foreclose potential new ways of knowing and legitimizing knowledge' (Svennson 2011). Juola similarly appreciates that killer applications could be more theoretical or conceptual in nature, rather than being software programs or communication protocols. He also shares Borgman and Svennson's appreciation and concern that, until the mid-1990s, the record of human experience included scholarly interpretations of our thoughts and actions, as well as the books, newspapers, photographs, diaries, letters, and other primary sources on which those interpretations rest. Should humanities scholars prefer the sureties of the Gutenberg era, and not actively contribute to the digital reorganization of our cultural heritage, the risk is that we will find ourselves in the position of the 'raw data' sources of human memory being widely and freely available in digital forms, but not the social and ethical benefits that humanities scholarship creates through connecting us with our heritage.

*   *   *

Collingwood memorably observed that the historian's business is knowing the past, not the future. However, I have dared to suggest here that past experience inclines one to think that the potential of digitally based research seems likely to be best realized by our focusing our energies on developing digital humanities as an interdiscipline whose members are likely to have many different interests beyond a common desire to use technologies to pursue those interests. By the same token we cannot afford to ignore what is happening in the mainstream of established disciplines. As the late Rob Kling, creator of the field of social informatics, convincingly argued, computation and information technologies are most likely to be successful when they are integral parts of human-centred systems—enabling constituencies to do what they want to do better (Kling 1999). Much is to be said for strategically investing, as Juola advocates, in the development of killer applications that are of immediate value to scholars across the spectrum of humanities who until now have had little interest in the scholarly application of digital technologies.

Space prevents detailed discussion of other key issues. Implicit in Juola and Prescott's assessments of the fortunes and future prospects of digital humanities is that the work of reorganizing, reediting, and interpreting human memory will increasingly rely on technology capable of automatically understanding and expressing the meanings of digital content. Digital humanists thus face the dual challenge of connecting with mainstream humanities scholarship, while fostering explorations with computing and information scientists of the potential of semantic computing. Also, making digital humanities more mainstream depends on our success in preparing the generations to come. Prescott argues that the real reason why younger scholars find it difficult to secure advancement in the academy is not the continuing cultural investment in the book, but the failure of digital humanities to produce scholarship of sufficient value to attract wide interest. The extent of disciplinary conservatism varies, but in general the continuing centrality of specialist monographs and articles within disciplinary cultures is a significant problem and will remain so unless undergraduate and graduate curricula equip students to use technology with disciplinary insights and imagination.

In this chapter I have offered some reflections grounded in my own engagement with technology and thoughts on two articles that seems to raise many of the key issues for digital humanists. My own experiences make me sympathetic to the argument that digital humanities needs to engage with traditional disciplinary interests and methods, but it seems to me that, on balance, we are better served by focusing our energies on finding interdisciplinary solutions to the cultural, social, and technical challenges I have sought to draw attention to in this chapter. If the past is any guide, it seems likely that digital humanists will have a meagre impact within established disciplines, won at the expense of diverting our energies away from creating an interdisciplinary formation that would develop new methods, lead the development of new research questions, and possibly thereby in the longer term have a greater impact within established disciplines.

## Notes

1. The Cambridge School drew on the work of Oxford philosopher of language J. L. Austin, who proposed that we can distinguish between statements that can be shown to be either true or false (what he termed 'constantives'), and utterances that are performances of an action by the use of words (what he called 'performatives'). In describing the performative dimensions of language, Austin highlighted how when saying things one does something else (Austin 1967). The Cambridge School thus construed the symbolic traces of past behaviour as 'performative' speech acts. As performatives have fairly well-defined and widely known rules governing their utterance, they presumed that one should be able to establish with reasonable confidence the meanings of what a historical actor intended to do by the utterance of performatives, on reconstructing the rules which at the time were agreed to determine what the utterance would have meant.
2. Braudel, however, had relatively little interest in the influence of ideas and emotions, despite the commitment of other historians with whom he interacted closely to the study of mentalities. For example, there is virtually no mention of religion in his monumental study of the Mediterranean world (Braudel 1972). The most substantial discussion of the Reformation occurs in six pages of an introductory chapter to the first volume, and the wars of religion in France during the second half of the sixteenth century merit a section of around 15 pages.

## Works cited

Austin, J. L. (1967). *How to Do Things With Words*. Cambridge, MA: Harvard University Press.
Borgman, Christine L. (2007). *Scholarship in the Digital Age: Information, Infrastructure, and the Internet*. Cambridge, MA: MIT Press.
Braudel, Fernand. (1972). *The Mediterranean and the Mediterranean World in the Age of Philip II*. New York: Harper & Row.
Braudel, Fernand. (1980). *On History*. Chicago: University of Chicago Press.
Bridenbaugh, Charles. (1963). 'The Great Mutation'. *American Historical Review* 68, no. 2: 315–31.
Burton, Orville Vernon. (2005). 'American Digital History'. *Social Science Computer Review* 23, no. 2: 206–07.
Dursteler, Eric R. (2010). 'Fernand Braudel (1902–85)'. In *French Historians 1900–2000: New Historical Writing in Twentieth-Century France*, ed. Philip Daileader and Philip Whalen, 62–76. Oxford: Blackwell.
Fischer, David Hackett. (1970). *Historians' Fallacies; Toward a Logic of Historical Thought*. New York: Harper & Row.

Fogel, Robert William, and Stanley L. Engerman. (1974). *Time on the Cross*. 1st ed. Boston: Little, Brown.

Gascoigne, John. (2007). *Captain Cook: Voyager Between Worlds*. London: Hambledon Continuum.

Halpern, Sue. (2013). 'Are We Puppets in a Wired World?' *New York Review of Books* 60, no. 17: 24–28.

Israel, Jonathan. (1983). 'Cracks in the Second Storey: Review of Civilization and Capitalism, 15th–18th Century: Volume 2, The Wheels of Commerce'. *Times Literary Supplement* 4164: 63.

Juola, Patrick. (2008). 'Killer Applications in Digital Humanities'. *Literary and Linguistic Computing* 23, no. 1: 73–83.

Kling, Rob. (1999). 'What Is Social Informatics and Why Does It Matter?' *D-Lib Magazine* 5, no. 1. Available at: http://www.dlib.org.

Laslett, Peter. (1977). *Family Life and Illicit Love in Earlier Generations: Essays in Historical Sociology*. Cambridge: Cambridge University Press.

Laslett, Peter. (1999). 'Signifying Nothing: Traditional History, Local History, Statistics, and Computing'. *History and Computing* 11, nos 1–2: 129–33.

Le Roy Ladurie, Emmanuel. (1979). *The Territory of the Historian*. Hassocks, Sussex: Harvester Press.

Locke, John, and Peter Laslett. (1960). *Two Treatises of Government*. Cambridge: Cambridge University Press.

McCarty, Willard. (2005). *Humanities Computing*. London: Palgrave Macmillan.

McGann, Jerome. (2010). 'Introduction'. In *Online Humanities Scholarship*, ed. Jerome McGann. Houston: Rice University.

NEH (National Endowment for the Humanities), Office of Digital Humanities. (2010). 'Summary Findings of NEH Digital Humanities Start-Up Grants (2007–2010)'.

Oakeshott, Michael. (1983). *On History and Other Essays*. Oxford: B. Blackwell.

Paper Miner. Available at: http://www.paperminer.org.au/.

Pocock, J. G. A. (2009). *Political Thought and History: Essays on Theory and Method*. Cambridge: Cambridge University Press.

Prescott, Andrew. (2011). 'Consumers, Creators, or Commentators? Problems of Audience and Mission in the Digital Humanities'. *Arts and Humanities in Higher Education* 11, nos 1–2: 61–75.

Pumphrey, Steven. (2012). 'Experiments in 17th-Century English: Manual versus Automatic Conceptual History'. *LCC: The Journal of Literary and Linguistic Computing* 27, no. 4: 395–408.

Ramsay, Stephen. (2011). *Reading Machines: Toward an Algorithmic Criticism*. Urbana: University of Illinois Press.

Stone, Lawrence. (1973). *Family and Fortune: Studies in Aristocratic Finance in the Sixteenth and Seventeenth Centuries*. Oxford: Clarendon Press.

Stone, Lawrence. (1977). *The Family, Sex, and Marriage in England, 1500–1800*. New York: Harper & Row.

Stone, Lawrence. (1979). 'The Revival of Narrative: Reflections on a New Old History'. *Past and Present* 85, no. 1: 3–24.

Svensson, Patrik. (2011). 'From Optical Fibre to Conceptual Infrastructure'. *Digital Humanities Quarterly* 5, no. 1. Available at: http://digitalhumanities.org.

Thomas, William. G. (2004). 'Computing and the Historical Imagination'. In *A Companion to Digital Humanities*, ed. Susan Schreibman, Ray Siemens, and John Unsworth, 56–68. Oxford: Blackwell Publishing.

Tulchin, Allan. (2010). 'Geneva by the Sea: The Reformation in Nîmes in Historiographical Context'. In *Braudel Revisited: The Mediterranean World, 1600–1800*, ed. Abi Piterberg, Teo Ruiz, and Geoffrey Symcox, 151–76. Los Angeles: University of California Press.

Turnbull, Paul. (2004). *South Seas: Voyaging and Cross-Cultural Encounters in the Pacific (1760–1800)*. Available at: http://southseas.nla.gov.au/.

Turnbull, Paul. (2010). 'Historians, Computers, and the World-Wide-Web'. *Australian Historical Studies* 41, no. 2: 131–48.

Vann, Richard. T. (1969). 'History and Demography'. *History and Theory* 9: 64–78.

Wachter, Kenneth W., Eugene A. Hammel, and Peter Laslett. (1978). *Statistical Studies of Historical Social Structure*. New York: Academic Press.

# 18
# The Big Bang of Online Reading

*Alan Liu*

*'Reading' has adapted to multimedia, networking, mobile computing, and text-encoding, even as, reciprocally, the new technologies actively remember older habits of reading. Using a browser, search engine, or blog site, for instance, subtly inflects reading; but, equally, familiarity with historical reading technologies—with 'documents', 'pages', or 'indexes'—shapes the use of new technologies. Despite such cross-adaptation, however, we hardly understand the relation between older and newer ways of reading.... Online reading is Transliteracies's topic because this is the staging ground where humanists, social scientists, and computer scientists all have equal contributions to make.*

Transliteracies 2005, 2

The epigraph for this chapter is taken from the original funding proposal for the Transliteracies Project, a University of California multicampus research group under my direction that ran from 2005 to 2010 with the assistance of research faculty, graduate students, and guest industry researchers from many institutions. Transliteracies explored the technological, social, and cultural practices of online reading. Its working groups on the history of reading, new reading interfaces, and social computing began by conducting an extensive survey of the topic, resulting in a large number of research reports and papers now available through the project's online Research Clearinghouse. Ultimately, Transliteracies focused on one research area especially ripe for innovation: the use of social computing to augment traditional scholarly reading methods with Web 2.0 reading practices. For example, the project created an experimental system called RoSE: Research-oriented Social Environment (subsequently further developed to beta state on a NEH Digital Humanities Start-up grant) that fashions bibliographies into interactive social networks of authors and documents.

The overall result of Transliteracies (and of such similarly wide-angled projects as the Transliteracy Research Group in the United Kingdom, INKE: Implementing New Knowledge Environments in Canada, and more recently the TRANSLIT project in France) was to expose to view the sheer breadth and multifariousness of the phenomenon of online reading.[1] Above all, the study of digitally networked reading shows that only by perceiving the totality of recent changes in reading technologies and practices can we grasp the unfolding new universe of literacy. I choose the metaphor 'universe' (rather than the more conventional 'age', 'epoch', or 'revolution') to draw a specific analogy to cosmology. The analogy is to the big bang. Today, we are witnessing a big bang of online reading whose early stages are like the first instants of the universe as now theorized by physicists—an explosively rapid generative sequence of phases from which emerges, almost all at once, a multiplicity of forces, materialities, forms, and dimensions.[2] To understand 'transliteracies' as a general idea—that is, reading in all its media and networked forms today—requires a similarly cosmological horizon of perception in which we focus less on particular changes than on the totality of changes. Seen as a whole, I speculate, this totality becomes a research problem in its own right—one whose technological, social-policy, and philosophical implications do not appear at lower levels of scale and that the digital humanities have an opportunity to approach in ways that intersect with, yet also differ from, those of other fields and stakeholders.

But first let me start by commenting on some of the chief particular changes in reading—literacy reconfigurations, as I call them—enabled by the new technologies, each of which is a digital humanities research opportunity. *Reconfiguration* implies that the essential change occurs at the level not of discrete novelties but of phase shifts in ensembles of new technologies and practices remixed with older ones.

## Media reconfiguration

Online reading, obviously, is enabled by a reconfiguration of literacy media. But this statement alone tells us little, since the concept of 'media' currently functions as a kind of black box for *something* that is happening among older or underlying concepts such as technology, communication, information, and language for which we lack an adequate explanation. This is why, for example, one can't predict whether online reading is referred to in the research literature as a 'media technology', 'information technology', 'information media', 'information and communication technology' ('ICT', as it is called in the social sciences), and so on. Whereas in the past the mature codex book locked together the ideas of technology, communication, information, and language in a stable configuration (so that one could simply say 'print,' for example, without needing to specify 'print technology used to communicate information and language'), today's technologies have destabilized the configuration. Wrapping the idea of *media* around everything that is happening among underlying elements creates the illusion of a unified new 'convergence'.[3] It's as if media were an API (application programming interface) allowing us to concentrate on the inputs and outputs of the new system without needing to program the circuits inside the black box.

## Reconfiguration of materialities

Much of the current discussion of new-media literacy concerns specific new material technologies—for example, e-books, tablets, mobile phones, flexible screens, augmented reality interfaces, and so on. The Transliteracies Project also studied less commonly discussed materialities of literacy such as readers for the visually impaired, digital scrolls, digital coffee tables, retinal projection displays, interactive 'FogScreen' projection systems, and so on (as well as digital art projects or installations that invent surprising new materialities of literacy—e.g., riding a bicycle to navigate text).[4]

However, focusing on specific material instruments is deceptive because ultimately it is the *idea* of materiality that the new media reconfigures. This reconfiguration is occurring in two steps. First comes the realization that the virtual is indeed fully material. One of the important recent developments in the digital humanities relevant to the study of online literacy is thus a material-history approach similar to that in the history of the book field. Just as scholars of book history such as Peter Stallybrass, Roger Chartier, and others have innovatively studied the material surfaces of writing in the Renaissance (for example, erasable notebooks or tablets [Stallybrass et al. 2004]), so Matthew G. Kirschenbaum—whose training originally spanned textual and digital studies—explores with theoretical generality the materiality of digital inscription 'mechanisms' (Kirschenbaum 2008). Jean-François Blanchette (2011a) similarly emphasizes the materiality of the digital in discussing the way 'trade offs' between efficiency and abstraction in modern modular software betray the irresistible gravity of materiality. Meanwhile, the computing industry itself is well aware of the material constraints of the digital. Not only is 'Moore's Law' (of exponentially increasing density of transistors) running up against the fundamental limits of physics at the nano and atomic scales, but at the macro scale computing is confronting the limits of Earth's ecosystem. Heeding the early warning of such activist organizations as the Silicon Valley Toxics Coalition, the industry has evolved 'green' computing initiatives and become sensitive about its carbon footprint.[5]

Second comes the realization that while the virtual is material, it also changes our very understanding of materiality. Steam, gas, and electrical machinery (all the way through the era of the mainframe computer) were associated with mass and energy effects. But today's digital machineries are increasingly also associated with network and system effects. They witness the fact that today our idea of materiality is morphing into one of systematicity. After all, for decades, late- or post-Marxist, postmodern, and other theorists (for example, Harvey 1989; Soja 1989; Deleuze and Guattari 1987), complexity theorists in the sciences (for example, Nicolis and Prigogine 1989), and others have argued that old-fashioned ideas of materialism have been superseded by new geographies of space-time compression, 'a thousand plateaus', chaotic systems, and so on. Matter today is a differential substrate (like a semiconductor) on which, at nodal points, specific material intensities or knottings rise like signal from noise to mark out—and, in a sense, to fabricate—the structure of what really 'matters', which is a system of configurations, spacings, timings, channels, and flow rates. An example is the way that it is impossible to discuss Apple's iPod, iPhone, and iPad as material devices without appreciating the entire iTunes and apps system that multiplies the value of those devices. With regard to digital literacy, the Amazon Kindle is tied into the whole Amazon cloud service in a similar way.

## Sensory reconfiguration

The computing industry continues to experiment rapidly with the tactile, visual, and audio modalities of digital literacy—for example, exploring new formats of e-readers and tablets, trying out new combinations of multimedia in online newspapers or magazines, and so on. It may be that in the near future the clichéd complaint of book lovers that 'you can't take a computer to bed [or the bath, the beach, and so on] with you' will be obsolete. Not even the smell of books may be unique much longer, since a parfümeur recently bottled the smell of books in a fragrance called 'Paper Passion', which could conceivably enhance future e-reader technologies for readers who desire a retro literacy ambience.[6]

All of this speaks to changes in what may be called, using vocabulary that remembers the historical book, the sensory bindings of literacy or, choosing alternative vocabulary connoting open-ended complexity rather than closure, the sensory manifold of literacy. I refer to the way that the sensory experience of reading coheres as an operational and phenomenological whole.[7] A simple illustration: Any parent can remember wincing as their child first learns how to turn the pages of a book, crumpling and twisting each page to discover though trial and error (and imitation) exactly how the surprisingly complex tissues and joints of the codex work together. Functional literacy, we may say, begins even before the mastery of written language when one first internalizes the book as a unified perceptual field in which simply seeing, touching, and smelling the codex summons up bodily/mental programs for making it 'work' (as Johanna Drucker puts it).[8]

Currently, online reading is reconfiguring the sensory bindings or manifold of literacy. For example, as I write I am sitting in an American microbrewery pub with a codex book propped open next to a laptop computer. I also have on the side my iPad, which I use to consult e-books (linked to the Google and Amazon clouds) as well as articles in PDF format (linked to my other computing devices through the Dropbox online storage service). This is a reconfigured cocoon of phenomenological experience that remixes old and new literacy media. What essential difference the new sensory bindings or manifold of online literacy will make on reading is an open research question.

## Social reconfiguration

It is a short step from the sensory reconfiguration of online reading to the social reconfiguration of such reading.[9] My example of writing this essay in a pub surrounded by other people and also by ambient network connectivity is telling. The example makes it clear that whether we think of newspapers, books, laptop computers, tablets, e-readers, or smartphones, the sense-surround of reading is inseparable from social surroundings. Literacy is an experience that is not just bound in upon itself in stand-alone forms but also closely mapped over spatial, architectural, and social habitats. Consider, for example, the period from the Enlightenment through the nineteenth century when both manuscript correspondence and print publication were at a height. In that era, literacy acquired its distinctively split modern personality as both an individual and social act: one enjoys a letter or novel in solitude, but one also wants to chat over a newspaper in a coffeehouse (as Habermas theorized in his notion of the 'public sphere' (1989)). The identity of the modern democratic individual, in other words, arose in a dialectic of retreat from and immersion in sociality in conjunction with habits of literacy. Now consider the way our present era of Web 2.0, social media, and mobile computing is characterized by an equivalent, but reconfigured, sociality of literacy. Netizens today are torn dialectically between protecting privacy (a voyeuristic individualism allowing one to be in public while retreating from publicity) and valuing social computing (which is like chatting over a newspaper in a coffeehouse or pub, except in distributed and asynchronous fashion through blogs, wikis, Facebook, Twitter, and so on).[10]

## Cognitive reconfiguration

It is also a short step from considering the sensory reconfiguration of online reading to hypothesizing that such reading may lead to cognitive reconfiguration. After all, the relation between 'percept' and 'concept' in cognitive science research is a close one (the well-known cognitive science and artificial intelligence researcher Douglas Hofstadter, for example, builds models of cognition based on the computational equivalent of underlying processes of perception (Hoftstadter et al. 1995, esp. 192–93, 210–11).[11] More broadly, the cognitive science (and artificial intelligence) fields are fascinated by the relation between lower and higher cognitive events—for example, between neuronal activity, on the one hand, and ideas or feelings, on the other; or between cellular automata and emergent higher patterns. The so-called F-Shaped pattern of visual scanning that online readers follow when browsing web pages (observed by Jakob Nielsen through eye-tracking studies (Nielsen 2006)) is thus an example of lower- and middle-level sensory literacy practice that may correlate with mentalities such as the hyperattention of scanning or skimming theorized by N. Katherine Hayles in her 'Hyper and Deep Attention' (2007) and 'How We Read: Close, Hyper, Machine' (2010).

At least in regard to individual human thought (leaving aside the largely metaphorical discussion of Web 2.0 social thought as 'collective intelligence', 'hive mind', and so on), cognitive and neuroscience research into digital literacy has boomed in recent years. Publications such as Nicholas Carr's *The Shallows: What the Internet Is Doing to Our Brain* (2010) and the Hayles articles have surveyed and publicized research on the topic. Interdisciplinary research communities such as the Society for Text and Discourse place a strong emphasis on neurocognitive approaches to both print and digital literacy.[12] The Transliteracies Project itself included some attention to the approach by studying such software projects as the University of Memphis's Coh-Metrix online tool for measuring the cognitive coherence of prose texts, publishing Monica Bulger's 'Beyond Search: A Preliminary Skill Set for Online Literacy' ((2006) which in part discusses cognitive science approaches to new-media reading), and hosting participants such as Nicholas Dames and Andrew Elfenbein who work on cognitive science approaches to literature.[13]

The result of neurocognitive research into online reading is that we are now able to ask such questions as follows: Does the Internet constrain us to 'shallow' or 'hyper' reading? Or, instead, will new nuances of digital reading evolve to expose the limitations of metaphors like 'shallow' themselves? After all, the common metaphors used to debate the mental experience of digital reading—shallow versus deep, extensive versus intensive, hypertextual versus linear, focused versus distracted, or close versus distant—tend to be skeuomorphic sensory or physical tropes inherited from past ages of reading. In the past, 'shallow versus deep' may have been more analytically meaningful because literacy engaged with flat pages of text suggesting a phenomenology of surface (what Plato called 'external written characters' in his critique of the invention of writing) versus depth (what Plato called true 'memory' and 'wisdom').[14] But the 'shallow versus deep' binary is clumsy today when the screens of online reading devices are not flat in the same way; they are complexly both shallow and deep because they interact with underlying software 'layers' or 'stacks' and bottomless (or ceilingless) 'cloud services' so as to augment human reading with clever machine literacies (as Hayles emphasizes (2010)) for which we lack adequate descriptive terms. For example, could we instead say that a reading screen linked to a database or the Internet is deeply shallow? Or comprehensively, complexly, and emergently shallow?

## Reconfiguration of form (and scale)

Form is a new horizon in research on online literacy. A comparison to print is again useful. As a generalization we can say that once the platform of print media became standardized in its medial, material, sensory, social, and cognitive affordances—so that books or pages came in certain common sizes, circulated in known social or economic tranches (for example, trade publications versus mass market), and established particular conventions of sensory, social, and mental use—then discussion of print literature could proceed in terms of form. Thus, literary criticism from the Enlightenment onward made an art of critiquing forms from genres down to stylistic syntax or vocabulary. This was even more the case in the early to mid-twentieth century, when the Russian Formalists studied generic and stylistic forms with technical precision (for example, 'systems of genres', 'devices', 'motifs', 'rhythms') and, in parallel with the New Critics, raised awareness of form to a philosophical level as the *differentia specifica*, or essential distinguishing feature, of literary language.[15]

In the realm of online literacy, by contrast, platforms are still so changeful that formal thought continues to focus on underlying technical protocols, schema, and templates. Consider, for example, such content management systems as WordPress that publish many of today's database-driven websites. These systems evolve so rapidly through multiple updates each year that their formal 'themes' (template files and CSS style sheets, augmented with plug-ins) often require fine adjustments to maintain.[16] Ambitiously customized WordPress themes require even bolder hacks (sometimes of the core WordPress system files themselves). The most careful formal thought is thus still impelled by concern for the platform, with the result that true formal discussion remains rudimentary or, at best, descriptive. In terms of genre, for instance, we simply describe, *This is a listserv, blog, tweet, wiki,* or *social network site.*[17] And in terms of the digital microforms that are today's equivalent of rhetorical topoi (commonplaces), we similarly just say, *This is a banner, sidebar, post, comment,* or *hashtag.* Advanced formal critique occurs only in the specialized fields of human computing interface (HCI) research, graphic design, or usability research (for example, Nielsen 1999). The bottom line is that we do not yet have an adequate common framework in which to address such formal questions as: What difference does it make that we choose the form of a blog, tweet, or online magazine to narrate beautiful, comic, or tragic events? Are there formal or stylistic differences between tweets on public and private events? What haiku- or graffiti-like formal effects arise from the 140-character limit of a tweet (and how would it be different if everyone used 247 characters, at one point the actual secret maximum that Twitter's back end accepted through its application programming interface (Caufield 2009))?

The fact that my formal questions above end on a question of scale (140 versus 247 characters) is emblematic because the lack of an adequate framework of formal analysis often forces us to treat fine features of form as if they were just gross effects of scale. For example, an inordinate amount of recent debate concerns the properties of short online forms (such as posts and tweets) versus long forms. It's as if we were to say that the only essential difference between an epic and lyric poem, or between a novel and a letter, were length.

However, the ease with which analysis of form slides into measurement of scale does reveal something fundamental about the nature of online form. To suggest why, let me try out the following conceptual equation: *modularity + transmissibility + indexibility = form.* Again, the history of the book (and, more generally, of writing) is a good thinking tool. In the West, we know, early writing was relatively void of form. Designed to be recited by oral speakers who gave it form through pauses and emphases as they spoke, writing was a *scriptio continua* or undifferentiated stream of alphabetic characters without even spaces or punctuation (Svenbro 1999; Cavallo 1999). Gradually (as simulated in an elegant Flash animation of the history of the book that the Transliteracies Project produced (Warner et al. 2007)), form arose through the invention of word spacing, punctuation, capitalization, paragraph breaks, chapter titles and divisions, and so on. The lesson is that writing evolved to meet the combined demands of *modularity* (standard component units such as words, sentences, paragraphs, chapters), *transmissibility* (when transmitting a communication to another, it is important to be able to do so modularly so that only a sentence, paragraph, page, or book can be handed off), and *indexibility* (referring to the entire repertory of metadata and management devices such as chapter titles, tables of contents, page numbers, or indexes that made books one of our most important random access media even before computational media). All of that is what produced form. Modular, transmissible, and indexible structures are form.

This understanding of form has important implications for the study of online forms. For instance, it brings into question the foundational principles of text-encoding protocols such as TEI designed to encode written works for presentation and manipulation in digital media (so that a stanza in a poem, for instance, might be tagged digitally <lg> for 'line group'). Implemented in XML, TEI practices the general philosophy of modern semantic encoding: separating the form of content into two components, logical structure and presentation (or formatting) structure.[18] The goal is to allow a publisher, for example, simply to tag a set of lines with the logical descriptor <lg>, leaving it up to the reader's computer to decide what line and margin spacings to use to present a stanza. But if my conceptual equation above is correct, then the separation of logical structure from presentation structure cannot be correct all the way down, since the principles of modularity, transmissibility, and indexibility lie at the root of both kinds of structure to create the full sense of form. This is especially true in the era of modern graphic and typographic design (after the New Typography and International Style in the twentieth century), when designers exposed in their presentation style itself the principles of modularity, transmissibility, and indexibility—for example, through such elements as grid layouts allowing for modular design, sans serif fonts symbolizing the transmissive efficiency of communication, and dramatic white spaces and asymmetry used to give indexical emphasis.[19] At the deepest level, in other words, logical and presentation structures are integral in the experience of form, and any attempt to separate them is arbitrary. In practice, therefore, creators of digital media find it difficult to be purist in keeping metadata and formatting structures separate. It always seems that *something*—whether imposed by a particular platform, program, plug-in, or design—forces the use of ad hoc workarounds that transgress the divide between logic and presentation (resulting, for example, in occasional lapses of 'in-line' formatting code mixed in with the source code for a web page when all such formatting is supposed to be regulated by a CSS style sheet in an autonomous file).

Now we can see why formal issues are commutable with scale issues—something that is true for all media but especially for computational media where speed, efficiency, and flexibility depend on trade-offs between humanly recognizable form (for example, a document) and humanly unreadable scale (for example, an individual data packet or 'big data'). The reason that form is convertible with scale is that modularity, transmissibility, and indexibility all bear on the form *and* size of the communicational act. For example, modules have to be defined by indexical metadata at a size balanced between the formal integrity of the communication (for example, a whole document) and the efficiency and flexibility of transmission (optimized at the packet level). All of this means that it should be possible to decompose recent experiments in the scale of online reading into elemental terms of modularity, transmissibility, and indexibility that allow us to understand how such experiments in scale are a surrogate for formal experimentation. Consider, for example, the recent trend towards short, pamphlet-like online books (for example, Amazon Kindle Singles, Apple iBooks Quick Reads, TED Books, Atavist publications) as that trend is counterbalanced dialectically against corpora-scale reading ('distant reading' and 'culturomics' as popularized, for example, by the Google Books Ngram Viewer). Modularity, transmissibility, and indexibility are remaking online literacy into something like a playlist of songs in a gigantic, literate iTunes. The threat this poses for the 'album' (in this case, the book) is a matter both of scale and form.

## Reconfiguration of the value of reading

Other reconfigurations of literacy enabled or expressed by online media could be mentioned. But I will stop by reflecting on just one more, which may in fact be the most important of all: reconfiguration of the value of reading. Consider by comparison how different values of reading collaborated or competed in past media ages—for example, to bring the codex into dominance. The early codex Bible acquired very high value for religious, social, and personal purposes. But precisely the same lower and middle classes that were the early milieu of the Christian faith also valued the little codex notebooks they used for ordinary life and accounting. Codex literacy, in other words, advanced over the previous authority of the Roman and Jewish scroll through a conjuncture of high and mundane literacy values.[20] In the later print age, the literacy values of typeset sermons, ballads, newspapers, novels, and so on also variously came into convergence or divergence according to a complex dynamics of social, economic, aesthetic, entertainment, and other factors. Each past regime of reading never fully stabilized its literacy values, partly because new media of the time like broadside ballads in the Renaissance, television in the twentieth century, or blogs in the twenty-first century kept challenging established literacy values with what at first seemed to be trash, popular, or partisan devaluations of literacy. Yet over time any media age established a hierarchy of literacy values, or at least enough of an apparent hierarchy to sustain debate about what mattered most. Thus, for instance, novels were once supposed to be less valuable than just about anything else 'respectable' people read, whereas now we bemoan the loss of reading fiction amid the flood of trashy new popular media.

Today, online literacy is once more altering the hierarchy of reading values. Most importantly, what the highest value of reading will be in online society is unclear: information, opinion, entertainment, knowledge, or wisdom. As in the past when demotic discourses challenged established discourses, much of the current change is occurring in the chaotic gap between expert knowledge (discourse produced or filtered by academics, professionals, journalists, government agencies, etc.) and the new networked public knowledge (for example, Wikipedia, the blogosphere, viral media). Not only has an overall hierarchy not been established to regulate this gap, but the boundary-spanning instruments for negotiating between expertise and networked public knowledge—technologies, practices, rewards, and institutional protocols for encouraging academics to write for Wikipedia or the blogosphere, for example, or for the latter to be used in the classroom—have only begun to be invented.

The following seem to be some of the most important questions for the future of online literacy: What do we value about online reading? Who is the *we* (for example, expert, employer, regulator, consumer, worker, or citizen) who lies behind that question? And how will online reading strengthen or undermine the value of reading generally?

\* \* \*

I conclude as promised by returning to a cosmological perspective on the multiplicity and rapidity of the reconfigurations surveyed above, whose sum amounts to what I have called the big bang of online literacy. As I suggested, seeing the totality of these changes leads to a research problem in its own right (the 'transliteracies' problem proper) with important implications for how society develops its technologies, policies, and philosophies of online reading.

Let me now reveal my underlying reason for analogizing online reading to the big bang, which might otherwise seem just a colourful metaphor. Contemporary theoretical physicists think about the big bang (more generally, about both the origin and future of the universe) in such new frameworks as string theory, M-theory, and multiple universes theory.[21] All these compensate for the fact that while the accepted macrocosmological and microphysical models of the universe (for example, the 'standard model' of particles and forces) have proven to be precisely descriptive and predictive, they are not satisfying explanations that offer a picture of why the universe is the way it is (for example, why these kinds of particles and forces are related by these arbitrary physical constants) The greatest stumbling block continues to be the one that Einstein spent the latter part of his life wrestling with: how to reconcile the universe at the macro scale of gravitational effects to the universe at the micro scale of quantum mechanics. The two universes seemed to be theoretically incommensurable to the point of mathematical absurdity. The recent physics frameworks I mentioned all try for such a reconciliation, which is why they emphasize concepts like 'supersymmetry', a primordial unification of at least the three nongravitational cardinal forces (and, with M-theory, possibly also gravity to complete the set) preceding their differentiation after the earliest instants of the big bang. Thus, they foreground the essential metaphysical question in contemporary physics: Is there a so-called theory of everything (TOE)? In other words, is the universe fundamentally a unity that can be explained by a single comprehensive theory governing both the macro and micro?

A similar question applies to research into online reading, but with an important difference. Like physicists wondering about the theory of everything, we might ask, Is there *one* phenomenon of online literacy whose media, materialities, sensory experiences, social formations, cognitive operations, formal features, and values converge in an epochal transformation of literacy? The difference is that online reading is an artefactual rather than natural phenomenon, meaning that it occurs as much in the social as the physical universe. Therefore, while theoretical physics is relatively free to be biased towards the mathematical elegance of unity (leaving for experimental physics the untidiness of a fractured universe), research on technologies such as online reading is not free of debate on the very ideal of unified explanation because that ideal is entangled in some of today's most pressing ideological contests about the future of society. The closest equivalent now of a 'theory of everything' relating to information technology, it might be suggested, is economic neoliberalism, which develops technologies for online reading (and everything else) in ways that steer all transactions between private citizens and the public sphere into the economically 'privatized' containment structures—aggregator databases, technological protocols, intellectual property laws, organizational forms, and so on—of the corporate sphere along with privatized aspects of the governmental, health, media, educational, and other sectors that this sphere increasingly colonizes. Such is a vision of cultural rather than technological 'singularity'. The cultural singularity will occur when all knowledge and experience—in the present case, reading—are corralled into a single consolidated system of e-books, tablet computers, 'app stores', digital text publishing formats, operating systems, and so on. We are far along that path of consolidation now, with several well-known information technology corporations contesting to be the supreme singularity rewarded by the underlying cultural singularity for which they serve so prominently as the proxy on the stock market: capitalism.

Arrayed against the vision of cultural singularity are a set of other understandings, institutional settings, and 'counterpublics' of information technology. It is here that the digital humanities have a chance to contribute to, yet also differ from, the way other stakeholders conduct research and development. The digital humanities are inextricably (if not exclusively) rooted in a larger contemporary humanities milieu that in the past half century committed itself to *dis*unity as a matter both of ethical and research-driven principle under such names as *difference, otherness, historicism, contingency*, and so on. While just a few years ago it was sensible to ask about the digital humanities in its formative phase, 'Where is cultural criticism in the digital humanities?' (Liu 2012b), now in the wake of the field's heightened attention to theory (for example, Cecire 2011) and cultural criticism (for example, #transformDH n.d. and #DHPoco n.d.), it is clear that the successor question is not *whether* but *how* it will advance the most deep-seated, passionate, distinctive, and, of course, controversial principles and methods of the contemporary humanities. Should society, or should it not, be building a unified field of technologies for online reading? Should there be a single socioeconomic policy or legal-governmental framework for regulating such technologies? And should the value of online literacy lie in knowledge—or knowledges? A goal for the digital humanities should be to research and develop answers to such questions that make a difference in two directions. Endogamously in the humanities themselves, the digital humanities should inflect the discourse of difference in new ways—for example, adapting the ethos of poststructuralism or critique to that of 'building' through what James Smithies (2014) calls 'postfoundationalism'. Exogamously in relation to other research-and-development communities, the digital humanities should contribute the very emphasis of the humanities on difference. For example, digital humanities research is urgently needed to help shape online reading technologies that can serve scholars in their dual roles as general citizens of the reading public *and* denizens of a differentiated social sector and institution with special needs for fair use, citation, collaboration, presentation, and other practices. What is needed, in other words, are technologies that build in, plug in, extend, or otherwise enable a fundamentally differenti-ated yet also organic relation between scholarship and the public sphere—not just PowerPoint™s but also OtherViewPoints, SharedViewPoints, and ultimately PublicPoints.

By addressing such issues, the digital humanities field could both advance its humanities heritage and share that heritage with society at large. It could help society envision that the most humanly good future for the multiple reconfigura-tions of literacy is not a single coming age of online reading but instead emancipa-tory multiplicities of reading obeisant to the needs of people, institutions, nations, and cultures each to 'read' humanity differently.

## Notes

An earlier version of this essay was published in French translation in 2012 in INA's *E-Dossiers de l'audiovisuel* (Liu 2012a).

1. The Transliteracies Project, Transliteracy Research Group, and TRANSLIT Project are autonomous initiatives, though they share interests and their principal investigators have collaborated at some of each other's inaugural conferences. For the Transliteracies Project at the University of California and the Transliteracy Research Group in England, see their home pages. (On the relation between the two, see Thomas et al. 2007.) On the TRANSLIT project, see the French National Research Agency's announcement (n.d.).
2. See Greene (1999/2000, esp. 345–56) on the sequence of events at the origin of the universe.
3. For a study of the way the term 'convergence' is used in research on new media to stand for some combination of 'alignment, interoperability, optimization, recombination, and correspondence', see Herzhoff 2009.
4. See the Transliteracies Research Clearinghouse n.d. On the FogScreen display technol-ogy, which uses a thin layer of vapour for a projection surface, see Breisinger and Ford 2006. On the *Legible City* art installation in which a reader sits on a physical bicycle to navigate though a virtual architecture composed of text, see Swanstrom 2006.
5. On the Silicon Valley Toxics Coalition (SVTC), see the coalition's home page and my dis-cussion in Liu 2004, 267–68. In regard to the sensitivity of today's computing industry to its carbon footprint, see, for example, Fahey 2011. In his ' "Infrastructural Think-ing" as Core Computing Skill' (2011), Blanchette discusses the energy requirements and environmental impact of Google's server farms to illustrate a thesis about the unacknowledged materiality of 'cloud computing'.
6. I refer to the perfume called 'Paper Passion' originally reported to have been created by designer, artist, and bookstore owner Karl Lagerfeld in collaboration with parfümeur Geza Schön (Kaiser 2011; see also *Wallpaper* 2012). (Lagerfeld denied being involved after news of the perfume circulated widely in newspapers and blogs; see *The Independent* 2011). There was also an earlier perfume called 'In the Library' ('Katherine' 2012).
7. Compare with Andrew Piper: 'Books have been important to us not just as vehicles of mental transport, but because our interactions with them span so many domains of sensory and physical experience. Whether it is through the acts of touch, sight, sound, sharing, play, or acquiring a sense of place, these embodied, and at times interpersonal, ways of interacting with books coalesce to magnify the learning that takes place through them. The same information processed in different ways and woven together is one of the profound secrets of bookish thought' (2012).
8. Drucker observes that one effect of thinking about digital e-books may be to force us to reconceptualize 'traditional books' in terms 'based less on a formal grasp of layout, graphic, and physical features and more on an analysis of how those format features

effect the functional operation and activity of the work done by a traditional book'. 'Or, to put it more simply', she immediately continues, 'rather than think about simulating the way a book *looks*, we might consider extending the ways a book *works* as we shift into digital instruments' (Drucker 2007, 217).

9. For fuller thoughts on the relation between social reading and 'social computing', see Liu 2013.

10. 'Netizens' is a now obsolete term for socially or politically engaged online citizens dating from an earlier, cyberlibertarian moment in the political awakening of the Internet (see, for example, Katz 1997). I use the term here because it captures the sense of the transition between private- and public-sphere online literacy that I am describing.

11. See Hoftstadter et al. 1995, esp. 192–93, 210–11.

12. See, for example, the programmes for the Society for Text and Discourse annual conferences—for example, the 16th Annual Meeting, Minneapolis, 13–15 July 2006.

13. For a Transliteracies report on the Coh-Metrix project, see Knight 2006. Dames, who participated in a Transliteracies conference in 2005, is author of *The Physiology of the Novel: Reading, Neural Science, and the Form of Victorian Fiction* (2007). Elfenbein presented a lecture for Transliteracies on 'The Humanities and the Science of Comprehension' on 3 May 2007. Transliteracies researchers also discussed his essay, 'Cognitive Science and the History of Reading' (2006).

14. From Plato's myth of the invention of writing in the *Phaedrus*: 'But when they came to letters, This, said Theuth, will make the Egyptians wiser and give them better memories; it is a specific both for the memory and for the wit. Thamus replied: O most ingenious Theuth, the parent or inventor of an art is not always the best judge of the utility or inutility of his own inventions to the users of them. And in this instance, you who are the father of letters, from a paternal love of your own children have been led to attribute to them a quality which they cannot have; for this discovery of yours will create forgetfulness in the learners' souls, because they will not use their memories; they will trust to the external written characters and not remember of themselves. The specific which you have discovered is an aid not to memory, but to reminiscence, and you give your disciples not truth, but only the semblance of truth; they will be hearers of many things and will have learned nothing; they will appear to be omniscient and will generally know nothing; they will be tiresome company, having the show of wisdom without the reality' (2013).

15. The Russian Formalist principle of 'defamiliarization' in literature, for example, was linked to the principle of awareness of form. Victor Shklovsky wrote, 'The technique of art is to make objects "unfamiliar", to make forms difficult' and 'poetic speech is *formed speech*' (1965, 12, 23). The phrase *differentia specifica* was famously used by Roman Jakobson (1960/1985, 147) to refer to the special nature of poetic language. 'Systems of genres', 'devices', 'motifs', and 'rhythms' are typical examples of the vocabulary and topics of Russian Formalist literary analysis.

16. WordPress may be run locally on servers under the control of an individual or organization through open source software downloaded and installed from WordPress.org. Running the PHP and MySQL files of the platform on a local server leads to the problems I indicate of continually keeping the system up to date and adjusting themes. However, WordPress is also commonly implemented through the hosting provider WordPress.com, which provides free WordPress sites on its servers. In this case, the user does not have to update the system or worry as much about adjusting theme files, but the cost is that the ability to experiment with form is constrained to mixing and matching off-the-shelf themes (with such fine control features as custom CSS style sheets, for example, available only with a paid account). ('CSS' stands for Cascading Style Sheets, the standard formatting language and protocol for controlling the presentation of online documents structured through markup languages such as HTML.)

17. A clear exception is John Frow's chapter on 'Digital Genres' in the forthcoming revised edition of his *Genre*. Frow includes detailed discussion of such online discourse genres

as email, blogs, and microblogs. (My thanks to Frow for the draft manuscript of his chapter.)

18. For example, Sperberg-McQueen and Burnard's influential 'A Gentle Introduction to XML' declares that 'XML is more interested in the meaning of data than in its presentation' (2013, Section 5.1). The stronger phrasing in an earlier version was, 'XML focuses on the meaning of data, not its presentation.'

19. For my fuller discussion of these design issues, see the chapter titled 'Information Is Style' in Liu 2004.

20. On explanations that have been offered for the rise of the codex into cultural dominance, see Hall 2004, 7–8. He discusses the argument of Guglielmo Cavallo that early Christians from the lower and middle classes grew accustomed to the codex through the notebooks they used for everyday and commercial business.

21. I should make it clear, of course, that my knowledge of contemporary physics and cosmological theory is a layman's informed by some of today's articulate public-intellectual scientists who try to explain such theory in nonmathematical terms. My summary below (limited by my own understanding, and possibly misunderstanding) is especially informed by books from Greene (2000, 2005); Hawking (1998); Herbert (1985); Kaku (1994, 2006); and Kaku and Thompson (1995).

## Works cited

Blanchette, Jean-François. (2011a). '"Infrastructural" Thinking as Core Computing Skill'. Presentation at the Digital Humanities 2011 Conference, Stanford University, Palo Alto, CA, 21 June.

Blanchette, Jean-François. (2011b). 'A Material History of Bits'. *Journal of the American Society for Information Science and Technology* 62, no. 6: 1042–57.

Breisinger, Marc, and James K. Ford. (2006). 'Research Report on FogScreen'. *Transliteracies Project*, 12 March. Available at: http://transliteracies.english.ucsb.edu.

Bulger, Monica. (2006). 'Beyond Search: A Preliminary Skill Set for Online Literacy'. *Transliteracies Project*, 13 September. Available at: http://transliteracies.english.ucsb.edu.

Carr, Nicholas. (2010). *The Shallows: What the Internet Is Doing to Our Brains*. New York: W. W. Norton.

Caufield, Brian. (2009). 'The Longest Tweet in History'. *Forbes*, 9 July. Available at: http://www.forbes.com.

Cavallo, Guglielmo. (1999). 'Between Volumen and Codex: Reading in the Roman World'. In *A History of Reading in the West*, ed. Guglielmo Cavallo and Roger Chartier, trans. Lydia G. Cochrane, 64–89. Amherst: University of Massachusetts Press.

Cecire, Natalia. (2011). 'Introduction: Theory and the Virtues of Digital Humanities'. *Journal of Digital Humanities* 1, no. 1: 44–53. Available at: http://journalofdigitalhumanities.org/files/jdh_1_1.pdf.

Dames, Nicholas. (2007). *The Physiology of the Novel: Reading, Neural Science, and the Form of Victorian Fiction*. Oxford: Oxford University Press.

Deleuze, Gilles, and Félix Guattari. (1987). *A Thousand Plateaus: Capitalism and Schizophrenia*. Trans. Brian Massumi. Minneapolis: University of Minnesota Press.

#DHPoco (Postcolonial Digital Humanities). (nd.). Home page. Available at: http://dhpoco.org.

Drucker, Johanna. (2007). 'The Virtual Codex from Page Space to E-space'. In *A Companion to Digital Literary Studies*, ed. Ray Siemens and Susan Schreibman, 216–32. Malden, MA: Blackwell.

Elfenbein, Andrew. (2006). 'Cognitive Science and the History of Reading'. *PMLA* 121, no. 2: 484–502.

Elfenbein, Andrew. (2007). 'The Humanities and the Science of Comprehension'. Presentation for Transliteracies Project, University of California, Santa Barbara, 3 May.

Fahey, Jonathan. (2011). 'Google Reveals Energy Use to Show Search Is Green'. *Yahoo News*, 8 September. Available at: http://news.yahoo.com.

French National Research Agency. (nd.). 'Métamorphoses des sociétés. Emergences et évolutions des cultures et des phénomènes culturels. (CULT) 2012: projet TRANSLIT'. Available at: http://www.agence-nationale-recherche.fr.

Frow, John. (2006). *Genre*. London: Routledge.

Greene, Brian. (1999/2000). *The Elegant Universe: Superstrings, Hidden Dimensions, and the Quest for the Ultimate Theory*. New York: Vintage.

Greene, Brian. (2005). *The Fabric of the Cosmos: Space, Time, and the Texture of Reality*. New York: Vintage Books.

Habermas, Jürgen. (1989). *The Structural Transformation of the Public Sphere: An Inquiry into a Category of Bourgeois Society*. Trans. Thomas Burger with Frederick Lawrence. Cambridge, MA: MIT Press.

Hall, Stuart G. (2004). 'In the Beginning Was the Codex: The Early Church and Its Revolutionary Books'. In *The Church and the Book: Papers Read at the 2000 Summer Meeting and the 2001 Winter Meeting of the Ecclesiastical History Society*, ed. R. N. Swanson, 1–10. Woodbridge, UK: Boydell & Brewer, 2004.

Harvey, David. (1989). *The Condition of Postmodernity: An Enquiry into the Origins of Cultural Change*. Oxford: Basil Blackwell.

Hawking, Stephen. (1998). *A Brief History of Time*. 10th ed. New York: Bantam.

Hayles, N. Katherine. (2007). 'Hyper and Deep Attention: The Generational Divide in Cognitive Modes'. *Profession 2007*: 187–99.

Hayles, N. Katherine. (2010). 'How We Read: Close, Hyper, Machine'. *ADE Bulletin*, no. 150: 62–79.

Herbert, Nick. (1985). *Quantum Reality: Beyond the New Physics*. New York: Anchor.

Herzhoff, Jan. (2009). 'The ICT Convergence Discourse in the Information Systems Literature: A Second-Order Observation'. *ECIS 2009 Proceedings*. Paper 407. 8 June. Available at: http://csrc.lse.ac.uk.

Hofstadter, Douglas, and the Fluid Analogies Research Group. (1995). *Fluid Concepts and Creative Analogies: Computer Models of the Fundamental Mechanisms of Thought*. New York: Basic Books.

*The Independent*. (2011). 'Karl Lagerfeld Denies Involvement in Paper Perfume'. 26 April. Available at: http://www.independent.co.uk.

INKE: Implementing New Knowledge Environments. (2013). *Home page*. Available at: http://www.inke.ca.

Jakobson, Roman. (1960/1985). 'Closing Statement: Linguistics and Poetics'. In *Semiotics: An Introductory Anthology*, ed. Robert E. Innis, 147–75. Bloomington: Indiana University Press.

Kaiser, Alfons. (2011). 'Lagerfeld: Mit einer fettigen Note'. *Frankfurter Allgemeine Zeitung*, 16 April. Available at: http://www.faz.net.

Kaku, Michio. (1994). *Hyperspace: A Scientific Odyssey Through Parallel Universes, Time Warps, and the Tenth Dimension*. New York: Doubleday.

Kaku, Michio. (2006). *Parallel Worlds: A Journey Through Creation, Higher Dimensions, and the Future of the Cosmos*. New York: Anchor.

Kaku, Michio, and Jennifer Thompson. (1995). *Beyond Einstein: The Cosmic Quest for the Theory of the Universe*. Rev. ed. New York: Anchor Books.

'Katherine'. (2012). 'Nose in a Book: "In the Library" by CB I Hate Perfume and "Paper Passion" by Geza Schoen'. *Mad Perfumista*, 24 April. Available at: http://madperfumista.com.

Katz, Jon. (1997). 'Birth of a Digital Nation'. *Wired* 5.04, April. Sequence of eight web pages beginning at: http://www.wired.com/wired/archive/5.04/netizen.html.

Kirschenbaum, Matthew G. (2008). *Mechanisms: New Media and the Forensic Imagination*. Cambridge, MA: MIT Press.

Knight, Kim A. (2006). 'Research Report on the Coh-Metrix Project'. *Transliteracies Project*, 15 September. Available at: http://transliteracies.english.ucsb.edu.

Liu, Alan. (2004). *The Laws of Cool: Knowledge Work and the Culture of Information*. Chicago: University of Chicago Press.

Liu, Alan. (2012a). 'Translitteraties: le big bang de la lecture en ligne'. Trans. Françoise Bouillot. *E-Dossiers de l'audiovisuel*, January. INA Expert. Available at: http://www.ina -expert.com.

Liu, Alan. (2012b). 'Where Is Cultural Criticism in the Digital Humanities?' In *Debates in the Digital Humanities*, ed. Matthew K. Gold, 490–509. Minneapolis: University of Minnesota Press.

Liu, Alan. (2013). 'From Reading to Social Computing'. In *Literary Studies in the Digital Age: An Evolving Anthology*, ed. Kenneth M. Price and Ray Siemens (n.p.). MLA Commons. Modern Language Association of America. Available at: http://dlsanthology.commons .mla.org.

Nicolis, Grégoire, and Ilya Prigogine. (1989). *Exploring Complexity: An Introduction*. New York: W. H. Freeman.

Nielsen, Jakob. (1999). *Designing Web Usability: The Practice of Simplicity*. Indianapolis: New Riders.

Nielsen, Jakob. (2006). 'F-Shaped Pattern for Reading Web Content'. *Nielsen Norman Group*, 17 April. Available at: http://www.nngroup.com.

Piper, Andrew. (2012). 'The Past, Present, and Future of the Book'. *Chronicle of Higher Education* (*Chronicle Review*), 5 November. Available at: http://chronicle.com.

Plato. *Phaedrus*. (2013). Trans. Benjamin Jowett. Project Gutenberg, 15 January. Available at: http://www.gutenberg.org.

RoSE (Research-oriented Social Environment). 2012. *Home Page*. Available at: http://rose .english.ucsb.edu.

Shklovsky, Victor. (1965). 'Art as Technique'. In *Russian Formalist Criticism: Four Essays*, ed. and trans. Lee T. Lemon and Marion J. Reis, 3–24. Lincoln: University of Nebraska Press.

Silicon Valley Toxics Coalition (SVTC). (2013). *Home page*. Available at: http://svtc.org.

Smithies, James. (2014). 'Digital Humanities, Postfoundationalism, Postindustrial Culture'. *Digital Humanities Quarterly* 8, no. 1. Available at: http://www.digitalhumanities.org/dhq/ vol/8/1/000172/000172.html.

Society for Text and Discourse. (2006). 'Sixteenth Annual Meeting Program and Abstracts'. Available at: http://www.societyfortextanddiscourse.org.

Soja, Edward W. (1989). *Postmodern Geographies: The Reassertion of Space in Critical Social Theory*. London: Verso.

Sperberg-McQueen, C. M., and Lou Burnard. (2013). 'A Gentle Introduction to XML'. In *P5: Guidelines for Electronic Text Encoding and Interchange*, version 2.5.0 (26 July), by the Text Encoding Initiative Consortium (TEI), Section V. Available at: http://www.tei-c.org.

Stallybrass, Peter, Roger Chartier, J. Franklin Mowery, and Heather Wolfe. (2004). 'Hamlet's Tables and the Technologies of Writing in Renaissance England'. *Shakespeare Quarterly* 55, no. 4: 379–419.

Svenbro, Jesper. (1999). 'Archaic and Classical Greece: The Invention of Silent Reading'. In *A History of Reading in the West*, ed. Guglielmo Cavallo and Roger Chartier, trans. Lydia G. Cochrane, 37–63. Amherst: University of Massachusetts Press.

Swanstrom, Lisa. (2006). 'Research Report on the Legible City'. *Transliteracies Project*, 12 March. Available at: http://transliteracies.english.ucsb.edu.

Thomas, Sue, Chris Joseph, Jess Laccetti, Bruce Mason, Simon Mills, Simon Perril, and Kate Pullinger. (2007). 'Transliteracy: Crossing Divides'. *First Monday* 12, no. 12 (December 2007). Available at: http://firstmonday.org/article/view/2060/1908.

#transformDH (Transformative Digital Humanities). (nd.). *Home page*. Available at: http:// transformdh.org.

Transliteracies Project [University of California initiative]. (nd.). *Home page*. Available at: http://transliteracies.english.ucsb.edu.

Transliteracies Project [University of California initiative]. (nd.). 'Transliteracies Research Clearinghouse'. Available at: http://transliteracies.english.ucsb.edu.

Transliteracies Project [University of California initiative]. (2005). 'Transliteracies MRG Proposal (Abbreviated Version)'. 2 May. Available at: http://transliteracies.english.ucsb.edu.

Transliteracy Research Group [De Montfort University initiative]. (nd.). 'Transliteracy Research Group Archive, 2006–13'. Available at: http://transliteracyresearch.wordpress.com/.

Wallpaper. 2012. 'Paper Passion by Geza Schoen, Steidl, Wallpaper and Karl Lagerfeld'. 12 July. Available at: http://www.wallpaper.com.

Warner, William, Kim A. Knight, and the Transliteracies Project History of Reading Group. (2007). 'In the Beginning Was the Word: A Visualization of the Page as Interface'. Transliteracies Project. Available at: http://transliteracies.english.ucsb.edu.

# 19

# Getting There from Here

## Remembering the Future of Digital Humanities

Roberto Busa Award lecture 2013[1]

*Willard McCarty*

## Prologue

The text which follows was written as a lecture for a specific audience on a unique occasion, in a social setting that is now irretrievably gone. This setting allowed freedoms that are apt to seem out of place in the present context. But I exercised them for a reason which survives: in the spirit of Bruno Latour's advice in 'The Politics of Explanation', to foreground the struggle of making an argument rather than to give an impression of having captured some truth or other (1988: 162–3). On behalf of digital humanities I wanted to foreground the poverty of language (some would say of theory, others of criticism) that for most if not all of its history has made this struggle so difficult. As Clifford Geertz said on behalf of anthropology, 'We are reduced to insinuating theories because we lack the power to state them' (1973: 24). Whether my suggestion of a language gains purchase among those for whom the lecture was written remains to be seen. I do not insist on it as the sole possibility or even the best. But I do insist that this poverty of language should rank first among items on the agenda to be addressed and that its solution is to be found by putting the field into its historical context.

## Retrospective introduction

I am greatly honoured by the Busa Award, especially because it is given by the community of people among whom a quarter-century ago I found the intellectual home where I have thrived and prospered. I've thought long and hard about what to say: whether to present new results or to make something of how I got here from there. I've decided to do both: new results because I suffer from intellectual claustrophobia and want reactions to the cure I'm taking; retrospection because this occasion demands that a 'life of learning' be told as a meaningful story.[2]

**Retrospection first**. I cannot describe anything remotely like a career path because there was none. My trackless wanderings were affected by far too many accidents, though (I like to think) steadily driven by hunger for learning. Let me just say that I came to the PhD in Milton studies in 1976 with training in physics, English,

German and Latin literature and mathematics, and years spent as a programmer in Fortran and assembly language on some big machines. Eight years of obsessive devotion to John Milton's biblical and classical sources earned me the degree in 1984. The plan was to become a professor of English, but that didn't happen, despite powerful help. I spent a dozen years in academic limbo. While there I reverted to computing, moved into humanities computing (as we called it then),[3] learned a lot about other people's research and fell into a prolonged study of Ovid's *Metamorphoses*, by which I had become captivated. Its structure fascinated me. How, I wondered, did the poem manage so successfully to tease us with promise of structure yet always elude our grasp? Like Father Busa before me I turned to computing for help, on a smaller scale but for the same reasons.

Markup seemed the obvious way to go. SGML was the standard, TEI as yet unborn. I created my own scheme, rejecting SGML to make sure that my thinking would be as free from pre-existing theoretical commitments as possible.[4] I targeted names, which I reasoned were literary enough to tell me about structure, verbal enough to handle with a machine. Names quickly became all devices of language indicating persons. About 60,000 tags resulted, that is, an average of five per line of poetry. I worked on it both alone and with research assistants,[5] in Toronto and then in London after moving there in 1996, finally abandoning it when at last I realized that markup was radically wrong for the job, indeed that no conceivable technology would prove remotely adequate. But no matter: those years of work had already led me to the vein of gold I have been following ever since: an idea of what happens when Mr Turing's implemented idea of mathematical rigour meets the fluid, metamorphic genius of poetry.

Back up some years. In April 1987 at the International Conference for Computers and the Humanities in Columbia, South Carolina, I met Michael Sperberg-McQueen, whose eloquent rhetoric stirred up the righteous discontent of colleagues who like me were languishing on the academic periphery. *Humanist* was the result.[6] I threw myself into it, never for a moment thinking it would pay off. How wrong I was! Nearly a decade later, in 1996, Harold Short, whom I met in Toronto because of *Humanist*, changed everything by seeing to it that I was propelled quite unexpectedly across the pond into my first academic appointment, which I still hold. *Humanist* continues to be my primary academic forum.

I take the moral of this story from the great twelfth-century Jewish philosopher Moshe ben Maimon's *Commentary on the Mishnah*:

כל שאתם עושים לא תעשו אלא מאהבה

whatever you do, do it only out of love.[7]

And from the physician Thomas Fuller's *Gnomologia* (1732), I draw these helpful proverbs to hammer it home:

> He that hath Love in his Breast, hath Spurs at his Heels (2160);
> Love will creep, where it cannot go (3301);

Love lives more in Cottages than Courts (3290); and finally,
The Soul is not where it lives, but where it loves (4761).

To put the matter more personally and viscerally, I didn't walk a career path but followed the smell of food on the wind. And here I am, to say thank you all for the friendship, inspiration, sustenance, audience and now this, in the name of the great Jesuit scholar, Roberto Busa. *Mille grazie!*

But I do wonder, why me? I am a quite old-fashioned scholar, who works by himself, shuns collaborative teams and the grants that fuel them, who has written no code for decades, knows not TEI and teaches solely face to face. For many years I have insisted, contrary to Ronald Reagan when he worked as promo-man for General Electric (Reagan 1961), that failure is our most important product, partly for the shock value, as antidote to the hype of pervasive techno-triumphalism, but also to stress that computing is an ongoing, never-ending *experimental* process.[8] I've argued that the main thing is to fail so well that all you can see is Jerome McGann's 'hem of a quantum garment' (2004, 201)—a phrase he used, you may recall, to describe the intractable non-residual leftovers markup cannot capture, hence its potential for illumination.

My struggle with the *Metamorphoses* laid groundwork for my book *Humanities Computing* (2014/2005). Twenty years earlier Brian Cantwell Smith had observed that computers can only approximate reality according to a necessarily simplified, hence incorrect model of it (Smith 1985). So I could see that in principle my attempts to pin Ovid down were bound to fail. But by the time I came to think about Ovid two things had happened: progress had liberated digital computing from its confinement to mainframes, giving me a little machine of my own to play with; and I had met the great Australian ethnohistorian Greg Dening, who introduced me to the present participle (Dening 2002, 1993). So I could see that Brian had fastened on the wrong part of speech: *modelling,* not *model,* had to be the central idea. In other words I rediscovered the essential truth of the hackers' 'Hands-on Imperative' against the industrializing effects of batch-mode computing (Levy 2010/1984, 28). And so the book. But then, as always, intellectual claustrophobia took hold. By demonstrating the conceptual inadequacy of our tools, modelling the *Metamorphoses* had left me nowhere to go. And modelling itself was at once too pat an answer and unable to do more than work through consequences of interpretation that had already happened—elsewhere by other means.

Coming to the end of my own road alerted me to the others whose fate I shared, and so to wonder if I might figure a way out by finding out what it had been like for them. Hence my turn to history.

## A history of the present from an emotional past

What I found, and what I think it amounts to, forms the remainder of this lecture. But I am going to tell you a particular *kind* of story, which I learned about from Ian

Hacking (to whom I owe so much), who learned about it from Michel Foucault: a 'history of the present', Foucault called it, because it sets out to 'recognize and distinguish historical objects in order to illumine our own predicaments'.[9] Writing in 1940 with the Gestapo at his heels, Walter Benjamin put the case more starkly, just as we need it to be:

> To articulate the past historically does not mean to recognize it 'the way it really was' (Ranke). It means to seize hold of a memory as it flashes up at a moment of danger.... In every era the attempt must be made anew to wrest tradition away from a conformism that is about to overpower it.... Only that historian will have the gift of fanning the spark of hope in the past who is firmly convinced that *even the dead* will not be safe from the enemy if he wins. And this enemy has not ceased to be victorious.
>
> (1968/1955, 255)

For us the danger is that our being *of* as well as *in* the humanities remains an unanswered, even unasked, question. It is the predicament Steve Ramsay describes in *Reading Machines* (2011): the almost total grip of hermeneutical inhibitions on digital humanities, to the point of willful blindness to the centrality of interpretation. The primary historical object I want to bring into focus and call on for help with this predicament is the uncanny *otherness* of computing, its anomalous existential ambiguity. I will argue that the surviving evidence of fear this otherness once provoked, and continues occasionally to stir up, is a clue to a common ground with the humanities beyond utilitarian value or social impact.

But to avoid misunderstanding I must pause a moment to clarify what I mean by *fear*. The difficulty I have begins with a reluctance I think we share: to admit fear or attribute it to anyone whom we respect, in particular (given our profession) fear of computing. When the subject comes up, as it will in this lecture again and again, reluctance may bolster the common assumption that the emotions are natural or at least fixed psychological kinds and are an interference to, rather than component of, intelligence. In ordinary life we are wiser: thus the *Oxford English Dictionary* glosses the word as denoting 'all degrees of the emotion'[10] that (like the Devil) is known under so many names. I need the continuum this implies to be able to make sense of the historical actors and actions that are the focus of attention here, and so cannot risk the assumption that fear has an objective taxonomy of clear-cut and stable distinctions. It simply doesn't, as its history and current research in psychology demonstrate.[11] So in the following let us agree that *fear* has many guises, and—allow me to go out on a limb—that the presence of one degree of it does not preclude the presence, however hidden, of others.

I concentrate on fear rather than positive emotional response because dystopic visions of computing and reactions to them tell us far more about the psychological, intellectual and professional disruptions it brought about (see, for example, Hatfield 1928, 10). These were not just to the humanities and other technologically undereducated cohorts. The fearful threat of profound change was felt likewise in the sciences. Thus in the early 1970s the physicist Leon Kowarski, writing about 'The Impact of Computers on Nuclear Science', expressed much the same existential and cognitive worries as did his humanist colleagues:

> The vision of these huge and costly machines...is in a way terrifying. The era of the ingenious scientist...seems to be past. The machine will have to run just 'because it is there', and according to its own rules. And from each run—there will be not much sense in calling them experiments any more—there will be a rich harvest of recorded data, like a deep-sea dredge.... There will be a lot of attempts to judge such new situations by old value criteria. What is a physicist? What is an experimenter?...Is the man who accumulates print-outs of solved equations a mathematical physicist? And the ultimate worry: are we not going to use computers as a substitute for thinking?[12]

Furthermore, I will argue, the fear this threat provoked, though negative, is more than simply negative: it is in fear's nature to fore-feel the unknown, the new, the anomalous, as I said, the uncanny.[13]

I begin where I will end, in the digital humanities, first by probing its professional literature. Then I will move outward in three stages, expanding the historical context as I go: first to daily life during the early period; then to the scientific programme from which computing arose; then very briefly (and *very* ambitiously) to an historical process that Agamben, with reference to our current preoccupation, calls the anthropological machine (2004/2002). I shall concentrate on literary computing to simplify, I hope not falsify, the bigger picture.

## Shall we come rejoicing?

Allow me first to moralize a bit more, this time to advance the cause of acquisitive hunger for learning. This hunger is obviously one of my besetting sins. But I have a good reason for not repenting, despite good advice that I simply say what *I* think. In fact this *is* the way I think, by assembling scraps from other disciplines and making a kind of intellectual quilt suitable for our radically interdisciplinary and quite immature amalgam of interests.[14] Nelson Goodman has observed that quotation is a tool of worldmaking (1978, 56). We have a world to make.

Do you know the biblical story of Ruth the Moabite, of her gleaning in Boaz's field in order to feed her mother-in-law and herself? So, I say, are we: Ruth-like as a young discipline, migrants in need of the food of others, which is lying on the ground, that is, in libraries and online, freely for the taking, in seemingly endless and compelling abundance.

Make no mistake: we are *surrounded* by mature, subtle civilizations of enquiry, whose intellectual resources dwarf our own in volume, variety and sophistication. I think, for example, of philosopher Myles Burnyeat's 'Message from Heraclitus' (2012/1982) or of G. E. R. Lloyd's *Cognitive Variations* (2007; Inwood and McCarty 2010). I wonder, after catching my breath, when will *we* be able to write with such deep and far-reaching power? We may be smart, with the wind in our sails, but raw intellect alone and popularity aren't enough. Being in possession of our own island of knowledge, autonomous, with our own agenda (when at last we have one), conferences and publications, all that is necessary *but not enough*. We need far more than the luck of the moment, dozens of sessions at the MLA, THATCamps everywhere, millions of tweets, thousands of blogs and so on and so forth. We need *resonance* with the intellectual cultures of the arts and humanities, just as a great organ needs an acoustically adequate space for its music to move the listener. (There, that's me, saying *exactly* what I think.)

We need the techno-sciences just as much, more than many of us realize, more than some of us fear. Scientism is a problem, but without the sciences we denature the technological side of our discipline by severing it from its epistemological roots. We turn our backs on a literature full of wonders, on intellectual excitement and real help. We need to understand, for example, the implications of introducing experiment—which is exactly what we do—into the humanities.[15] And we need to recognize the other 'styles of scientific reasoning', as Hacking has called them (2002), which have come into the humanities via the back door of computing (McCarty 2008).

We have much to learn from the technologically aware artists such as Stelarc[16] and Marcel-lí Antúnez Roca,[17] who are far less confused about the sciences than we seem to be. Both of them performed at the recent IEEE International Conference on Robotics and Automation, where a number of us spoke (please note: at the invitation of the roboticists) on 'Robotics and the Humanities'.[18] I was reminded of the 1968 *Cybernetic Serendipity* exhibition in London, at which artists and engineers experimented with ideas so far ahead of their time they remain mostly ahead of ours.[19]

We have much to learn as well from the scholar-writers with strong scientific interests, such as Gillian Beer, who works on Darwin (2009/1983); Laura Otis, on nineteenth-century technology (2001); and A. S. Byatt (2005, 2000), whose fascination with the sciences informs her fiction. And near at hand is the disciplinary bridge built by historians, philosophers and sociologists of science, opened to us in the early 1960s when, in Hacking's words, philosophers 'finally unwrapped the cadaver [they had made of science] and saw the remnants of an historical process of becoming and discovering' (1983, 1). To many of us, alas, there is *still* only the cadaver. Some hallucinate a zombie.

Where and what are we amidst all this abundance? Do we even know it exists? I've imagined us as maritime explorers in an archipelago of disciplines, peripatetic, prowling the margins; I've imagined us with the novelist David Malouf, adventurous youth discovering life and death in a wild, dangerous acre of bush (McCarty 2006); with Greg Dening, 'on the edge of things in a great ring of viewers' (1998, 183); with historian Peter Galison, in the trading zone (Gorman 2010), or as Dening says, on the 'beaches of the mind' (1998, 85–88). And this is why I am so pleased to have been named at Digital Humanities 2013 the 'Obi-Wan Kenobi of digital humanities':[20] to be honoured for the marginal, peripatetic life of learning I have been able to lead and continue, *deo volente*, to live with you.

I am pleased to have been considered, just for that moment now gone, an eremitic elder possessed of powers beyond the ordinary, kindly but serious and *not to be messed with.* I am thrilled to be linked through Obi-Wan to Sir Alec Guinness, who made the part come alive (and had the good sense to shun the connection later). When Sir Alec was interviewed on the BBC Radio 4 programme *Desert Island Discs* in 1977, just prior to the release of *Star Wars*, he was asked what role he was playing in that film.[21] He answered, 'I don't know what I play—a wise old—an allegedly wise old character from outer space.' But however Obi-Wan'ish, I cannot agree to 'wise'; 'old' I will not admit to; and as far as I know, I came into the world in the way of all flesh and was raised in a small California town, though (I understand from the locals) flying saucers have been seen in the area.[22]

## Courting catastrophe

But now back to Earth, to the present, to our world-building. The raw material is abundantly to hand. What do we do with it? What governs the design of our quilt?

After a talk at Cambridge in 2012 I was asked by the historian of ancient science Geoffrey Lloyd one of those questions I live to be asked: where would we be with our digital scholarship in 20 years? On what did I think our sights could be set most ambitiously? What I fumbled then to say I am still fumbling with, but here's another go.

I spoke earlier of computing's otherness—a more dramatic way of referring to the distancing effect Julia Flanders has gently called 'productive unease' (2009). She makes a strong case for the contribution of the digital humanities in foregrounding 'issues of how we model the sources we study, in such a way that [these issues] cannot be sidestepped' (2009, 22). I know this to be true from long experience unable to sidestep them. But what about those for whom digital resources are made, who aren't themselves makers? I know I'm not the first to find fault with principles of design that conceal the difficulties and provide no means of struggling with them. There are deep, tough questions here as to how and at what level the essential struggle is enacted. But Flanders's point remains: *the struggle is the point of it all.* And we do *not,* or should not, emerge from it unscathed! (Again and again I will insist on this: being scathed is paradoxically our salvation.) Love may be 'an ever-fixéd mark'; we humans aren't. If we are not changed in response to computing, we imprison ourselves with it.

This struggle is a nascent form of reasoning that we have done for millennia with tools. But the potential—here is the answer to Lloyd's question—is for reasoning to evolve in concert with a radically adaptive tool, something more than the steersman's tiller that inspired cybernetics,[23] less perhaps than a conversational partner—but almost that, or perhaps exactly that. As we get close to conversational machines, our attempts produce, in Robert Hughes's famous phrase, 'the shock of the new'.[24] We share with the roboticists the chance, in Warren McCulloch's words, to ride the shock wave by engaging deliberately with 'that miscegenation of Art and Science which begets inanimate objects that behave like living systems' (1968, 9). I call the result *catastrophic* in Stephen Jay Gould's evolutionary sense, as that which punctuates the equilibrium of which we are a living part and so initiates developmental change.[25]

Such catastrophe implies a deep, not merely utilitarian, relationship between machine and human. Again the artists are there. In 1935 the Polish artist Bruno Schulz compared the work of art to a baby *in statu nascendi*, in the midst of being born, still operating 'at a premoral depth'. 'The role of art', he wrote, 'is to be a probe sunk into the nameless' (1998/1935, 368–70). What comes out is uncannily us and other, or to put it another way, an invitation to a becoming. So also for technologies. Those who attended the ACH-ALLC conference at Queen's in 1997 will have heard the Canadian cognitive psychologist Merlin Donald describe how from earliest times we have externalized ourselves in tools that have then remade us by changing what we can do, how we see the world and each other (Donald 1991). Thus the technological shape of early biocultural co-evolution in concert with material affordances, as Gary Tomlinson has argued for music (2013). Laura Otis, whom I mentioned earlier, has traced just such an interrelation of inventor and invention much closer to our own time in communication technologies and ideas of human neurophysiology from the mid-nineteenth century (Otis 2001).

In the twentieth century, computer and brain formed just such a co-developmental relation, or what Ian Hacking, in a very different context, calls 'looping effects' (1995): from Alan Turing's abstract machine in 1936, itself based on how a bureaucrat would do his sums,[26] to Warren McCulloch's and Walter Pitt's model of the brain as a Turing machine (1943); from their neurophysiological model to John von Neumann's computer architecture (1945), which he, inspired by McCulloch and Pitts, described in neurophysiological terms (Aspray 1990, 40, 180–81); and from that architecture to a modular conception of mind which reflected it (for example, Fodor 1983). Back and forth, back and forth. In 1948 von Neumann proposed that the problem of imitating natural intelligence might better be done 'with a network that will fit into the actual volume of the human brain' (1951, 34; 1958, 48). At the time of writing, the DARPA SyNAPSE program is working towards precisely that goal,[27] using neuromorphic hardware which reflects current ideas of neurological plasticity.[28] The pace of development is now so fast that neurophysiological models of consciousness and architectures of computing are a blurry chicken-and-egg. But that's precisely my point: the traffic between self-conception and invention goes in a loop. I want to ask what we can do to make that loop go for us and for the humanities.

## Stalemate

Another bit of autobiography to get us there.

By the time I was done with *Humanities Computing*, McGann had come up with some powerful theories we might use to get us moving beyond the forecourts of interpretation, where from the perspective of the interpretative disciplines digital humanities had stalled early in its development.[29] Being stuck myself, I went for his gift basket of theories but could not see any rationale for choice. Since theories to some degree set forth the direction of future research and embody assumptions about the world in which they operate, choice is crucial, the wrong choice potentially ruinous. To ask whether the research of a field should go in the direction expressed or implied by a theory, practitioners must have a good idea of where the field has been. They need history.[30]

I decided to focus on the history of what I will call the incunabular period, from a beginning in the late 1940s to the public release of the Web in 1991. I had two reasons: the period is neatly delimited, but more importantly it defines a time we have good cause to believe was formative.[31] This gave me confidence to think that despite the dramatic changes brought about by the Web, I could determine at least some parameters for a trajectory and so uncover a range of genuine possibilities for the future.

I found abundant raw material for such a history in the professional literature,[32] but constraints of time force me to give only the briefest sketch here.

Within the incunabular period the relevant literature in the Anglophone world defines a core of three decades, from the early 1960s to the early 1990s. These decades are bracketed by two pairs of evaluative statements. The authors of the first pair argued that the then-dominant use of computing to alleviate drudgery was skewing the focus of research towards problems of drudgery and away from imaginative exploration (Masterman 1962; Milic 1966). The authors of the second pair, summing up what had been done by 1991, argued that the field had failed in its ambitions, that its work had been steadfastly ignored by mainstream scholars because it was theory-poor (Potter 1991) or wrongly directed and should turn to what Franco Moretti was almost a decade later to call 'distant reading' (Olsen 1991).[33] During those three decades Busa was among the very few who insisted that the point was not saving labour but 'more human work, more mental effort... to know, more systematically, deeper, and better' (1976, 3). Few insisted along with him that the point was not to design for efficient service but to realize that computing was something altogether new and to find out what that was. The brilliant experiments of cybernetic artists to which I referred earlier, not just in London but also in Zagreb, Paris, New York, Sydney and elsewhere, gave glimpses of what could be done with very little. Thus the poignancy of Busa's question in 1976 on behalf of philology: 'Why can a computer do so little?'

From his analytic, philological perspective Busa pointed to the sophistication of human language. His response serves well to explain why the pioneering work in computational stylistics, first by John Burrows, then also Hugh Craig, David Hoover, Tomoji Tabata, Jan Rybicki and others, and now for literary history by Matt Jockers (2013) and former colleagues at the Stanford LitLab,[34] has been long in the oven. It is the great exception to the stalemate that concerns me here. It is exceptional, and really should rock our colleagues, because it has produced 'mounting evidence', as Burrows has said, that literature is probabilistic—hence that the most elusive of cultural qualities behaves in roughly the same way as both the natural and social worlds.[35] But the cause of this work's obscurity to most of us—fear of the mathematical—returns us to the stalemate that concerns me here. What is it about numbers that frightens us away? What are we frightened of? What does this fright tell us about our relationship to digital machinery?

Let me work towards an answer by revising Busa's question: not why can the computer do so little, but why were those historical scholars doing so little with it? What was stopping or inhibiting them? We know, thanks to the cybernetic artists, that primitive kit cannot be blamed and that the kit itself had as much or more potential to inspire and excite creative work as it did to inhibit. We know from those who experimented that the concerns of the humanities were a fertile ground for experiment with computing.[36] We know that at the time a few saw what was not being done and were distressed.

As the evidence shows,[37] computer-using scholars commonly worried about lack of progress and its causes. Blame for the problem was variously fixed. But what matters historically and tells us far more of use to us now is not the causes they assigned but the fact of their persistent worrying, repeatedly, from the early 1960s on. Sensitivity to this fact foregrounds the anomalous expressions of concern about computing not merely in the professional literature of digital humanities but scattered all across the academic and popular writings of the time. However directed to whatever subject, these expressions of concern looked to an unknown future with varying degrees of predictive assertiveness and disquiet. Then as now the popular press exaggerated both, and by doing that showed that a nerve had been touched.[38] It is easy for the knowledgeable practitioner to dismiss such reactions, as Parrish did in 1962 when he scorned the fearful who, he alleged, were indulging themselves 'with terrors that are meaningless to people who know anything about computers' (1962, 2). But as I have suggested, even techno-scientific competence was no shield to the important and significant fear of the computer becoming human. Supposed evidence, formed as such in no small measure by thinking of the human in computational terms, made this becoming seem inevitable.

In an old but still valuable 'synthetic genetic study' of fear, pioneering child psychologist G. Stanley Hall wrote that the emotion is 'not prevision but only a highly generalized fore-feeling...a primitive *Anlage* of futurity' (1914, 149). I quote him not merely to underscore congruence between two forward-looking kinds of imaginative activity, computing (by design) and fear (by nature). Rather, as I suggested earlier, I want to complete my rescue of the emotion from dismissal as only, purely negative, therefore unhelpful. Thus his crucial point for my purposes: 'but for fear pain could do little of its prodigious educative work in the animal world. Fear is thus...*the chief spur of psychic evolution*' (my emph.). I will return to human psychic evolution later. For now let us agree that fear is a treasure to the historian, if a mixed blessing to those afflicted.

Fear was variously expressed in the professional literature of digital humanities: fear of the distortions computing would work on the humanities if taken seriously, evinced by the work and words of those who did take it seriously;[39] fear of its mechanization of scholarship,[40] parallel to the mechanization of which public intellectuals had been warning;[41] fear of its revolutionary force, threatening to cast aside old-fashioned ways of thinking, as literary scholar Stephen Parrish declared was about to happen;[42] and fear expressed in reassurances, such as literary critic Alan Markman's, that the computer is no threat to scholarship or a dehumanizing machine to be feared (1965, 79), or historian Franklin Pegues' in a review of the conference at which Parrish spoke, that all would be well, that the scholar still had a role to play and would not be put out of work (1965, 107). It was fundamentally an existential angst, a 'fear and trembling', as one scholar said (Nold 1975), quoting Søren Kirkegaard.

How do we explain such evidence? Here is where the harder task of history-writing begins, in the first of the two dilations I promised earlier: outward from the professional literature, heavily filtered by academic decorum, into the social setting in which our predecessors lived. Blaming (as some have done) a bogey-man of their particular disliking—French critical theory is a favourite among empiricists—only grants it causal powers it did not have.[43] All were part of the same world. What was that world like? Our predecessors were ordinary people as we are, living more or less ordinary lives. What was ordinary life like for them?

Readings can be taken in various ways, for example from imaginative literature of the time, including science fiction, or from the cinema. Best for my purposes are the ambient bearers of information we can plausibly assume ordinary people, including academics, would have encountered casually, accidentally in daily life: newspapers and magazines, neighbours, shopkeepers, radio and television. The abundance I must skip over is painful to omit, as it conjures the scene so effectively. Let me recommend that you seek out a few images that the complications of copyright and expense of reproduction prevent me from offering you: some utopic, some dystopic, with which the media were then saturated.[44] First the utopic: the computer depicted in *Saturday Evening Post* for 16 December 1950 in an advert, 'Oracle on 57th Street', showing a giant Sibylline figure sitting atop IBM World Headquarters in Manhattan, a scroll of printout tumbling from her outstretched arms; the computer as 'giant brain' (a viral phrase at the time) in Boris Artzybasheff's *Time Magazine* cover for 2 April 1965; the computer, shown on the scale of the room-sized ENIAC, ejecting a greeting card with a red heart on it for the operator, a woman alone in the room, on the cover of *The New Yorker*'s Valentine's Day issue, 11 February 1961; and, in a Marvel Comic advert, a child's toy, 'miracle of the modern space age . . . . an actual working digital computer' designed and marketed by Edmund Callis Berkeley, author of *Giant Brains, or Machines that Think* (1949). Then the opposite of these: a photograph of the darkened control room of the Semi-Automatic Ground Environment (SAGE) system with the Whirlwind computer at its core, in effect a giant military cyborg for defence of the United States against nuclear attack, fictionalized in *War Games* (1983);[45] the computer on the cover of *Processed World* 12 (1984) as hydra-like PC automator of office work attacking a woman at her desk with its many tentacles while her boss looks on; a looming mainframe tape drive in an advert for the Electronic Computer Programming Institute, in the *Pittsburgh Press* for 6 November 1966, proclaiming 'Let this machine give you a new career before it takes away your old one'; and finally a photograph of a woman inside a mainframe, looking startled, accompanying an article by Warren R. Young in *Life Magazine* for 3 March 1961: 'The Machines Are Taking Over. Computers outdo man at his work now—and soon may outthink him.' Such images and sentiments were commonplace.

Granted: neither emotional extreme, jubilation or terror, were at all likely to have been observed in persons who viewed these images. What seems more likely would have been the feeling expressed in 1969 by the director of an intensive summer programme for disadvantaged students at Harvard, Yale and Columbia, Gordon K. Davies, who expressed 'the most typical anxiety concerning man's relation to computers': the fear of oneself being reduced to data processing cards. He wrote, 'we must be careful, or we shall all become rectangles of cardboard with holes punched in them' (Davies 1969, 283).

All of this, whether at home or at work, was enframed and informed by the defining context of computing in its infancy, the Cold War—so named by George Orwell two months after the atom bomb was dropped on Nagasaki, 9 August 1945.[46] Again, forced to be briefer than I would like, I offer another sampling of material typical of the time: a vividly illustrated *Life Magazine* article of 1950 based on a plan for survival of nuclear attack, hatched by Norbert Wiener and two colleagues from the History Department at MIT, with reference to the contemporary British film *Seven Days to Noon* (LM 1950); a 1961 article in *Reader's Digest* reporting on the widely publicized near miss of 5 October 1960, when an incorrect software model caused the rising moon to be falsely identified as a massive Soviet missile attack;[47] a paper in 1985 for the Symposium on Unintentional Nuclear War, in which Brian Cantwell Smith demonstrated that in principle no fool-proof system was possible—that there would always be another such moon-rise, as he said.[48] Children on both sides of the Atlantic (I, like historian Spencer Weart, was one of these) practiced variants of 'duck and cover', diving under desks in school to be ready for the bomb;[49] adults were instructed via Civil Defense bulletins and films.[50] Stanley Kubrick's *Dr Strangelove* (1964) told a story we recognized because we were almost living it.

## What the thunder said

What do we make of all this?

First the obvious: that the Cold War gives us a good if partial explanation for scholars' timidity in the real or imagined presence of mainframe systems that were *other* to most humanists because physically, culturally alien and obviously complicit. But it also helps to explain the curious departure of the scholarly mainstream from the kinds of enquiry computing was most nearly suited for just at the time when computers became available.[51] Anthony Kenny has speculated that the majority turned away from computing to critical theory in fear of quantification (1992, 9–10). There's truth to that guess, just as there is reason behind practitioners' opposition to abstract theory, but both underplay the positive, indeed visionary hunger for theorizing as a liberating practice (for example, Hooks 1994, 59). Students were, as one said, *theory-hungry* (Bowlby 2013, 32). The evidence suggests that they and their theorizing professors did not so much flee from computing as run towards and embrace new, powerful means of asking (in Terry Eagleton's words) 'the most embarrassingly general and fundamental questions, regarding [routine social practices] with a wondering estrangement which we...have forgotten'.[52] The mechanizers had nothing for them.

The public release of the Web in 1991, coinciding almost exactly with the end of the Cold War, was a radical game changer.[53] But as others have remarked, the Web did not address the stalemate in analytical computing, rather it shifted attention to the great stocking of the virtual shelves. The Web buried the problem rather than solved it, and by being so very useful and saleable to colleagues, Web-based resources did little to bring our discipline in from the cold intellectually.

Hence, with the thrusting of digital humanities into the limelight, the old complaints and problems have resurfaced unresolved: first, the internal relation of theorizing to making, and of scholarship to technical skills; second, the external relation of digital practices to the techno-sciences on the one hand and to the non-technical humanities on the other; third, the still unknown basis for a 'normal discourse' (Rorty 1979, 320) that would allow us to speak coherently to each other and to others. Alan Liu (2011) and Fred Gibbs (2011) have both asked the question I am struggling here to answer: where is the criticism in the digital humanities? Where indeed? The danger is temptation 'to trope away from specificity and to generalize hyperbolically...through an extremely abstract mode of discourse that may at times serve as a surrogate' for experience (LaCapra 1998, 23). Ungrounded theorizing is as much an enemy as no theorizing at all. But the absence Liu and Gibbs illumine is the theoretical poverty I spoke of at the beginning. It was noted at the end of the incunabular period by Rosanne Potter in her survey of previous work (1991). This poverty vexes us still. It may seem with all the activity we are witnessing, so much we cannot see it all, that the long-awaited revolution has begun (Jockers 2013, 3–4). But actually it's been proclaimed before—e.g., by literary critic Stephen Parrish at the first conference in the field in 1964[54]—but then 'postponed owing to technical difficulties' (Mahoney 2011, 56). The truth is that the great cognitive revolution for us has not begun even once. Natalia Cecire is right on when she argues that for humanities *plus* computing the central problematic—Bachelard's 'matrix or angle from which it will become possible and even necessary to formulate a certain number of precise problems' (Maniglier 2012)—is that *plus*; so far, as she says, we've construed the joining to be merely additive rather than transformative (Cecire 2011, 55). The growing mass of well-presented data is continuing to change conditions of scholarly work, and with them (I suspect) much else, but this is *not* addressing the old problem of how we are *of* the humanities. It does not help us with what that *plus* means, what it portends, what it entails.

That's why I've embarked on a history of the present. Such a history demands use of the past to point the way forward. If long ago scholars came to the crossroads, to that plus sign, and were frightened either into retreating or into reducing the challenges of the machine to something comfortable, like minimizing drudgery or mining data; if we find now that we are still there wondering what to do analytically but cannot, despite healthy scepticism, shake the sense that what we know to do is only a poor beginning; then that old fright is a treasure to be *used*, not just understood. It directs us to the uncanny moment; what matters is our response to it, as Benjamin said. What matters is our trajectory into the future.

When Father Busa asked why the computer could do 'so little' for philology, he meant in relation to the 'monumental services' done elsewhere, especially in the sciences. In the mid-1960s, in artificial intelligence, machine translation and humanities computing, the honeymoon period came almost simultaneously to an end.[55] All three suffered 'notorious disappointments', as Cambridge Lucasian Professor Sir James Lighthill said of machine translation in 1972 (Lighthill 1973/1972, 10). His sentence for AI can stand for them all: 'In no part of the field have the discoveries made so far produced the major impact that was then promised'.[56] (8). But note: AI absorbed the shock and continued; computational linguistics was born out of machine translation and thrived; digital humanities, as a theoretical, critically self-aware and persuasive discipline, remained *in potentia*.[57] Changing the name from 'humanities computing' and being popular with the boys and girls does not solve the fundamental problem.

And so my second dilation: from the social world of digital humanists circa 1949–91, to the world from which digital computing arose, that of the technosciences, first as we know them now, then as they have been since Bacon and Galileo.

The extent of computing's influence on these sciences is unabashedly summarized by philosopher Paul Humphreys in his book *Extending Ourselves: Computational Science, Empiricism, and Scientific Method* (2004).[58] Because of computing, Humphreys observes, 'scientific epistemology is no longer human epistemology' (2004, 8). He concludes in language reminiscent of Milton's *Paradise Lost*: 'The Copernican Revolution first removed humans from their position at the center of the physical universe, and science has now driven humans from the center of the epistemological universe.'[59] Whether he is right is for my purposes beside the point. What matters is his language, specifically his echo of Adam and Eve's expulsion from Paradise.[60] What's going on?

The best known and most fruitful pronouncement of the kind is Sigmund Freud's. Twice in 1917 he declared that scientific research had precipitated three great crises in human self-conception, or as he put it, three 'great outrages' ('große Kränkungen'):[61] first, as with Humphreys, by Copernican cosmology, which decentred humankind; then by Darwinian evolution, which dethroned us, setting in motion discoveries of how intimately we belong to life; and finally by his own psychoanalysis, which showed we are not even masters of own minds. Less often noticed is his suggestion (implicit in the German *Kränkung*, from *krank*, 'ill, sick, diseased') that these dis-easings of mind can be turned to therapeutic effect. We are apt to see only the physician here, but Freud was in fact showing his inheritance from the whole moral tradition of the physical sciences. At least from Bacon and Galileo in the seventeenth century this tradition had identified the cognitively and morally curative function of science acting against fanciful or capricious knowledge—'the sciences as one would', Bacon called it.[62] Science for them was a corrective, restorative force: 'the moral enterprise of freedom for the enquiring mind', historian Alastair Crombie has written.[63] We now know that in its origins science was not anti-religious; its aim was restoration of cognitively diseased humankind to prelapsarian Adamic intelligence (McCarty 2012a, 9–11). The religious language has gone from science (with the occasional exception, as we have seen), but the moral imperative remains. Freud's series of outrages is thus radically incomplete: they do not stop with him because the imperative to correct 'the sciences as one would' is integral to the scientific programme.

But the high moral purpose darkens when the scientific perspective is taken to be absolute, reducing human imaginings to narcissism on a cosmic scale. Consider, for example, cosmologist and Nobel Laureate Steven Weinberg, who like Freud takes aim at this narcissism, proclaiming that we live in 'an overwhelmingly hostile universe' whose laws are 'as impersonal and free of human values as the laws of arithmetic', 'that human life is...a more-or-less farcical outcome of a chain of accidents reaching back to the first three minutes' after the Big Bang.[64] Or consider the words of geneticist and Nobel Laureate Jacques Monod, who aims at the same target, proclaiming 'that, like a gypsy, [man] lives on the boundary of an alien world that is deaf to his music, and as indifferent to his hopes as it is to his suffering or his crimes'.[65] A Blakean Nobodaddy is in the pulpit, gleefully telling us deluded children to grow up and face facts. However severe Weinberg and Monod may be, they are indicative of a much broader sense of a mounting attack of ourselves as scientists upon ourselves as humans, summed up by biological anthropologist Melvin Konner: 'It would seem', he concludes, 'that we are sorted to a pulp, caught in a vise made, on the one side, of the increasing power of evolutionary biology...and, on the other, of the relentless duplication of human mental faculties by increasingly subtle and complex machines.' He asks, 'So what is left of us?' (1991, 120).

This question and the vision it encapsulates lie close to the recent origins of the so-called posthuman condition, which is likewise both feared and celebrated by cultural critics as the end to the old conception of humanity.[66] I will return to it in a moment. But note: doesn't Konner's question sound familiar? Isn't it formally the same question that Flanders's encoder constantly asks, mindful of the 'productive unease' from which she struggles to learn? Isn't it the same question Jerry McGann has illumined by that reach for the 'hem of a quantum garment' when all else but the inexplicable anomaly has been nailed down? Again: the claustrophobia which signals a world outgrown and a transformed one in the offing, a catastrophe which punctuates the old equilibrium, precipitating a new order of things, a new idea of the human.

The cultural criticism that Alan Liu says we lack converges on much the same crisis of the human as the sciences (though it does not spare them). 'A good many theorizations of the postmodern', Hans Bertens writes, 'suggest that for some time now we have been finding ourselves in the middle of a moral, political and cognitive mohole'—Don DeLillo's fictional cosmic zone where physical law is suspended—'and, indeed, may never get out on the other side' (1995, 230). The question is again, what is left of and for us?

And so to my third dilation, ambitious in the extreme, as I warned, but promising so much. Here I can only indicate where I think it takes us.

I have argued that we are situated at the posthumanizing juncture where computing meets the humanities and so replicates the larger cultural transformation expressed in and through Turing's machine. But the historical *longue durée* of becoming human shows this juncture to be one of many punctuating catastrophes. This is the story told for example by Roger Smith in *Being Human: Historical Knowledge and the Creation of Human Nature* (2007). It is the process sketched across the millennia by Giorgio Agamben in *The Open: Man and Animal* (2004/2002), in which he cites Carolus Linnaeus's eighteenth-century classification of us as human by virtue of our perpetually coming to know ourselves, *homo nosce te ipsum*. And, at the other end of the scale, is our every moment's 'going on being' in the anxious construction of self that Anthony Giddens brilliantly describes in *Modernity and Self-Identity* (1991). This same anxiety is legible in the attempts, such as René Descartes's in 1637, to counteract perhaps the most psychologically corrosive discovery of his age, the Great Apes, so physiologically similar to humans, physician Nicolaes Tulp wrote in 1641, 'that it would be difficult to find one egg more like another'.[67] There is, I think, no more powerful expression of this anxiety than Jonathan Swift's depiction of Lemuel Gulliver driven insane after willingly embracing the lustful, brutish nature he had denied was his, in the form of a female Yahoo in heat. Ejected by the creatures of perfect reason for copulating with her and so revealing what he is, he returns home to find himself repelled by the smell of 'that odious animal' his wife, preferring the company and smell of his horses and of the groom who takes care of them.[68]

Marvin Minsky reminds us that in making any model of what's happening (as we do when we speak of a crossroads or plus sign) we must never forget that the modelling relation is ternary, in other words that our plus sign is three dimensional, that it signifies nothing independently of us:[69] we are individually, personally, morally, psychologically involved. We are *attacked*, as Lionel Trilling said, by forces we would be foolish to underestimate (1967/1961). But for us the catastrophic attack is no longer animal. Our digital machine has shifted the locus of engagement.

In 1970 the Japanese roboticist Masahiro Mori (whom I mentioned earlier) proposed that as robots become more recognizably anthropomorphic, we react more favourably to them, until suddenly their resemblance to us becomes uncanny and so provokes a strongly negative reaction. He called this plunge into fright 'the uncanny valley phenomenon' (Mori 2012/1970). Then and in a recent interview Mori has emphasized the benefit of remaining deliberately in the uncanny valley, so as better to know what it means to be human (Kageki 2012). Those of you who have seen the Bollywood film *Enthiran* (2010), Spanish *Eva* (2011), the Swedish *Äkta Människor* ('Real Humans' 2012) or 'Be Right Back' from the British *Black Mirror* (2013) will know how current in our thoughts this valley remains. For us in digital humanities the locus of engagement may well be—I think it must be—with the embodied artificial intelligence of robots. But my point for now is the uncanny valley which that plus sign denotes.

This valley is our place of beginnings. All disciplines are that, of course—starting points for a mental expanding that is transgressive but not possessive. 'It doesn't matter so much what you learn', Northrop Frye wrote in *On Education*, 'when you learn it in a structure that can expand into other structures' (1988, 10). Our structure is the crossroads of the techno-scientific and the humanistic. That's where we begin, whether we mine individually for diamonds or collaboratively for coal (Kowarski 1972, 29).

## The unknown, remembered gate

So, how do we get there? What do we do about the situation I have depicted?

'Turing's "Machines" ... ', Wittgenstein wrote in the mid to late 1940s, 'are *humans* who calculate' (1980, 191e §1096), and that's exactly what we find when we go back to Turing's paper of 1936, his originating metaphor of 'a man in the process of computing a real number'. So we find ourselves reduced to a 'computer' (as that man would then have been called, and as we now call the device he became). In it we discover a bare-bones stamp of the human that can do so much that is so little. Again, Fr Busa asked, why can it do so little? Now, I suggest, we must ask, how is all that it can do, and all that is imagined it will do, still so little? Or better: how do we come to know, however able it becomes, that it *is* so little? If it isn't, how do we make it so?

These are the questions that constitute the next step towards a digital practice that is *of* as well as *in* the humanities. This next step is the learned practitioner's open-eyed, technologically informed, imaginative, critical, hands-on *questioning* of what happens at the crossroads of actual work, where computing, scholar-practitioners and the humanities meet. It opens up the shocking yet familiar otherness that is rough midwife to ourselves as will be. It *defamiliarizes,* as Viktor Shklovsky said, so to recover 'the sensation of things as they are perceived and not as they are known' (1965/1917, 12). And while all that is going on, digital humanities needs use its more than 60 years of fumbling to gain leverage for a great inductive leap to a vantage point from which its disciplinary shape and trajectory, sighted dimly here, can be clearly seen. The key to its future—and in some measure the future of all the related humanities—is its history. This history we must remember.

Remember: not a tablet fetched from a storehouse just as it was written—a metaphor from classical antiquity that found at last a fitting referent in digital computing machinery—rather the creative, storytelling activity we now know it to be. I leave you with this: remembrance of what our predecessors did and did not do, and the conditions under which they worked, so that we may fashion stories for our future and the language in which to tell them. Remember that the struggle is the point of it all. Remember the humanities.

## Notes

1. The Busa Award lecture was presented at the 2013 conference of the Alliance of Digital Humanities Organizations, Lincoln, Nebraska, 16–19 July, for which see dh2013.unl.edu/. For the lecture as delivered see www.youtube.com/watch?v=nTHa1rDR680.

2. For the autobiographical thread of this lecture my model is the inspirational American Council of Learned Societies' Charles Homer Haskins lecture series, 'A Life of Learning', www.acls.org/pubs/haskins/.

3. Henceforth, to indicate the essential continuity (not identity) for which I am arguing, I will use the term 'digital humanities' for the activity from 1949 to the present. To dismiss the earlier period as somehow essentially different and so irrelevant is a serious, damaging error. As Agamben said, quoting Deleuze, 'terminology is the poetic moment of thought' (2009, 1).

4. The final state of *An Analytical Onomasticon to the* Metamorphoses *of Ovid* is preserved at www.mccarty.org.uk/analyticalonomasticon/.

5. I owe a great debt of gratitude to two in particular: Burton Wright at Toronto for his persistent other-mindedness, and Monica Matthews at King's College London.

6. See www.dhhumanist.org/.

7. 'Introduction to Perek Helek', on his 13 principles of faith. The Hebrew is thanks to Ms Debora Matos; the translation is taken from the Maimonides Heritage Center's version at www.mhcny.org/qt/1005.pdf.

8. This is a serious qualification and represents, I think, a new departure for the humanities. See especially Gooding 1990; Galison 1987; see also McCarty 2008.

9. Hacking 2002, 202; compare with 70, 71.

10. *OED* n.1, 2.a.

11. Distinctions, for example between fear and anxiety, are unclear (Bourke 2005, 189–92) except in quite specific circumstances, for example for psychiatric diagnosis (DSM-5 2013 makes *anxiety* the standard term). Note also that categories of emotion are not only blurred but also historically contingent: see, for example, Plamper 2012; Eustace et al. 2012; and compare with Danziger 2008. For general studies of fear see Plamper and Lazier 2012; Dyer et al. 2008; Bourke 2005; Hollander 2004; Massumi 1993; Gray 1991; Hall 1914. Fear of computer technology is well documented in psychology (for example Bozionelos 2001, Brosnan 1998 and many earlier), postmodern and posthuman studies (Dinello 2005; Hayles 1999), for automation (Zuboff 1988) and elsewhere. Fear has been a constant companion of AI (McCorduck 2004/1979) and, of course, robotics (Mori 2012/1970; Kageki 2012), to which I will return. For the arts, humanities and librarianship see Kohrman 2003; Holland and Burgess 1992; Kenny 1992; Nold 1975; Daigon 1969; Efron 1966; Pegues 1965; Handlin 1964; Brower 1964; Jenkins 1962; Parrish 1962; Schofield 1962. See also note 27, below.

12. Kowarski 1972, 38 and 1975; see also Aborn 1988 and Denning 1986; compare with Galison 1996, 139–40.

13. For the uncanny in the context of recent automata, see Galison 1994, 242–43 on Norbert Wiener's wartime research, with reference to Cavell 1988/1986 on Freud's analysis of E. A. Hoffmann's *Der Sandmann* (Freud 1955/1919); see also Mori 2012/1970 and Kageki 2012, discussed below. For more recent work see Masschelein 2011.

14. Such quilt-making, at least in the preliminary stages of research, would seem to be a default condition nowadays. See Richard Rorty's exploration with reference to Gadamer (Rorty 2004), for what I've called going wide rather than deep, that is, doing what we do as researchers in a fundamentally different way (McCarty 2013). The dangers are, I think, both non-trivial and obvious.

15. See note 8.

16. See stelarc.org. For a discussion of his work see Massumi 2002, 89–132.

17. See marceliantunez.com/.

18. See www.icra2013.org/?page_id=1272.

19. Reichardt 1969; see also Brett 1968; Klütsch 2005; Fernández 2008. For cybernetic art as a whole see Brown et al. 2008; Shanken 2002; Reichardt 1971; for larger contexts see Apter 1969; Malina 1989; Husbands, Holland and Weaver 2008; Gere 2008, 51–115; Pickering 2010.

20. Matthew Jockers has told the sort of my *creation* (*OED* 'create', 2.a.) as Obi-Wan in his blog entry for 19 July, at www.matthewjockers.net/2013/07/19/obi-wan-mccarty/; for the background see Glen Worthey's blog at digitalhumanities.stanford.edu/obi-wan -mccarty-episode-1.

21. www.bbc.co.uk/radio4/features/desert-island-discs/castaway/204bd479#p009mszc.

22. See, for example, www.youtube.com/watch?v=_RI99bG_-6A and www.youtube.com/ watch?v=9FqoOvUymfE, both sightings close to my place of birth.

23. Wiener 1961/1948, 7; compare with Hutchins 1995; Menary 2010.

24. Hughes 1991/1980; compare with the essays in Herbert 2000/1964 for the supporting words of the artists themselves and Shlovsky 1965/1917.

25. The theory from which evolutionary catastrophe comes is 'punctuated equilibrium', first proposed by Gould and Eldridge 1977. Note Gould's later synopsis: 'The history of life is not a continuum of development, but a record punctuated by brief, sometimes geologically instantaneous, episodes of mass extinction and subsequent diversification' (1989, 54). See also Eldredge's cautionary remarks on the use of the evolutionary metaphor outside the biological sciences (Eldredge 2009).

26. 'We may compare a man in the process of computing a real number to a machine which is only capable of a finite number of conditions...' (Turing 1936–1937, 59, 49). Note the relationship of Turing's machine and its progeny to governmental bureaucracy in Agar 2003.

27. See www.artificialbrains.com/darpa-synapse-program (visited on 5 April 2013).

28. As the editors of *Critical Neuroscience* note in their Introduction, 'Evidence of genomic and neural plasticity ... forces scientists to rethink the primacy given to biophysical levels of explanations, and challenges us to destabilize the dichotomy of nature/culture and instead address the fundamental interaction of mind, body, and society' (Choudhury and Slaby 2012, 34); see also the contributions throughout this volume and Pascual-Leone et al. 2005, Buonomano and Merzenich 1998.

29. McGann 2004. Stalled development is attested from the early 1960s by a mixture of (a) persistent nervousness over 'evidence of value', as the test of worth was later to be called (McCarty 2012b, 118), and inability to demonstrate any such evidence persuasively; (b) closely related agonizing over lack of influence on mainstream disciplines; and (c) preoccupation with the menial applications of computing, and so failure to deal with the theoretical problem of a digital hermeneutics. To 1991 the best state-of-the-art summary (of literary computing) is Potter 1991; see also Masterman 1962; Fogel 1964; Busa 1976 and 1980; Corns 1986; Zwaan 1987; Irizarry 1988; Potter 1989; DeRose et al. 1990; Corns 1991; Olsen 1991. Subsequently see the retrospective studies by Kenny 1992; Fortier et al. 1993; Miall 1995; McGann 2001; Ramsay et al. 2003; Rommel 2004; McGann 2004; Hoover 2007; Juola 2008; McCarty 2008; Ramsay 2011; McCarty 2012a; Jockers 2013.

30. The most recent attempts, Hockey 2004 and the other contributions to Schreibman, Siemens and Unsworth 2004, Part I, 'History', are but first steps toward a genuine history; see White 1980 on the distinction between chronology and history. For the dimensions of the problem of writing a history of computing, see Mahoney 2011, especially 'The Histories of Computing(s)', 55–73; for the importance of history to the formation of a discipline see Frye 1957, 15.

31. On the formative effects of early developments in social institutions see Stinchcombe 1965; Baum and Singh 1994, 12 and under the heading 'imprinting'; compare with Lounsbury and Ventresca 2002; Tillyard 1958, 11–12.

32. See, for example, the references in note 29.

33. For the revised and published version of Olsen 1991 see Olsen 1993 and note Fortier's introductory remarks in Fortier 1993. For 'distant reading' see Moretti 2000; Bode and Dixon 2009; Bode 2012; Jockers 2013.

34. See the series of pamphlets at http://litlab.stanford.edu/?page_id=255, and compare with Liu 2013.

35. Burrows 2010. On statistics across the disciplines see Gigerenzer et al. 1989; Hacking 1990; see also Hacking 1995.
36. Automated poetry writing seems to have made the biggest stir, but experiments in the other creative arts should not be ignored (for which see note 19, above). For poetry, see Funkhouser 2007; also 1971; Masterman and McKinnon Wood 1970; 'Computer poems and texts' in Reichardt 1969, 53–62, including Scottish national poet Edwin Morgan's 'Note on simulated computer poems'. We can be reasonably certain from his language that F. R. Leavis's violent objections to the very idea of computer-generated poetry (Leavis 1970) were aimed at Masterman; they betray just the kind of underlying fear I have been arguing for, though Leavis was also quite prescient. See Oliphant 1961–62; Newell 1983; Ernst 1992; Van Dyke 1993. Compare with Weaver 1961; Nemerov 1967.
37. See note 29.
38. For example the weekly magazine *U.S. News and World Report*, which in a pair of articles for 24 February 1964, 'Is the Computer Running Wild?' and 'Machines Smarter than Men?' (an interview with Norbert Wiener) hinted at if not predicted a very dark future (USN&WR 1964a and b).
39. Kenny 1992, 9; McKenzie 1991, 161; Banz 1990, 28; Mesthene 1969; Milic 1966.
40. Prescott 1999, 73; Mitchell 1967, 22–23; Lindsay 1966, 28; Hymes 1965. Mechanization of scholarship also occurs in highly positive contexts, however, for example in the first six contributions to TLS 1962; note Margaret Masterman's serious objections in that volume (Masterman 1962).
41. Purdy 1984; Leavis 1970; McDermott 1969; Mumford 1967 and 1970a, 1970b; Pooley 1961; Ellul 1964/1954; Wiener 1954/1950, 136–62. Compare with Husbands, Holland and Wheeler 2008; Morgan 2006, 11–31; Agar 2003; Zuboff 1988; Giedion 1948.
42. Parrish 1964; note commentary by Pegues 1965.
43. An example is Hoover 2007; compare with Miller 1991.
44. Some glimpse of these may be obtained from YouTube, http://www.youtube.com/watch?v=nTHa1rDR680.
45. See especially Edwards 1996 and note LM 1957; Ghamari-Tabrizi 2000.
46. Orwell 1968/1945, 9. On the Cold War see Ball 2004/1998; Whitfield 1996; Hennessy 2002; Grant 2010; Kahn 2007/1960; Leffler and Painter 1994.
47. Hubbell 1961. According to MacKenzie 2001, 340 no. 4, this remains 'the best available account of the incident'. For others see Borning 1987; www.nuclearinfo.org/.
48. Smith 1985, rpt. Johnson and Nissenbaum 1995, 456–69; compare with Shore 1985, 161–84 on 'Myths of Correctness'; see also Dyer 1985, reporting on the conference at which Smith 1985 was given.
49. The phrase 'duck and cover' refers to the 1952 film of that title (www.imdb.com/title/tt0213381/fullcredits); for an early draft of the script see www.scribd.com/doc/45799687/Duck-and-Cover-Script. See Weart 1988; Brown 1988; McEnaney 2000; Masco 2009; www.conelrad.com/.
50. For example for the UK see HMSO 1963; for the United States see OCD 1968; see also the Civil Defense Museum's collection, www.civildefensemuseum.com/docs.html. The Internet Archive and YouTube are rich sources for the many instructional films produced in both countries.
51. Connor 1991, 58–59 observes this curiosity for Classics, but it is true for literary studies as a whole; see Kenny 1992, 9–10, who cites Connor.
52. Eagleton 1990, 34. See also Hooks 1990 and the work of Raymond Williams and Richard Hoggart during the incunabular years.
53. The Berlin Wall fell 9 November 1989; the Soviet Union was officially dissolved by the signing of the Belavezha Accords 8 December 1991. Tim Berners-Lee proposed what later became the World Wide Web in March 1989; the Web was released to the public, on alt.hypertext, 7 August 1991.
54. Parrish, who had attended C. P. Snow's 'Two Cultures' lecture in 1959 and had sided with the scientists, declared a consensus, 'that we understand ourselves to be living though the early stages of a revolution, perhaps a quasi-scientific revolution, which cannot fail

to touch us all in everything we do' (1964, 3–4). For the 1964 conference see Bessinger, Parrish and Arader 1964; Pegues 1965.

55. For machine translation see ALPAC 1966; for artificial intelligence see Dreyfus 1965; for digital humanities see Milic 1966. There were prior difficulties for all three, but it is interesting that prominent public declarations or accusations of failure occurred in the United States almost simultaneously.

56. Lighthill 1973/1972, 8, 10. See also 'Controversy: The General Purpose Robot is a Mirage' ('The Lighthill Debate', YouTube, in six parts), pitting Lighthill in debate against Donald Michie (Edinburgh), John McCarthy (Stanford) and Richard Gregory (Bristol).

57. For a summary form of the argument for this statement see note 29.

58. Compare with Humphreys 2009; see also Lenhard 2007.

59. Humphreys 2004, 156. Mahoney shows that it is possible to avoid the apocalyptic, biblical language: 'the artefact as formal (mathematical) system has become deeply embedded in the natural world, and it is not clear how one would go about re-establishing traditional epistemological boundaries among the elements of our understanding' (2011, 179).

60. On this sort of language see especially Keller 1991 and Midgley 2002/1989.

61. Freud 1920/1917a and 1920/1917b; compare with Mazlish 1967 as well as Mazlish 1993 and Bruner 1956. Note, however, that I argue for a cyclical, creative tragicomedy, whereas Mazlish argues for a progressive teleological comedy.

62. id quod generat ad quod vult scientias, in *Novum Organum*, I.xlix.

63. Crombie 1994, 8; for Bacon see also Crombie 1994, 1208–09 and 1572–86.

64. Weinberg 1983/1977, 148 and 1974, 43, respectively; see Keller 1991, 87–88.

65. Monod 1972/1970, 160; see Midgley 2002/1985; Keller 1991.

66. Hayles 1999; see also Bertens 1995; compare with Giddens and Pierson 1998, 116f.

67. 'cum homine similitudinem: ut vix ovum ovo videris similis', Tulp 1641, 3.56, p. 274; compare with de Waal and Lanting 1997, 7.

68. See especially Hugh Kenner's brilliant story of Gulliver's place in an intellectual history stretching through Charles Babbage and Alan Turing to Andy Warhol, among others (2005/1968).

69. Minsky 1995/1968; compare with Peirce's discussion of 'thirdness, for example in his third Harvard lecture, 'The Categories Defended' (Peirce 1998, 160–78).

# References

Aborn, Murray. (1988). 'Machine Cognition and the Downloading of Scientific Intellect'. *Annals of the American Academy of Political and Social Science*, 495: 135–43.

Agamben, Giorgio. (1999/1993). 'Bartleby, or On Contingency'. In *Potentialities: Collected Essays in Philosophy*, ed. and trans. Daniel Heller-Roazen. Stanford: Stanford University Press, 243–71.

Agamben, Giorgio. (2004/2002). *The Open: Man and Animal*. Trans. Kevin Attell. Stanford: Stanford University Press.

Agamben, Giorgio. (2009). *What Is an Apparatus? And Other Essays*. Trans. David Kishik and Stefan Pedatella. Stanford: Stanford University Press.

Agar, Jon. (2003). *The Government Machine: A Revolutionary History of the Computer*. Cambridge, MA: MIT Press.

ALPAC (Automatic Language Processing Advisory Committee). (1966). *Language and Machines: Computers in Translation and Linguistics*. Report 1416. Washington, DC: National Academy of Sciences, National Research Council. Available at: http://www.nap.edu/html/alpac_lm/ARC000005.pdf (accessed 26 November 2013).

Apter, Michael J. (1969). 'Cybernetics and Art'. *Leonardo* 2, no. 3: 257–65.

Aspray, William. (1990). *John von Neumann and The Origins of Modern Computing*. Cambridge, MA: MIT Press.

Ball, S. J. (2004/1998). *The Cold War: An International History, 1947–91*. London: Arnold.

Banz, David A. (1990). 'The Values of the Humanities and the Values of Computing'. In *Humanities and the Computer: New Directions*, ed. David S. Miall, 27–37. Oxford: Clarendon Press.

Baum, Joel A. C. and Jitendra V. Singh, eds. (1994). *Evolutionary Dynamics of Organizations*. New York: Oxford University Press.

Beer, Gillian. (2009/1983). *Darwin's Plots: Evolutionary Narrative in Darwin, George Eliot and Nineteenth-Century Fiction*. 3rd ed. Cambridge: Cambridge University Press.

Benjamin, Walter. (1968/1955). *Illuminations*. Ed. Hannah Arendt, trans. Harry Zohn. New York: Schocken Books.

Berkeley, Edmund Callis. (1949). *Giant Brains or Machines That Think*. New York: John Wiley & Sons.

Bertens, Hans. (1995). *The Idea of the Postmodern: A History*. London: Routledge.

Bessinger, Jess B., Stephen M. Parrish, and Harry F. Arader, eds. (1964). *Literary Data Processing Conference Proceedings*, 9–11 September. Armonk, NY: IBM Corporation.

Bode, Katherine. (2012). *Reading by Numbers: Recalibrating the Literary Field*. London: Anthem Press.

Bode, Katherine and Robert Dixon, eds. (2009). *Resourceful Reading: The New Empiricism, eResearch, and Australian Literary Culture*. Sydney: Sydney University Press.

Borning, Alan. (1987). 'Computer System Reliability and Nuclear War'. *Communications of the ACM* 30, no. 2: 112–31.

Bourke, Joanna. (2005). *Fear: A Cultural History*. London: Virago.

Bowlby, Rachel. (2013). 'Waiting for the Dawn to Come. Rev'. *Reading for Our Time: 'Adam Bede' and 'Middlemarch' Revisited*. By J. Hillis Miller. *London Review of Books* 35, no. 7: 32–34.

Bozionelos, Nikos. (2001). 'Computer Anxiety: Relationship With Computer Experience and Prevalence'. *Computers in Human Behavior* 17: 213–24.

Brett, Guy. (1968). 'The Computers Take to Art. The Arts'. *The Times*, 2 August: 7.

Brosnan, Mark. (1998). *Technophobia: The Psychological Impact of Information Technology*. London: Routledge.

Brower, Brock. (1964). 'Of Nothing but Facts'. *The American Scholar* 33, no. 4: 613–14, 616, 618.

Brown, JoAnne. (1988). ' "A is for Atom, B is for Bomb": Civil Defense in American Public Education, 1948–63'. *The Journal of American History* 75, no. 1: 68–90.

Brown, Paul, Charlie Gere, Nicholas Lambert, and Catherine Mason, eds. (2010). *White Heat Cold Logic: British Computer Art 1960–80*. Cambridge, MA: MIT Press.

Bruner, Jerome. (1956). 'Freud and the Image of Man'. *American Psychologist* 11, no. 9: 463–66.

Buonomano, Dean V. and Michael M. Merzenich. (1998). 'Cortical Plasticity: From Synapses to Maps'. *Annual Review of Neuroscience* 21: 149–86.

Burnyeat, M. F. (2012/1982). 'Message from Heraclitus'. In *Explorations in Ancient and Modern Philosophy*. Vol. II. 195–204. Cambridge: Cambridge University Press.

Burrows, John. (2010). 'Never Say Always Again: Reflections on the Numbers Game'. In *Text and Genre in Reconstruction: Effects of Digitization on Ideas, Behaviours, Products & Institutions*, ed. Willard McCarty. Cambridge: Open Book Publishers, 13–35.

Busa, Roberto. (1976). 'Why Can a Computer Do so Little?' *ALLC Bulletin* 4, no. 1: 1–3.

Busa, Roberto. (1980). 'The Annals of Humanities Computing: The Index Thomisticus'. *Computers and the Humanities* 14: 83–90.

Byatt, A. S. (2000). *On Histories and Stories: Selected Essays*. Cambridge, MA: Harvard University Press.

Byatt, A. S. (2005). 'Fiction Informed by Science'. *Nature* 434: 294–96.

Cavell, Stanley. (1988/1986). 'The Uncanniness of the Ordinary'. *The Tanner Lecture*. Stanford University. 153–78. Chicago IL: University of Chicago Press.

Cecire, Natalia. (2011). 'When Digital Humanities Was in Vogue'. *Journal of Digital Humanities* 1, no. 1: 54–59.

Choudhury, Suparna and Jan Slaby, eds. (2012). *Critical Neuroscience: A Handbook of the Social and Cultural Contexts of Neuroscience*. Chichester: Wiley-Blackwell.

Connor, W. R. (1991). 'Scholarship and Technology in Classical Studies'. In *Scholarship and Technology in the Humanities. Proceedings of a Conference Held at Elvetham Hall*, Hampshire, UK, 9–12 May, ed. May Katzen, 52–62. London: British Library Research, Bowker Saur.

Corns, Thomas N. (1986). 'Literary Theory and Computer-based Criticism: Current Problems and Future Prospects'. In *Méthodes quantitatives et informatiques dans l'étude des textes. Computers in Literary and Linguistic Research*. Colloque International CNRS, Université de Nice, 5–8 June, 1985. Genéve: Slatkine-Champion.

Corns, Thomas N. (1991). 'Computers in the Humanities: Methods and Applications in the Study of English Literature'. *Literary and Linguistic Computing* 6, no. 2: 127–30.

Corns, Thomas N. and Margarette E. Smith. (1987). 'Literature'. In *Information Technology in the Humanities: Tools, Techniques and Applications*. Chichester: Ellis Horwood, 104–15.

Crombie, A. C. (1994). *Styles of Scientific Thinking in the European Tradition. The History of Argument and Explanation Especially in the Mathematical and Biomedical Sciences and Arts*. 3 vols. London: Duckworth.

Daigon, Arthur. (1969). 'Literature and the Schools'. *The English Journal* 58, no. 1: 30–39.

Danziger, Kurt. (2008). *Marking the Mind: A History of Memory*. Cambridge: Cambridge University Press.

Davies, Gordon K. (1969). 'Describing Men to Machines: The Use of Computers in Dealing with Social Problems'. *Soundings: An Interdisciplinary Journal* 52, no. 3: 283–98.

Dening, Greg. (1993). 'The Theatricality of History Making'. *Cultural Anthropology* 8, no. 1: 73–95.

Dening, Greg. (1998). *Readings/Writings*. Melbourne: University of Melbourne Press.

Dening, Greg. (2002). 'Performing on the Beaches of the Mind: An Essay'. *History and Theory* 41: 1–24.

Denning, Peter. (1986). 'The Science of Computing: Will Machines Ever Think?' *American Scientist* 74, no. 4: 344–46.

DeRose, Steven J., David G. Durand, Elli Milonas, and Allen H. Renear. (1990). 'What is Text, Really?' *Journal of Computing in Higher Education* 1, no. 2: 3–26.

de Waal, Frans, and Frans Lanting. (1997). *Bonobo: The Forgotten Ape*. Berkeley: University of California Press.

Dinello, Daniel. (2005). *Technophobia! Science Fiction Visions of Posthuman Technology*. Austin: University of Texas Press.

Donald, Merlin. (1991). *Origins of the Modern Mind: Three Stages in the Evolution of Culture and Cognition*. Cambridge, MA: Harvard University Press.

Dreyfus, Herbert L. (1965). *Alchemy and Artificial Intelligence*. Paper P-3244. Santa Monica, CA: Rand Corporation. Available at: http://www.rand.org/pubs/papers/P3244/ (visited on 26 November 2013).

DSM-5. (2013). *Diagnostic and Statistical Manual of Mental Disorders*. 5th ed. Washington, DC: American Psychiatric Association.

Dyer, Geoff, Charlie Haas, Robert Reich, Elizabeth Tallent, Daisy Fried, Lynne Sharon Schwartz, Morris Dickstein, and W. S. Di Pier. (2008). 'A Symposium on Fear'. *Threepenny Review* 115: 14–17.

Dyer, Robert R. (1969). 'The New Philology: An Old Discipline or a New Science?' *Computers and the Humanities* 4, no. 1: 53–64.

Dyer, Jim. (1985). 'Cooperation not confrontation: the imperative of a nuclear age' *British Medical Journal* 291: 191–3.

Eagleton, Terry. (1990). 'The Significance of Theory'. *Bucknell Lectures in Literary Theory* 2. Oxford: Basil Blackwell.

Edwards, Paul N. (1996). *The Closed World: Computers and the Politics of Discourse in Cold War America*. Cambridge, MA: MIT Press.

Efron, Arthur. (1966). 'Technology and the Future of Art'. *The Massachusetts Review* 7, no. 4: 677–710.

Eldredge, Niles. (2009). 'Material Cultural Macroevolution'. In *Macroevolution in Human Prehistory: Evolutionary Theory and Processual Archaeology,* ed. Anna Marie Prentiss, Ian Kuijt and James C. Chatters. New York: Springer, 297–316.

Ellul, Jacques. (1964/1954). *The Technological Society.* Trans. John Wilkinson. Intro. Robert K. Merton. New York: Random House.

Ernst, Josef. (1992). 'Computer Poetry: An Act of Disinterested Communication'. *New Literary History* 23, no. 2: 451–65.

Eustace, Nicole, Eugenia Lean, Julie Livingston, Jan Plamper, William M. Ready, and Barbara H. Rosenwein. (2012). 'AHR Conversation: The Historical Study of Emotions'. *American Historical Review* 117, no. 5: 1487–1531.

Fernández, Maria. (2008). 'Detached From HiStory: Jasia Reichardt and Cybernetic Serendipity'. *Art Journal* 67, no. 3: 6–23.

Flanders, Julia. (2009). 'The Productive Unease of 21st-century Digital Scholarship'. *Digital Humanities Quarterly* 3, no. 3. Available at: http://www.digitalhumanities.org/dhq/vol/3/3/000055/000055.html (visited on 26 November 2013).

Fodor, Jerry A. (1983). *The Modularity of Mind.* Cambridge, MA: MIT Press.

Fogel, Ephraim. (1964). "The Humanist and the Computer: Vision and Actuality". In Bessinger, Parrish and Arader 1964: 11–24. Rpt. *Journal of Higher Education* 36.2 (1965): 61–8.

Fortier, Paul A. ed. (1993). 'A New Direction for Literary Studies?' Special issue of *Computers and the Humanities* 27: 305–400.

Freud, Sigmund. (1920a/1917). *A General Introduction to Psychoanalysis.* Trans. G. Stanley Hall. New York: Boni and Liveright.

Freud, Sigmund. (1920b/1917). 'One of the Difficulties of Psychoanalysis'. Trans. Joan Riviere. *International Journal of Psychoanalysis* 1: 17–23.

Freud, Sigmund. (1955/1919). 'The "Uncanny"'. In *An Infantile Neurosis and Other Works.* Vol. XVII of *The Standard Edition of the Complete Psychological Works of Sigmund Freud.* Trans. James Strachey. London: The Hogarth Press, 217–52.

Frye, Northrop. (1957). *Anatomy of Criticism: Four Essays.* Princeton: Princeton University Press.

Frye, Northrop. (1988). *On Education.* Toronto: Fitzhenry and Whiteside.

Fuller, Thomas. (1732). *Gnomologia: Adagies and Proverbs; Wise Sentences and Witty Sayings, Ancient and Modern, Foreign and British.* London: for B. Barker.

Funkhouser, C. T. (2007). *Prehistoric Digital Poetry: An Archaeology of Forms.* Tuscaloosa AL: University of Alabama Press.

Galison, Peter. (1987). *How Experiments End.* Chicago: University of Chicago Press.

Galison, Peter. (1994). 'The Ontology of the Enemy: Norbert Wiener and the Cybernetic Vision'. *Critical Inquiry* 21, no. 1: 228–66.

Galison, Peter. (1996). 'Computer Simulations and the Trading Zone'. In *The Disunity of Science: Boundaries, Contexts, and Power,* ed. Peter Galison and David J. Stump. Stanford: Stanford University Press, 118–57.

Geertz, Clifford. (1973). 'Thick Description: Toward an Interpretive Theory of Culture'. In *The Interpretation of Cultures: Selected Essays.* New York: Basic Books, 3–30.

Gere, Charlie. (2008). *Digital Culture.* 2nd ed. London: Reaktion Books.

Ghamari-Tabrizi, Sharon. (2000). 'Simulating the Unthinkable: Gaming Future War in the 1950s and 1960s'. *Social Studies of Science* 30, no. 2: 163–223.

Gibbs, Fred. (2011). 'Critical Discourse in Digital Humanities'. *Journal of Digital Humanities* 1, no. 1: 34–42.

Giddens, Anthony. (1991). *Modernity and Self-Identity: Self and Society in the Late Modern Age.* London: Polity.

Giddens, Anthony, and Christopher Pierson. (1998). *Conversations With Anthony Giddens.* London: Polity.

Giedion, Siegfried. (1948). *Mechanization Takes Command: A Contribution to an Anonymous History*. New York: Oxford University Press.

Gigerenzer, Gerd, Zeno Swijtink, Theodore Porter, Lorraine Daston, John Beatty, and Lorenz Krüger. (1989). *The Empire of Chance: How Probability Changed Science and Everyday Life*. Ideas in context. Cambridge: Cambridge University Press.

Gooding, David. (1990). *Experiment and the Making of Meaning: Human Agency in Scientific Observation and Experiment*. Dordrecht: Kluwer Academic Publishers.

Goodman, Nelson. (1978). *Ways of Worldmaking*. Indianapolis, IN: Hackett Publishing.

Gorman, Michael E., ed. (2010). *Trading Zones and Interactional Expertise*. Cambridge, MA: MIT Press.

Gould, Stephen Jay. (1989). *Wonderful Life: The Burgess Shale and the Nature of History*. New York: W. W. Norton and Company.

Gould, Stephen Jay, and Niles Eldredge. (1977). 'Punctuated Equilibria: The Tempo and Mode of Evolution Reconsidered'. *Paleobiology* 3, no. 2: 115–51.

Grant, Matthew. (2010). *After the Bomb: Civil Defence and Nuclear War in Britain, 1945–68*. Houndmills, Basingstoke: Palgrave Macmillan.

Gray, Geoffrey A. (1991). 'Fear, Panic, and Anxiety: What's in a Name?' *Psychological Inquiry* 2, no. 1: 77–78.

Greenly, Mike. (1988). 'Computerphobia'. *The Futurist* 22, no. 1: 14–18.

Hacking, Ian. (1983). *Representing and Intervening: Introductory Topics in the Philosophy of Natural Science*. Cambridge: Cambridge University Press.

Hacking, Ian. (1990). *The Taming of Chance*. Ideas in Context. Cambridge: Cambridge University Press.

Hacking, Ian. (1995). *Rewriting the Soul: Multiple Personality and the Sciences of Memory*. Princeton: Princeton University Press.

Hacking, Ian. (2002). ' "Style" for Historians and Philosophers'. In *Historical Ontology*. Cambridge, MA: Harvard University Press, 178–99.

Hall, G. Stanley. (1914). 'A Synthetic Genetic Study of Fear: Chapter I and A Synthetic Genetic Study of Fear: Chapter II'. *The American Journal of Psychology* 25, no. 2; 25, no. 3: 149–200; 321–92.

Handlin, Oscar. (1964). 'Man and Magic: First Encounters With the Machine'. *The American Scholar* 33, no. 3: 408–19.

Hatfield, H. Stafford. (1928). *Automation, or the Future of the Mechanical Man*. To-Day and To-Morrow. London: Kegan Paul, Trench, Trubner & Co.

Hayes, Brian. (1999). 'Computing Science: Computational Creationism'. *American Scientist* 87, no. 5: 392–96.

Hayles, N. Katherine. (1999). *How We Became Posthuman: Virtual Bodies in Cybernetics, Literature, and Informatics*. Chicago: University of Chicago Press.

Hennessy, Peter. (2002). *The Secret State: Whitehall and the Cold War*. London: Allen Lane.

Herbert, Robert L. (2000/1964). *Modern Artists on Art*. 2nd ed. Mineola, NY: Dover Publications.

HMSO. (1963). *Advising the Householder on Protection Against Nuclear Attack*. Civil Defence Handbook No. 10. London: Her Majesty's Stationery Office. Reproduction without the covers. Available at: http://www.mgrfoundation.org/libro.pdf (visited on 27 November 2013).

Hockey, Susan. (2004). 'A History of Humanities Computing'. In *A Companion to Digital Humanities*, ed. Susan Schreibman, Ray Siemens, and John Unsworth, 3–19. Oxford: Blackwell. Available at: http://www.digitalhumanities.org/companion/.

Holland, Simon, and Gordon Burgess. (1992). 'Beauty and the Beast: New Approaches to Teaching Computing for Humanities Students at the University of Aberdeen'. *Computers and the Humanities* 26, no. 4: 267–74.

Hollander, John. (2004). 'Fear Itself'. *Social Research* 71, no. 4: 865–86.

Hooks, Bell. (1994). 'Theory as Liberatory Practice'. In *Teaching to Transgress: Education as the Practice of Freedom*. London: Routledge, 59–75.

Hoover, David. (2007). 'The End of the Irrelevant Text: Electronic Texts, Linguistics, and Literary Theory'. *Digital Humanities Quarterly* 1, no. 2. Available at: http://www.digitalhumanities.org/dhq/vol/001/2/.

Hubbell, John G. (1961). ' "You Are Under Attack!": The Strange Incident of 5 October'. *Reader's Digest*, April: 37–41.

Hughes, Robert. (1991/1980). *The Shock of the New: Art and the Century of Change.* Rev. ed. London: Thames and Hudson.

Humphreys, Paul. (2004). *Extending Ourselves: Computational Science, Empiricism, and Scientific Method.* Oxford: Oxford University Press.

Humphreys, Paul. (2009). 'The Philosophical Novelty of Computer Simulation Methods'. *Synthese* 169, no. 3: 615–26.

Husbands, Phillip, Owen Holland, and Michael Wheeler, eds. (2008). *The Mechanical Mind in History.* Cambridge, MA: MIT Press.

Hutchins, Edwin. (1995). *Cognition in the Wild.* Cambridge, MA: MIT Press.

Hymes, Dell. (1965). 'Introduction'. In *The Use of Computers in Anthropology*, ed. Dell Hymes. The Hague: Mouton & Co.

Inwood, Brad, and Willard McCarty, eds. (2010). 'History and Human Nature: An Essay by G. E. R. Lloyd With Invited Responses'. *Interdisciplinary Science Reviews* 35: 3–4.

Irizarry, Estelle. (1988). 'Literary Analysis and the Microcomputer'. *Hispania* 71, no. 4: 984–95.

Jenkins, William A. (1962). 'Time That is Intolerant'. *Elementary English* 39, no. 2: 84–90.

Jockers, Matthew L. (2013). *Microanalysis: Digital Methods and Literary History.* Illinois, IN: Indiana University Press.

Johnson, Deborah G. and Helen Nissenbaum. (1995). *Computers, Ethics and Social Values.* Upper Saddle River NJ: Prentice Hall.

Juola, Patrick. (2008). 'Killer Applications in Digital Humanities'. *Literary and Linguistic Computing* 23, no. 1: 73–83.

Kahn, Herman. (2007/1960). *On Thermonuclear War.* New Brunswick, NJ: Transaction Publishers.

Kageki, Norri. (2012). 'An Uncanny Mind'. *IEEE Robotics and Automation Magazine* (June): 112, 106, 108.

Katzen, May, ed. (1991). *Scholarship and Technology in the Humanities. Proceedings of a Conference held at Elvetham Hall,* Hampshire, UK, 9–12 May 1990. London: British Library Research, Bowker Saur.

Keller, Evelyn Fox. (1991). 'Language and Ideology in Evolutionary Theory: Reading Cultural Norms into Natural Law'. In *The Boundaries of Humanity: Humans, Animals, Machines*, ed. James J. Sheehan and Morton Sosna, 85–102. Berkeley: University of California Press.

Kenner, Hugh. (2005/1968). *The Counterfeiters: An Historical Comedy.* Normal, IL: Dalkey Archive Press.

Kenny, Anthony. (1992). *Computers and the Humanities.* Ninth British Library Research Lecture. London: The British Library.

Klütsch, Christoph. (2005). 'The Summer 1968 in London and Zagreb: Starting or End Point for Computer art?' Proceedings of the 5th conference on Creativity & Cognition, New Cross, London, 12–15 April, 109–117. New York: Association of Computing Machinery.

Kohrman, Rita. (2003). 'Computer Anxiety in the 21st Century: When You Are Not in Kansas Any More'. Association of College and Research Libraries Eleventh National Conference, Charlotte, North Carolina, 10–13 April. Available at: http://www.ala.org/acrl/sites/ala.org.acrl/files/content/conferences/pdf/kohrman.pdf.

Konner, Melvin. (1991). 'Human Nature and Culture: Biology and the Residue of Uniqueness'. In *The Boundaries of Humanity: Humans, Animals, Machines*, ed. James J. Sheehan and Morton Sosna, 103–24. Berkeley: University of California Press.

Kowarski, L. (1972). 'The Impact of Computers on Nuclear Science'. In *Computing as a Language of Physics.* International Centre for Theoretical Physics, Trieste, 27–37. Vienna: International Atomic Energy Agency.

Kowarski, L. (1975). 'Man-Computer Symbiosis: Fears and Hopes'. In *Human Choice and Computers*, ed. Enid Mumford and Harold Sackman. Amsterdam: North Holland, 305–12.

LaCapra, Dominick. (1998). *History and Memory After Auschwitz*. 2nd ed. Ithaca: Cornell University Press.

Latour, Bruno. (1988). 'The Politics of Explanation: An Alternative'. In *Knowledge and Reflexivity: New Frontiers in the Sociology of Knowledge*, ed. S. Woolgar. London: Sage, 155–76.

Leavis, F. R. (1970). ' "Literarism" versus "Scientism": The Misconception and the Menace'. *Times Literary Supplement*, 23 April: 441–44. Rpt. in *Nor Shall My Sword: Discourses on Pluralism, Compassion and Social Hope*. London: Chatto and Windus, 1972, 135–60.

Leffler, Melvyn P. and David S. Painter, eds. (1994). *Origins of the Cold War: An International History*. London: Routledge.

Levy, Steven. (2010). *Hackers: Heroes of the Computer Revolution*. Sebastopol, CA: O'Reilly Media, Inc.

Lenhard, Johannes. (2007). 'Computer Simulation: The Cooperation Between Experimenting and Modeling'. *Philosophy of Science* 74, no. 2: 176–94.

Lighthill, Sir James. (1973/1972). 'Artificial Intelligence: A General Survey. Part I of Artificial Intelligence': a paper symposium. London: Science Research Council. Available at: http://www.chilton-computing.org.uk/inf/literature/reports/lighthill_report/contents.htm.

Lindsay, Kenneth C. (1966). 'Art, Art History, and the Computer'. *Computers and the Humanities* 1, no. 2: 27–30.

Liu, Alan. (2011). 'Where Is Cultural Criticism in the Digital Humanities?' In *Debates in the Digital Humanities*, ed. Matthew K. Gold, 490–509. Minneapolis: University of Minnesota Press.

Liu, Alan. (2013). 'The Meaning of the Digital Humanities'. *PMLA* 128, no. 2: 409–23.

Lloyd, G. E. R. (2007). *Cognitive Variations: Reflections on the Unity and Diversity of the Human Mind*. Oxford: Clarendon Press.

LM. (1950). 'How U.S. Cities Can Prepare for Atomic War'. *Life Magazine*, 18 December: 77–86.

LM. (1957). 'Pushbutton Defense for Air War'. *Life Magazine*, 11 February: 62–67.

Lounsbury, Michael, and Marc J. Ventresca. (2002). 'Social Structure and Organizations Revisited'. *Research in the Sociology of Organizations* 19: 3–36.

MacKenzie, Donald A. (2001). *Mechanizing Proof: Computing, Risk, and Trust inside Technology*. Cambridge MA: MIT Press.

Mahoney, Michael Sean. (2011). *Histories of Computing*, ed. Thomas Haigh. Cambridge, MA: Harvard University Press.

Malina, Roger F. (1989). 'Computer Art in the Context of the Journal *Leonardo*'. *Leonardo* (Supplemental issue, Vol. 2, Computer Art in Context: SIGGRAPH '89 Art Show Catalogue): 67–70.

Maniglier, Patrice. (2012). "What is a problematic?" Dossier: Bachelard and the concept of the problematic. *Radical Philosophy* 173. www.radicalphilosophy.com/article/what-is-a-problematic.

Markman, Alan. (1965). 'Litterae ex Machina: Man and Machine in Literary Criticism'. *The Journal of Higher Education* 36, no. 2: 69–79.

Masco, Joseph. (2009). 'Life Underground: Building the Bunker Society'. *Anthropology Now* 1, no. 2: 13–29.

Masschelein, Anneleen. (2011). *The Unconcept: The Freudian Uncanny in Late-Twentieth-Century Theory*. Albany: State University of New York Press.

Massumi, Brian, ed. (1993). *The Politics of Everyday Fear*. Minneapolis: University of Minnesota Press.

Massumi, Brian, ed. (2002). *Parables for the Virtual: Movement, Affect, Sensation*. Durham, NC: Duke University Press.

Masterman, Margaret. (1962). 'The intellect's New Eye'. In *Freeing the Mind: Articles and Letters from The Times Literary Supplement During March–June, 1962*, 38–44. London: The Times Publishing Company.

Masterman, Margaret. (1971). 'Computerized Haiku'. In *Cybernetics, Art and Idea*, ed. Jasia Reichardt, 175–83. London: Studio Vista.

Masterman, Margaret, and Robin McKinnon Wood. (1970). 'The Poet and the Computer'. *Times Literary Supplement*, 18 June, 667–68.

Mazlish, Bruce. (1967). 'The Fourth Discontinuity'. *Technology and Culture* 8, no. 1: 1–15.

Mazlish, Bruce. (1993). *The Fourth Discontinuity: The Co-Evolution of Humans and Machines*. New Haven: Yale University Press.

McCarty, Willard. (2014/2005). *Humanities Computing*. Rev. edn. Houndmills, Basingstoke: Palgrave Macmillan.

McCarty, Willard. (2006). 'Tree, Turf, Centre, Archipelago – or Wild Acre? Metaphors and Stories for Humanities Computing'. *Literary and Linguistic Computing* 21, no. 1: 1–13.

McCarty, Willard. (2008). 'Being Reborn: The Humanities, Computing and Styles of Scientific Reasoning'. In *New Technologies and Renaissance Studies*, ed. William R. Bowen and Raymond G. Siemens. Tempe: Iter Inc. and the Arizona Center for Medieval and Renaissance Texts.

McCarty, Willard. (2012a). 'The Residue of Uniqueness'. *Historical Social Research/Historische Sozialforschung* 37, no. 3: 24–45.

McCarty, Willard. (2012b). 'A Telescope of the Mind?' In *Debates in the Digital Humanities*, ed. Matthew K. Gold, 113–23. Minneapolis: University of Minnesota Press.

McCarty, Willard. (2013). 'Getting into the driver's seat'. Rev. of *Histories of Computing*, by Michael S. Mahoney. *Metascience* 22: 99–104.

McCorduck, Pamela. (2004/1979). *Machines Who Think: A Personal Inquiry into the History and Prospects of Artificial Intelligence*. Rev ed. Nattick, MA: A. K. Peters, Ltd.

McCulloch, Warren S., and Walter Pitts. (1989/1943). 'A Logical Calculus of Ideas Immanent in Nervous Activity'. In *Embodiments of Mind*, ed. Warren McCulloch, 10–39. Cambridge, MA: MIT Press.

McCulloch, Warren S. (1968). 'Preface'. In *An Approach to Cybernetics*, ed. Gordon Pask. London: Hutchinson.

McDermott, John. (1969). 'Technology: The Opiate of the Intellectuals' Rev. *The Fourth Annual Report of the Harvard Program on Technology and Society*. *New York Review of Books*, 31 July. Rpt. "Technology: The Opiate of the Intellectuals, with the Author's 2000 Retrospective", in Robert C. Scharff and Val Dusek, eds., *Philosophy of Technology: The Technological Condition: An Anthology*. 693–705. Chichester: John Wiley & Sons.

McEnaney, Laura. (2000). *Civil Defense Begins at Home: Militarization Meets Everyday Life in the Fifties*. Princeton: Princeton University Press.

McGann, Jerome. (2001). *Radiant Textuality: Literature after the World Wide Web*. Houndmills, Basingstoke: Palgrave.

McGann, Jerome. (2004). 'Marking Texts of Many Dimensions'. In *A Companion to Digital Humanities*, ed. Susan Schreibman, Ray Siemens, and John Unsworth, 198–217. Oxford: Blackwell. Available at: http://www.digitalhumanities.org/companion/.

McKenzie, D. F. (1991). 'Computers and the Humanities: a Personal Synthesis of Conference Issues'. In *Scholarship and Technology in the Humanities. Proceedings of a Conference held at Elvetham Hall*, Hampshire, UK, 9–12 May, ed. May Katzen, 157–69. London: British Library Research, Bowker Saur.

Mead, Margaret. (1970). *Culture and Commitment: A Study of the Generation Gap*. New York: Doubleday, 1970.

Menary, Richard, ed. (2010). *The Extended Mind*. Cambridge, MA: MIT Press.

Mesthene, Emmanuel. G. (1969). 'Technology and Humanistic Values'. *Computers and the Humanities* 4, no. 1: 1–10.

Miall, David. S., ed. (1995). *Humanities and the Computer: New Directions*. Oxford: Clarendon Press.

Midgley, Mary. (1985). *Evolution as a Religion: Strange Hopes and Stranger Fears*. London: Routledge.

Milic, Louis. T. (1966). 'The Next Step'. *Computers and the Humanities* 1: 3–6.

Miller, J. Hillis. (1991). 'Literary Theory, Telecommunications, and the Making of History'. In *Scholarship and Technology in the Humanities. Proceedings of a Conference held at Elvetham Hall*, Hampshire, UK, 9–12 May, ed. May Katzen, 11–20. London: British Library Research, Bowker Saur.

Miller, Perry. (1962). 'The Responsibility of Mind in a Civilization of Machines'. *The American Scholar* 31, no. 1: 51–69.

Minsky, Marvin L. (1995/1968). 'Matter, Mind and Models'. Available at: http://web .media.mit.edu/~minsky/papers/MatterMindModels.html (visited on 27 November 2013).

Mitchell, S. O. (1967). 'Larger Implications of Computerization'. *Journal of General Education* 19: 216–23.

Monod, Jacques. (1972/1970). *Chance and Necessity: An Essay on the Natural Philosophy of Modern Biology*. Trans. Austryn Wainhouse. London: Collins.

Moretti, Franco. (2000). 'Conjectures on World Literature'. *New Left Review* 1: 54–68.

Morgan, Gareth. (2006). *Images of Organization*. Rev. ed. Thousand Oaks, CA: Sage Publications.

Mori, Masahiro. (2012/1970). 'The Uncanny Valley'. Trans. Karl F. McDorman and Norri Kageki. In *IEEE Robotics and Automation Magazine* 19, no. 2 (June): 98–100.

Mumford, Louis. (1967 and 1970a). *The Myth of the Machine*. 2 vols. New York: Harcourt Brace Jovanovich.

Mumford, Louis. (1970a). 'The Megamachine'. *New Yorker*, 31 October: 10.

Nemerov, Howard. (1967). 'Speculative Equations: Poems, Poets, Computers'. *The American Scholar* 36, no. 3: 394–414.

Newell, Kenneth B. (1983). 'Pattern, Concrete, and Computer Poetry: The Poem as Object in Itself'. *The Bucknell Review* 27, no. 2: 159–73.

Nold, Ellen W. (1975). 'Fear and Trembling: The Humanist Approaches the Computer'. *College Composition and Communication* 26, no. 3: 269–73.

OCD. (1968). *In Time of Emergency: A Citizen's Handbook on . . . Nuclear Attack . . . Natural Disasters*. H-14, Washington, DC: Office of Civil Defense, Department of Defense.

Oliphant, Robert. (1961–62). 'The Auto-Beatnik, the Auto-Critic, and the Justification of Nonsense'. *The Antioch Review* 21, no. 4: 405–29.

Olsen, Mark. (1991). 'What can and cannot be done with electronic text in historical and literary research'. Unpublished paper for the Modern Language Association of America Annual Meeting, San Francisco CA, December 1991.

Olsen, Mark. (1993). 'Signs, Symbols and Discourses: A New Direction for Computer-Aided Literature Studies'. In Fortier 1993: 309–14.

Orwell, George. (1968/1945). 'You and the Atom Bomb'. In *The Collected Essays, Journalism and Letters of George Orwell*, volume IV, ed. Sonia Orwell and Ian Angus, 6–10. London: Secker & Warburg.

Otis, Laura. (2001). *Networking: Communicating with Bodies and Machines in the Nineteenth Century*. Ann Arbor: University of Michigan Press.

Parrish, Stephen M. (1962). 'Problems in the Making of Computer Concordances'. *Studies in Bibliography* 15: 1–14.

Parrish, Stephen M. (1964). 'Summary'. In *Literary Data Processing Conference Proceedings, 9–11 September*, ed. Jess B. Bessinger, Jr., Stephen M. Parrish and Harry F. Arader, 3–10. Armonk, NY: IBM Corporation.

Pascual-Leone, Alvaro, Amir Amedi, Felipe Fregni, and Lotfi B. Merabet. (2005). 'The Plastic Human Brain Cortex'. *Annual Review of Neuroscience* 28: 377–401.

Pegues, Franklin J. (1965). 'Editorial: Computer Research in the Humanities'. *The Journal of Higher Education* 36, no. 2: 105–08.

Peirce, Charles Sanders. (1998). *The Essential Peirce: Selected Philosophical Writing*. Vol. 2. Peirce Edition Project. Bloomington: Indiana University Press.

Pickering, Andrew. (2010). *The Cybernetic Brain: Sketches of Another Future*. Chicago: University of Chicago Press.

Plamper, Jan. (2012). *Geschichte und Gefühl: Grundlagen der Emotionsgeschichte*. München: Seidler.

Plamper, Jan, and Benjamin Lazier, eds. (2012). *Fear Across the Disciplines*. Pittsburgh, PA: University of Pittsburgh Press.

Pooley, Robert C. (1961). 'Automatons or English Teachers?' *The English Journal* 50, no. 3: 168–73, 209.

Potter, Rosanne G. (1991). 'Statistical Analysis of Literature: A Retrospective on Computers and the Humanities, 1966–1990'. *Computers and the Humanities* 25: 401–29.

Potter, Rosanne G., ed. (1989). *Literary Computing and Literary Criticism. Theoretical and Practical Essays on Theme and Rhetoric*. Philadelphia: University of Pennsylvania Press.

Prescott, Andrew. (1999). 'Commentary'. In *Information Technology and Scholarship: Applications in the Humanities and Social Sciences*, ed. Terry Coppock, 72–78. Oxford: Oxford University Press.

Purdy, Strother B. (1984). 'Technopoetics: Seeing What Literature Has to Do with the Machine'. *Critical Inquiry* 11, no. 1: 130–40.

Ramsay, Stephen. (2011). *Reading Machines: Toward an Algorithmic Criticism*. Urbana: University of Illinois Press.

Ramsay, Stephen, Stéfan Sinclair, John Bradley, Geoffrey Rockwell, and Thomas N. Corns. (2003). 'Reconceiving Text Analysis. Special Section of Four Articles and an Afterword'. *Literary and Linguistic Computing* 18, no. 2: 174–223.

Reagan, Ronald. (1961). 'Frontiers of Progress'. National Sales Meeting, General Electric Corporation, Apache Junction, Arizona, 15–18 May. Available at: http://www.smecc.org/frontiers_of_progress_-_1961_sales_meeting.htm#reagan (visited on 27 November 2013).

Reichardt, Jasia, ed. (1969). *Cybernetic Serendipity*. New York: Frederick A. Praeger, Inc.

Reichardt, Jasia, ed. (1971). *Cybernetics, Art and Ideas*. London: Studio Vista.

Rommel, Thomas. (2004). 'Literary Studies'. In *A Companion to Digital Humanities*, ed. Susan Schreibman, Ray Siemens, and John Unsworth, 88–96. Oxford: Blackwell. Available at: http://www.digitalhumanities.org/companion/.

Rorty, Richard. (2004). 'Being That can be Understood Is Language'. In *Gadamer's Repercussions: Reconsidering Philosophical Hermeneutics*, ed. Bruce Krajewski. Berkeley: University of California Press.

Rorty, Richard. (1979). *Philosophy and the Mirror of Nature*. Princeton: Princeton University Press.

Schofield, Mary-Peale. (1962). 'Libraries are for Books: A Plea from a Lifetime Customer'. *ALA Bulletin* 56, no. 9: 803–05.

Schreibman, Susan, Ray Siemens, and John Unsworth, eds. (2004). *A Companion to Digital Humanities*. Oxford: Blackwell. Available at: http://www.digitalhumanities.org/companion/.

Schulz, Bruno. (1998/1935). 'An Essay for S. I. Witkiewicz'. In *The Collected Works of Bruno Schulz*, ed. Jerzy Ficowski. London: Picador 367–70.

Shanken, Edward A. (2002). 'Art in the Information Age: Technology and Conceptual Art'. *Leonardo* 35, no. 4: 433–38.

Sheehan, James J. and Morton Sosna, eds. (1991). *The Boundaries of Humanity: Humans, Animals, Machines*. Berkeley: University of California Press.

Shklovsky, Viktor. (1965/1917). 'Art as Technique'. In *Russian Formalist Criticism: Four Essays*, ed. and trans. Lee T. Lemon and Marion J. Reis, 3–24. Lincoln: University of Nebraska Press.

Shore, John. (1985). *The Sachertorte Algorithm and Other Anecdotes to Computer Anxiety*. New York: Viking Penguin.

Smith, Brian Cantwell. (1985). 'Limits of Correctness. ACM SIGCAS'. *Computers and Society* 14–15, nos 1–4: 18–26. Rpt. 1995 In *Computers, Ethics & Social Values*, ed. Deborah G. Johnson and Helen Nissenbaum, 456–69. Englewood Cliffs, NJ: Prentice Hall.

Smith, Roger. (2007). *Being Human: Historical Knowledge and the Creation of Human Nature*. New York: Columbia University Press.

Stinchcombe, A. L. (1965). 'Social Structure and Organizations'. In *Handbook of Organizations*, ed. J. G. March, 142–93. Chicago: Rand McNally & Company.

Tillyard, E. M. W. (1958). *The Muse Unchained: An Intimate Account of the Revolution in English Studies at Cambridge*. London: Bowes & Bowes.

TLS. (1962). *Articles and Letters From The Times Literary Supplement During March–June, 1962*. London: Times Publishing Company.

Tomlinson, Gary. (2013). 'Evolutionary Studies in the Humanities: The Case of Music'. *Critical Inquiry* 39: 647–75.

Trilling, Lionel. (1967/1961). 'On the Teaching of Modern Literature'. In *Beyond Culture: Essays on Literature and Learning*. 19–41. London: Penguin.

Tulp, Nicolaes. (1641). *Observationum Medicarum. Libri Tres. Cum aeneis figuris*. Amsterdam: Ludovicus Elzevirium.

Turing, A. M. (1936–37). 'On Computable Numbers, With an Application to the Entscheidungsproblem'. *Proceedings of the London Mathematical Society*, ser. 2, no. 42: 230–65.

USN&WR. (1964a). 'Is the Computer Running Wild?' *U.S. News & World Report*, 24 February: 81–84.

USN&WR. (1964b). 'Machines Smarter than Men? Interview With Dr. Norbert Wiener, Noted Scientist'. *U.S. News & World Report*, 24 February: 84–86.

Van Dyke, Carolynn. (1993). ' "Bits of Information and Tender Feeling": Gertrude Stein and Computer-Generated Prose'. *Texas Studies in Literature and Language* 35, no. 2: 168–97.

von Neumann, John. (1945). *First Draft of a Report on the EDVAC*. Contract W-670-ORD-4926, US Army Ordnance Department and the University of Pennsylvania. Philadelphia, PA: Moore School of Electrical Engineering. Rpt. *IEEE Annals of the History of Computing* 15, no. 4 (1993): 27–43.

von Neumann, John. (1951). 'The General and Logical Theory of Automata'. In *General Mechanisms in Behavior: The Hixon Symposium*, ed. Lloyd A. Jeffress, 1–41. New York: John Wiley & Sons.

von Neumann, John. (1958). *The Computer and the Brain*. Mrs. Hepsa Ely Silliman Memorial Lectures, Yale University. New Haven: Yale University Press.

Weart, Spencer R. (1988). *Nuclear Fear: A History of Images*. Cambridge, MA: Harvard University Press.

Weaver, Warren. (1961). 'The Imperfections of Science'. *American Scientist* 49, no. 1: 99–113.

Weinberg, Steven. (1974). 'Reflections of a Working Scientist'. *Daedalus* 103, no. 3: 33–45.

Weinberg, Steven. (1983/1977). *The First Three Minutes: A Modern View of the Origin of the Universe*. London: Flamingo.

White, Hayden. (1980). 'The Value of Narrativity in the Representation of Reality'. *Critical Inquiry* 7, no. 1: 5–27.

Whitfield, Stephen. J. (1996). *The Culture of the Cold War*. 2nd ed. Baltimore: Johns Hopkins University Press.

Wiener, Norbert. (1961/1948). *Cybernetics, or Control and Communication in the Animal and the Machine*. 2nd ed. Cambridge, MA: MIT Press.

Wiener, Norbert. (1954/1950). *The Human Use of Human Beings: Cybernetics and Society*. Boston, MA: Houghton Mifflin Co.

Wittgenstein, Ludwig. (1980). *Bemerkungen über die Philosophie der Psychologie/Remarks on the Philosophy of Psychology*. Ed. and trans. G. E. M. Anscombe and G. H. von Wright. Vol. I. Oxford: Basil Blackwell.

Zuboff, Shoshana. (1988). *In the Age of the Smart Machine: the Future of Work and Power*. Oxford: Heinemann Professional.

Zwaan, R. A. (1987). 'The Computer in Perspective: Towards a Relevant Use of the Computer in the Study of Literature'. *Poetics* 16: 553–68.

# Index

Note: Locators in *italics* indicate figures and tables. Locators followed by the letter 'n' and 'nn' refer to notes.